AN INTRODUCTION

TO THE STUDY OF

JUSTINIAN'S DIGEST

CONTAINING AN ACCOUNT OF ITS COMPOSITION AND
OF THE JURISTS USED OR REFERRED TO THEREIN

TOGETHER WITH

A FULL COMMENTARY ON ONE TITLE
(DE USUFRUCTU)

BY

HENRY JOHN ROBY

FORMERLY
CLASSICAL LECTURER IN ST JOHN'S COLLEGE, CAMBRIDGE
AND PROFESSOR OF JURISPRUDENCE IN UNIVERSITY COLLEGE, LONDON.

EDITED FOR THE SYNDICS OF THE UNIVERSITY PRESS.

THE LAWBOOK EXCHANGE, LTD.
Clark, New Jersey

ISBN 9781584770732 (hardcover)
ISBN 9781616192631 (paperback)

Lawbook Exchange edition 2000, 2012

The quality of this reprint is equivalent to the quality of the original work.

THE LAWBOOK EXCHANGE, LTD.

33 Terminal Avenue
Clark, New Jersey 07066-1321

Please see our website for a selection of our other publications
and fine facsimile reprints of classic works of legal history:
www.lawbookexchange.com

Library of Congress Cataloging-in-Publication Data

Roby, Henry John, 1830-1915.
   An introduction to the study of Justinian's digest ; containing an account of its
composition and of the jurists used or referred to therein / by Henry John Roby.
     p. cm.
   "Edited for the syndics of the University Press.
   Originally published: Cambridge: University Press, 1884.
   Includes bibliographical references.
   ISBN 1-58477-073-2 (cloth : alk. paper)
    1. Roman law. 2. Usufruct. 3. Digesta. I. Title.

KJA1112.2 2000
   340.5'4—dc21   99-059331

Printed in the United States of America on acid-free paper

AN INTRODUCTION

TO THE STUDY OF

JUSTINIAN'S DIGEST

CONTAINING AN ACCOUNT OF ITS COMPOSITION AND OF THE JURISTS USED OR REFERRED TO THEREIN

TOGETHER WITH

A FULL COMMENTARY ON ONE TITLE
(DE USUFRUCTU)

BY

HENRY JOHN ROBY
FORMERLY
CLASSICAL LECTURER IN ST JOHN'S COLLEGE, CAMBRIDGE
AND PROFESSOR OF JURISPRUDENCE IN UNIVERSITY COLLEGE, LONDON.

EDITED FOR THE SYNDICS OF THE UNIVERSITY PRESS.

Cambridge:
AT THE UNIVERSITY PRESS.
1884

Cambridge:
PRINTED BY C. J. CLAY, M.A & SON,
AT THE UNIVERSITY PRESS.

„ Und was darfs viel Worte? das kayserliche Recht nach welchem das Römische Reich noch heutiges Tags geregiert wird, ist ja Nichts anders denn heydnische Weißheit, welches die Römer, ehe denn Roma von Christo gehört hat, gesetzt und geordnet haben. Und ich acht wohl wann itzt alle Juristen in einen Kuchen gebacken und alle Weisen in einen Trank gebraut würden, sie sollten nicht allein die Sachen und Händel unangefasset lassen, sondern auch nicht so wohl davon reden noch denken können. Denn solche Leute haben sich in großen Händeln müssen üben, sind darzu mit großer Vernunft und Verstand begabet geweßt. Summa sie haben gelebt und werden nicht mehr leben, die solche Weißheit im weltlichen Regiment gehabt haben." LUTHER[1] (*Opp. Altenb. T.* 6. f. 203 sq. *Ien.* 6. p. 156).

"Dixi saepius post scripta geometrarum nihil extare quod ui ac subtilitate cum Romanorum Iureconsultorum scriptis comparari possit, tantum nerui inest, tantum profunditatis." LEIBNITZ[1] (*Op.* 4, 3. 267).

Unter ungünstigen Verhältnissen wurden Justinians Sammlungen unternommen, und dennoch geschah die Auswahl mit so viel Sinn und Liebe, daß wir nach Dreizehenhundert Jahren fast bloß aus diesen Büchern, und bei großen Lücken unsrer historischen Kenntniß, den Geist des Römischen Rechts begreifen können....Die eigenen Constitutionen Justinians sind allerdings von verschiedenem Werthe, aber ein großer Theil derselben verdient das Lob der vollständingingsten Einsicht und Zweckmäßigkeit, und Vieles, was uns als Verunstaltung des alten Rechts erscheint, ist nur der verständige Ausdruck der Aenderungen, welche ganz von selbst, und ohne Zuthun eines Gesetzgebers, eingetreten waren. SAVIGNY (Gesch. I. § 5).

"With all their errors and imperfections, the Pandects are the greatest repository of sound legal principles applied to the private rights and business of mankind that has ever appeared in any age or nation." CHANCELLOR KENT (*Comm.* i. p. 541).

"Hoc non ignoro ueram utilitatem libri pendere ab uniuersa horum studiorum condicione, maxime a felici iuris prudentiae litterarumque Latinarum communione, quae hodie iacet, nec iuri magis operam dant Latine docti quam iurisprudentes Latine sciunt. sunt qui dum huic meae operae fauent putant fieri posse ut studia reuirescant: nec desperandum est. uideant qui hodie iuri operam dant adulescentes ingenui: apud eos enim stat, utrum perduratura sit ars iuris nobilis et liberalis an in artificium sordidum degeneratura. ius Romanum creatum ingenio populi ad id ipsum nati, perpolitum decursu illo mirabili per uiginti saecula nationesque quae fuerunt quaeque sunt omnium principes, tamquam nobile aurum identidem decoctum splendet hodie splendore non imminuto aetate, sed adaucto: et ut causarum patroni idonei iudicesque sagaces et religiosi etiam eo non adhibito institui possint, tamen ut studium efficiatur liberali homine dignum, id est eo qui hoc intellexit neminem plene uiuere diem praesentem nisi memorem dierum praeteritorum, opus est iure Romano, coniuncto cum ipsorum populorum tam Romani quam nostri creatione et formatione, uitae communi autem neque ita applicato ut animus adulescentis a libero motu statim in sordium eius uincula abripiatur neque ita ab ea alieno ut ex tirocinio ad arma difficilis transitus sit." TH. MOMMSEN (*Praef. ad Digest.* p. lxxx).

[1] These two passages are given as quoted by Rudorff, *Gesch.* i. p. 364.

PREFACE.

It is not unusual for students who have read the Institutes of Gaius and Justinian to proceed to the Digest. But the Digest is not easy. Neither the arrangement nor the method nor in some respects the phraseology is the same as that of the Institutes, and whatever title is taken up seems to presume a knowledge of a good many other titles. Yet, so far as I am aware, there is no edition of any part of it, at least in modern times, which furnishes help of the same kind as that, which is expected and given in many editions of classical authors. The present book is an attempt in some degree to supply this want.

The first part gives an account of the composition of the Digest and a brief notice of each of the jurists, both those from whose writings the Digest has been compiled and those who are cited or referred to in it. Some information of this kind is given in Histories and Institutional treatises on Roman law, but neither the order of the titles nor the order of the extracts seems to me treated satisfactorily. On the latter point no doubt everyone mentions Bluhme's discovery, but I am not aware of any exposition of it, except Bluhme's own, going into sufficient detail to shew its importance in the practical study and interpretation of the Digest. Further, I have thought it well to shew clearly by juxtaposition of some extracts with the originals, what the character of Tribonian's revision was.

The account of the Jurists is fuller than is found in general histories of Roman law. That this account is after all in

many cases very meagre, is due, mainly at least, to the want
of trustworthy materials. I have refrained here and elsewhere
from giving reins to imagination, and have endeavoured to let
my readers see what may fairly be treated as known and what
is matter of inference and conjecture.

One title fully explained seemed to me more likely to
introduce a student to the intelligent study of the Digest than
a longer portion less thoroughly treated. Accident determined
the selection of the title *de usufructu*, but I have seen no
reason for regretting the choice. There is much in the doctrine
of usufruct which closely resembles our law of life interests,
but there is also much which is specially Roman; and, as will
be seen, a good many other parts of the law come naturally into
notice in dealing with this. It is also not a little advantage
that the corresponding title of the *Basilica* is one of those
which have been edited by Zachariä von Lingenthal, with the
Byzantine comments conveniently arranged. The Vatican
Fragments contain a number of extracts on Usufruct, which
furnish important comparisons with the Digest.

The text of the title *de usufructu* is that of Mommsen, with
a few conjectural alterations. Whenever it deviates in any
matter of moment from the Florentine text (i.e. represents
neither that of the original copyist nor of the corrector) the
fact is noted at the foot of the page. The arrangement of the
text is my own.

My notes it will be seen are legal, philological, and antiquarian. They are of course much longer and more numerous
than would properly accompany an edition of the Digest or of
a large part of it. It seemed desirable to explain the meaning
of a word or expression, not merely so far as the particular
passage in question was concerned, but also as the student
might find it in other parts of the Digest. A brief summary

of the law on many matters has been given, partly to remind
the student of its relation to the particular question in hand,
and partly because what may be already familiar to him from
the Institutes will be found to assume a somewhat different
aspect under different treatment.

Having had no predecessors in this particular field of annotation I have no special obligations to acknowledge here.
Throughout the book I have tried to take my information
from the original sources, and to depend on others only when
the matter in question was large in itself and not closely
connected with my subject. Whenever I have made any distinctive use of modern writers, or have thought the reader
might like a fuller or different statement, I have given the
requisite reference.

But a vast general debt I am anxious to proclaim. No
one who cares for Roman law and philology can fail to feel
the heartiest gratitude to the noble school of workers and
writers, of whom as jurists, historians and philologers the leaders
and types in their respective generations and lines are Savigny
and Mommsen.

I have to express my thanks to the Syndics of the University Press for undertaking the publication of this book ; and
to the Rev. Joseph B. Mayor, Editor of Cicero's *de Natura
Deorum,* for having kindly read and criticised some of the
proof sheets.

Corrections will be welcome. One who writes on subjects
of this nature, without the assistance and check of colleagues
or pupils, and with the resources of a private library only,
stands especially in need of criticism from his readers.

H. J. ROBY.

Wood Hill, Pendleton,
May 1884.

CONTENTS.

PART I.

PART II.

INDEX.

CORRIGENDA ET ADDENDA.

(This list contains several errors and omissions which were not noted at the time of the earlier issues.)

Page xxii, line 14 from bottom, for 'Theodosian' read 'Theodosius'.

„ xxvii, note, add 'H. Pernice (*Miscellanea* p. 107 sqq.) makes it probable that *dupondius* referred originally to the small daily pay of gladiator-pupils who were thence called *dupondii* or *dipundii* (pp. 143, 150). This term for 'recruits' was transferred to young soldiers, and hence to jurists in training (cf. Lyd. περὶ μηνῶν p. 109 Bekk.)'.

„ xxxiv, lines 5, 6 from bottom, dele 'as in Gaius'.

„ xxxv, line 18 from bottom, for vi. read v.

„ xxxix, line 18 from bottom, for xiv.—xvii. read xiv.—xvi.

„ lix, line 11 from bottom, for '§ 2' read 'pr.'.

„ lxxx, line 6 from bottom, for 'context' read 'content'.

„ lxxxiv, line 7 from top, after 'we know not' add 'but a probable explanation is given by Huschke *Jur. Antejust.* p. 436, ed. 4, who compares Cod. Theod. ix. 43 init.'.

„ xciii, line 10 from bottom, for 'Sex.' read 'L.'

„ ci, line 8 from bottom, for 'Curius' read 'Canius'.

„ ci, line 6 from bottom, after *Rutilius* insert (Cic. *Or.* ii. 69).

„ cviii, line 4 from top, add 'For the so-called *Muciana praesumtio* see D. xxiv. i. 1 51; Cod. Just. v. 16, 1 6'.

„ cxvii, line 27 from bottom, for 'conspiracy' read 'auspices'.

„ cxxi, line 20 from top, for '*Ars Poetica* 37' read '*Ars Poetica* 371'.

„ cxxxiii, line 6 from top, add 'But most modern jurists hold that Justinian sanctioned the Sabinian view. See Arndts-Glück xlviii. p. 264 sqq.'

„ cxxxiv, line 15 from bottom, for 'Proculian view (*Inst.* iii. 19. § 11)' read 'Sabinian view (*Inst.* ii. 14. § 10; *Dig.* xxxv. 1. 1 3; 1 6. § 1)'.

„ cxxxvii, line 18 from bottom, for *perpetuo* read *perpetua*.

„ cxlii, line 19 from bottom, for 'A.D. 16' read 'A.D. 13'.

„ cxlii, line 6 from bottom, after 'Caesar' insert (Cic. *Fam.* viii. 8. §§ 5, 6).

„ clix, Iauolenus. Mommsen refers to this jurist the following inscription from Nadinum in Dacia. *Corp. I. L.* iii. No. 2864 : add. iii. p. 1062. C. Octauio Fidio Tossiano Iaoleno Prisco l(egato) leg(ionis) iv Flau(iae), l(egato) leg(ionis) iii Aug(ustae), iuridico prouinc(iae) Brittaniae, leg(ato) consulari prouinc(iae) Germ(aniae) Superioris, legato consulari prouinc(iae) Syriae, proconsuli prouinc(iae) Africae, pontifici P. Mutilius P. F. Cla. Crispinus t(estamento) p(oni) i(ussit) amico carissimo. A grant of privileges to veterans (found at Mayence) mentions I. Iauolenus Priscus as commander in Upper Germany A.D. 90. The praenomen Caius in the Dacian inscription and I (which may stand for I, L or T, but apparently as Mommsen argues from the name of a priest's freedman *Corp. I. L.* VI. 2184, 2185 stands here for Lucius), is however a difficulty. See Mommsen *Eph. Epig.* v. p. 655.

Page clxviii, line 16 from top. This unknown jurist 'Tuscianus' perhaps owes his existence to a misunderstanding of 'Tossianus' which the inscription just quoted gives as one of the names of Iauolenus.

„ clxxxv, line 4 from bottom, after 'sent' insert '*anno* 184'.

„ clxxxix, line 11 from bottom, for 'XLI. 1' read 'XLI. 2'.

„ ccxiii, line 5 from bottom. It should be remembered that such forms as *mandauero* are called futures subjunctive by Priscian (*Inst.* VIII. §§ 55, 57).

„ ccxvi, line 13 from bottom, for 'present' read 'perfect'.

„ ccxlix, line 2 from bottom, for '2 vols.' read '1877'.

„ ccliv, line 20 from bottom, for 'Particular' read 'General'.

„ cclxxvii, line 27 from bottom, for 977 read 997.

„ cclxxviii, line 15 from bottom, for 'Ualentinianus' read UALENTINIANUS.

„ 20, add marginal note to l 48 '*Heir repairs without direction*'.

„ 30, line 19 from bottom, for '*Grom.* p. 56' read '*Grom.* p. 36'.

„ 40, line 8 from bottom, for 'Distinction' read 'Destruction'.

„ 45, line 6 from bottom, after 'practice' insert 'confirmed or suggested by a constitution of Seuerus (Cod. VIII. 56, 1 2. § 2)'.

„ 84, line 9 from top, for 'sale' read 'hire'.

„ 87, last line, for '*Inst.*' read 'Cod. Iust.'

„ 103, lines 27 and 29 from top, for 'Negligence' read 'Mere omission'.

„ 144, line 19 from top, for '*traditis*' read '*tradidero*'.

„ 149, line 17 from top: Studemund in his second edition of Gaius (p. xxxi) states that the MS in III. 42 has *proinde*.

„ 151, line 2 from top, for 'Ulpian' read 'Paul'.

„ 194, line 7 from top, after 'free' insert 'by will'; and add at end of sentence: 'The case is otherwise, if he is set free by his master in his lifetime; (Vat. Fr. 261; D. XVI. 1. l 53)'.

„ 196, note on **inhabitare**. Add 'Justinian's constitution (Cod. III. 33, l 13) determines some of these questions differently from the Digest'.

„ 198, line 13 from top, for '50' read '60'.

„ 198, line 5 from bottom, at end of paragraph (*d*) add 'Justinian altered this, (*Inst.* II. 13. § 5)'.

„ 222, line 19 from top, for 'l 16' read 'l 3'.

„ 236, line 7 from top, for 'making' read 'marking'.

PART I.

CHAPTER I.

INTRODUCTORY.

WHEN Uprauda the Slave or Goth, reigning under the name of Justinian, essayed the reformation of the laws of Rome and accomplished it in seven years, he undertook and performed a task which, in point of difficulty and usefulness, is not undeserving even of the highflown praise which he has himself bestowed upon it. It is remarkable that the nephew of a barbarian peasant should, in the first year of his obtaining the Empire of the East, have conceived or adopted so bold a design: it is much more remarkable that within so few years he should have executed in masterly fashion the codification of the jurisprudence and legislation of more than seven hundred years, from Cato the Censor to his own time. But it is a still more striking fact that the law books, issued at Constantinople by Justinian for the lands surrounding the Eastern half of the Mediterranean in the beginning of the sixth century of our era, should be directly or indirectly a large, or even the principal, source of private law in all the civilized countries of the world in the nineteenth century. As a basis for the scientific study of law Justinian's law books have still no rival. We in England do not stand in the same close and direct connexion with them that our continental neighbours do. No part of the Digest or Code is law with us, or is now of more than illustrative or casual bearing on the decisions of our courts. But partly through the early law-writers, much more through the Chancellor's jurisdiction, and partly, perhaps in an increasing degree, through intercourse with other nations and through literary and professional training, the Roman law has materially helped, and is still helping, to form our rules for the business of life. It may be that a cultivated nation having to form laws for itself would naturally devise a body of rules in many respects very similar to those actually in force here or on

the continent: but cultivated nations do not exist without laws
already; and laws are not sudden creations but the slow growth of
time, in other words their shape is due to a nation's past history
as well as to the practical exigencies of life. The intellect of the
nineteenth century can no more deny or shake off its hereditary
allegiance to the law of Rome, than it can to the philosophy and
art of Greece. And for the law of Rome we have to thank Justinian
and his great minister Tribonian.

Whether the Emperor or his minister have the largest claim to
our respect is rather a curious than a fruitful question. One may
well guess, that the scheme originated with the skilled lawyer, who
afterwards assisted in and presided over its practical execution. But
the Emperor had at least the ability to comprehend its importance,
the courage to adopt it, and the energy and persistence to carry
it through. An absolute monarch has not indeed the special difficulties to contend with, that a constitutional sovereign or a parliamentary minister has, in dealing with legal reform, but the isolation
and uncertainty of an absolute monarch's position, the danger of
waywardness, the influence of private temptations are so great, that
there is as much to claim our respect and gratitude in the resolve of
the Emperor as in the excellence of his instruments. The good
judgment that found Belisarius and Narses for the work of war was
shewn previously in the selection of Tribonian for the work of peace:
and while fully admitting that Justinian has often the praise and
blame which more strictly may belong to Tribonian, and that
Tribonian in the same way stands responsible for the merits and
demerits of Theophilus and Dorotheus and their colleagues, I am
content to use the names almost indiscriminately as symbols of a
great achievement, and leave to others the hopeless problem whether
he who wisely selects the instruments or he who faithfully and skil-
fully executes can best claim the credit of the work.

But there is another point of view from which one part, and
that the most important, of Justinian's legislation deserves to be
regarded. The Digest is not only, or for us chiefly, a law book with
Justinian's sanction, but it is a collection of fragments, mutilated
and interpolated to some extent, but still fragments, of some of
the great masters of Roman jurisprudence. Latin literature from
Nerva to Alexander Severus comprises Tacitus, Pliny the younger,
Juvenal, Suetonius, the short but elegant apology of Minucius
Felix, the antiquarian Gellius, the affected Fronto, and the lively

though very different African writers, Apuleius and Tertullian.
And those are all that deserve mention. But the first two names
drop off with Trajan, and from Hadrian onwards the real strength of
Roman literature was in law. Celsus and Julian, Pomponius and
Gaius, Marcellus and Cervidius Scaevola, Papinian, Paul, and Ulpian
are the writers who represent Roman thought for a period of more
than 100 years, and have been the teachers to the subsequent world
of one of the chief divisions of systematic knowledge and practical
literature. In this light, it is true, Justinian and Tribonian have an
ambiguous reputation. It is common enough to visit them with
scorn and blame for what they have destroyed, rather than praise for
what they have preserved; to reproach them with their alterations
and interpolations; and in fact to treat them more as slaves who
have plundered their masters' treasures and not known how to use
them, than as guardians who have saved what was possible from a
general conflagration. But after all they have a sufficient and a
twofold answer. First, it is very improbable that much of the
original works of the Roman jurists would have come down to us
at all, if it had not been for their collection and abridgment under
imperial sanction; and secondly, the primary and paramount use of
law is to be a practical guide in the business of men. No consideration of antiquarian wishes ought for a moment to prevent the
thorough adaptation of the law to the real needs and conveniences
of the time. Happily for us Justinian felt the authority the law
derived both from its antiquity and from the great names of the
ancient jurists, and found a means, rough and unscientific but practical, of working in the spirit of the great lawyers themselves and
preserving much of the past without doing injustice to the wants of
the present.

There is no more difficult task of practical literature than the
codification of the law of a nation, and it is connected with the
equally difficult task of arranging for the practical application of the
code by the judges and for its continual amendment. Written law
is like a forest: if underwood be allowed to grow freely, the forest
becomes impenetrable. Justinian forbad commentaries and all comparison of his new Digest with the writings from which it was
compiled. Napoleon's exclamation on seeing a commentary on the
Code Civil was " *Mon Code est perdu.*" Doubtless it is impossible to
prevent explanations of the law from being written, and it would
be undesirable if it were possible. The writings of jurists have a

twofold purpose and effect : they tend to improve the law itself as a system of principles and rules, and they bring the conceptions of the judges and practitioners and of the general public itself into accord or intelligent relation with the system. Reports of decided cases come under the same category. The decision itself has only a special and limited bearing, but the arguments of counsel and the reasons of the judge are essentially the discussions of jurists, and, when reported, become part of the class of juristic literature. They are the only discussions which the people in general read at all, and in fact are the main source of legal education to laymen. Reports are however destined for a further purpose, and one for which jurists' writings are at least not so openly used. They are quoted in the courts not merely to instruct the mind of the judge but to influence his decision ; not merely to let him see all the bearings of the case at issue, but to impose on him a somewhat vague necessity of making his decision in the case before him consistent with that given by a judge in a previous case of a similar character. When this principle is once fully admitted, reports are multiplied without limit, the law, whether codified or not, becomes dispersed through hundreds and thousands of volumes, and there is ultimately, owing to the mass of literature, the inevitable progress of thought, and the ineradicable divergency of human minds, no more security for consistency of decision than there would be, if no reported cases were quoted at all. In the vain desire to prevent or remedy one evil another still greater is forgotten and encouraged.

For there is a real and constant opposition between the interests of the suitor and the tendency of scientific law. I put aside the vulgar opposition between the interests of practitioners in the law's being complicated and dear, and the interests of suitors in its being simple and cheap. That opposition may under certain circumstances exist, but it is one which the public can in time overcome. The opposition that I refer to is inherent in the nature of the subject. Legal conceptions, however you may define and explain, will not have the same content in all minds, and the facts to which they are applied will wear a different aspect according to the presumptions which the judge brings to bear on them. The more thoroughly a matter is investigated, the more fully it is compared with other cases, the more the application of different legal principles or categories to it is discussed, the greater chance there would appear to be of the right decision being arrived at in the particular case, and of the

general law being set in clearer light. But the process is long and
costly, and, cases being thus selected only by accident[1], the general
improvement of the law is very slight and very slow. The suitor's
real interest is forgotten. It may seem paradoxical, but I believe it
is on the whole true, that, apart from questions of life, freedom and
honour, a suitor's real interest lies not so much in a just decision as
in a speedy and final decision. *Summum jus summa iniuria* is true
in more senses than one. A perfectly just decision would often be
badly purchased by the loss of time, temper and money, and by the
paralysis of uncertainty. And that the decision, when obtained, is
perfectly just, is a proposition of the truth of which the successful
party is often the only person to be confident. There is usually in a
disputed question some right or reasonable claim on each side : the
decision must of course turn on the balance of probabilities and
equities ; but if the balance is eventually not quite rightly adjusted,
a bystander will console himself for the failure of justice by the
reflexion, that the law no longer prevents the parties from adjusting
themselves to their now ascertained circumstances, and seeking in a
wise and energetic future the remedy for the mistake of the past. A
statesman will try to improve the law by other means than the
prolongation of a private suit between those, to whom the immediate
interests are of more importance than the solution of legal difficulties
or the improvement of legal procedure.

Ultimately it will I believe be found best to leave each private
suit as much as possible to the *viri boni arbitratus* acting authorita-
tively and publicly, whether he be called judge or arbitrator. Let
the preparatory stages be under his control : let him order the
proceedings as in the particular case may be best calculated to bring
the issues out clearly : let all witnesses be examined who can throw
light on the matter, whether the parties call them or not : let him
stop the inquiry whenever it is being carried, even by the parties'
consent, to an unreasonable length. It is *pessimi exempli* to have
litigation run on, till the cost in time and money to the public and
the parties is out of proportion to the attainable object of the suit.

In points of law no decision in a parallel case should be quoted
except that of an appeal court[2], and the decision itself should be

---

[1] See Maine's *Ancient Law*, chap. ii. pp. 38, 39.
[2] I recently examined the decisions in one Part of the Law Reports, containing a large number of appeal cases. In one half the judgment of the Court
of first instance was reversed. If this be a fair sample, it is an even chance

subject to review only once, and that, at least in most cases, only with the consent of the judge.

But the law itself must be better ascertained. There must be a code, or something like one, and there must be means for its continued improvement. As a scientific consolidation of the law no jurist would approve Justinian's plan. It had however two great merits; it was actually done within a very short time, and it gave the people and the practitioners the law to which they were accustomed, with only such alterations as probably had long been desired. A new code, with new definitions, method and arrangement, may or may not, according to the skill of the draughtsman, be greatly superior, but there is more difficulty in its execution, more criticism to be encountered, and more risk of its not being understood. Few of the judges who have to apply it will be scientific jurists, and it is easy to be too logical for the mass. The problem of consolidating the common law must in every country be an arduous one, but the difficulty is not insuperable, and one gets weary of finding an imagined future perfection made a bar to present improvement. The better should not for ever be an enemy to the good.

Almost more important than the code is the means for keeping it abreast of the development of men's minds and of new circumstances. A standing Commission having a small nucleus of scientific and practising lawyers, with large power of temporary and special addition, should be continually considering the code and preparing such alterations as may be shewn, either by reports of cases or by scientific criticism, to be desirable. The decisions of appeal courts should be specially considered with a view to incorporation. A revised code should be issued at regular intervals, say every five or ten years, and the previous decisions even of the appeal courts should then be no longer citable in cases commenced subsequently.

With these brief remarks suggested naturally by the subject of the Digest, I pass to the subject itself.

The reign of Justinian occupies five brilliant chapters of Gibbon's history, and I shall therefore content myself with a brief notice. It is only the first few years of it which concern the present subject. His father's name was Iztok, his mother's Bigleniza, which were translated or latinized into Sabatius and Vigilantia. He was born

whether the first decision be right or wrong, according to the judgment of the Appeal Court, and cannot therefore be trusted as a guide in other cases.

in 482 or 483 A.D. at the village Tauresium, near the site of the modern Sophia. His uncle, a peasant, whom we know as Justin I. became a soldier, rose from the ranks to the command of the Guards, and on the death of Anastasius was made emperor by the soldiers A.D. 518. He adopted his nephew Uprauda, who succeeded him in the year 527, and reigned for more than 38 years. Justinian at once commenced the reform of the law, and did not allow it to be delayed by a sedition in Jan. 532, which was excited by the rivalry of the blue and green factions of the circus. They set fire to the city and demanded and obtained the removal from office of the ministers Tribonian and John of Cappadocia; and the tumult was only quelled by a massacre of the greens, effected by three thousand veteran soldiers and the orthodox blues. The conquest of the Vandals in Africa, and of the Goths in Italy, and the defeat of the Persians, all by Belisarius, and a renewed conquest of Italy by Narses, were the principal military glories of Justinian's reign. His buildings were no less remarkable. In Constantinople and its suburbs alone he raised 25 churches, and amongst them the church of St Sophia is as memorable in architecture as his other achievements in their respective lines. 'There was nothing erected during the ten centuries from Constantine to the building of the great mediæval cathedrals which can be compared with it. Indeed it remains now an open question, whether a christian church exists anywhere of any age, whose interior is so beautiful as that of this marvellous creation of old Byzantine art[1].' A chain of more than 80 forts from Belgrade to the Black Sea was formed to protect the empire from the northern barbarians, but this was only part of the system of fortification which was carried out on many other borders. Justinian was courteous and patient, temperate and frugal, constantly engaged in the work of administration: 'he professed himself a musician and architect, a poet and philosopher, a lawyer and theologian. But he was not a successful ruler: the people were oppressed and discontented; his wife and many of his ministers abused their power: his name was eclipsed by those of his victorious generals. He died A.D. 565[2].'

'Tribonian was a native of Side in Pamphylia, and his genius 'embraced all the business and knowledge of the age. He composed

---

[1] Fergusson, *Hist. of Arch.* vol. II. pp. 444.
[2] An interesting notice of Justinian by Prof. Bryce is entombed in the new edition of the *Encyclopaedia Britannica*.

'both in prose and verse on a strange diversity of curious and abstruse
'subjects: a double panegyric of Justinian and the life of the
'philosopher Theodotus; the nature of happiness and the duties of
'government; Homer's catalogue and the four and twenty sorts of
'metre; the astronomical canon of Ptolemy; the changes of the
'months; the homes of the planets and the harmonic system of the
'world. From the bar of the praetorian prefects he raised himself to
'the honours of quaestor, of consul, and of master of the offices'. His
gentleness and affability were admitted, but he was charged with
impiety and avarice. In the sedition of 532 he was removed from
office, but was speedily restored, and continued to enjoy the confidence of the emperor till his death in 546[1].

CHAPTER II.

JUSTINIAN'S LEGISLATION.

OUR knowledge respecting the method adopted by Justinian in
his rearrangement and codification of the law is derived from the
decrees which were issued by him for the direction of the work, and
which are prefixed to the several parts of it.

The first step was to compose one Code which should contain
the imperial constitutions which were comprised in the Codes of
Gregorian, Hermogenian and Theodosian, and those subsequently
issued. But collection was not the whole task: the laws were to be
edited as well. 1. Superfluous matter, not touching the real purport
of the constitution, but inserted merely as preface, was to be omitted.
2. The constitutions were to be compared, and repetitions and
contradictions to be removed, excepting so far as the division of the
law into different parts required their preservation (*praeterquam si
juris aliqua divisione adiuuentur*. Cf. Const. *Summa*). 3. What
was obsolete was to be removed. 4. Additions, omissions and
changes were to be made in the constitutions themselves, where convenience required it. 5. The constitutions were to be classified
according to their subject matter into different titles. 6. They were

---

[1] Condensed from Gibbon, chapp. xliii. xliv. The description of Tribonian
does not rest on sure evidence.

to be arranged in each title in chronological order, with their dates appended, the absence of a date not however to detract from the authority of the constitution. 7. Rescripts addressed to individuals and pragmatic sanctions (i. e. charters addressed to communities. Cf. Cod. I. 23. 1 7), if included in the Code, were to have the force of general law. This Code was to be compiled by a commission of ten persons, of whom Johannes was named first and Tribonian sixth. Seven were high officials, a professor of law at Constantinople, Theophilus, was the eighth; and two practising lawyers made up the number. The Constitution was dated 13 Febr. 528 A.D. (Const. *Haec quae necessario.*)

In little over a year the task was completed. On the 7th April, A.D. 529, Justinian issued a constitution announcing the completion of the *Codex Justinianus,* and directing it to have exclusive validity from the 16th of that month. No constitutions were to be cited in the courts, except such as were contained in the Code; and whatever alterations had been made were not to be impugned. Cases in the courts were to be decided on the basis of the old legal commentators and this Code. No constitutions not contained therein were to be valid, except such 'pragmatic sanctions' as only granted special privileges to communities or corporations, and such as dealt only with special points (*pro certis capitulis factae*), and were consistent with the code. (Const. *Summa.*)

The next step was a more difficult one. Justinian determined to do, what as he says no one had attempted before, to collect, amend and digest the authorized Roman law from the writings of the old lawyers (see below, ch. VI.). Having found Tribonian, from his labours on the Code, to be well qualified for the task, he entrusted it to him and to such colleagues, both professors and practising lawyers, as he should select. The writings of those lawyers only who had received official recognition were to be taken ; all selected passages were to have the force of law equally; neither the number of authorities nor the importance of some (e. g. Papinian) were to affect the question. Contradictions and repetitions were to be cut out; even what was already to be found in the Code was not to be repeated in the Digest, except so far as circumstances might require or justify some repetitions ; and such additions and corrections were to be made both in the writings of the lawyers and in any constitutions quoted in those writings, as might be necessary for the perfection of the Digest. Any obsolete laws were to be omitted, the test being the practice of the courts and the custom of Rome, both old and new (i. e. Constantinople). No commentaries were to be written in future on the Digest, and no contractions or abbreviations to be used in writing it out, even the numbers of the books to be written in full. The matter was to be arranged in fifty books and subordinate titles, in accordance with the Code already published and the perpetual edict of Julian. This constitution is addressed to Tribonian and dated 15 Dec. 530 A.D. (Const. *Deo auctore.*)

In the performance of this task it was found necessary to settle a number of much disputed points, and to abolish some distinctions and obsolete practices. For this purpose Justinian issued a series of fifty decisions on disputed points, and many other constitutions for the amendment of the law (Const. *Cordi* § 1 ; Inst. I. 5. § 3). The ground being thus cleared, Tribonian and his assistants completed the Digest. In two constitutions, one in Latin (commencing *Tanta*), one in Greek (commencing Δέδωκεν), issued for its confirmation on the 16th Dec. 533 A.D., Justinian gives an account of the work. The two constitutions are very similar, but are both originals, and sometimes one is fuller and clearer than the other. Tribonian chose for his assistants one high official, Constantinus, two professors of law at Constantinople, Theophilus and Cratinus, two professors of Berytus, Dorotheus and Anatolius, and eleven lawyers practising at Constantinople, Stephanus, Menas, Prosdocius, Eutolmius, Timotheus, Leonides, Leontius, Plato, Jacobus, Constantinus and Johannes (§ 9). A large number of books were collected, principally from Tribonian's own library, some of the books being rare and even their titles unknown to most of the lawyers of high repute (§ 17). Some were found to contain nothing worth extracting. Those which furnished materials for the Digest are stated to be named in a list prefixed to the Digest (§ 20). This list (or at least a list of this kind) is preserved in the Florentine MS., and contains the names of 38 authors, 207 treatises, and a total of 1544 books[1], i. e. volumes or rolls; many of the treatises being very voluminous. The list, however, is not quite accurate, some treatises not having supplied extracts, and some treatises which have supplied extracts not being named, but the discrepancies are not important[2]. Tribonian had suggested to Jus-

---

[1] One book of Paul's is named twice over.

[2] These discrepancies are noted in the list drawn up by Krüger and appended to Mommsen's larger edition, vol. II. p. 59*. It appears that one author, Aelius Gallus (from whom a single extract is taken) is omitted, as well as 26 treatises, apparently small, and usually supplying only one extract each. Of these 11 are

tinian that there were almost 2000 books containing 3,000,000 lines
which ought to be examined. Instead of these three million lines
Justinian's Digest contains as he states about 150,000[1], the matter
being arranged in seven parts and fifty books (§ 1). The full powers
of correction, omission and addition granted by the constitution *Deo
auctore* were exercised, but the name of the author from whose
writings the extract was taken, was invariably prefixed (§ 10).
Matters dealt with by imperial constitutions were as a rule omitted
from the Digest (§ 14). Any apparent contradiction would be found
on attentive examination to disappear, owing to some delicate point
of difference (§ 15). The Digest (with the other imperial law books)
was made the exclusive legal authority, no one being allowed to
compare its provisions with the writings from which it was taken,
or to cite them in court or in any legal proceeding (§ 19). No abbreviations in writing the Digest and no commentary were to be allowed.
No one was to cite from a copy containing abbreviations in court,
and the copyist was to forfeit twice the value to the owner of the
book and to incur the penalty of forgery (*falsi*, § 22). Under the
same penalty it was forbidden to make any commentary on the
Digest; only literal (κατὰ πόδα) translation into Greek, and παράτιτλα

---

by Paulus, 5 by Gaius, 4 by Ulpian. *Alfeni Digesta* is mentioned, the Epitome
by Paulus is not; Labeo's *Posteriores* are mentioned, *Javolenus ex posterioribus
Lab.* is not; others appear to be wrongly described. Again, one author,
Sabinus, and 15 treatises are named in the Index, but no extract from them is
found in the Digest. These are chiefly single-book treatises of Paulus.

[1] The Florentine MS. (according to Mommsen vol. I. p. xi.) contains, besides
index and prefatory constitutions and title, 887 leaves, of 4 pages each, each
page having 44 or 45 lines, i.e. in all between 156,000 and 160,000 lines.

Some estimate of the work of Justinian may be made in this way. As a
basis for comparison I take Mommsen's Digest (stereotype edit.) which has 873
pages of (say) 5900 letters of text; each page averaging 2 cols × 72 lines × 41
letters). The Digest itself, apart from prefaces, &c. contains about one-third
more matter than Kerr's Blackstone (1st edit.), if Kerr's appendices be disregarded
and the space occupied by the notes be estimated as if filled with text. Then if
the Digest is equal to 5¼ vols. of the average size of Kerr's Blackstone, and the
ratio of the Digest to the treatises from which it was compiled was, as Justinian says, 1 to 20, we get the result that Justinian compressed a law library
of 106 vols. into one of 5¼ vols. If there were contractions in the old books
as in the MS. of Gaius, and these were compared by Justinian to his un-
contracted Digest, we should have to increase the quantity in old books by an
addition of one-fourth (25 per cent.)

If there were 2000 books, the average size of each book would be about 8¾
pages of Mommsen (= 30 pages of Kerr); if there were only 1600 (see p. xxiv and
note) each book would average nearly 11 pages of Mommsen. An average book
of Gaius' *Institutes* is equal to 11½ pages Mommsen; of Justinian's *Institutes*
13¼ pages; of Quintilian's *Institutes* 14 pages. A book of the Digest itself
averages 17½ pages. Hence we may *guess* at the length of Ulpian's *Commentary
on the Edict* (83 books × 14 pages Mommsen = 7½ Kerr's vols.?)

were to be allowed (§ 21).   What were παράτιτλα, Zachariae a Lingenthal has shewn by examples actually found in some Byzantine
compilations.   They were short summaries added to each title, giving
references to other parts of the law books where the same matter was
treated, and a brief account of such passages (Heimbach *Proleg.* ad
Basil. vol. vi. p. 4).   The Digest was to have the force of law from
30 Dec. 533.

To complete the reformation of the law Justinian provided for
the education in the schools a new book of elements and a new course
of study.   In the instructions for preparing the Digest he had
already hinted at the possibility of a new book of Institutes (Const.
Deo auctore § 11).   Accordingly he directed Tribonian, with the
assistance of Theophilus and Dorotheus, to examine the institutional
treatises then used, and compile, with due corrections and notices of
the amending constitutions, new Institutes in four books (Const.
Tanta § 11).   In the preface to the Institutes Justinian says they
were compiled from all the Institutes of the old writers, but especially
from the *Institutiones* and *Res cottidianae* of Gaius.   The constitution approving of them was dated on the 21 Nov. 533, but was to
take effect from the same day as the Digest, viz. 30 Dec. 533.

Directions for a new course of study were issued on the 16 Dec.
533, in a Constitution addressed to Theophilus, Dorotheus, Theodorus,
Isodorus, Anatolius, Thalelaeus, Cratinus and Salaminius, all described as professors (*antecessores*).   Justinian describes the course of
study then in use as spread over five years but badly arranged, the
order of the edict being disregarded, and an injudicious selection
being made out of a number of books, with useful and useless mixed
together.   The first year's instruction was from six books, viz. two
books of Gaius' institutes (perhaps the Epitome which forms part of
the *lex Romana Uisigothorum:* cf. Dernburg, *Gaius,* p. 132) and
his four one-book treatises (*libri singulares*) on Wife's property, Guardianships, Wills and Legacies.   The second year was given to the
matter of Justinian's first part, i.e. Jurisdiction and Procedure,
and after that to portions of Justinian's second or third parts, i.e.
actions *in rem* and commercial contracts.   In the third year was
taken whichever of these second and third parts was not taken before:
and eight out of Papinian's nineteen books of answers (*Responsa*) were
added, but only in short selections.   This was all that the professors
lectured on.   The Answers of Paulus (*Pauliana responsa*) the
students had to read by themselves in the fourth year.   What was

learnt in the fifth year is not stated, but from the preface to the Institutes it may be inferred that it was some of the Imperial Constitutions. The customary names of the students were in the 1st year, Dupondii[1]; in the 2nd, Edictales; in the 3rd, Papinianistae; in the 4th, Λύται (i.e. freed from lectures); in the 5th, προλύται ('advanced Λίται').

Justinian's new plan was based on the old one, but adapted to the Digest and made more definite. He gave his own name to the first year students—*Justiniani novi*. They were to be lectured first on the Institutes and then on the first 4 books of the Digest (Jurisdiction and Preliminary matters). For the second year the whole either of the second part (Books v.—xi.) or of the third part (Books xii.—xix.), and in addition the first of the three books on Dowry (Book xxiii.), the first of the two books on Guardianship (Book xxvi.), the first of the two on Wills (Book xxviii.), and the first of the seven on Legacies (Book xxx.). For the third year was to be taken whichever of the second or third parts was not taken in the second; and in addition the three books following, viz. on Pledge (xx.), on the Aediles' Edict and Eviction (xxi.), and on Interest, Evidence, &c. (xxii.). Of the book on Pledge five out of six titles are made to commence with an extract from Papinian, so that the name of *Papinianistae* for the students might still have some justification. To the fourth year were allotted for private study the remaining ten books of the series (xxiii—xxxvi.), which were not taken in the third year. The fifth year was to be devoted to the Code. Law schools were sanctioned only in Constantinople, Rome and Berytus; those in Alexandria, Caesarea and elsewhere being suppressed, under the penalty for a teacher of a fine of 10 lbs. of gold and banishment from the town. This constitution was dated 16 Dec. 533 p. Chr. (Const. *Omnem*.)

Justinian speaks with natural pride of the completion of this work. But Tribonian was not satisfied. The composition of the Digest had necessitated so many new Constitutions that the Code was no longer sufficient, and a new edition (*repetita praelectio*) was requisite. The task was given to Tribonian, Dorotheus, Menas, Constantinus and Johannes to incorporate the new Constitutions in

---

[1] The origin of this term is obscure; Justinian calls it *tam frivolum quam ridiculum cognomen* (Const. *Omnem*. § 2). *Dupondius* may denote either two pounds, or a brass coin in value half a sesterce, or two feet. If we compare *Pers.* v. 76 *Dama est non tressis agaso*, 'a groom not worth threepence', we may guess that the freshmen were called contemptuously 'Twopennies'.

fitting places in the Code, and boldly to amend, omit, amplify and make clear.   The work was finished by the 16 Nov. 534, and directed to take effect from the 29 Dec. 534, the former Code and all other Constitutions being abrogated (Const. *Cordi*).

This second edition of the Code is the one which we have.   The earliest constitution contained in it is one of Hadrian's, and there are in all only 23[1] before the reign of Severus.   After that they are frequent.   (See the chronological table appended to Krüger's edition). The earlier constitutions, so far as they were of general and permanent character, were incorporated in the jurists' writings, and form part of Justinian's law only so far as the extracts in the Digest or the Institutes may chance to contain them.   The Theodosian Code, the Vatican Fragments, and general literature have preserved others. (See Hänel's *Corpus Legum*.)

After the publication of this second edition of the Code, Justinian issued from time to time other Constitutions, mostly in Greek.   Of these about 170 are still extant, and form part of the *Corpus Iuris*. They are called *Novellae* (new Constitutions).   Zachariae a Lingenthal has arranged them[2], with a few others probably issued before the second Code, in chronological order, 174 in all, the last of which belongs to the year 565 p. Chr., in which Justinian died, aged 83. Of these Novels one is of great importance as altering the order of intestate succession to the form which has since been prevalent in Europe, and which mainly rules intestate succession to personalty in England at the present time.   It is Nov. 118 = 143 Zach. published 543 p. Chr.   It is a significant fact that only 20 of the whole number are later than the year of Tribonian's death, 545 p. Chr.

CHAPTER III.

DIVISION OF THE DIGEST AND ORDER OF THE TITLES.

JUSTINIAN divided the Digest into 7 Parts and 50 Books.   In each book the matter is further subdivided into Titles, of which there are 432.   Three books however (*De legatis* XXX—XXXII.) are

---

[1] Rudorff (*Rechtsgesch.* i. p. 314) speaks of 180 constitutions from the Divi Fratres and 192 from Commodus.   This is quite wild.   Cf. Zimmern, i. p. 179.

[2] Published in the Teubner series of classical authors.

not subdivided at all. Each Title consists of one or more extracts, the total being 9142. Some of these extracts are very short, others of considerable length, and in the middle ages were divided into several paragraphs, each containing as a rule a different case or point of law. I estimate the total number of paragraphs and undivided laws together at about 19000.

Of the Parts the 1st is called by Justinian πρῶτα, containing Books I.—IV.; the 2nd *de judiciis* (V.—XI.), from the initial words of the first title; the 3rd *de rebus* (XII.—XIX.), on the like ground; the 4th, *Umbilicus Pandectarum*, is the central Part (XX.—XXVII.); the 5th *De testamentis* (XXVIII.—XXXVI.); the 6th contains XXXVII.—XLIV.; the 7th, XLV.—L. This division rested probably on some usual classification of the matter, at least as regards the first three and the fifth parts. The sixth part to a large extent is dominated by the idea of possession, the fourth and seventh are clearly made up of heterogeneous materials, and their size was dictated by the desire of symmetry or by mystic associations. A similar notion seems to have existed in grouping the titles into books. The total number of books was prescribed beforehand (Const. *Deo auctore* § 5).

Justinian's words are very noticeable. *Et in septem partes eos digessimus, non perperam neque sine ratione, sed in numerorum naturam et artem respicientes et consentaneam eis diuisionem partium conficientes. Igitur prima quidem pars totius contextus, quae Graeco uocabulo* πρῶτα *nuncupatur, in quattuor libros seposita est* (Const. *Tanta* §§ 1, 2). So in the Greek Const. Δέδωκεν we have καὶ τοῦτο οὐ παρέργως, ἀλλὰ τῆς τῶν ἀριθμῶν φύσεώς τε καὶ ἁρμονίας στοχασάμενοι. Hofmann (*Z. R. G.* XI. 340 sqq.) points out the probable connexion of these words with the later Pythagorean mysticism respecting numbers (cf. Ritter and Preller *Hist. Phil.* §§ 104, 116. ed. 2), and gives some details, of which I extract the most striking. The number 50 for the books was fixed on beforehand: we may remember also the 50 Decisions. The nearest root of 50 is 7 ($50 = 7 \times 7 + 1$). Justinian makes 7 parts, not however, as one might have expected, six parts of 7 books each and one of 8 books for the middle, but he commences with a first part of 4 books. Four (Tetractys) is the mother of the perfect number 10 ($= 1 + 2 + 3 + 4$), and is the 'root of all things[1] and source of nature'. So Justinian directed Tribonian to

---

[1] Hofmann refers to Irenaeus and Themistius. 'See also Sext. Emp. *Math.* iv. 3; vii. 94, with Fabricius' notes; Hierocles *Carm. Aur.* p. 166 (Fragm. Phil. ed. Didot. I. 464). See Zeller, I. p. 368 n. ed. 4. where the ancient Pythagorean oath by the Tetractys is given. Macrob. *Som. Scip.* i. 6. § 41'. Jos. B. Mayor.

make an introductory treatise (the Institutes), and in that also *quidquid utile...sit, quattuor libris reponere, et totius eruditionis prima fundamenta atque elementa ponere.* (Gaius divided his subject into three (§ 8), but made four books of Institutes). The remaining six parts are divisible into halves (II.—IV. and V.—VII.) each containing 23 books. Again the three middle parts (III.—V.) have 25 books, and the four outside books (I. II. VI. VII.) have also 25 books. The last part has 6 books, which with the first part makes the perfect 10. Students were to be instructed in 36 of the 50 books, *ut ex triginta sex librorum recitatione fiant iuuenes perfecti* (Const. *Omnem* § 5). Now 36 is the 'great tetractys' and denotes the universe. Its perfection consists in being the sum of the first four odd, and the first four even, numbers $(1 + 3 + 5 + 7 + 2 + 4 + 6 + 8 = 36)$. Fourteen of the fifty books are left for subsequent study (ib. § 5 and cf. § 3). Fourteen is twice seven. There were also fourteen *libri singulares*, viz. 3 on marriage (XXIII.—XXV.), 4 on guardianship and wills (XXVI.—XXIX.), and 7 on legacies (XXX.—XXXVI.). But the number 3 was an especial favourite. *Omni igitur Romani iuris dispositione composita et in tribus uoluminibus, id est Institutionum, et Digestorum...necnon Constitutionum perfecta, et in tribus annis consummata* (Const. *Tanta* § 12). *Leges autem nostras suum optinere robur ex tertio nostro felicissimo sancimus consulatu, praesentis duodecimae indictionis tertio Kalendas Januarias....Bene autem properauimus in tertium nostrum consulatum et has leges edere, quia...in hunc...et bella Parthica abolita sunt et tertia pars mundi (Libya) nobis adcrevit, et tanto operi legum caput inpositum est, omnia caelestia dona nostro tertio consulatui indulta* (Ib. § 23). In another paper (*Z. R. G.* XII. 180 sqq.) Hofmann shews that a contemporary of Justinian, Cassiodor, attaches the like importance to numbers, especially 50, 7, 12, 4, 3, and makes the division of his books accordingly.

In truth neither parts nor books have as a whole a natural justification. The divisions between them correspond sometimes with the division of the subject, but often appear to be more or less arbitrary. The real unit is the title, which however, according to the quantity and character of the matter, will sometimes be part of a series on the same subject, sometimes itself contain several subdivisions which might be made into separate titles. I proceed to discuss the principles followed by Tribonian in his arrangement of the matter, or in other words, in his arrangement of the series of titles.

Most students of the Digest are at first bewildered with the apparently strange and haphazard distribution of the matter. And this feeling is the stronger because the student is usually acquainted with the arrangement of Gaius or Justinian in their Institutes, and finds that of the Digest very different. Gaius first treats of persons, their position in the state and in the family, i.e. of citizenship, freedom, marriage and guardianship. Then comes the law of property, its acquisition and loss, both as regards aggregates (*universitates*) and as regards individual things. A large portion of this relates to inheritance and bequest, this last being taken out of its proper place among singular successions and placed immediately after heirship by will, and followed by the rules of intestate succession. The law of obligations follows, divided into obligations arising from contract, and obligations arising from tort (*ex delicto*); those from contract being divided into real, verbal, literal, and consensual, and discussed both as to their rise and extinction: those from tort being represented by theft, violent robbery, physical injury to person or property, and insult. Procedure is the subject of the last book; first the old forms of statutable procedure, then the procedure by written *formulae*, i.e. instructions from the praetor to a judge to try particular issues of law or fact: then the parties to an action, including the liability of a father or master for the acts of his children and slaves, and the mode and conditions of appointing an attorney to conduct the case. Special pleas, injunctions, the penalties of improper litigation, and the means of enforcing appearance to a summons close the book. On the whole the matter is arranged in five masses: law of persons, things, inheritance (in the large sense of succession to property vacant by death), obligations, and procedure, the law of inheritance being however incorporated as a whole in the law of things.

These five divisions are very usual in modern writers on Roman law, who, however, often prefix a collection of definitions, rules, and considerations affecting all or many of the parts of law, and called the general part. Procedure is often omitted or only partially represented in the general or introductory part. The order of the rest however is frequently things, obligations, family, inheritance; sometimes family, things, obligations, inheritance; sometimes otherwise. Criminal law is occasionally appended at the end.

These masses are found in the Digest. Speaking roughly, jurisdiction, appearance and preliminary objections, Books I.—v. 1; things,

v. 2—XI.; obligations (real and consensual), XII.—XXII.; family,
XXIII.—XXVII.; inheritance and bequest, XXIX.—XXXVIII.   But after
that we have danger to neighbours, and gifts, Book XXXIX. ; manumission, Book XL.; acquisition of ownership, XLI.; judgment and
execution, XLII.; interdicts, XLIII.; pleas, XLIV.; verbal obligations
and their extinction, XLV., XLVI. ; torts, XLVII.; criminal law, XLVIII. ;
appeals, municipal administration and interpretation, XLIX. and L.
And confusion seems to be caused by the strange position of some
titles, e.g. acquisition of property widely separated from the law of
things; verbal contracts separated from bargains (II. 14), and both
from real and consensual obligations ; damage under the Aquilian
statute put far away from theft and insult; action for fraud in Book
IV. and plea of fraud in Book XLIV., &c.

Justinian directed the compilers to follow in the arrangement his
own Code and the Perpetual Edict, (see ch. xii.) as should be found
most convenient (Const. *Deo auctore* § 5).   The code thus referred to
is not now extant.   The second edition which we have agrees in the
main arrangement with the Digest, but there are some minor divergencies.   Possibly some of these may be due to the revision.   In any
case the main lines seem to coincide with the Edict, which had
probably served as the guide in the arrangement of the first code.

Though the Edict itself is not preserved, its arrangement may be
confidently gathered from the sequence of matters in the *Digesta* of
Julian, its framer, and in the three commentaries by Gaius, Ulpian
and Paulus, numerous fragments from which occur in the Digest.   In
many parts indeed the Commentary of Ulpian furnishes the bulk of
the titles in the Digest on matters treated in the Edict.   The principal differences in the arrangement of the matter in the Digest from
that in the Edict appear to be (1) that the Edict put theft immediately after guardianship and before the law of patrons and of
succession to property of deceased persons ; (2) that intestate succession preceded wills and legacies; (3) that action for tumult, robbery
by violence, and insult preceded judgment and execution; (4) that
the edict of the Curule Aediles was appended at the end of the
Praetor's edict instead of being incorporated with it; (5) that the
Praetorian recognisances (*stipulationes*) were put all together after
interdicts and pleas, instead of some in the Digest being put with the
law to which they specially related.

Rudorff and others speak of the Digest as following the order of
Gaius' Institutes, viz. persons in I. title 5—7 ; things in I. title 8,

and actions I. title 9—L. 15, but say that the material part of Gaius' law of persons and things has been brought into the law of actions (*Rechtsgesch.* I. p. 302). This seems to me to be a delusive comparison. Partly from the different character and object of the Institutes and the Digest, partly from the changes in the law, the treatment and order of the matter is really quite different, the resemblances as regards the matter of persons and things being superficial and almost accidental, and as regards other matters being due either to the natural connexion of the subjects or to the Praetor's edict.

The Digest is a handbook for practitioners, not a systematic treatise for students. It treats of who are judges, who are plaintiffs and how they can get defendants into court, what matters are actionable, the effect of a judgment and the means of enforcing it, and then other remedies such as injunctions and recognisances. Matter necessary for the explanation of the various actions is prefixed, often in separate titles, and cognate matter is sometimes appended in other titles. It is the insertion of these prefatory and explanatory titles and occasional digressions, which often prevents a student from catching the main lines of the arrangement.

I proceed to examine more in detail the order of the titles.

Book I. titles 1—4 contain introductory, general and historical matter.

Titles 5—7 treat of the distinction of free and slave, father and child, regarded as subjects of rights and capable or incapable of suing or being sued.

Title 8 treats of the distinction between things which can and can not be private property, and therefore objects of a suit.

Titles 9—22 of officials, so far as their private rights are affected by their position or as they have jurisdiction over suits.

Book II. treats of jurisdiction (titles 1—3) and of the means of securing a defendant's appearance to the suit (titles 4—12).

Title 13 is *de edendo*, i.e. of production of documents in judicial proceedings, and especially of the plaintiff's duty, fully to state the nature of his action ; and of bankers' duty to produce their accounts with their customers.

Title 14 (*de pactis*) treats of bargains not to sue, i.e. of agreements for the settlement or waiving of claims before action brought, with some general remarks on bargains and contracts.

Title 15 is *de transactionibus*, i.e. of compromises of a doubtful claim, but specially treats of compromises of claims for annuities.

Book III. is of the parties to a suit, i.e. of those who are disqualified to bring an action, of agents and defenders, both those duly appointed and those acting without appointment (*de negotiis gestis*), and of those who are bribed to bring, or not to bring, an action (*de calumniatoribus*).

Book IV. treats mainly of the cases, where the ordinary effect of actions and pleas is defeated by annulling the acts on which they rest, in consequence of intimidation or fraud, or of the insufficient age or other disability of the party attacked. *Restitutio in integrum* is here regarded as a bar to the ordinary procedure. Then in title 7 comes another bar of the like kind, that of endeavours to avoid trial by alienating the object of the suit. Title 8 deals with the duty of an arbitrator who has accepted a reference of a suit to him. Title 9 is peculiar. Its connexion seems to be accidental. *De receptis: qui arbitrium receperint*, i.e. undertakings to act as arbitrator (tit. 8), seems to have attracted to it the law on the duty of shipcaptains and innkeepers to give up what they have received (*ut recepta restituant*). One would have thought the end of the thirteenth book a more appropriate position. But its position in this neighbourhood is not a hasty act on the part of Tribonian, but at least as old as the Commentaries of Ulpian on the Edict.

Book v. title 1 is on the place of trial, and here ends the part of the Digest on procedure and preliminary objection. Title 1 was placed here rather than in one of the earlier books either to make the bulk of the books more equal, or because the initial words of the rubric '*de iudiciis*' happen to be identical with those of the description of the subject-matter, which occupies this and the following books, and formerly made one of the important divisions of law, viz. trials for recovery of things called *de iudiciis* (*rei persequendae gratia*). Cf. Just. IV. 6. §§ 16, 17.

The discussion of the subject-matter of suits then follows.

First come *actiones in rem*, e.g. actions by owners, and here, as in Gaius, we have claims to a mass of property put before claims to individual things. The third title, *de petitione hereditatis*, is the principal instance of a claim to a *uniuersitas*, and occupies with smaller connected matters the rest of the book. The second title 'of an undutiful will' is appropriately prefixed to it. It also was an action which gave a man if successful the position of heir, and it has a resemblance to the matters treated of in the preceding book, because it aims at the annulment of the will.

Book VI. contains the claim to recover your own property: and this is treated in two headings, first where the claimant has a good legal title (*de rei uindicatione*), secondly where he has an honest title, but requires longer possession to cure defects in the conveyance to him (*de Publiciana in rem actione*); thirdly when he has a perpetual lease.

Books VII. and VIII. treat of servitudes, and deal with the matter generally, setting forth the nature and creation of servitudes as well as the actions for enforcing them. This action is in each case a *uindicatio*. Book VII. treats of personal servitudes, usufruct, use, claim to services: Book VIII. of rights of light, of prospect, of support, of drip (*seruitutes urbanae*), rights of road, of taking water, of pasture, of winning stone and chalk (*seruitutes rusticae*). The discussion of the bond given by a fructuary has been transferred by the compilers to Book VII. from its place with other bonds at the end of the Edict.

Book IX. treats chiefly of the actions for damage caused by fault and negligence, as provided by Aquilius' statute expanded by the lawyers. It is not at first sight obvious why this action is treated here rather than with theft and robbery, as Gaius treats it. Heffter (*Rhein. Mus.* I. p. 54) has suggested that Books VI. 2—VIII. represent the old action *sacramento*, Books IX.—XI. the actions *per iudicis postulationem*, after which we have actions *per condictionem*. There is a good deal to be said for this view, though Rudorff criticises it unfavourably (*Z. R. G.* III. p. 53), but even without it the place assigned to the matters of Book IX. seems appropriate. Tribonian has separated those torts which have more of a civil character from those which, although they have a civil side, are also frequently criminal. The actions *de pauperie, damni iniuria, de his qui effuderint*, &c. and noxal actions as a whole, are actions for recovering not indeed your property but a substitute for it. They are in fact actions by owners of what has been damaged or destroyed: they are not the result of any contract; they are aimed not like a *condictio* at some one with whom we have formed a business connexion, but like a vindication at any person who has deprived us of our property by his own or his family's or his cattle's fault. They do not prosecute an offender as a criminal, from vindictive feelings, but in order to put the injured party in the position as far as possible that he was in before. And they are characterized by the peculiar option given to the defendant, either to pay the damages awarded or to surrender to the plaintiff (*noxae dedere*) the delinquent slave or beast.

Book x. treats of actions of a special character, in which any one of several persons may be plaintiff and the other or others defendants. Such are suits for division of property: viz. *finium regundorum*, for settling the boundaries of landed estates between neighbours; *familiae erciscundae*, for the division of an inheritance between coheirs; *communi diuidundo*, for the division of any other property between tenants in common. In all these cases the parties claim property as their own and seek to have their right established: those who have no right as holders of conterminous estates, or as coheirs, or as tenants in common cannot bring the action; but the judgment is not simply for or against the plaintiff, but for and against both parties, by ascertaining and definitely allocating to them their proper shares, so that they no longer hold with uncertain boundaries or in ideal shares, but each is lord over a specific domain or property.

To this book is added *ad exhibendum*, an ancillary action for the purpose of compelling the production before the judge of any thing in which you have a proper cognisable interest. It was at the service of those who were about to sue *in rem*, or had, or were in the way to have, a claim to the possession of a thing. It lay against any one who had the actual possession, and is called a personal action, because it is not confined to those who assert a claim as owner either of the property in a thing or of a limited right in it, but is open to all *quorum interest rem exhiberi*. It is thus not unnaturally placed at the end of the class of actions which have occupied Books v. 1—x.

Book xi. is a supplementary book. It contains various actions not specially apposite elsewhere, and all more or less connected with those discussed. The first title 'on Interrogatories' is one of several relating to procedure, which we might have expected to see collected into one book and placed after the first title of the fifth book. The others are xii. 2, 3 on oaths; and the last four of Book xxii., viz. title 3 on proofs and presumptions, title 4 on documentary evidence, title 5 on witnesses, title 6 on ignorance of law and fact. The place of the title on interrogatories is due to the edict, and the subject is by Justinian mainly illustrated with references to interrogatories for the purpose of a suit against heirs (e. g. *familiae erciscundae*) and noxal suits. Much the same applies to the short title xi. 2.

Titles 3, 4 and 5 (of Book xi.), on suits for spoiling a slave (*de seruo corrupto*), and against those who conceal runaway slaves and on dice players are perhaps appendages to the action *damni iniuria*. Title 6 on the suit against a surveyor who has given a false measure is an appendage to x. 1 on boundaries. Titles 7 and 8 deal with those rights or restrictions on rights, which arise from pieces of land having acquired a religious character by the burial in them of the dead. To these are appended suits for funeral expenses, which begin with 7. 1 12. § 2. The 8th title might have been put in Book XLII. with other injunctions. But the connexion of subject, viz. injunctions against interference with a right of burial or erecting a monument has led Tribonian to place it here, just as he transferred the treatment of the usufructuary's bond to Book VII.

Book XII. commences an important class of actions which extend to Book XXII. As opposed to the class already dealt with they are (a class of) actions *in personam*, i.e. not claims as owners against all the world, but claims in consequence of a special relation by contract. They may be described as Commercial Actions—loan, pledge, deposit, sale, hire, exchange, agency, partnership, acknowledgement of debt stated, recovery of moneys unduly paid, set-off, claims for interest and mesne profits. To a considerable extent they coincide with the actions arising from real and consensual contracts.

Books XII. XIII. 5 contain *condictiones certi*, and *incerti*, and practically deal chiefly with claims arising from the payment of money, of which a loan of money (*mutuum* XII. 1) is the most typical. With this is connected recovery of moneys paid without consideration (XII. 4 and 7), or for an improper cause (XII. 5), or by mistake (XII. 6). The second title of this book seems oddly placed. It is on oaths. Rudorff (on Puchta's *Cursus* § 162 note *f*) suggests that the original action *per condictionem* favoured a summary settlement of the matter by allowing the praetor to tender an oath to the parties and thus dispense with strict proof and cut short dispute. The next title (XII. 3) is evidently in close connexion, as in case of the defendant declining to obey the sentence and make restoration, the plaintiff was allowed to settle the value of the thing thus wrongfully retained by stating its value on oath : and judgment was then given for the amount of the plaintiff's estimate, the judge however having a discretion to reduce it.

Book XIII. has some supplementary cases of condiction and also (title 5) the action *de pecunia constituta* for a stated sum of money acknowledged to be due. The two last titles of this book are on *commodatum*, i. e. loan of an article which has to be specifically returned; and *de pigneraticia actione*, i. e. the right of a debtor to reclaim the pledged property, on paying his debt and any expenses which the pledgee may have been put to in respect of the pledge. (See below on Book XX.) In both cases however, that of *commodatum* and that of *pignus*, the scope of the action is not mere recovery of possession of the object lent or pledged. Vindication would be enough for that. But the object lent or pledged may have been lost, or the borrower or pledgee may have incurred expenses in relation to it. These actions then were granted by the Praetor to deal with the reasonable claims arising out of the contract, and which were much wider than the mere claim to a bare restitution of the particular object.

The connexion with the preceding titles is easy. The discussion of a loan of money is naturally soon followed by that of a loan of specific articles, and pledge is in fact a loan not for use, but as a security for a debt. It is noticeable that both these actions are spoken of as having been treated in the Edict under the general heading of *de rebus creditis* (D. XII. 1. 1 1. § 1).

Books XIV. XV. XVI. 1 contain the various actions by which contracts are enforceable against others than those who made them, and especially of slaves and children by and against their owners or fathers, either wholly or partially according to circumstances. The group is headed by the two actions of most general application, those which made a principal liable for the contracts of his agent, whether free or slave, who has been entrusted with the management of a ship (XIV. 1 *de exercitoria actione*), or of a shop or other business (tit. 3 *de institoria actione*). Actions concerned with those who are in another's power follow. Amongst these is inserted a title (XIV. 6) on the *S. consultum Macedonianum* which annulled all right of action by lenders of money to sons who were still in the power of their father, and one on the *S. consultum Uellaeanum* (XVI. 1), which annulled any guarantee or security given by a woman for others' debts. To the title which made a shipmaster's contracts enforceable against the owner is not unnaturally appended (XIV. 2) a title on the *Lex Rhodia*, which enforced a general average, i. e. a contribution on the part of all who have goods on board and of the shipowner to make good the loss of any whose goods have been sacrificed to save the rest.

At first sight it is not evident why the question of liability of *A* for debts contracted by *B* should be discussed in the midst as it were of the commercial contracts. That this order was in compliance with the Edict only puts the question further back. Why were matters so arranged in the Edict? Perhaps the answer is this. The most typical cases of condiction were comprised in Books XII. and XIII. Before passing to more complicated contracts the large question of liability on another's contracts is taken, and discussed not in relation to the subject-matter of those contracts, as sale, hire, &c., but simply as liability for others' debts. The simplest form of liability, that arising from a loan, is enough to illustrate the principles, and it was not desirable to put off longer than was necessary dealing with such typical contracts as loans to children and to slaves on their father's or master's account.

Book XVI. 2 treats of set-off; a title which is naturally connected with loans and particularly affected bankers (Gai. IV. 64).

With title 3 we commence a new division of contracts. In the old law *fiducia* would have come first. Its connexion with deposit is seen in Gai. II. 60. And these with *actio mandati*, *pro socio* and others formed a class of actions, condemnation in which was followed by ignominy (Gai. IV. 182 ; D. III. 2. 1 1), a consequence which did not belong to actions *de rebus creditis*.

The actions in XIV.—XVII. naturally lead up to that on *mandatum* (agency), and *pro socio*, which occupy Book XVII. Books XVIII. and XIX. 1 treat of the contract of sale and various special contracts and considerations connected with sale. The remaining titles of Book XIX. deal with analogous contracts, that of hire, that of exchange, and others which did not come precisely within the technical definition of either sale or hire.

Book XX. is on Pledge and is mainly occupied with different aspects of the relation from that treated in XIII. 7. The *pigneraticia actio* was concerned simply with the debtor's recovery of his property after he has paid the debt for which it was pledged. Book XX. deals rather with the rights of the pledgee or successive pledgees against one another and against third parties, and generally with the modes in which pledge is created and extinguished. There were formerly three kinds of pledge : *fiducia*, by which the property was conveyed as in our mortgage ; *pignus*, in which not property but possession was transferred; and *hypotheca*, where neither property nor possession were transferred but only a personal contract entered into. Justinian ignored the first (*fiducia*) and abolished all legal distinctions between *pignus* and *hypotheca* (cf. D. xx. 1. 1 5. § 1 ; Just. iv. 6. § 4). This change has made it unnatural to separate XIII. 7 from xx. But *hypotheca* is the main subject of Book xx. as *pignus* is of XIII. 7. There the question is what is the purview of the debtor's action for recovery of possession of things pledged : in Book xx. what are the circumstances and rights attending *hypotheca*. So that here belongs the *hypothecaria* or *quasi Seruiana actio*, the pledgee's action against third parties. And the work from which a great deal of this book is taken is Marcian's treatise *ad formulam hypothecariam*, which has been in arrangement subordinated to extracts from Papinian in order to preserve old traditions in the course of study (see above, p. xxvii).

Book xxi. (title 1) contains important supplements to the law of sale, treating of the right of rescission where there has been any concealment of faults in the thing sold contrary to the rules of the Aediles' Edict ; and (title 2) of the consequences of eviction from the vendor's want of title. One would have rather expected that these two titles should have been put before the discussion of pledge. The arrangement suggests that some analogy was seen between a mortgagee, and a purchaser who under the circumstances had only a temporary hold of the thing purchased.

Book xxii. is one of the books made up of titles having no special connexion with each other. The first title is on interest and produce (*fructibus*), and other considerations accessory to sales and to other transfers, and contracts for transfer, of property. The second is on interest in the contract of bottomry. The other titles are quite general ; title 3 of proofs and presumptions; 4 of deeds and their loss ; 5 of witnesses ; 6 of the effect of ignorance of law and fact. They are placed here rather to make up the usual size of a book, and because a large new division of subject-matter is approaching, than because of any special logical connexion.

Book xxiii. commences the matter of Family law, which is treated of under the heads of marriage, dowry, guardianship, and is naturally followed by inheritance, patronage and manumission reaching to Book xl. though with some inconsistent interpolations in Book xxxix.

Book xxiii. is (title 1) of betrothal, (title 2) of marriage, and (titles 3—5) of the creation of dowry. Book xxiv. treats (title 1) of gifts between husband and wife, (title 2) of divorce, (title 3) of recovery of dowry after dissolution of marriage. Book XXV. treats (titles 1 and 2) of the claims of husband and wife against one another in respect of dowry and other property. Titles 3—6 deal with another branch of family law, viz. of the rights of children not yet born at the time of dissolution of marriage, and (title 3. 1 5—1 9) of the reciprocal claims of parents and children for necessary sustenance. The book is closed by a short title, 7, on concubines.

Books XXVI. and XXVII. deal with guardians, their mode of appointment and their duties and responsibilities: of the grounds of excuse from acting: of the responsibility of magistrates who appointed unsuitable guardians: and the restrictions on sale of a ward's property.

Books XXVIII. and XXIX. deal with testamentary inheritance. Book XXVIII. regards wills from the side of the testator, i.e. treats of making wills and the necessary conditions of validity. The last title of XXVIII. and several titles of XXIX. regard wills from the side of the heir, i.e. treat of acceptance or refusal of the position of heir. The first title of Book XXIX. treats of a military will and might perhaps have been better put in Book XXVIII., if connexion of subject rather than symmetrical size had dictated the distribution of the titles into books. The last title XXIX. 7 on codicils is naturally placed just before legacies and trusts.

Books XXX.—XXXVI. treat of legacies, both direct and by way of trust.

Books XXX.—XXXII. are really one book, or rather one title, and symmetry only has dictated their distribution into three books, with no further distribution into titles. The matter is somewhat general. The first has, amongst others, large extracts from Julianus, Africanus and Marcianus, the second from Modestinus and Papinianus, the third from Scaevola. The last part of XXXII. (l 44 to end) was probably originally intended to form a separate title 'on the interpretation of words in legacies'. (Bluhme, *Z. G. R.* IV. p. 299.)

Book XXXIII. deals with special legacies, e.g. of annuities, usufruct, servitudes, dowry, options, land and houses as stocked or furnished, *peculium*, store of provisions, furniture. Book XXXIV. continues special legacies, of aliment, gold and silver, release from debt (*de liberatione legata*), and then (title 4) treats of withdrawal of legacies and of gifts over, alterations, &c. Minor matters occupy the remaining titles. Books XXXV. and XXXVI. treat of conditional legacies, of the fourth reserved by the Falcidian law for the heir, of the *S. consultum Trebellianum* which transferred to the heir in trust the burdens and benefits which legally fell on the heir-at-law appointed by the will; then of the time of vesting of legacies, and of the security of the legatees either by the heir's bond or by actual possession.

Books XXXVII. and XXXVIII. treat of inheritance other than testamentary. The old law, which gave the inheritance of an intestate first to the *sui heredes* and, failing those, to *agnati*, was so largely altered in practice through the praetor's recognising natural claims by the grant of the *bonorum possessio*, that the legitimate intestate succession is treated in the Digest as subordinate to the *bonorum possessio*. After a general title (*de bonorum possessionibus*, XXXVII. 1) we have a series of titles (4—8) dealing with the grant of Possession of the Goods contrary to the devolution prescribed by the will and with the consequent arrangements for upholding legacies and making the persons so favoured by the praetor bring their property into hotchpot. These are followed by title 9 dealing with the case of an unborn child, and title 10 (*de Carboniano edicto*) with the case of one whose claim to be a child of the deceased is disputed. Title 11 deals with the grant of possession in accordance with the will. Title 12 which gives a parent the same rights to the inheritance of his emancipated son that a patron has in his freedman's forms a transition to the treatment of the patron's right, which is discussed, first generally (XXXVII. 14); then in title 15 his right to his freedman's respect; (XXXVIII. 1) to his services; (titles 2, 3) to a share of his property; followed by (title 4) the law on the distribution of the deceased's freedmen amongst his sons as patrons, and title 5 evasion by the freedman of his patron's rights.

The rules of intestate succession begin with XXXVIII. 6, and extend to the end of the book. The praetor's grant of possession is taken first, and then we come (tit. 16) to the legitimate succession of the *sui* and *agnati* and patron, and (tit. 17) to the reciprocal rights of the mother and children in their respective inheritances, which rights were granted by the senate's decrees called *Tertullianum* and *Orphitianum*.

Book XXXIX. has somewhat heterogeneous contents. The first three titles deal with rights against one's neighbour who is constructing or destroying some work, or who neglects to repair property which has become dangerous, or who is altering the flow of rainwater, or drawing off water to which he is not intitled. In the case of persistent neglect to repair, the praetor gave a right to the complainant to enter into possession of the land where the building was; and this grant of possession appears to be the link which has led to the position of the title *damni infecti* here (XXXIX. 2). The two others (title 1) *operis noui nuntiatio* and (title 3) *aquae pluuiae arcendae* come in its company. Title 4 *de publicanis* is more difficult to account for. We can only suppose that the matter was treated in some such connexion by the writers extracted (cf. 1 7), and that the links have been omitted by Justinian. (Compare its place in Cod. Theodos. IV. 12.) The last title in the book *de donationibus mortis causa* is required before the doctrine of inheritance is concluded, and the preceding title *de donationibus* is inserted as dealing with gifts in general and therefore introductory to gifts in view of death. The remarks of Bluhme (*Z. G. R.* IV. p. 285 sq.; p. 364, n. 19) tend to shew that the compilers hesitated about the arrangement of the matter in this book.

Book XL. is linked to the preceding books by two attachments, one the law of patrons and freedmen, which formed part of Books XXXVII. and XXXVIII., and the other the frequent occurrence of manumissions by will. This book treats (title 1) of manumission in general; title 3 of manumission *inter uiuos;* (title 4) of manumission by will, and (title 5) by way of trust, (title 7) of the position of slaves whose freedom was postponed till a future day or made dependent upon some condition (*de statuliberis*); then (title 8) of cases where freedom was obtained without the master's act, and (title 9) where freedom was not obtained notwithstanding manumission had taken place; titles 10 and 11 of freedmen being made or recognised as if they were free-born, and the remaining titles of supposed slaves claiming to be really free-born, and the like. This book closes the important part of the Digest formed by the law of Family and Inheritance.

Book XLI. opens with a title on the acquisition of property and appears disconnected from the preceding. In fact it is only introductory to those which follow. The real link is Possession, which begun with *bonorum possessio* in Book XXXVII. (or perhaps XXXVI. 4) and of which other phases occur in Books XLII. and XLIII. The present book treats (title 2) of acquiring and losing possession, and title 3 and subsequent titles of the acquisition of property by uninterrupted possession (*usucapio*). The first title therefore is contrasted with the second as property to possession, and with the third and others as the acquisition of property in general to the special acquisition by means of possession.

Book XLII. thus introduced by XLI., contains a new division. Hitherto we have had the various kinds of suits. We now have (title 1) the result of the suit, viz. judgment and its effect. Title 2 is on confession, title 3 on voluntary surrender of goods, and the remaining titles on the execution of judgment by seizure (*missio in possessionem*) and sale of the debtor's property, and rescission of acts done to defraud the creditors.

Book XLIII. deals with interdicts or injunctions, which form a separate class of suits, originally more or less of a temporary and interlocutory character, directed to obtain the permission or prohibition of certain acts rather than damages for loss of property or for injury. Many interdicts are for gaining or retaining possession, and hence are connected with the matter of the two preceding books.

Book XLIV. treats of pleas, especially (title 2) the plea of the case having been already decided ; (title 3) of the statute of limitations, (title 4) of fraud and intimidation, and (titles 4 and 5) some others. The last title in the book, (tit. 7) on obligations and actions, is partly supplementary and partly introductory. It contains a brief notice of some contractual actions not before specifically treated, and some general notices on the different kinds of actions.

Books XLV. and XLVI. deal with stipulation, the only form of strict verbal obligation which remained in Justinian's legislation. Title 1 of Book XLV. is on stipulation in general; title 2 on joint stipulations ; title 3 on stipulations made by slaves; Book XLVI. title 1 on sureties; title 2 on the use of stipulations to give a new valid form to existing obligations (*de nouationibus et delegationibus*) ; title 3 on payments and discharge of obligations in general, and title 4 on the formal discharge of a verbal obligation; title 5 on the stipulations directed by the praetor and then (in the three remaining titles) of three stipulations in particular ; that for safe-keeping of a ward's property, for the payment of a judgment debt, and for the ratification of an agent's acts.

It is indeed these last stipulations which appear to have attracted the general doctrine of verbal obligations to this part of the Digest. For doing justice between parties the court had sometimes not so much to give judgment on the past as to secure certain conduct for the future. Injunctions or interdicts were one mode of doing this : another was to compel the party or parties to enter into recognisances for their own acts in future. And the recognisance was a bond, i.e. a verbal obligation entered into by the one party to the other, and confirmed by similar verbal obligations of others as sureties for them. Some of these usual stipulations were transferred by Justinian to earlier parts of the Digest from the place in the Edict corresponding to this. (See VII. 9 ; XXXVI. 3.)

Books XLVII. and XLVIII. treat of penal actions : Book XLVII. of torts, especially, titles 2—9, of thefts, and robbery of various kinds; title 10 of insult, including libel and defamation; and the other titles of various torts, such as violating graves, collusive conduct of a suit, disturbing boundary stones, illicit societies, &c. Some or all of these torts might also be treated as crimes, and subject the offender to punishment as well as, or in lieu of, damages. Book XLVIII. treats of crimes and criminal procedure, especially title 4 of treason ; 5 of adultery ; 6 and 7 of violence ; 8 of assassination and poisoning ; 9 of parricide ; 10 of forgery ; 11 of extortion ; 16 of false accusation. Criminal procedure is treated in some titles viz. title 2 of indictments ; 3 of the custody of the accused ; 17 of dealings with those who do not appear to take their trial ; 18 of inquiry by torture ; 19 of punishments ; 20 and 21 of dealing with the property of criminals ; 22 of banishment.

Book XLIX. titles 1—13 treats of appeal ; title 14 of the rights of the crown (*fiscus*) to escheats in certain cases; 15 of the restoration of rights to one restored from captivity (*de postliminio*), and, this naturally having most frequently application to soldiers, we then have 16 of the position of soldiers ; 17 of the privilege accorded to soldiers of having property of their own, though otherwise in their father's power, and 18 of certain privileges of veterans.

Book L. is mainly on a part of public law, viz. title 1—12 on the administration of municipal affairs and the duties of the citizens to take their share of the burdens : title 13 on certain extraordinary jurisdiction ; 14 on brokerage ; 15 on public registers of taxable property (*de censibus*). The last two titles are collections respectively (title 16) of a large number of passages explaining the import of particular words when used in law, and (title 17) of a number of legal maxims.

The result of this examination tends to shew that while some suggestions have been adopted first from the old procedure by statutable actions, and secondly from the Praetor's edict, the dominant idea in the arrangement is that of the order of matters to be considered in the conduct of a suit[1]. I. Jurisdiction, parties to the action and bars to action. II. Import of actions divided into (1) recovery of what is still your property; repair of damage; ascertainment or partition of property; (2) commercial dealings; (3) relations between husband, wife and children; (4) succession to property vacant by death. III. Judgment and Execution. IV. Injunctions, Special Pleas, Bonds and Sureties. Here ends the matter of purely civil actions. Then follow V. Punishment of Wrongs by civil action or by criminal proceedings; VI. special and public Law and Interpretation.

The principal disturbances or apparent disturbances to this order are first, three miscellaneous books, viz. Books XI., XXII. and XXXIX., and secondly the interference of other principles with the main lines. To this latter head belong (a) the treatment of suits for an inheritance as a whole (v. 2, 3) before suits for individual things instead of leaving them to the section on succession by death, (b) the attention paid to the idea of possession which, originating with the grant of possession in execution of a judgment, has probably first dictated the position of inheritance, and, through that, of other branches of family law; and secondly has led to the position of acquisition by possession and therefore of acquisition in general in Book XLI., and thirdly has placed *damni infecti* and kindred actions in Book XXXIX., (c) the treatment of obligations in general and verbal obligations in particular in connexion with, and as it were introductory to, the Praetorian Recognisances.

CHAPTER IV.

ORDER OF EXTRACTS IN THE TITLE.

HAVING discussed the order of the titles, I pass to the order of the extracts in the titles. And here we are even less assisted by any authoritative information than we were in the case of the larger division of the matter. Justinian tells us who were the Commis-

---

[1] O. Lenel's exposition of the principles of arrangement of the Edict has much which resembles and supports this view (*Edict. Perp.* pp. 9—22), but I am concerned with Tribonian, not (except indirectly) with Julian.

sioners, what was the number and quantity of the books from which the extracts were taken, their descriptions, and the large powers given to the Commissioners to deal with them. What is more than this we have to discover from the Digest itself.

The first thought, no doubt, is that each title will have been made by this kind of mosaic to contain an orderly discussion of the branch of law denoted by the title. And this idea is confirmed by our frequently finding at the commencement of the title a definition or brief description of the subject-matter or some neat division of it. And not uncommonly this is followed by some regular treatment of one or more branches of the subject. Some extracts are found, as it were, fused together into an intelligible account. Other extracts are left separate, but seem to throw light on one another, and to limit or extend the notion which each would have given singly. Few readers but must in studying a title have fancied they found, or at least have tried to find, a clue to the arrangement of the extracts in the connexion and development of the thought; and nothing can have appeared a more legitimate source of assistance in the comprehension of an extract than the train of ideas suggested by the extracts on each side of it.

Yet no long study is required before it is seen that, at least in many cases, this hope is fallacious. Neighbouring extracts are found to be in no wise specially connected, and the same extract is found to contain sometimes an orderly discussion, sometimes a collection of isolated, or at least not closely connected, points. Even if one title conforms more or less to what might be expected in the treatment of a branch of law, the next defies all attempts to justify the notion of arrangement which may have been gained from the preceding.

But Justinian left a clue to the arrangement when he (or Tribonian) directed the compilers to give with each extract a reference to the work from which it was taken. Probably all he aimed at by this means was to give to the new digest the authority which was still justly attributed to the lawyers, whose writings were used. The law, which Justinian gave and meant to give, was the law sanctioned by his predecessors, recognised by custom, and illustrated by writers of renown: it was the old law, but purified, amended, made accessible to all students and practitioners, and suitable to the needs and habits of the time. But these references have been found in fact to have a further value. On patient examination they reveal the mode in which the compilers went to work. The inscriptions, as they are called, attracted the attention of Augustin and others in the sixteenth century, but it was reserved for Friedr. Bluhme in a masterly essay (of which the learning, thoughtfulness, and composure are very striking for a young man of only twenty-three years of age) to solve the problem in a manner which has since met with all but universal acceptance[1]. This essay was published in 1820 in Savigny's *Zeitschrift für gesch. Rechtswiss.* Vol. IV.[2]

On examining the inscriptions in any title containing a large number of extracts it will be noticed that the extracts from each work, say for instance Ulpian's Commentary on Sabinus, follow each other in the order of the work itself. Take the last title in the Digest (L. 17, *de diuersis regulis*); the second extract is from the first book of Ulpian's commentary, the third extract is from the third book, the fourth extract from the sixth book, the sixth extract from the seventh book, the ninth extract from the fifteenth book, the thirteenth extract from the nineteenth book, and so on, the intermediate extracts being from other works, which again are quoted in their own order. Further, if the different works, from which extracts are made in this title, are taken in the order in which they occur in this title, and this list of works be compared with the works from which extracts are made in another title (say that *de uerborum significatione*, L. 16), it will be seen that, so far as the same works occur at all, there is a great similarity in the order, accompanied with certain differences which, when the comparison is extended to several titles, assume a marked character, clearly not accidental. The works are seen to be grouped in three large masses and one smaller one. In each of these groups the order of works is in the main the same in each title (so far as it contains extracts from these works at all), but the groups themselves change their positions. Thus in XLV. 1, the order of these groups may be represented by $A\ B\ C\ c$; in L. 16, it becomes $B\ A\ c\ C$; in L. 17, $A\ c\ C\ B$. ($C\ c$ or $c\ C$ will be generally treated as one group, of which a small number of works are sometimes suffixed, sometimes prefixed, to the bulk of the group.) On carrying the examination throughout the Digest it is found that

---

[1] F. C. Schmidt in his well-written work, *Methode der Auslegung der Justinianischen Rechtsbücher*, 1855, §§ 30—36, is an exception. But his objections and illustrations are quite inadequate, and not in themselves maintainable.

[2] He published separately an essay on the repetitions in the Digest (*De geminatis* &c., Jenae, 1820).

these groups are persistent, but that there are, on the whole not unfrequently, slight displacements of the order of the works in the several groups, and intrusions of one or more extracts from one group into the midst of another group.   The most noticeable displacements are of two kinds, first, the alternation of some works with others of similar contents, and secondly, the displacement of a few extracts from their regular order to the commencement of the title, where they form a sort of introduction to the subject.   These facts clearly suggest a theory of the course of proceedings followed by the compilers, which may be illustrated by considering the natural probabilities of the case.

A long task, a short time, and a large body of Commissioners naturally lead to division of the work.   The work to be done was, in this case, first the reduction of the large mass of writings of lawyers of recognised authority into a manageable compass, by the omission of what was obsolete, the decision of disputes, the removal of contradictions and repetitions, and then the consolidation of the matter into fifty books under titles selected from the Code or the Perpetual Edict.   To divide the Commissioners into committees and to assign to each committee a fair share of the treatises to read and manipulate seems an obvious course.   The task of removing repetitions and contradictions would be greatly facilitated, if works dealing with the same subject-matter were assigned to the same section and were read and examined in connexion with one another. Doubt would be sure to arise as to the precise title (the Code contains 765) to which any part of the book which they were reading should be referred, and whether it would be better to make longer and more continuous extracts with fewer titles, or shorter extracts under more numerous titles.   Such points would be more capable of at least a provisional solution, if each committee worked first on some comprehensive work or works which kept before them the extent and connexion of the matter.   And it would probably be thought advisable to select for this purpose the latest of the important authors, as shewing most completely what opinions had met most general acquiescence, and what contradictions and disputes still remained for decision. The Roman writers on law were evidently in the habit of quoting largely from their predecessors (as was indeed almost necessary at a time when books were all manuscript and copies therefore rare and costly), and thus a later work might well give not only a general account of the matter from the writer's own point of view, but also an account of the different views and illustrations of others.   After each committee had done its own work the consolidation of the whole would have to be undertaken.   Sometimes no doubt the division of subject-matter would be so clean, or the matter itself so scanty, that the title would remain unaltered from the form in which it left the committee.   But few writers are so logical in their divisions and so stern in restricting their discussion, that under each head only that matter is found which is suitable there and not suitable else-where.   Certainly such was not the character of the Roman jurists : they treated in the same book questions which are fruitfully discussed under more than one head.   The result would be that all the com-mittees would have contributions to make to many titles.   The easiest way to compose what was ultimately to form a title of the Digest would be to put the several contributions one after the other, without attempting any arrangement of the fragments according to their meaning.   But the same process of striking out repetitions and contradictions would have to be gone through with the title as a whole, which each committee had gone through with its own part.

This account of what, considering the instructions and the nature of the material, would be *a priori* probable, or at least very possible, fits in with what has been gathered from an attentive examination of the Digest, especially of the inscriptions.   It is hardly therefore an assumption to say that this is what was done.   Tribonian divided his Commission into three committees and the books to be extracted into three groups, or masses.   The first group is headed by Ulpian's commentary on Sabinus ; the second group by two-thirds of Ulpian's commentary on the Edict, viz. the first third and the last third ; the third group is headed by Papinian's works.   From a comparison of the commentaries on Sabinus by Ulpian, Paul, and Pomponius, we can see that the subject-matter of Sabinus must have been, speaking generally, inheritance, consensual contracts, family law, theft, con-dictions, stipulations and perhaps some other matters, but the evidence is conflicting[1].   The part of the commentaries on the Praetor's Edict which dealt with the same heads of law, i.e. the middle third, was given to the same section.   The Sabinian group then would contain the principal materials for Books XII.—XL. and a good proportion of Books XLV.—L.   The Edictal group would contain the principal materials for Books II.—XI. and XLI.—XLIV. and a proportion of the

[1] See Leist's *Versuch einer Geschichte des römischen Rechtsystem* (1850) p. 44 sqq. and table appended: also account of Sabinus, below ch. x.

final books. Of Justinian's Parts, Parts I. II. would belong to the Edictal group, Parts III.—V. to the Sabinian group, Parts VI. and VII. were divided between them. The Sabinian group stood relatively in a closer relation to the old civil law, the Edictal group to the praetorian law. The Papinian group would be supplementary to both. It is noticeable that these groups correspond to the course of study in the law schools before Justinian reformed it. The first year's course (marriage, guardianship, inheritance) and part of the second year's course in alternate years (commercial contracts) are included in the Sabinian group; the constant part of the second year's course, viz. Procedure (Pars I. = Books I.—IV. of Digest), and actions for the recovery of property, which alternated with commercial contracts for the second year's course, are included in the Edictal group; the constant part of the third year's course (Papinian) and the fourth year's study (Pauli Responsa) were included in the Papinian group. Among the compilers were four Professors of Law, who may naturally be supposed to have been allotted to the group principally treated in their lectures.

Besides the works already mentioned each group contained some other important treatises and a number of smaller writings on special points of law. It would seem that these smaller writings were allotted to the three committees more to make an equal distribution of the mass to be dealt with than from any strict division of subject-matter. A complete list of the works extracted is given in Appendix B. It shews the distribution between the several committees, the order in which the works were taken, and the subordinate groups of works dealt with at the same time, so that parts of the one work were taken before parts of the others, as if they had been separate works. For instance the whole of Ulpian's commentary on the Urban Edict does not precede the whole of Paul's commentary, nor do these two precede the whole of Gaius' commentary on the provincial Edict; but, beginning with the first six books of Ulpian, with the first five of Paul, and with the first of Gaius, we then go on to the seventh book of Ulpian, the sixth and seventh of Paul, and the second of Gaius, and so on. Thus of the Sabinian group there were taken together, and broken up into smaller groups, the commentaries on Sabinus, those on the middle part of the Edict, the various books of Institutes, the books on Adultery, the collections of Rules and the books on Appeals. Of the Edictal group there were broken up and grouped in sections the commentaries on the Edict, the books on Plautius, the Digests of Celsus and Marcellus, the books on the Julian and Papian law, and others. Of the Papinian group the *Quaestiones* of Paul and Scaevola, the answers of Paul and Scaevola, the books on Trusts, the *Receptae sententiae* of Paul with the Epitome of Hermogenian, and others were respectively grouped.

Out of nearly 230 works bearing separate titles, extracts from which appear in the Digest, a small number have composed the bulk of the Digest. The works first taken in hand were large and comprehensive treatises or collections, and naturally extracts from them rendered it superfluous to make many or large extracts from most of the others, except on special points. Hommel has rearranged all the extracts under the head of the works from which they were taken, and although from the necessity of the case his book falls far short of justifying its ambitious title as a 'New birth of the Old Law-Books' (*Palingenesia librorum iuris ueterum*, Lipsiae, 1767) it is convenient for many purposes, and affords us a ready means of determining the proportion in which each work and each author has been made to contribute to the Digest. (See App. C.)

The extracts from Ulpian's commentary on the Edict form between a fourth and a fifth, or, if we add his *Libri ad Sabinum*, nearly one-third of the whole Digest. If we add to these the like treatises of Paul, Pomponius' books on Sabinus, Julian's *Digesta*, Gaius' commentary on the Provincial Edict, Papinian's *Quaestiones* and *Responsa*, and Scaevola's *Digesta*, we have one half of the Digest. Six more works, viz. Ulpian's *Disputationes*, Paul's *Quaestiones*, *Responsa* and books *ad Plautium*, African's *Quaestiones* and Scaevola's *Responsa*, making sixteen works by eight authors, raise the proportion to nearly two-thirds. About twice this number, or thirty-three works by sixteen authors give four-fifths of the whole Digest. The remaining one-fifth is contributed by nearly 200 treatises, none of which however have supplied extracts sufficient to fill much more than four pages of Mommsen's stereotype edition, and some of which have supplied only two or three lines.

The proportion of extracts supplied by each of the three groups is estimated by Bluhme approximately as the numbers 5 for the Sabinian group, 4 for the Edictal group, 3 for the Papinian group. The thirty-three important works, which, as I have stated, furnish together four-fifths of the Digest, are distributed between the groups as follows. I have added my estimate of the pages of Hommel respectively occupied by them.   The order of extraction is preserved, the works dealt with simultaneously being bracketed.

			Hommel's pages
SABINIAN GROUP :			
Ulpiani	*Libri ad Sabinum*	. . . . .	130
Pomponi	„ „	. . . .	37
Pauli	„ „	. . . .	31
Ulpiani	*Libri* XXVI.—LI. *ad edictum*	. . .	125½
Pauli	*Libri* XXVIII.—XLVIII. *med.*	. . .	26
Gai	*Libri* IX.—XVIII. *ad edictum prouinciale*	.	14
Ulpiani	*Disputationes*	. . . . .	25
Ulpiani	*Opiniones* .	. . . . .	9½
Iuliani	*Digesta*	. . . . .	58
Africani	*Quaestiones*	. . . .	23½
Marciani	*Institutiones*	. . . .	16½
Ulpiani	*Libri de officio proconsulis*	. . .	15
			—— 511
EDICTAL GROUP :			
Ulpiani	*Libri* I.—XXV.; LII.—LXXXI. *ad edictum*	.	216½
Ulpiani	*Libri ad edictum aedilium curulium*	.	10½
Pauli	*Libri* I.—XXVII.; XLVIII. *med.*—LXXVIII. *ad edictum*	. . . . .	66
Gai	*Libri* I.—VIII.; XIX.—XXX. *ad edict. prouinciale*	19
Pauli	*Libri ad Plautium*	. . . .	22
Celsi	*Digesta* .	. . . . .	14
Marcelli	*Digesta* .	. . . . .	16
Modestini	*Excusationes*	. . . .	8
Modestini	*Responsa* .	. . . .	11
Iavoleni	*Epistulae*	. . . . .	9
Pomponi	*Libri ad Q. Mucium*	. . .	13½
Callistrati	*Libri de cognitionibus*	. . .	9½
Ulpiani	*Libri ad legem Iuliam et Papiam*	.	8
			—— 423
PAPINIAN GROUP :			
Papiniani	*Quaestiones*	. . . .	45
Papiniani	*Responsa* .	. . . .	40
Pauli	*Quaestiones*	. . . .	29
Scaevolae	*Quaestiones*	. . . .	9
Pauli	*Responsa* .	. . . .	20
Scaevolae	*Responsa* .	. . . .	20

		Hommel's pages.
Ulpiani	*Fideicommissa*	17
⌠Pauli	*Sententiae*	15
⌡Hermogeniani	*Iuris epitomae*	9½
Tryphonini	*Disputationes*	18½
		—— 223

APPENDIX TO PAPINIAN GROUP:

Scaevolae *Digesta*   44

                                                1201

N.B. The total number of extracts in the Digest occupy about 1510 of Hommel's pages.

The group called Appendix to the Papinian group, and which is found sometimes to precede the bulk of that group, sometimes to follow it, contains one very important work, Scaevola's Digest, and also some books of Labeo abridged by Javolenus, and by Paulus. It is probable that they were discovered later than the rest, and given out, probably to the Papinian Committee, separately from the other works assigned to them.

Another case of indecision is shewn by the position of some books of Ulpian's, and the others' Commentaries on the Edict. The whole of Books 52—81 of Ulpian's were given to the Edictal Committee, but they were extracted in this order: Books 56—81, then the Commentary on the Aediles' Edict, then Books 54, 55, and lastly Books 52, 53. Possibly these books 52—55 were originally assigned to the Sabinian Committee, and they being overworked eventually passed them on to the Edictal Committee. But it is very likely that the subject-matter had something to do with it. Book 52 (besides treating of the security to be given to the legatee) dealt with *operis noui nuntiatio ;* Book 53 with *damni infecti* and *aquae pluuiae arcendae ;* Books 54, 55 with claims to freedom and with the *publicani.* These are just matters of which the position in the Digest is somewhat difficult to account for. See what is said of Dig. XXXIX. and XL above p. xliii. The position of the Commentary on the Aedile's Edict in the order of extracting probably indicates that that Edict was by Julian made an Appendix to the Praetor's Edict. (Hence the Florentine Index gives the number of Ulpian's books on the Edict as 83, and of Paul's as 80.)

If we turn for a minute from the works to the authors it may be noted that the extracts from Ulpian's various works are in bulk 39 per cent. of the whole Digest.   Paulus has nearly 18 per cent.; Papinianus, Scaevola, Pomponius, Julianus and Gaius have together more than 24 per cent.; Modestinus, Marcianus, Africanus, Javolenus and Marcellus 9½ per cent.;' Tryphoninus, Callistrátus, Celsus and Hermogenianus nearly 4 per cent.   Thus the sixteen authors of the thirty-three works mentioned above have, when their other works are taken into account, supplied 94½ per cent. of the whole.   The remaining 5½ per cent. was supplied by extracts from 22 writers.

If we make a chronological division, classing as older writers all down to and inclusive of Gaius, and as later writers the rest, beginning with Uenuleius and Marcellus, one-fifth of the Digest is taken from the older writers and four-fifths from the later.   The Republican writers (Q. Mucius, Aelius Gallus) and the other writers before Trajan (Alfenus, Labeo, Proculus) are insignificant in bulk (not 2 per cent. of the whole): the writers after Alexander Severus, or at any rate after Gordian (Hermogenianus, Arcadius) are doubly insignificant (not we may safely say 1 per cent.).   Over 95 per cent. of the Digest was originally written from cir. 100 to 230 A.D.

Such then being the authors and works used, what is the nature of the Digest as revealed by the observed order?   Clearly it is not a systematic treatise on each separate head of law, composed after consultation of these authorities.   Nor is it a skilful mosaic in which fragments carefully selected from these works are disposed, each in the place and order calculated to give the effect of original treatment, because permeated with consecutive thought.   It is simply the result of taking the selected treatises and arranging them, partly in one line, partly in parallel lines, and then as it were squeezing them together, so as to throw out what was antiquated or superfluous, and leave only what was practical, with no more repetition than was needed for clearness.   Where Ulpian, Pomponius and Paul had treated the same matter, the most comprehensive, usually Ulpian, sometimes Paul (e.g. D. XLI. 2), was made the groundwork, and the others were either dovetailed into it or clipt and appended.   The larger treatises being exhausted, supplementary remarks or illustrations were taken from the multifarious string of minor works which each committee had received for examination.   The same process was repeated when the contributions of the three committees were combined, but there is less fusing of the extracts together: the largest and most important string of extracts being put first, the other two contributions were clipt and appended.

But there are, as has been said and as would naturally result from such treatment, signs of the operations of the compilers having been in a limited degree guided by the connexion of thought. First, not unusually some extracts are taken from the regular order of the works and placed at the beginning of the title as an introduction (see ll 1—6 of this title). Secondly, some extracts have been evidently mutilated so as to form part of a sentence in another extract from a different work (see e.g. l 8; l 14; l 16; l 69 of this title, and especially III. 3; IV. 3 *passim*). Thirdly, successive extracts are connected by particles, e.g. *quodsi, uero, autem, enim, ergo*, &c., which may or may not have been in the original work, but at any rate have, it is fair to suppose, been either left there or inserted there on purpose to connect the meaning of the two fragments. Fourthly, repeated alternation of extracts from the same books indicates the selection or compression of the one with an eye to the other. Where there is no such connexion visible, we should not be justified in imagining that the compilers intended to imply any connexion in thought between two successive extracts, unless one at least of the extracts is found in a different part of the title from that which the known order of the treatises would assign to it. And even if it is found in such an abnormal position, we cannot at once conclude that the law given in the extract is meant to be explained or qualified or supplemented by the adjoining extracts or *uice uersa*. The position may be merely accidental—a slip of the compilers or their copyists, a consequence of the exigencies or convenience of the work. For there is no ground for thinking that the compilers set any special value on preserving the order. The order, which we observe, is one which was natural for them to fall into, but not one thoughtfully adopted and religiously retained and protected. They struck out parts of the manuscripts before them, amended the rest where necessary, and gave them to be copied one by one or section by section as they finished with them.

But even when we can see some design in the displacement of a fragment, it is not always a design of real importance for the interpretation of the law. The connexion may be due to a much slighter cause. Thus Bluhme (p. 293) suggests that the extract from Papinian forming l 33 of our title has been put out of its place, merely because Julian is mentioned, and the position thus serves to introduce the

extracts from Julian's own works. Possibly Papinian had quoted
the part of Julian which the compilers have given from the original.
In D. I. 6 the extract from Gaius (1 1) is interrupted in order to give
the full text of Pius' rescript, and for this purpose Ulpian's book *de off.*
procons. is resorted to (1 2). Again Bluhme suggests that ll 5—8 of
D. XXXIII. 6 have been placed after l 4 merely because they, like l 4,
speak of quantity, not quality, of wine, oil, &c. contained in a bequest.
In fact a disturbance of order may be due to accident or temporary
forgetfulness, or may be due to design, but design may be moved by
only a superficial resemblance or by an external connexion. Justinian
appears to have hurried the Commissioners in order to signalize his
third consulship with the additional distinction of the publication of
the Digest (Const. *Tanta* § 23). Bluhme (p. 372) notes that the later
books of the Digest contain less evidence of comparison of the work
of the three sections than the earlier books do—a fact which the
compilers' weariness or Justinian's haste may well account for. The
titles containing most disarrangement of the order are, according to
Bluhme, I. 3, 5, 7. In Book XX. the desire to put Papinian first has
avowedly (Const. *omnem* § 4) been the main motive. Thus the extract
from Gaius now standing fourth was clearly intended originally to
head the first title of that book.

Under the light thrown by Bluhme's discovery the Digest
assumes a different aspect to what might otherwise be taken.
The internal connexion of thought was not the motive of the
arrangement, and the arrangement cannot therefore be made the
guide of interpretation. What connexion of thought there is comes
mainly from the compilers having taken as the foundation several
systematic works, compared them with one another, and given us
blocks of them pared away to avoid repetitions. These blocks may
coincide with a natural division of the subject-matter, or may contain parts of two or more sections, or may be merely a string of
disconnected cases on different parts of the subject. Mommsen's
edition, like some other modern editions, prints each fragment con-
tinuously and separates successive fragments. This is quite right
when the composition of the Digest has to be shewn. I have however thought it advisable to distinguish in the printing the parts of
some fragments and to join together some separate fragments, the
order however being preserved. A rearrangement of the matter in
each title of the Digest, so as to make an orderly discussion, has
been executed by Pothier, but the result is not very satisfactory;

the difficulty of reference is considerable; and we have a subjective instead of an objective basis to rest on.

As an illustration of the compilers' work, we may examine the order in our present title. The first six fragments are from the work of different committees. Of these the first two are from the Edictal series; l 3 is from the Sabinian series; l 4 from the Edictal series, l 5 from the Papinian, and again l 6 from the Edictal. Moreover ll 4, 6 are from an earlier part of the Edictal series than ll 1 and 2. On examination it is clear that these six fragments have been arranged so as to form an introduction, containing definition, character, mode of constitution, acquisition and loss. With l 7 we begin the extracts from Ulpian *ad Sabinum* which form the bulk of the title. Ulpian's seventeenth book is interrupted by short interpolations (l 8) from the fortieth book of his commentary on the Edict (one of the Edict books assigned to the Sabinian Committee), and from Pomponius' fifth and Paul's third book *ad Sabinum*. L 11 is from Paul's epitome of Alfenus, also in the Sabinian series. L 15 begins the eighteenth book of Ulpian *ad Sabinum*, which is similarly interrupted. L 21 and l 23 are interpolations from the seventeenth book of Ulpian, which had evidently been postponed on account of the fuller treatment of the subject of acquisition by slaves in the eighteenth book. There is also an interpolation, l 24, from the tenth book of Paulus *ad Sabinum*, i. e. a later book than would naturally be taken with Ulpian's eighteenth book. Then follows another extract from Paul's tenth book *ad Sabinum*, which, if the connexion of thought had been regarded, must have been placed after l 23 or in some such place. It is put here simply because it was extracted after Paul's third book, and before Julian. The like reason accounts for l 32. Then comes a curious interpolation from the Edictal series, viz. an extract from Papinian for which Bluhme, as I have said, accounts by the reference in it to Julian. Extracts from Julian, African, Marcian, Ulpian's Rules and Neratius follow in due order: but (l 39) an extract from Gaius *ad Edictum prouinciale* (one of the Edictal series) is fused with Marcian. We then proceed in l 45 with the Edictal series, and the first here is another extract from the same book of Gaius. Evidently the Edictal series has been made slightly to overlap the end of the Sabinian, and thus l 39 has been squeezed into the Sabinian group instead of following l 44. The extracts from the books on Plautius and from Paul's edition of Vitellius duly follow. After l 50 should have come the other extract from the same third book on Vitellius and an extract from Celsus which have been transferred to head the title (ll 1, 2). Modestin's various works and Pomponius *ad Q. Mucium* follow duly. An extract from Gaius *ad Edict. prou.* follows. According to the Florentine MS. it is from the seventeenth book, and if so, belongs to the Sabinian series, but the inferior MSS. give the seventh book, and then it belongs to the Edictal series, and is an after-thought of the Edictal compilers, not an intermixture of the two series. With l 57 begins the Papinian series, the extract from the *Quaestiones* having been already taken to make l 33. The series duly extends to l 63. After this comes a number of extracts from the Sabinian series interrupted by l 65 and l 71, and concluded by l 74 from the Edictal section. And this collection is composed of two sets of extracts, ll 64—67 and ll 68—73, the former set consisting of extracts from the books on the Edict and a treatise of Julian's, the latter of extracts from Ulpian's seventeenth book and Pomponius' fifth book *ad Sabinum*. In the order of extraction by the Sabinian Committee, the latter set would precede the former. It is difficult to find any reason for this recurrence of Sabinian extracts at the end of the title and in an inverted order. Probably they were intended for insertion in another title, and have thus fallen out of their normal position. Certainly the connexion of thought can have had nothing to do with this postponement and with the arrangement as we now have it.

If the connexion of thought had been the ruling principle the arrangement in our title is inexplicable. Why should ll 18—20 be put where they are, instead of being partly put amongst the other miscellaneous extracts and partly interpolated in appropriate places? Why separate l 10 from l 48. § 1? and why connect the latter with l 48. § 2, except because they were, after perhaps divers omissions, left continuous in the book from which they were taken? And the same may be said of the present continuity of l 19. pr. and l 19. § 1. Surely l 12. pr., l 18, l 19. § 1, l 59 ought to come together; and so also l 7. § 2 fin. with l 27. § 3 and l 52; and l 44 with l 7. § 3; and so on.

In some titles the three series occur twice over. Books XXX.— XXXII. are as it were one title. The Sabinian mass (with a considerable number of interpolations from the others) occupies Book XXX. Book XXXI. as far as l 63 is Edictal. The rest of XXXI. and the first 42 extracts of XXXII. are Papinian and post-Papinian.

Then we recommence with Sabinian l 44—l 75 ; Edictal l 76—l 90 ; Papinian l 91 to end.   Evidently these last extracts (XXXII. l 44 to end) were intended to form a separate title *de uerborum et rerum significatione*, as in the Code VI. § 8 such a title immediately follows the title *de legatis*.   So the title *de ritu nuptiarum* (D. XXIII. 2) has what was intended for two titles, ll 1—51 corresponding to Cod. v. 4, and the rest corresponding to Cod. v. 5, *de incestis et inutilibus nuptiis*.   The three series occur twice over here, as they do also in I. 3, where l 32 to end appears to have been meant for a title *de consuetudine ;* in XXI. 2, where l 13 to end may have been for a separate title *de duplae stipulatione ;* and in XXXIV. 2, where the three series recommence at l 19, Bluhme suggests that *uestimenta* and *ornamenta* seem the principal matters in the former part of the title, and *aurum* and *argentum* in the latter.   In other titles one mass only is repeated, e.g. D. XXXIII. 7, where the Papinian mass occurs first in ll 2—7, and then again ll 19—29.   Our title appears to be another instance, though not expressly mentioned by Bluhme under this head.

In the long title *de uerb. obl.* (XLV. 1) the first hand of the Florentine MS. has put a new rubric τὸ B τοῦ *de uerborum obligationibus* after l 47, and a similar one Γ after l 122, thus dividing the title into three unequal portions.   It is noticeable that the first section thus terminates with the extracts from the books on Sabinus ; the second begins with the books on the Edict which were taken by the Sabinian Committee, proceeds with the Edictal series and with Papinian's *Quaestiones* and *Responsa*, and ends with a long extract from Scaevola's Digest : the third section has the rest of the Papinian series.   This looks as if the division in the Florentine MS. witnessed to some minor distribution of work among the committees.

CHAPTER V.

COMPARISON OF EXTRACTS WITH THEIR ORIGINALS.

IF Justinian's Commissioners had adopted a different course and compiled each title as a systematic account of the subject-matter, using such materials as they found, but welding them into a new mass, regardless of preserving the words or identity of the authors, they would have produced what would at first sight have been better for practical purposes and more worthy of the idea of a scientific digest of the law. But we should have been much worse off. We should have had the law as conceived by Byzantine lawyers in the sixth century instead of numerous, often large, extracts mutilated and disarranged, but still preserving much of the practical results and of the characteristic form of the writings of the most brilliant period of Roman Jurisprudence. So far as they used the writings of the old lawyers the work might yet have been valuable, as we can see from Justinian's Institutes, but the historical interest would have largely suffered. If the compilers had been at liberty to compile as they pleased and give no authorities, we should have had much less of the old lawyers than we have, thanks to Tribonian's direction to preserve the names of the authors and to the compilers' method of giving the extracts (at least usually) in the order in which they extracted them. But the question still remains, how far have these extracts been altered by the Commissioners? Justinian gave large powers of correction, and was so stringent in forbidding any comparison of the result with the originals, that we might be sure *a priori* that these large powers were used. A comparison of Justinian's Institutes with Gaius (as made in Gneist's *Syntagma*) is not good evidence on this point, because the procedure there was not strictly analogous to that in the case of the Digest. The Institutes were to be a new work, and only a general acknowledgment was made to Gaius and others. The Digest was to be a consolidation of the old lawyers' writings, corrected and compressed. It is well therefore to compare[1] the passages of the old lawyers which have been independently preserved to us, with the form which they have assumed in the Digest under the manipulation of Justinian's Commissioners. The comparison is not reassuring. Amendment of the law, decision of controversies, omission of repetitions and of obsolete matters were the duty of the Commissioners, and could not but largely alter the shape of the material. It is clear from this comparison that they *have* often largely altered it. Though much of the writing of the old jurists is left us in the Digest, and some passages coincide precisely with the words otherwise preserved to us, it is yet somewhat hazardous to say of any fragment, where we have not

---

[1] Something of this kind has been done, not very satisfactorily, by Istrich, *Quomodo versati sint compilatores Dig.* &c. 1863. I have taken one reference from it.

independent evidence of its being a faithful extract, that it represents exactly the view of the author, and still more hazardous to say that it represents his mode of stating it[1]. And unfortunately the independent evidence that we have covers the merest fraction of the Digest. The Vatican Fragments (first published 1823), Gaius' Institutes, the *Collatio Mosaicarum et Romanarum Legum*, and Paul's *Sententiae*, are almost our only independent sources. And most of the passages thus comparable (I count over 80 in all) are very short. I append a comparison of the more important passages and of some of the smaller ones, which bear characteristic traces of Tribonian's 'short method'. The parts printed in Roman letters are those which Tribonian has left unaltered. The parts printed in Italic letters shew the alterations. Consequently in the left hand column italics represent what Tribonian has omitted; in the right hand column what he has added or substituted.

In considering these extracts it is desirable to remember that partly by the effect of time, partly by imperial constitutions and especially by those which Justinian issued for the express purpose of preparing the Digest, changes had taken place which necessitated large alterations or omissions. The following are the most important. The abolition of *Latinitas* and granting of full citizenship to all freemen whether Italians or foreigners (D. I. 5. 1 17[2]; Cod. VII. 5, 6); the gradual extinction of *mancipatio* and *in iure cessio* (p. 36); the consolidation of *usucapio* and *longi temporis possessio* (p. 138); the abolition of the distinction between land in Italy and in the provinces; the disuse of the forms of marriage which made the woman pass into the power of her husband (p. 163); the abolition of *fiducia*, and amalgamation of *pignus* and *hypotheca* (p. xxxix); the abolition of *sponsores* and *fidepromissores* leaving only *fideiussores*; the abolition of *adstipulatores*; the extinction of the old *litterarum obligatio*; the large reforms in the law of wills, *cretio* (Cod. VI. 30. 1 17), and all distinction between the several kinds of legacies being abolished, and

---

[1] Compare for instance xxxii. 1 55 with L. 16. 1 167. Ofilius' authorship is suppressed, and Ulpian's arrangement, as shewn by the former extract, is altered in the latter. On the general question Puchta makes some remarks, Cursus § 104, with Rudorff's notes *nn*.

[2] While Caracalla made all freemen Roman citizens, we find in Ulpian, Paul, and the Theodosian Code *Latinitas* &c. treated as still subsisting. The most satisfactory explanation is that Caracalla gave citizenship to all Roman freemen of inferior status at the time but did not prevent such growth of *Latinitas* and *Peregrinitas* as arose from informal manumission, or from punishment &c. Cf. Zimmern § 123; Walter § 352; Kuntze § 326: &c.

legacies and *fideicommissa* being put on the same footing, accompanied
by the greatest freedom which either possessed before ; the consolidation of the *S.Cta Pegasianum* and *Trebellianum ;* the alterations
in the course of intestate succession ; the practical repeal of the *lex
Cincia* and of the *Iulia* and *Papia Poppaea,* and finally the change
of the judicial system under Diocletian by which the *formulae* and
much of the consequent language passed away.

Another cause of omissions may be found in the directions of
Justinian (Const. *Deo auctore,* § 9) that matter already placed in the
Code should not be repeated in the Digest. How far these directions
were observed we do not know. It is possible that Tribonian may
have allowed much to stand in the Digest, which he would have
omitted, if he had not contemplated the revision of the Code, which was
afterwards carried into effect. Of this we have no means of judging.
(See however Const. *Cordi,* §§ 1—3.)

Gai. *Inst.* i. 48—55.	Dig. i. 6. l 1.
	Gaius libro primo institutionum.
Sequitur de iure personarum alia diuisio. *Nam* quaedam personae sui iuris sunt, quaedam alieno iuri subiectae sunt. *Rursus earum personarum quae alieno iuri subiectae sunt, aliae in potestate, aliae in manu, aliae in mancipio sunt.* Uideamus *nunc* de his quae alieno iuri subiectae si̇nt. Si cognoverimus quae istae personae sunt, simul intellegemus quae sui iuris si̇nt. *Ac prius* dispiciamus de *i̇is* qui̇ in aliena potestate sunt.	De iure personarum alia diuisio sequitur, *quod* quaedam personae sui iuris sunt, quaedam alieno iuri subiectae suṅt. Uideamus *itaque* de his quae alieno iuri subiectae suṅt : *nam* si cognoverimus quae istae personae sunt, simul intellegemus quae sui iuris sunt. Dispiciamus *itaque* de *hi*s quae in aliena potestate sunt. *Igitur* in potestate sunt serui dominorum. Quae quidem potestas iuris
In potestate *itaque* sunt serui dominorum. Quae quidem potestas iuris gentium est : nam aput omnes peraeque gentes animaduertere possumus dominis in seruos uitae necisque potestatem *esse*; et quodcumque per seruum adquiritur id domino adquiritur. Sed hoc tempore *neque ciuibus Romanis nec* ullis *aliis* hominibus qui sub imperio *populi* Romani sunt, licet supra modum et sine causa in	gentium est : nam apud omnes peraeque gentes animaduertere possumus dominis in seruos uitae necisque potestatem *fuisse*; et quodcumque per seruum adquiritur, id domino adquiritur. Sed hoc tempore nullis hominibus qui sub imperio Romano sunt, licet supra modum et sine causa *legibus cognita* in

seruos suos saeuire. Nam ex con-
stitutione *imperatoris* Antonini qui
sine causa seruum suum occiderit,
non minus *teneri* iubetur quam qui
alienum seruum occiderit. Sed et
maior *quoque* asperitas dominorum
per eiusdem principis constitution*em*
coercetur: *nam*[1] *consultus a quibusdam praesidibus prouinciarum de
his seruis qui ad fana deorum uel
ad statuas principum confugiunt,
praecepit, ut, si intolerabilis uideatur
dominorum saeuitia, cogantur seruos
suos uendere. Et utrumque recte fit:
male enim nostro iure uti non debemus; qua ratione et prodigis inter-
dicitur bonorum suorum administratio. Ceterum*[2] *cum aput ciues
Romanos duplex sit dominium, (nam
uel in bonis uel ex iure Quiritium
uel ex utroque iure cuiusque seruus
esse intellegitur), ita demum seruum
in potestate domini esse dicemus, si
in bonis eius sit, etiamsi simul ex
iure Quiritium eiusdem non sit: nam
qui nudum ius Quiritium in seruo
habet, is potestatem habere non intellegitur.* Item in potestate nostra
sunt liberi nostri quos iustis nuptiis procreauimus: quod ius proprium ciuium Romanorum est.

seruos suos saeuire. Nam ex con-
stitutione *diui* Antonini qui
sine causa seruum suum occiderit
non minus *puniri* iubetur, quam qui
alienum seruum occiderit. Sed et
maior   asperitas dominorum
eiusdem principis constitution*e*
coercetur.

(1 2)

1 3. Gaius libro primo institutionum.

Item in potestate nostra
sunt liberi nostri quos *ex* iustis nuptiis procreau*erimus*: quod ius proprium ciuium Romanorum est.

Gai. Inst. I. 98—107.

Adoptio   *autem*   duobus
modis fit, aut *populi* auctoritate
aut imperio magistratus *uel*[3] *praetoris. Populi* auctoritate adoptamus eos qui sui iuris sunt: quae

Dig. I. 7. 1 2.

Gaius libro primo institutionum.
Generalis enim adoptio duobus
modis fit, aut *principis* auctoritate
aut magistratus imperio.
  Principis auctoritate adoptamus eos qui sui iuris sunt: quae

---

[1] In place of this paragraph the Digest contains an extract from Ulpian which gives the rescript of Antoninus at length.

[2] This is wholly omitted in the Digest because the distinction was abolished by Justinian. See Cod. VII. 25.

[3] *Veluti* Stud. *Velut* Huschke.

species adoptionis dicitur adrogatio, quia et is qui adoptat rogatur, id est interrogatur, an uelit eum quem adoptaturus sit iustum sibi filium esse, et is qui adoptatur rogatur an id fieri patiatur; *et populus rogatur an id fieri iubeat.* Imperio magistratus adoptamus eos qui in potestate parentium sunt, siue primum gradum liberorum optineant, qualis est filius et filia, siue inferiorem, qualis est nepos neptis, pronepos proneptis. *Et quidem illa adoptio quae per populum fit, nusquam nisi Romae fit*[1]*; ad*[2] *haec etiam in prouinciis aput praesides earum fieri solet. Item per populum feminae non adoptantur, nam id magis placuit*[3]*; aput praetorem uero uel in prouinciis aput proconsules legatumue etiam feminae solent adoptari. Item inpuberem*[4] *aput populum adoptari aliquando prohibitum est, aliquando permissum est: nunc ex epistula optimi imperatoris Antonini quam scripsit pontificibus, si iusta causa adoptionis esse uidebitur, cum quibusdam condicionibus permissum est. Aput praetorem uero, et in prouinciis aput proconsulem legatumue cuiuscumque aetatis*[5] *adoptare possumus.* Illud *uero* utriusque adoptionis commune est, qu*ia* et hi qui generare non possunt, quales sunt spadones, adoptare possunt. *Feminae*[6] *uero nullo modo adoptare possunt, quia ne quidem naturales libe-*

species adoptionis dicitur adrogatio, quia et is qui adoptat rogatur, id est interrogatur, an uelit eum quem adoptaturus sit iustum sibi filium esse, et is qui adoptatur rogatur an id fieri patiatur.

Imperio magistratus adoptamus eos qui in potestat*e* parent*is* sunt, siue primum gradum liberorum optineant, qualis est filius   filia, siue inferiorem, qualis est nepos neptis, pronepos proneptis.

Illud   utriusque adoptionis commune est qu*od* et hi qui generare non possunt, quales sunt spadones, adoptare possunt.

---

[1] No restriction of place : Emperor's rescript required ; Cod. viii. 47. 1 6.

[2] *At* Stud. Huschke.

[3] Women *sui iuris* were by Justinian's legislation adopted only by Emperor's rescript ; Cod. viii. 47. 1 8 ; D. i. 7. 1 21, which passage is attributed to Gaius, but has doubtless been altered.

[4] See D. i. 7. 1 18 ; Cod. viii. 47. 1 2.

[5] Stud. inserts *personas*. Huschke inserts (before *aetatis*) *quemque*.

[6] Women were by Justinian's law sometimes allowed to adopt.   Cod. vii. 47. 1 5.

ros in potestate habent. Item si quis
per populum siue aput praetorem uel
aput praesidem prouinciae adoptaue-
rit, potest eundem alii in adoptionem
dare. Set illa quaestio, an minor
natu maiorem natu adoptare possit,
utriusque adoptionis communis est.
Illut proprium est eius adoptionis quae per *populum* fit, quod
is qui liberos in potestate habet, si
se adrogandum dederit, non solum
ipse potestati adrogatoris subicitur,
set etiam liberi eius in eiusdem fiunt
potestate tamquam nepotes.

Hoc uero proprium est eius adoptionis, quae per *principem* fit, quod
is qui liberos in potestate habet, si
se adrogandum dederit, non solum
ipse potestati adrogatoris subicitur,
sed *et* liberi eius in eiusdem fiunt
potestate tamquam nepotes.

Gai. Inst. ii. 86—93.

Dig. xli. 1. 1 10.

Idem (Gaius) libro secundo institutionum.

Adqui*ritur autem* nobis non solum
per nosmet ipsos, sed etiam per eos
quos in potestate *manu mancipioue*
habemus ; item per *eos* seruos in quibus usumfructum habemus ; item
per homines liberos et seruos alienos
quos bona fide possidemus : de quibus singulis diligen*ter* dispiciamus.
Igitur *liberi nostri quos in potes-*
tate habemus, item quod serui *man-*
cipio accipiunt uel ex traditione nan-
ciscuntur, siue quid stipulentur uel
ex *ali*qualibet causa adquirunt, id
nobis adquiritur : ipse enim qui in
potestate *nostra* est, nihil suum
habere potest ; *et* ideo si heres institutus sit, nisi nostro iussu hereditatem adire non potest ; et si
iubentibus nobis adierit, hereditas
nobis adquiritur, *proinde* atque si
nos ipsi heredes instituti essemus ;
et   conuenienter scilicet legatum
     per *eos*   nobis adquiritur :
dum tamen sciamus, si alterius
in bonis sit seruus, alterius ex iure

Adqui*runtur*   nobis non solum
per nosmet ipsos, sed etiam per eos
quos in potestate
habemus, item per   seruos in quibus usumfructum habemus ; item
per homines liberos et seruos alienos,
quos bona fide possidemus ; de quibus singulis diligen*tius* dispiciamus.
Igitur

           quod serui *nostri*
        ex traditione nan-
ciscuntur, siue quid stipulentur uel
ex qualibet *alia* causa adquirunt, id
nobis adquiritur : ipse enim, qui in
potestate *alterius* est, nihil suum
habere potest ; ideo*que* si heres institutus sit, nisi nostro iussu hereditatem adire non potest ; et si
iubentibus nobis adierit, hereditas
nobis adquiritur, *perinde* atque si
nos ipsi heredes instituti essemus ;
et *his* conuenienter scilicet legatum
nobis per *eundem* adquiritur.

Quiritium, ex omnibus causis ei soli per eum adquiritur cuius in bonis est. Non solum autem proprietas per eos quos in potestate habemus adquiritur nobis, sed etiam possessio : cuius   enim rei possessionem adepti fuerint, id nos possidere uidemur; unde etiam per eos *usucapio procedit. Per eas uero personas quas in manu mancipioue habemus, proprietas quidem adquiritur nobis ex omnibus causis sicut per eos qui in potestate nostra sunt; an autem possessio adquiratur, quaeri solet, quia ipsas non possidemus.* De his autem seruis in quibus tantum usumfructum habemus, ita placuit, ut quidquid ex re nostra uel ex operis suis adquirunt id nobis adquiratur; *quod* uero extra eas causas,   id ad dominum proprietatis pertineat : itaque si is*te* seruus heres institutus sit legatumue *quod*   ei *datum* fuerit, non mihi sed domino proprietatis adquiritur. Idem placet de eo qui *a* nobis bona fide possidetur siue liber sit siue alienus seruus : quod enim placuit de usufructuario, idem probatur etiam de bonae fidei possessore. Itaque quod extra duas *istas* causas adquiritur, id uel ad ipsum pertinet, si liber est, uel ad dominum,   si seruus *sit.* Sed bonae fidei possessor cum usuceperit seruum, quia eo modo dominus fit, ex omn*i*   *causa* per eum sibi adquirere potest.   Usufructuarius uero usucapere   non potest, primum quia non possidet sed habet ius utendi *et* fruendi, deinde *quia* scit alienum seruum esse.

Non solum autem proprietas per eos quos in potestate habemus adquiritur nobis sed etiam possessio : cuius*cumque* enim rei possessionem adepti fuerint, id nos possidere uidemur; unde etiam per eo*rum longam possessionem dominium nobis adquiritur.*

De his autem seruis, in quibus tantum usumfructum habemus, ita placuit, ut quidquid ex re nostra uel ex operis suis adquir*a*nt id nobis adquiratur; *si quid* uero extra eas causas *persecuti sint,* id ad dominum proprietatis pertinet : itaque si is seruus heres institutus sit, legatumue *quid aut* ei *donatum* fuerit, non mihi sed domino proprietatis adquiritur. Idem placet de eo qui   nobis bona fide possidetur siue liber sit siue alienus seruus : quod enim placuit de usufructuario, idem probatur etiam de bonae fidei possessore. Itaque quod extra duas   causas adquiritur, id uel ad ipsum pertinet, si liber est, uel ad dominum *eius,* si seruus *est.* Sed bonae fidei possessor cum usuceperit seruum, quia eo modo dominus fit, ex omn*ibus* caus*is* per eum sibi adquirere potest : usufructuarius uero usucapere *seruum* non potest, primum quia non possidet, sed habet ius utendi   fruendi, deinde *quoniam* scit seruum alienum esse.

e 2

Mosaic. et Roman. legum collatio (ed. Bluhme) vii. 3.

Ulpianus libro xviii. ad edictum sub titulo 'si quadrupes pauperiem dederit'.

Iniuria occisum esse merito adicitur, non enim sufficit occisum sed oportet iniuria id esse factum. *Proinde si quis seruum latronem occiderit, lege Aquilia non tenetur quia²non occidit.* Sed et quemcumque alium ferro se petentem qu*i* occiderit, non uidebitur iniuria occidisse. *Proinde si furem nocturnum, quem lex duodecim tabularum omnimodo permittit occidere, aut diurnum, quem aeque lex permittit, sed ita demum si se telo defendat, uideamus an lege Aquilia teneatur. Et Pomponius dubitat num haec lex non sit in usu.* Et si   quis *noctu* furem occiderit, non dubitamus quin lege Aquilia³ teneatur; sin autem cum posset adprehendere maluit occidere, magis est ut iniuria fecisse uideatur; ergo et*iam lege* Cornelia tenebitur. Iniuriam autem accipere hic nos oportet non, quemadmodum circa iniuriarum actionem, contumeliam quandam, sed, quod non iure factum est, hoc est contra ius, id est si culpa quis occiderit.

Dig. ix. 2. 1 3; 1 5. pr. § 1.

Ulpianus libro octauo decimo ad edictum.

Si seruus seruaue iniuria occisus occisaue fuerit, lex Aquilia locum habet.

Iniuria occisum esse merito adicitur, non enim sufficit occisum, sed oportet iniuria id esse factum¹.

Sed ets*i* quemcumque alium ferro se petentem qu*is* occiderit, non uidebitur iniuria occidisse.

Et si *metu* quis *mortis* furem occiderit, non dubita*bitur* quin lege Aquilia *non* teneatur; sin autem cum posset adprehendere maluit occidere, magis est ut iniuria fecisse uideatur: ergo et Cornelia tenebitur. Iniuriam autem hic accipere nos oportet non, quemadmodum circa iniuriarum actionem, contumeliam quandam, sed, quod non iure factum est, hoc est contra ius, id est si culpa quis occiderit.

---

¹ The treatment of the robber and the night thief slain are in the Digest given somewhat more fully in an interpolated extract from Gaius *ad Edict. prou.*

² Huschke inserts *iniuria*.

³ Huschke omits *non* two lines higher and adds it here after *Aquilia*.

Mosaic. et Roman. legum collatio (ed. Bluhme) xii. 7.

Ulpianus libro xviii. ad edictum, sub titulo 'si fatebitur iniuria occisum esse, in simplum ut condiceret'.

Item si *insulam meam adusseris uel* incenderis, Aquiliae actionem habebo. *Idemque est et si arbustum meum uel uillam meam. Quodsi dolo quis insulam exusserit, etiam capitis poena plectitur quasi incendiarius. Item* si quis insulam uoluerit   exurere, et ignis etiam ad uicini insulam peruenerit, Aquilia tenebitur *lege* uicino: non minus etiam inquilinis   ·   ob res eorum exustas, *et ita Labeo libro responsorum* xv *refert. Sed si stipulam in agro tuo incenderis, ignisque euagatus ad praedium uicini peruenerit, et illud exusserit, Aquilia lex locum habeat an in factum actio sit, fuit quaestionis. Et plerisque Aquilia lex locum habere non uidetur, et ita Celsus libro* xxxvii. *digestorum scribit. Ait enim, si stipulam incendentis ignis effugit, Aquilia lege eum non teneri, sed in factum agendum, quia non principaliter hic exussit, sed dum aliud egit, sic ignis processit. Cuius sententia scilicet rescripto Diui Seueri comprobata est in haec uerba: Praeses prouinciae si*[1] *propter ignem, (qui)*[2] *pabuli gratia factus culpa seruorum Ueturiae Astiliae euagatus agrum tuum, ut proponis, depopulatus est, ad exemplum legis Aquiliae noxali iudicio acturus (es)*[2]*, si litis aestimatio permittitur, iudicium accommodare potest. Uidelicet non est uisum Aquiliam suffi-*

Dig. ix. 2. l 27. § 7.

(Ulpianus libro octauo decimo ad edictum.)

Item si

arbustum meum uel uillam meam incenderis, Aquiliae actionem habebo.

Si quis insulam uoluerit *meam* exurere, et ignis etiam ad uicini insulam peruenerit, Aquilia tenebitur *etiam* uicino; non minus etiam inquilinis *tenebitur* ob res eorum exustas.

---

[1] *Praeses prou. si* is Bluhme's conj. for the ms. reading *profiteri.*
[2] Inserted by the Editors.

cere. Si *forte*   seruus coloni ad fornacem obdormisset et uilla fuerit exusta, Neratius scribit ex locato conuentum praestare debere, si neglegens in eligendis ministeriis fuit. Ceterum si alius ignem subiecit fornaci, alius neglegenter custodierit?

        nam qui *non* custodit, nihil fecit, qui recte ignem subiecit, non peccauit: *quemadmodum si hominem medicus*[1] *recte secuerit, sed neglegenter uel ipse uel alius curauerit, Aquilia cessat.* Quid ergo est? *Et hic* puto *ad exemplum Aquiliae dandam* actionem tam in eum qui ad fornacem obdormiuit uel

        neglegenter custodi*it, quam in medicum qui neglegenter curauit, siue homo periit siue debilitatus est.* Nec quisquam dixerit in eo qui obdormiuit rem eum humanam et naturalem passum, cum deberet uel ignem extinguere uel ita munire *ut non* euag*aret. Item libro* VI. *ex Uiuiano relatum est:* si furnum secundum parietem communem habeas, an damni iniuria tenearis? Et ait   agi non posse *Aquilia lege,* quia nec cum eo qui focum haberet: et ideo aequ*um* put*at* in factum actionem dandam. *Sed non proponit* exustum parietem. *Sane enim quaeri potest* (si)[2] nondum mihi damnum dederis, *et* ita ignem habeas ut metuam ne mihi de*tur, aequum sit me interim actionem in factum impetrare. Fortassis enim de hoc senserit Proculus: nisi quis dixerit* damni *non* facti   sufficere cautionem. *Sed et si qui serui in-*

Si *fornicarius* seruus coloni ad fornacem obdormi*ui*sset et uilla fuerit exusta, Neratius scribit ex locato conuentum praestare debere, si neglegens in eligendis ministeriis fuit. Ceterum si alius ignem subiecit fornaci, alius neglegenter custodierit, *an tenebitur qui subiecerit?* nam qui   custodit, nihil fecit, qui recte ignem subiecit, non peccauit.

        Quid ergo est? puto *utilem competere* actionem tam in eum qui ad fornacem obdormiuit *quam in eum qui* neglegenter custodit.

Nec quisquam dixerit in eo qui obdormiuit rem eum humanam et naturalem passum, cum deberet uel ignem extinguere uel ita munire *ne*   euag*etur*.
        Si furnum secundum parietem communem habeas, an damni iniuria tenearis? Et ait *Proculus* agi non posse   quia nec cum eo qui focum haberet: et ideo aequ*ius* puto in factum actionem dandam, *scilicet si*   paries exustu*s sit. Sin autem*   nondum mihi damnum dederis, *sed* ita ignem habeas, ut metuam, ne· mihi *damnum* des,

damni *infecti* puto sufficere cautionem.

---

[1] The case of the doctor's neglect is omitted in the Digest, because it has already been dealt with in an extract from Gaius which forms l 8 of this title.
[2] Inserted by the Editors.

quilini[1] *insulam exusserint, libro* x.
Urseius refert Sabinum respondisse,
lege Aquilia seruorum nomine domi-
num noxali iudicio conueniendum;
ex locato autem dominum teneri ne-
gat. Proculus *autem respondit,* cum
coloni serui uillam exusser*int,* colo-
num uel ex locato uel lege Aquilia
teneri ita, ut colonus seru*um* posset
noxae dedere, et, si uno iudicio res
esset iudicata, altero amplius non
agendum.

Proculus *ait*   cum
coloni serui uillam exuss*issent,* colo-
num uel ex locato uel lege Aquilia
teneri ita, ut colonus poss*it* seru*os*
noxae dedere, et, si uno iudicio res
esset iudicata, altero amplius non
agendum. *Sed haec ita si culpa*
colonus careret: ceterum si noxios
seruos habuit, damni eum iniuria
teneri, cur tales habuit. Idem[2] *ser-*
uandum et circa inquilinorum in-
sulae personas scribit: quae senten-
tia habet rationem. Si cum apes
meae ad tuas aduolassent, tu eas
exusseris,   legis
Aquiliae actionem competere Celsus
ait.

           Celsus libro XXVII.
digestorum scribit: si cum apes
meae ad tuas aduolassent, tu eas
exusseris, *quosdam negare* competere *legis* Aquiliae actionem, *inter*
quos et Proculum, quasi apes dominii
non fuerint. Sed id falsum esse
Celsus ait, *cum apes reuenire soleant*
et fructui mihi sint. Sed Proculus
eo mouetur quod nec mansuetae nec
ita clausae fuerint. Ipse autem Cel-
sus ait nihil inter has et columbas
interesse, quae si manu refugiunt,
domi[3] *tamen fugiunt.*

           Ulpianus *Reg.* xx. 6.

   Pater et filius qui in potestate
eius est, item duo fratres qui in
eiusdem patris potestate sunt, testes
utrique, *uel alter testis, alter libri-*

           Dig. XXII. 5. 1 17.
   Ulpianus libro singulari regularum.

   Pater et filius qui in potestate
eius est, item duo fratres qui in
eiusdem patris potestate sunt, testes
utrique *in eodem testamento uel eodem*

---

[1] The Digest has dealt with this case briefly after the case of the farmer's
slaves.
[2] This is an abridgment of Ulpian's treatment of the lodger's slaves before
the case of the farmer's slaves.
[3] *domitae* Huschke.

pens fieri possunt *alio familiam emente*, quoniam nihil nocet ex una domo plures testes alieno negotio adhiberi.

negotio fieri possunt,
     quoniam nihil nocet ex una domo plures testes alieno negotio adhiberi.

The chapter of Ulpian is dealing with wills and therefore it was unnecessary for Ulpian to mention here the subject-matter of the evidence spoken of. But the title of the Digest is 'on witnesses' in general, and hence we have the addition of *in eodem testamento uel eodem negotio*. The Institutes (II. 10. § 8) have the same passage, but there as the chapter is on wills, *in unum testamentum* only is added. Ulpian's reference to the *libripens* and *familiae emptor* is of course omitted by Justinian in both places, as obsolete in connexion with mancipation.

Paul. *Sent.* III. 6. § 15.

Qui se filio testatoris impuberi tutorem adscrips*er*it, *ut* suspectus a tutela *remouendus est, ad quam* ultro   uidetur adfectasse.

Dig. XLVIII. 10. l 18. § 1.
Paulus libro tertio sententiarum.

Qui se filio testatoris impuberi tutorem adscripsit, *etsi* suspectus *esse praesumitur, quod* ultro tutela*m* uide*b*itur affectasse, *tamen si idoneus esse adprobetur, non ex testamento sed ex decreto tutor dandus est. Nec excusatio eius admittetur, quia consensisse uidetur uoluntati testatoris.*

The Digest largely modifies the doctrine of Paul.

Paul. *Sent.* v. 11. § 6.

Ei qui aliquem a latrunculis uel hostibus eripuit, *in infinitum donare non prohibetur* (*si tamen* donatio et non merces eximii laboris appellanda est), qu*ia* contemplatione salutis certo ˙ modo aestimari non placuit.

Dig. XXXIX. 5. l 34. § 1.
Paulus libro quinto sententiarum.

Si qui*s* aliquem a latrunculis uel hostibus eripuit *et aliquid pro eo ab ipso accipiat, haec* donatio *irreuocabilis est:* non merces eximii laboris appellanda est, qu*od* contemplatione salutis certo modo aestimari non placuit.

See Savigny, *Syst.* IV. p. 97. *In infinitum* had reference to the restrictions of the *lex Cincia*, and was therefore changed in the Digest to a more general term. *Certo modo* had reference to the same, but by a change in the Digest we get the somewhat inept remark that the impossibility of accurately measuring the merit of saving life prevents *merces* being an appropriate term, instead of the appropriate remark of Paulus that a gift in such a case is not so much a gift as a well-earned payment. *Si tamen—appellanda est* is parenthetical in Paulus. The corrector of the Florentine Digest writes *nam* for *non*, which would greatly improve the sense.

Vat. Fr. 12.	Dig. xviii. 6. 1 19. (18.) § 1.
(Ex Papinian. *Responsor.* libro iii.)	Papinianus libro tertio Responsorum.
Ante pretium solutum dominii quaestione mota pretium emptor *restituere* non cogetur, *tametsi maxime* fideiussores	Ante pretium solutum dominii quaestione mota pretium emptor *soluere* non cogetur, *nisi*
euictionis offerantur, *cum ignorans possidere 'coeperit. Nam usucapio frustra complebitur anticipata lite, nec oportet euictionis securitatem praestari, cum in ipso contractus limine domini periculum immineat.*	fideiussores *idonei a uenditore eius* euictionis offerantur.

By the change of *tametsi* into *nisi*, the meaning is reversed. The alteration was evidently caused by Cod. viii. 44. (45.) 1 24. (Cf. Bruns *Quid conferant Vat. Fr.*, p. 25.)

Vat. Fr. 75—83.	Dig. vii. 2. 1 1. § 2.
(I omit the first part of this fragment as too imperfectly preserved for proper comparison. It seems to have corresponded pretty closely to Dig. vii. 2. 1 1. pr. and § 1, but contained a reference to the *do lego* form of bequest.)	(From Ulpian *ad Sabin.* xvii. 'Idem' means Julian.)
75. Idem ait et si commûni seruo et separatim Titio ususfructus legatus sit, amiss*am partem*	§ 2. Idem ait et si communi seruo et separatim Titio ususfructus legatus sit, amiss*um ab altero ex sociis* usumfructum non ad Titium
ususfructus non ad Titium, sed ad solum socium pertinere debere quasi solum coniunctum. *Quam* sententi*am neque Marcellus neque Mauricianus probant: Papinianus quoque libro* xvii. *quaestionum ab ea recedit. Quae sententia Nerati fuit, est libro* i. *responsorum relatum. Sed puto esse* uera*m Iuliani sententiam ;* nam quamdiu uel unus utitur, potest dici usumfructum in suo esse statu.	sed ad solum socium pertinere debere quasi solum coniunctum : *quae* sententia
	uera est.
	nam quamdiu uel unus utitur, potest dici usumfructum in suo statu esse.

Pomponius ait libro VII. *ex Plautio, relata Iuliani sententia, quosdam esse in diuersam opinionem; nec enim magis socio debere adcrescere, quam deberet ei, qui fundi habens usumfructum partem ususfructus proprietario cessit uel non utendo amisit. Ego autem Iuliani sententiam non ratione adcrescendi probandam puto, sed eo quod quamdiu seruus est, cuius persona in legato spectatur, non debet perire portio. Urgetur tamen Iuliani sententia argumentis Pomponi; quamquam Sabinus responderit ut et Iulianus*[1] *libro* XVIIII. *digestorum refert, eum qui partem ususfructus in iure cessit et amittere partem et ipso momento recipere. Quam sententiam ipse ut stolidam reprehendit; etenim esse incogitabile eandem esse causam cuique et amittendi et recipiendi.*

76. *Iulianus scribit, si seruo communi et Titio ususfructus legetur et unus ex dominis amiserit usumfructum, non adcrescere Titio, sed soli socio quemadmodum fieret* si duobus coniunctim et alteri separatim esset relictus. *Sed qui diuersam sententiam probant, quid dicerent? utrum extraneo soli an etiam socio adcrescere? et qui Iulianum consuluit, ita consuluit an ad utrum pertineat, quasi possit et ipsi socio adcrescere. Atquin quod quis amittit secundum Pomponi sententiam ipsi non accedit.*

Idem est si duobus coniunctim et alteri separatim *ususfructus* esset relictus.

77. Interdum tamen etsi non sint coniuncti, tamen ususfructus legatus alteri adcrescit, ut puta si mihi fundi ususfructus separatim totius et tibi similiter fuerit *usus-*

§ 3. Interdum tamen etsi non sint coniuncti, tamen ususfructus legatus alteri adcrescit : ut puta si mihi fundi ususfructus separatim totius et tibi similiter fuerit

---

[1] The Editors change *Iulianus* into *Celsus* and XVIIII. into XVIII.

fructus relictus; nam ut   Celsus libro XVIII.   digestorum et Iulianus libro XXXV. scribunt concursu partes habemus. Quod et in proprietate contingeret; nam altero repudiante alter totum fundum haberet. Sed in usufructu hoc plus est (*contra quam Atilicinum respondisse Anfidius Chius refert*) *quod* et constitutus   nihilo minus amissus ius adcrescendi a-mittit[1]. Omnes enim auctores apud Plautium de hoc consenserunt *ut et* Celsus et Iulianus eleganter aiunt, ususfructus cotidie constituitur et legatur, non ut proprietas eo solo tempore quo uindicatur. Cum primum itaque non inueniet alter*um* qui sibi concurrat, solus utetur totum. *Uindius tamen, dum consulit Iulianum, in ea opinione est ut putet non alias ius adcrescendi esse quam in coniunctis, qui responso ait: nihil* refert, coniunctim an separatim relinquatur.

78.   Iulianus libro XXXV.
scrib*it*, si duobus heredibus institutis deducto usufructu proprietas legetur, ius adcrescendi heredes non habere, nam uideri usumfructum constitutum[2], non per concursum diuisum.

79.   Neratius putat cessare ius adcrescendi libro I. responsorum. Cui*us* sententiae congruit ratio Celsi dicen*t*is totiens ius adcrescendi esse, quotiens in duobus

relictus : nam ut *et* Celsus libro octauo decimo digestorum et Iulianus libro tricesimo quinto scrib*it*, concursu partes habemus. Quod et in proprietate contingeret; nam altero repudiante alter totum fundum haberet. Sed in usufructu hoc plus est,

quia et constitutus *et postea* amissus nihilo minus ius adcrescendi *ad-*mittit. Omnes enim auctores apud Plautium de hoc consenserunt, *et ut* Celsus et Iulianus eleganter aiunt, ususfructus co*tt*idie constituitur et legatur, non ut proprietas eo solo tempore quo uindicatur. Cum pri-mum itaque non inueniet alter *eum* qui sibi concurrat, solus utetur *in* totum.

nec refert coniunctim an separatim relinquatur.

§ 4. *Idem* Iulianus libro trige-simo quinto digestorum scri*psit*, si duobus heredibus institutis deducto usufructu proprietas legetur, ius ad-crescendi heredes non habere ; nam uideri usumfructum constitutum, non per concursum diuisum.

2. *Africanus libro quinto quaes-tionum: ideoque amissa pars usus-fructus ad legatarium eundemque proprietarium redibit.*

3. *Ulpianus libro septimo decimo ad Sabinum. Idem* Neratius putat cessare ius adcrescendi libro primo responsorum : cui sententiae con-gruit ratio Celsi dicentis totiens ius adcrescendi esse, quotiens in duobus

---

[1] A mere copyist's error for *admittit*.
[2] Mommsen suggests the insertion of *partium*.

qui   solidum habuerunt concursu diuisus est.   80. Unde Celsus libro XVIII. :   si duo fundi domini deducto usufructu proprietatem *mancipauerint,* uter eorum amiserit, usumfructum ad proprietatem redire, sed non ad totam, sed cuiusque usumfructum ei parti accedere quam ipse *mancipauit ;* ad eam enim partem redire debet a qua initio diuisus est. *Plane inquit si partem ususfructus habeat et ego totam proprietatem cum partis usufructu, non posse me meam partem tibi mancipare quae est sine usufructu, quoniam nullam partem habeo in qua non est tibi ususfructus. 81. (Papinianus)[1] quoque libro* XVIII. *quaestionum sententiam Nerati probat quae non est sine ratione.*

82. *Poterit quaeri, si duobus seruis heredibus institutis deducto usufructu proprietas sit legata, an altero defuncto ususfructus proprietati adcrescat ; nam illud constat, ut et Iulianus libro* XXXV. *scribit et Pomponius libro* VII. *ex Plautio non reprobat, si duobus seruis meis ususfructus legetur et alter decesserit, cum per utrumque quaesissem usumfructum, ius adcrescendi me habere, cum, si alterius nomine repudiassem alterius quaesissem, haberem quidem usumfructum totum iure adcrescendi sed ex solius persona amitterem. In proposito autem si quidem pure fundus non[2] ex persona serui ; et ita Iulianus quoque libro* XXXV. *digestorum scribit, quamuis Scaeuola apud Marcellum dubitans notet. Ad[3] si*

qui *in* solidum habuerunt concursu diuisus est. § 1. Unde Celsus libro octauo decimo *scribit,* si duo fundi domini deducto usufructu proprietatem   *tradiderint,* uter eorum amiserit, usumfructum ad proprietatem redire, sed non ad totam, sed cuiusque usumfructum ei parti accedere, quam ipse *tradiderit ;* ad eam enim partem redire debet a qua initio diuisus est.

---

[1] Inserted by the Editors.

[2] Hollweg and Mommsen insert, as required by the sense *'sub condicione legatus sit, constituitur ususfructus '.* See also Huschke.

[3] Mommsen *dubitare se notet. At...*

sub condicione sit legatus, potius ex persona domini constitui usumfructum Marcellus libro XIII. *digestorum scribit. Ubi Scaeuola notat, quid si pure? Sed dubitare non debuit, cum et Iulianus scribat ex persona serui constitui. Secundum quae ius adcrescendi locum habere*[1] *in duobus seruis, si quis contrariam sententiam probaret. Sed nunc secundum Iuliani sententiam et Nerati cessat quaestio.*

83. Non solum autem, si duobus *do lego* ususfructus legetur, *erit* ius adcrescendi, uerum   si alteri ususfructus alteri *proprietas ;*

nam, amittente usumfructum altero cui erat legatus, magis iure adcrescendi ad alterum pertinet quam redit ad proprietatem. Nec nouum.

Nam et si duobus ususfructus legetur et apud alterum sit consolidatus, ius adcrescendi non perit nec ei apud quem consolidatus est neque ab eo, et ipse, quibus modis amitteret   ante   consolidationem, *ii*sdem et nunc *ipso quidem iure non* amittet, *sed praetor secutus exemplum iuris ciuilis utilem actionem dabit fructuario* et ita   Neratio et Aristoni uidetur et Pomponius probat.

§ 2.   Non solum autem, si duobus   ususfructus legetur, est ius adcrescendi, uerum *et* si alteri ususfructus, alteri *fundus legatus est :* nam, amittente usumfructum altero cui erat legatus, magis iure adcrescendi ad alterum pertinet quam redit ad proprietatem. Nec nouum.

Nam et si duobus ususfructus legetur et apud alterum sit consolidatus, ius adcrescendi non perit *neque* ei apud quem consolidatus est, neque ab eo, et ipse, quibus modis amitteret   ante   consolidationem, *is*dem et nunc amittet

et ita *et* Neratio et Aristoni uidetur et Pomponius probat.

Vat. Fr. §§ 86—88.

[Some pages (partly lost) after the above extract.]

Dig. VII. 2. 1 8.

Ulpianus libro septimo decimo ad Sabinum.

86. *Nouissime quod ait Sabinus,* si *uxori* cum liberis   ususfructus legetur, amissis liberis eam   habere, *quale sit uidendum. Et si quidem do lego legetur, tametsi quis filios legatarios acceperit, sine dubio locum habebit propter ius*

Si *mulieri* cum liberis *suis* ususfructus legetur, amissis liberis ea *usumfructum* hab*et:*

[1] *haberet* Edd.

adcrescendi ; sed si legatarii non
fuerint, multo magis, quoniam partem
ei non fecerunt, tametsi cum ea
uterentur. Matre *autem* mortua, *si*
quidem legatari fuerunt, soli habebunt
iure adcrescendi ; *si heredes non iure*
adcrescendi, sed iure dominii, si
fundus eorum est, ipsis adcrescit,
sin minus, domino proprietatis ; sed
si nec heredes fuerunt nec legatarii,
nihil habebunt. Quod si per damna-
tionem fuerit ususfructus legatus
matri, si quidem legatarii sunt fili,
partes sunt[1] *; si non sunt, sola mater*
legataria est, nec mortalitas liberorum
partem ei facit. 87. *Sabinus certe*
uerbis istis non ostendit utrum lega-
tarii fuerint necne. Sed Iulianus
xxxv.   digestorum *relata Sabini*
scriptura ait   intellegendum
e*um qui solos liberos heredes scri*b*it,*
    non ut legatario*rum fecisse men-*
tionem, sed ut ostenderet magis matrem ita se uelle frui ut liberos secum
habeat. *Alioquin, inquit, in damna-*
tione ratio non permittebat ius ad-
crescendi. Proposuit autem Iulianus
uel do lego legatum usumfructum
uel per damnationem, et sic sensit
quasi[2] *legatarii sint et heredes soli, in*
do lego legato non esse ius adcre-
scendi ; adque si alteri ab altero
legetur, quoniam a semet ipsis inuti-
liter legatum est, sibi non concurrunt,
matri uero non in totum concurrunt
sed alter pro alterius portione, et in eo
dumtaxat ius adcrescendi erit ; mater
tamen aduersus utrumque ius ad-
crescendi habet.
    88. *Iulianus subicit Sextum quo-*
que Pomponium praeferre[3] *si per*

sed et matre mortua *liberi*
eius nihilo minus usumfructum habent
iure adcrescendi.

Nam et Iulianus
libro trigensimo digestorum
    ait *idem* intellegendum *in*
*eo qui solos liberos heredes scri*p*serit,*
licet non ut legatario*s eos nomina-*
uerit, sed ut ostenderet magis uelle
se matrem ita frui ut liberos secum
habeat *fruentes*

---

[1] For *sunt* Hollweg suggests *habebunt* or *fiunt :* Mommsen gives *sumunt.*
[2] Mommsen and Huschke put *quamuis* for *quasi.*
[3] *referre,* Mommsen.

damnationem ususfructus et liberis uxori[1] *legetur, singulare hoc esse adque ideo fili personam matri*[2] *accederet, nec esse legatarios sed matre mortua liberos quasi heredes usumfructum habituros. Ego, inquit* Pomponius, quaero quid si mixti fuerint liber*is* extranei heredes ? ait et filios *pro* legatari*is habendos,*   et mortui partem interituram, Aristonem autem adnotare haec uera esse : et sunt uera.

sed et Pomponius quaer*it;* quid si mixti fuerint liber*i et* extranei heredes ? et ait filios legatari*os esse intellegendos,* et

per contrarium si uoluit eos liberos simul cum matre frui, debere dici matrem legatariam esse intellegendam et per omnia similem esse et in hoc casu iuris euentum.

Vat. Fr. 75, 76=Dig. vii. 2. 1 1. § 2.   Ulpian, or rather Julian, whom he quotes, discusses two questions.   1. Usufruct left to common slave and in a separate sentence left to Titius : one of the partners in the slave loses the usufruct: to whom does it accrue ?   2. Usufruct left to common slave and Titius in same clause : one partner loses his share : to whom does it accrue ?   Julian in both cases says the usufruct or part of the usufruct lost accrues to the partner in the slave only.   Ulpian, as regards the first case, holds that there is not strictly speaking any accrual, but that the partner retains the whole through the medium of the common slave.   The second case he does not decide expressly, but probably would treat it as the first case.   In the Digest we have the first case only given, with a slight change in the expression (*usumfructum* for *partem ususfructus*) borrowed from the other case, Ulpian's observations on which are then struck out entirely, except an illustration (*quemadmodum fieret si*), which is made into a substantive statement (*Idem est si duobus*).   See Arndts in Glück's *Pand.* xlviii. p. 145 sqq.

Vat. Fr. 78=1 1. § 4.   The Digest adds a sentence from Africanus (1 2) in order to make it clear what becomes of the usufruct, if lost in the case supposed.

Vat. Fr. 80—82.   This consists (*a*) of the case of two owners selling an estate and reserving the usufruct.   The usufruct, if lost by one, follows

---

[1] Mommsen reads *cum liberis uxori.*
[2] Mommsen inserts here *accedere, ne sine liberis ad usumfructum mater.*

the propriety, but only that part of the propriety to which it originally belonged. The two sellers were evidently not joint owners of the whole estate, but owners of separate portions (i.e. *fundum regionibus diuisum*). The Digest takes this, but changes *mancipare* to *tradere*), on which cf. Arndts in Glück XLVIII. p. 193.

(*b*) Then follows a case which is not very easy to understand. I take it that the case supposed is that of A owner of the propriety of the whole of an estate and of the usufruct only of part of it, desiring to arrange with B who has part of the usufruct of the whole, so that each may have a separate estate without the other having any usufruct in it. A tries to effect this by conveying to B the bare ownership in that part of the estate in which A has not the usufruct, and thinks by so doing B's partial usufruct will attach to this portion and drop away from the portion of the estate which A still retains. Celsus says no : B has a partial usufruct in the whole, and consequently after the mancipation will have the propriety in the portion of the estate so conveyed to him, but will still be partner with A in the usufruct of the estate retained by A. But this is not expressed in the passage, and perhaps on this account Tribonian cut it out. Arndts deals but slightly and unsatisfactorily with this case. Glück XLVIII. p. 194.

(*c*) Then fragment 82 contains a discussion of the question named in fr. 78 and beginning of 79, but takes the special suppositions of *slaves* being legatees of a usufruct, and the more difficult case of slaves being heirs, an estate bequeathed away and the usufruct reserved. The section concludes with the view that this case is ruled by the general principle laid down by Julianus and Neratius. Hence the Digest omits all this and ignores the subordinate question, whether there is a distinction between a pure and conditional legacy, so that in a pure legacy the duration of the usufruct depends on the slave's life, in a conditional legacy on the life of the master who acquires through the slave ; the reason of which distinction I do not see, unless the condition meant be one pointing to the interest of the master. See notes on l 6. § 2. p. 52; l 21. pp. 151, 152 and p. 178. There is however an omission in the middle of the passage, which is variously supplied by the editors. If we had the case as Ulpian wrote it, we should perhaps be saved much difficulty.

Vat. Fr. 83=l 3. § 2. The Digest of course omits *do lego* and thus makes the rule applicable to legacies in general. Then it alters *proprietas* to *fundus*, which I take to be an alteration merely of expression, for clearness sake, not of context. I suppose Ulpian in writing *proprietas* as given by the Vat. Fr., to have meant a legacy of *proprietas*, i.e. *plena proprietas*, the bequest running *proprietatem illius fundi do lego*. If he had said *proprietatem deducto usufructu do lego*, the legatee would have only had the bare ownership and there could have been no question of accrual, but only of reversion. See D. XXXIII. 2. l 19.

The latter part of the Vat. Fr. is based on the principle that where the usufruct is once merged, even though partially, it no longer exists as regards that part, and therefore cannot be lost (see note on p. 203). This principle of strict law was however modified by the Praetor, who was unwilling that one holder of a usufruct should, by acquiring the propriety, oust the other holder of his chance of an accrual. The Digest going on the principle of recognising the Praetor's action as law not merely practically but theoretically, lays down the rule absolutely.

Vat. Fr. 86—88 = D. VII. 2. 1 8. In this case the Digest is more of an abridgment than a corrected edition. The passage in Ulpian is largely composed of the contrast between the two principal forms of legacy, and the different cases which Sabinus may have meant. He may have intended to put the case of the children being heirs and the mother a legatee of the usufruct along with her children ; or of the mother only being a legatee, but the testator wishing her to enjoy the usufruct along with the children. And the propriety may be left with the heirs or may be bequeathed away. If the children are not legatees, along with their mother, there can be no accrual ; if they are heirs, they would take on the mother's death, but not by accrual but in virtue of their propriety. And this is supposing the legacy to have been made by *do lego*. If it was *per damnationem*, then in no case would there be accrual (cf. Gai. II. 205). Supposing however that the children were heirs and legatees with no outsider as heir, they cannot even by a *do lego* legacy have any accrual amongst themselves. For each must take his legacy not from himself as heir, but from one of his brothers, and thus their shares are as it were already marked off and do not admit of concurrence as regards one another, but only as regards their mother. With her there is a concurrence, but only as regards each several share. It seems to me that this supposes only two children : if there were three, the usufruct might be bequeathed from heir A to B and C and the mother ; and from heir B to A and C and mother, and so on ; in which case there might be accrual between the children among themselves as well as with their mother.

The passage is a striking example of the freedom with which the compilers of the Digest dealt with the old lawyers, and the little resemblance there may have been in the original text to the law given in the Digest with their name. Even when the words are more or less the same, the immediate context may have been, as here it is, very different, one of several alternatives being put as alone true, and the real points of the discussion being ignored or distorted. See Arndts in Glück XLVIII. p. 194.

I add merely by way of sample two specimens of the free way in which the compilers of the Code handled the matter submitted to them.

R.   *f*

Vat. Fr. 283.

Idem (sc. Diocletianus) Aurelio *Carr*enoni.

Si *stipendiariorum* proprietatem dono dedisti ita, ut post mortem eius qui accepit ad te rediret, donatio *inrita est*, cum ad *te*[1] *proprietas transferri nequiuerit. Si uero usumfructum in eam, contra quam supplicas, contulisti, usumfructum a proprietate alienare non potuisti.*

Proposita v. id. Mart. Maximo et Aquilino conss. [i.e. A.D. 286].

Cod. Just. VIII. 54 (55) l 2.

Impp. Diocletianus et Maximianus AA Zenoni.

Si *praediorum* proprietatem dono dedisti ita, ut post mortem eius qui accepit ad te rediret, donatio *ualet*, cum *etiam* ad *tempus certum uel incertum ea fieri potest, lege scilicet quae ei imposita est conseruanda.*

PP v. id. Mart. Maximo II. et Aquilino conss.

Cod. Theodos. II. 26. l 1.

(Ex Gromat. Script. p. 267, ed. Lachmann.)

Imp. Constantinus Aug. ad Tertullianum *Uirum perfectissimum comitem dioceseos Asianae.*

Si quis super *inuasis* sui iuris locis prior   detulerit quaerimoniam quae *finali* cohaeret *de* proprieta*e* controuersiae,

prius super possessione quaestio finiatur, et tunc agri mensor ire praecipiatur ad loca, ut patefacta ueritate huius modi litigium terminetur. Quod si altera pars, *locorum adepta dominium, subterfugiendo moras adtulerit ne possit controuersia definiri, a locorum ordine selectus* agri mensor *dirigatur ad loca; ut si fidelis inspectio tenentis locum esse probauerit, petitor uictus abscedat; at si controuersia eius claruerit qui primo iudiciis detulerit causam, ut*

Cod. Just. III. 39. l 3.

Imp. Constantinus A. ad Tertullianum.

Si quis super   iuris sui locis prior *de finibus* detulerit querimoniam, qu*ae*   proprietat*is* controuersiae cohaeret, prius super possessione quaestio finiatur, et tunc agri mensor ire praecipiatur ad loca, ut patefacta ueritate huius modi litigium terminetur. Quod si altera pars, ne *huius modi quaestio terminetur, se subtraxerit, nihilominus*

agri mensor *in ipsis locis iussione rectoris prouinciae una cum obseruante parte hoc ipsum faciens perueniet.*

D. VIII. k. Mart. Bessi Gallicano et Symmacho conss.

Cod. Just. VIII. 4. l 5.

Imp. Constantinus A. ad Tertullianum.

---

[1] The MS. has *te ;* Mommsen and Huschke read *tempus.*

inuasor *ille* poena teneatur *edicti*, si tamen ui *ea* loca eundem inuasisse constiterit : nam si per errorem aut incuriam domini loca *data* ab aliis possessa sunt, *ipsis solis* cedere debent.

Dat. VIII. kl. Mar. Gallicano et Symmacho consulibus (i.e. A.D. 330).

Inuasor *locorum* poena teneatur *legitima*, si tamen ui loca eundem inuasisse constiterit. Nam si per errorem aut incuriam domini loca ab aliis possessa sunt, *sine poena possessio restitui debet*.

D. VI. k. Mart. Gallicano et Symmacho conss.

CHAPTER VI.

INTRODUCTION TO ACCOUNT OF JURISTS.

JUSTINIAN in giving directions for the compilation of the Digest instructed Tribonian and his colleagues to collect the matter out of the writings of the ancient lawyers who had received imperial authority to compose and interpret laws. He added that there were other writers whose works had not been accepted by any authorities or used in practice, but that he did not consider these worthy of recognition in his Digest. The words are *Iubemus igitur uobis antiquorum prudentium, quibus auctoritatem conscribendarum interpretandarumque legum sacratissimi principes praebuerunt, libros ad ius Romanum pertinentes et legere et elimare, ut ex his omnis materia colligatur, nulla, secundum quod possibile est, neque similitudine neque discordia derelicta, sed ex his hoc colligi quod unum pro omnibus sufficiat. Quia autem et alii libros ad ius pertinentes scripserunt, quorum scripturae a nullis auctoribus receptae nec usitatae sunt, neque nos eorum uolumina nostram inquietare dignamur sanctionem* (Const. *Deo auctore*, § 4). The question arises upon this, who were the lawyers who had received the 'imperial authority to draw up and interpret laws'. Reference may be made to the practice introduced by Augustus of a license to certain lawyers to give authoritative answers (see notes, p. 102). Who (besides Sabinus to whom Tiberius gave a license, D. I. 2. 1 2. § 48) actually received such license we do not know, though several of the great lawyers issued books of *responsa* or *epistulae* or *quaestiones*, which probably contained cases on which they gave such authoritative opinions. Three

f 2

constitutions however (Cod. Theod. I. 4) appear to have a special
bearing on the application of Justinian's words.   One is by Constantine (A.D. 321) *Perpetuas prudentium contentiones eruere cupientes
Ulpiani ac Paulli in Papinianum notas, qui dum ingenii laudem
sectantur non tam corrigere eum quam deprauare maluerunt, aboleri
praecipimus* (cf. ib. IX. 43. 1 1).   What fit of spleen dictated this law
we know not.   Paul's writing met with more favour subsequently
from the same emperor (A.D. 327).   *Uniuersa, quae scriptura Paulli
continentur, recepta auctoritate firmanda sunt, et omni ueneratione
celebranda.   Ideoque Sententiarum libros, plenissima luce et perfectis-
sima elocutione et iustissima iuris ratione succinctos, in iudiciis
prolatos ualere minime dubitatur.*   So far however we have only
got the names of Papinian and Paul among writers and Sabinus
among the early authoritative advisers.   But in the year 426 A.D. a
constitution bearing the names of Theodosius II. and Valentinian
III. (often called Valentinian's *Citirgesetz*—with what justice may be
inferred from the fact that Valentinian was then seven years old)
was passed which gave a comprehensive decision on the question and
was probably what Justinian had in mind.   The constitution as we have
it (Cod. Th. I. 4. 1 3) speaks thus : *Papiniani, Paulli, Gaii, Ulpiani,
atque Modestini scripta uniuersa firmamus, ita ut Gaium, quae Paul-
lum Ulpianum et cunctos, comitetur auctoritas, lectionesque ('passages')
ex omni eius opere recitentur.   Eorum quoque scientiam, quorum
tractatus atque sententias praedicti omnes suis operibus miscuerunt,
ratam esse censemus, ut Scaeuolae, Sabini, Iuliani, atque Marcelli,
omniumque quos illi celebrarunt, si tamen eorum libri propter antiquitatis incertum codicum collatione firmentur.   Ubi autem diuersae
sententiae proferuntur, potior numerus uincat auctorum, uel si
numerus aequalis sit, eius partis praecedat auctoritas, in qua excellentis ingenii uir Papinianus emineat, qui, ut singulos uincit, ita
cedit duobus.   Notas etiam Paulli atque Ulpiani in Papiniani
corpus factas, sicut dudum statutum est, praecipimus infirmari.   Ubi
autem pares eorum sententiae recitantur, quorum par censetur auctoritas, quod sequi debeat, eligat moderatio iudicantis.   Paulli quoque
sententias semper ualere praecipimus.*   A good deal of discussion has
taken place on this law (see Jac. Gothofred. *ad loc.* ; Puchta *Rhein.
Mus.* v. 141 ; VI. 87 ; *Cursus* I § 134 ; Huschke *Z. G. R.* XIII. 18 ;
&c.).   The better opinion is that this law was caused by the difficulty
of the courts to know what writers they should admit as authorities,
and which they ought to follow in case of differences.   There was

probably no list of lawyers who had received license (as Gaius calls it, see p. 102) *iura condere*, and 250 years after Gaius, with scarce and old MSS. only to refer to, a judge might well be perplexed by advocates quoting, or perhaps misreading or inventing, ancient authorities. We can see from many passages of Ulpian that authorities were often much divided : the judge might indeed (see Gaius l. c.) follow in that case which he preferred, but most judges would like more definite guidance. The law before us appears to have dealt with all these difficulties. 1. It gives a list of authorities : Papinian, Paul, Gaius, Ulpian and Modestin, who (except Gaius) were in fact the latest of the great jurists. But to these must be added all whose discussions and opinions have been interspersed in the writings of any (*omnes* is not collective) of the above, and particularly Scaevola, Sabinus, Julian and Marcellus. As the habit of citation of predecessors was very prevalent, this brought in a great number of lawyers in addition to the five. 2. Further the law confirms the professional authority (*scientiam*) of all these lawyers, i. e. not merely the particular opinions cited by some of the five, but any of their writings that might be adduced. But a condition is appended. The cited authors were old : and manuscripts professing to be their works might easily be falsified. They would be rarer and therefore more open to accidental or purposed misrepresentation than the later and more usual works of the five. Consequently it is required that the passage adduced by the advocate as the opinion of Scaevola or Julian should be authenticated by the comparison of MSS. More than one copy at least must be shewn to contain the passage : on a conflict of testimony the judge would have to decide. (For *collatio* in this sense see Cod. IX. 22. 1 22 ; Cod. Theod. IX. 19. 1 2. § 1 ; and Jac. Gothofred. *ad loc.*) 3. The notes of Paul and Ulpian on Papinian are again disallowed, but, though this part of the constitution of 321 is repeated, the *Sententiae* of Paul are expressly sanctioned. What the effect of the disallowance would be is not clear. Was such an opinion of Paul's or Ulpian's not to be counted at all, even if another jurist agreed ? or was it merely meant that Papinian's opinion was not, in consequence of this annotation, to have less than its usual weight ? (Cf. *Deo auctore*, § 6.) As regards Gaius see below, ch. XIII. 4. A rule is given for deciding among divergent opinions. The majority decide ; if the numbers are equal, a casting vote is given to Papinian's opinion ; if his opinion is not given, the judge must himself decide between the authorities.

There can be little doubt that this is what Justinian mainly referred to, and accordingly it is from the writers so indicated that the bulk of the extracts in the Digest are taken. The only authors quoted later than Modestinus, who was himself the latest of the five, are Hermogenianus, Arcadius Charisius, and possibly Julius Aquila and Furius Anthianus. The extracts from the last three are very few, though those from Arcadius are of some length. In what way they are included in Justinian's instructions we do not know, but if Hermogenianus was the author of the collection of Rescripts called *Codex Hermogenianus*, which are referred to by Justinian in his constitutions for making and confirming his own code, we cannot be surprised at his works being used for the Digest.

The juristic literature consisted in ancient as in modern times of writings of different kinds. There were dogmatic treatises, exegetical, casuistical and institutional: in other words there were expositions of the law generally and expositions of a particular subject: there were explanations of the purview of statutes or edicts, and these might be commentaries on a large subject such as the Praetor's edict, or the twelve tables, or on one law of less or greater importance: there were collections of answers given to clients' inquiries, in fact reports of cases, only that the lawyer's opinion took the place now taken by the judge's decision: and there were introductions to the study of the law, short summaries of the principal doctrines, and collections of brief rules or principles for the practitioner's remembrance. Another class yet there was, which in some degree partook of the character of all, questions discussed in lectures with difficulties or new aspects suggested by the pupils, and with the teacher's solutions. The list prefixed to the Florentine MS. gives plenty of examples of each. I name some as samples.

I. DOGMATIC TREATISES. Such were Sabinus's *Ius Ciuile*, the books on trusts by Pomponius, Gaius, Ulpian and Paul, Gaius on verbal obligations, Venuleius on stipulations and on actions, Ulpian on the office of the proconsul, of the consul, of the praefect of the city, &c., Paul and Callistratus on the law of the *fiscus*, Menander and Macer on military law, Paul on adulteries, on interest, on wills, &c.

II. EXEGETICAL TREATISES. At the head of these stand the largest and most important works of the Roman jurists as we know them, viz. the Commentaries on Sabinus, which may perhaps be compared with Coke on Littleton; and the Commentaries on the Edict. These practically amounted to complete dogmatic treatises, only with a text of an ancient writer for a starting-point of discussion, instead of definitions or principles of the writer's own. Other exegetical treatises of moment were Gaius on the twelve tables Pomponius on Q. Mucius, Paul and other writers on the *lex Iulia* and *lex Papia Poppaea*, Paul on the *lex Falcidia*, *lex Uellaea*, *lex Cincia*, Marcian on the *S. consultum Turpilianum*, &c. ·

III.   CASES. These form an important part of the literature and head the Papinian series of books. Papinian's, Paul's, Scaevola's, and Modestin's *Responsa* are the principal, but Ulpian and Marcellus both have *Responsa* quoted; Paul's *Decreta*, Gaius' work *de casibus*, Javolen and Pomponius' *Epistulae* belong here; and other works of the same class may lie concealed under more general or ambiguous titles.

IV.   INSTITUTIONAL TREATISES. Such were no doubt the Institutes of Gaius, Ulpian, Marcian, Callistratus and Florentin; and though not so elementary, the *Regulae* of Neratius, Scaevola, Ulpian and Modestin; the *Sententiae, Manualia* and *Breuia* of Paul; the *Epitome* of Hermogenianus, the *Aurea* (or *Res cottidianae*) of Gaius, the Handbook of Pomponius. Perhaps also the *Definitiones* of Q. Mucius and Papinian, and *Differentiae* of Modestin.

V.   DISCUSSIONS. Such were the *Quaestiones* of Papinian, Africanus, Tertullian, and Paul, the *Quaestiones* and *Quaestiones publice tractatae* of Scaevola; the *Disputationes* of Ulpian and of Tryphoninus, and doubtless the *Publica* of Maecian, Marcian, Venuleius, and Macer. To this class belongs, according to Mommsen, the *Digesta* of Julian.

VI.   A number of other works, some of them of importance, bear ambiguous titles, so that we cannot refer them with any great probability to one class more than another. Such are the *Pithana* and *Libri Posteriores* of Labeo; the *Uariae lectiones* of Pomponius; the *Membranae* of Neratius; the Pandects of Ulpian and Modestin.

The *Digesta* of Julian, Celsus and Marcellus are similarly ambiguous. Mommsen (*Z. R. G.* VII. 480) holds that by *Digesta* was meant the collected works of an author. He adduces, as evidence of this, the fact that many references are double, both the book of the Digest and the book of an individual treatise being given, e.g. Gellius VII. (VI) 5 cites a passage from Alfenus' *Digestorum libro* XXXIV. *coniectaneorum autem secundo.* Again Ulpian quotes Celsus, *epistularum libro undecimo et digestorum secundo.* Further when the *Digesta* of a writer are quoted, other works are not quoted. The books of Julian *ad Urseium* and *ex Minicio* are only apparent exceptions, for they are probably works of Urseius or Minicius, edited with notes by Julian. Scaevola is an exception, for other works of his are quoted besides the *Digesta.* But this is an exception which helps to prove the rule, for many passages are quoted, evidently by an oversight, both from the *Digesta* and from the *Responsa,* &c., so that the contents were to some extent the same; and those jurists who quote the *responsa* or *quaestiones* do not quote the *Digesta.* Marcellus seems however to be a real exception and to go far to break the proof.

The books of Cassius, Urseius, Plautius, and Minicius, which later jurists edited with notes or commented on, are also of an undetermined character.

In the following pages I shall give a brief account of the lawyers named in the extract from Pomponius, which forms D. 1. 2. 1 2, and of all others named in the Digest, both those whose opinions or statements are cited, and those from whose writings actual extracts appear. The last class are almost all subsequent to the fall of the republic, Q. Mucius and Aelius Gallus being the only exceptions (unless Alfenus be one), and their contribution is quite insignificant. The republican jurists are however of interest, and some are striking figures. They are sometimes denoted collectively by the writers in the Digest by the term *Ueteres,* whereas those who were officially recognised as law advisers (cf. p. 102) were called *iuris auctores,* cf. D. XLI. 2. 1 3. § 18; II. 4. 1 4. § 2; XXXV. 2. 1 1. § 9; 1 31, &c. (Dirksen *Beitr.* pp. 120 foll.; 164 foll.) With Labeo the series of Digest-jurists worthily opens, but few of the subsequent jurists furnish extracts to the Digest till we come to Trajan's time. After that the series is continuous for about 130 years. There are some others whom we only know at second hand.

The information with respect to many is very meagre. I have given what seemed fairly trustworthy without endeavouring to clothe the skeleton by the aid of doubtful inferences. Fitting's tract *über das Alter d. Schriften d. römischen Juristen* (1860) has been of special service to me, besides the references in Zimmern, Rudorff and

Teuffel-Schwabe's histories[1]. But it is well to bear in mind the nature of the evidence on which the time of composition of the different writings is based. We have rarely any direct knowledge on this point, and are left to glean hints from the extracts of the book so described or inscribed in the Digest. Sometimes such extracts shew distinct acquaintance with a Constitution, the date of which may be otherwise ascertained ; or on the contrary shew what appears to be a significant ignorance of such a Constitution. Frequently they quote other writers, which gives at least a relative date. But the most frequent ground for referring a work to a particular time, or for referring parts of a long work to one time and part to another, is the mode in which they mention the emperors. The following is a summary of the results arrived at by Mommsen in his essay *Die Kaiserbezeichnung bei den römischen Juristen* in *Z. R. G.* IX. p. 97 sqq.

The designation of an emperor as *diuus* shews that the work in which it occurs was composed after the death of that emperor. But one cannot safely reverse this and say, that the omission of this title authorises us to conclude that the work was composed in the lifetime of the emperor. Moreover, the rule is applicable properly only to official language. Historians, e.g. Tacitus, and Pliny in his Epistles, do not consistently adopt it. An official document ought to have it, and its absence would be due to carelessness or to transcribers' errors. The jurists adopt it as a rule, but there are instances, relatively few, to the contrary.

On the other hand, the emperor reigning at the time is called *imperator,* more rarely *Augustus* or *princeps.* But it is a secular title and therefore is not attached to a consecrated emperor, now a god. There are some exceptions, most of which may be classed under three heads: (*a*) A constitution is sometimes given by a writer in its original terms. Then *imperator* is retained (e.g. D. I. 15. 1 4; XXXIV. 1. 1 13. § 1, &c.): (*b*) Papinian often omits *diuus* in his *Quaestiones,* but not in his *Responsa:* (*c*) Ulpian in the first thirty-five books of his Commentary on the Edict in twelve places denotes Severus as *imperator,* in more places as *diuus.* Probably these books were written before, and only imperfectly corrected and published after, the death of Severus, A.D. 211. Some other exceptions are due either to similar want of correction or to carelessness, or to confusion either of author, or scribe, or Justinian's compilers.

---

[1] Some use has also been made of Hommel and of Anton. Augustin's work *de nominibus propriis* Πανδέκτου (in Otto's Thesaurus, Vol. I.).

Mommsen adds a notice of the mode in which the different emperors called Antoninus (Pius, Marcus, Caracalla) are spoken of by the jurists.

1. Pius is properly *diuus Antoninus Pius*, frequently shortened to *diuus Antoninus* or *diuus Pius*. The jurists who wrote in Marcus' reign, Pomponius, Gaius, Marcellus, call him usually *diuus Antoninus*. Those who wrote after Marcus' death usually call him *diuus Pius*, sometimes *diuus Pius Antoninus* or *diuus Antoninus Pius*.

2. Marcus is properly *diuus M. Antoninus Pius;* by the jurists he is regularly called *diuus Marcus*.

His adoptive brother is officially *diuus Verus:* in the jurists he is sometimes called this and sometimes *diuus Lucius*, most commonly they are spoken of together as *diui fratres*.

3. Caracalla's full name of consecration was *diuus Antoninus Magnus*. No inscription or coin gives him the name of *Magnus* during life. In the jurists *Magnus* always implies that the work was written after his death. His usual name however is *diuus Antoninus;* but, where that was likely to lead to confusion, we have *diuus Magnus Antoninus*. So the father and son are regularly called *diuus Seuerus et Antoninus*.

The simple *diuus Antoninus* is used of all three; the circumstances being generally, though not always, sufficient to say which is meant.

It will readily be seen that, in thus estimating the date at which a work was composed, we are on very unstable ground. Where such use of *diuus* or *imperator* is frequent and consistent, it is fairly trustworthy, but where, as is frequently the case, there are only one or two instances in a work, the inference becomes more doubtful, because accident may have so easily interfered. And the inference from the apparent ignorance of a particular matter, e.g. of a constitution, is hazardous, considering that we have only parts, often short extracts, from most works, that these extracts are the results of free handling of the originals by omission, addition, and revision, and that we can only guess at the purpose of the authors in writing a particular work and know nothing of their process of composition and revision. We have not a single complete work of any ante-Justinian jurist. Gaius's Institutes is the only book approaching to this description. The little tract on the parts of the *as* by Volusius Maecianus, whether complete or not, is hardly in question here. So

that we have to presume the basis of our inferences unaffected
(1) by the purpose and method of the author, (2) by the revision of
the author, (3) by the transcription of the work before Justinian,
(4) by the handling of Tribonian and his colleagues, (5) by the
copyists of the Digest. But these are possibilities only of error,
and we have daily experience how many such possibilities may exist
while yet reports and inferences are substantially true for all that.
If excessive scepticism and suspicion would lead to practical paralysis
in the affairs of life, there is no reason in deferring too much to a
similar temper in matters of history and speculation. But the
superstructure cannot but be treated with caution, where the ground
is not assured.

The Florentine Index, i.e. the list of authors prefixed to the
Digest in the Florentine MS. (see p. xxiv), does not usually give the
full name of the author; and the titles of the works sometimes differ
slightly from the inscriptions of the extracts. The list is roughly
chronological, except that Julian and Papinian, no doubt from their
great eminence, are placed first and second in the list.

I give the jurists approximately in chronological order, many
however being more or less contemporaries. The division into
chapters is necessarily made by a somewhat arbitrary line, and in
the case of some jurists the date thus assigned to them is in truth
hardly more than a guess.

CHAPTER VII.

EARLY JURISTS.

OF the early jurists named by Pomponius in the famous extract
from his Handbook, which forms the second law of D. I. 2, some are
very little known; others were leading orators and statesmen, others
left books on law, which were in the hands of the jurists whose
writings contributed to the Digest.

SEX. PAPIRIUS according to Pomponius lived at the time of Tar-
quinius Superbus, and made a collection of the *leges regiae*, which
was called *ius ciuile Papirianum*. In another place he calls him
Publius Papirius (D. I. 2. 1 2. §§ 2, 36). According to Dionysius
(III. 36) Gaius Papirius, the chief priest, had the laws and religious
regulations, which had become obliterated, put up again in public

after the expulsion of the kings. That some collection of religious or other rules existed under the name of Papirius, is shewn by Granius Flaccus having written a book *de iure Papiriano* (D. L. 16. 1 144). See some other notices in Bruns' *Fontes*, p. 3. Cf. Mommsen *Staatsrecht* II. p. 43.

APP. CLAUDIUS, Consul B.C. 451, abdicated on becoming one of the *decemuiri* who drew up the Twelve Tables. His descendant was

APP. CLAUDIUS C. F. Caecus. His offices and deeds are recorded in an inscription at Arretium (*Corp. I. L.* I. p. 287, Wilmanns 628). According to this he was 'censor (B.C. 312, Liv. IX. 29), twice consul (B.C. 307 and 296, Liv. IX. 42; X. 16), dictator, thrice interrex, twice praetor, twice curule aedile, quaestor, thrice tribune of the soldiers; he took many towns of the Samnites, routed the army of the Sabines and Tuscans, prevented peace being made with Pyrrhus, paved the Appian road' from Rome to Capua, and 'brought water into the city', from seven or eight miles off on the Praenestine road (Frontin. I. 5), 'erected a temple to Bellona'. The speech which he made in the senate (B.C. 269), when Cineas came as ambassador from Pyrrhus, was extant in Cicero's time (Cic. *Sen.* 6). But his place in the law list is due to his composing forms of actions, (which were afterwards published by Cn. Flavius), and to a book *de usurpationibus* (Pompon. D. I. 2. 1 2. §§ 7, 36). Livy (X. 22) calls him *callidus sollersque iuris atque eloquentiae consultus*. Pomponius gives him the name of '*Centemmanus*' and does not mention *Caecus*.

SEMPRONIUS, i.e. P. Sempronius Sophus, consul B.C. 304 (Liv. IX. 45), was elected B.C. 300 one of the first plebeian pontifices after the passing of the Ogulnian law, which App. Claudius opposed; in the next year, censor (Liv. X. 9) and, B.C. 296, praetor. His cognomen was, Pomponius says, derived from his great wisdom (i.e. legal knowledge?).

C. SCIPIO NASICA, according to Pomponius, had a house on the *Sacra via* given him by the public in order that he might be more readily consulted, and was called by the senate *Optimus*. There seems here to be some confusion with the consul of B.C. 191, who was chosen B.C. 204 as the best man in the state to receive the image of the *magna mater* (Liv. XXIX. 14). There is also a blunder in the next-named Q. MUCIUS (Q. Fabius Maximus?).

TIB. CORUNCANIUS, from Tusculum (Cic. *Planc.* 8), first avowed himself a public jurisconsult (*primus profiteri coepit*). He was

consul 280 B.C., and the first *pontifex maximus* who was a plebeian
(Liv. *Ep.* 18). Cicero calls him *peritissimus pontifex* (*Dom.* 54),
and frequently refers to him as a model of legal and general wisdom,
e.g. *Or.* III. 33; *Sen.* 6; 9; *Am.* 5; *N. D.* I. 41; II. 66, &c.

SEX. AELIUS, whose cognomen was Paetus, was aedile B.C. 200;
consul 198; censor 193 (Liv. XXXI. 50; XXXII. 7; XXXV. 9). He is
said by Cicero to have been *iuris quidem ciuilis omnium peritissimus
sed etiam ad dicendum paratus* (*Brut.* 20), is put beside Manilius
and P. Mucius (*Or.* I. 48; *Sen.* 9). The same width of instruction is
attributed to him as to Manilius (see p. xcvii). A line of Ennius
describing him *egregie cordatus homo Catus Aelius Sextus*, 'a man of excellent wits, Aelius Sextus, the shrewd', is often quoted (Cic. *T. D.* I. 9,
&c.), and, if Gellius IV. 1. § 20 is right, we must treat *Catus* as an
additional name. He wrote according to Pomponius (D. I. 2. 1 2.
§ 38) a work called *Tripertita*, 'which contains the cradle of the
law'. It gave in three divisions the text of the Twelve Tables, then
an explanation of them, then 'the statutable action', i.e. the form of
procedure applicable to the case. He is also said to have increased
the forms of procedure as set forth by Appius Claudius and published
by his clerk Cn. Flavius, and to have published these additional
forms, which were called *ius Aelianum* (ib. § 7). Pomponius mentions three other books which however were of doubtful genuineness
(ib. § 38). Crassus in Cic. *Or.* I. 56 speaks of having read something in *Sex. Aelii commentariis*. Whether the *ius Aelianum* and
the *commentarii* were different from the *Tripertita* we do not know.
Cicero elsewhere calls him an old interpreter of the Twelve Tables
(*Legg.* II. 23). Gellius l. c. says that he was of opinion that incense
and wax tapers were included under the term *penus*, and hence in
D. XXXIII. 9. 1 3. § 9 we should correct *Sex. Caecilius* into *Sex. Aelius*.

It is important to distinguish this jurist from Sex. Aelius Stilo,
the accomplished philologer and Roman knight (Cic. *Brut.* 56; Suet.
Gr. 3; &c. Cf. Cic. *Or.* I. 43. § 193 *haec Aeliana studia*, as we read
from Madvig's conjecture.

Pomponius speaks of a brother of Sex. Aelius Paetus, viz.

P. AELIUS. The two brothers with P. Atilius ('a mistake for L.
Acilius, see Cic. *Am.* 2', Mommsen) are said by Pomponius to have
had the greatest knowledge as professed jurisconsults. P. Aelius
was successively aedile, praetor, master of the horse, consul, censor,
and augur, dying B.C. 174 (Liv. XLI. 21).

M. PORCIUS CATO is mentioned by Pomponius in his account of the jurists, but belongs more to general Roman history than to this special class. He was born at Tusculum B.C. 234, was quaestor in 204, aedile 199, praetor 198, consul 195, and censor 184. He may justly be regarded as a type of the Roman character at the time when our first authentic information begins. Cicero (*Or.* III. 33), Livy (XXXIX. 40), Cornelius Nepos (*Cat.* 3), Quintilian (XII. 11. § 23) sing his praises. With grey eyes, red hair and a strong voice, of an iron constitution and hardy life, thrifty, laborious, straightforward and incorruptible, coarse in habits and feelings, with a vigorous and downright eloquence, and humorous though biting tongue, indefatigable in whatever he undertook, and pushing his own opinions and his country's interests in all directions, eager to attack and ready to reply, farmer and statesman, trader and soldier, orator and lawyer, speaking, writing and studying to the age of 85, he left an abiding impress on Roman character and history. He was accused forty-four times but never condemned (Plin. VII. 100). Cicero had read one hundred and fifty of his speeches; we know the names of 80, and of some have brief fragments (Cic. *Brut.* 16, 17, 85). He wrote the first Roman history in Latin (*Origines* in 7 books), and was indeed the earliest Roman prose writer of whom we have any specimens. His treatise on farming is preserved—as some think, in a later revision. Its contents are very various : the whole duty of the farm-bailiff and his wife; forms of contracts for the sale of produce; an exact inventory of the plant required; charms for dislocated limbs; prayers before harvest and against blight; receipts for making cakes and erecting an olive press, all in brief confident language, mingle with instructions for the economical management of the farm. Cato supported the *lex Cincia* (see p. cxxxvii) in B.C. 204 (Liv. XXXIV. 4. § 9), and unsuccessfully opposed the repeal of the *lex Oppia* in B.C. 195, which, passed in the midst of the second Punic war, restricted the jewels and dress women might wear and the carriages they might use. In B.C. 170 he supported the *lex Uoconia*, which limited the share which any citizen enrolled in the first class might leave to any woman (Gell. XVII. 6; Cic. *Verr.* Act. I. 41, 42; Gai. II. 274).

As regards law Cicero calls him *iuris ciuilis omnium peritissimus* (*Or.* I. 37), that is, of his time, and similar expressions are used by others. Pomponius (D. I. 2. 1 2. § 38) speaks of books of his, apparently on law, being extant in his time, but adds that there are more of his son's. Cicero introduces him in the *de Senectute* in his 84th year occupied among other things in dealing with *ius augurium, pontificium, ciuile* (*Sen.* II. § 38), and in *Or.* II. 33 speaks of books of Cato and Brutus, which gave law cases with the actual details and the answers of the jurist. But this last reference may belong really to his son.

CATO THE YOUNGER, son of Cato Censorinus by his first wife, died when Praetor designate in his father's life time, and left *egregios de iure ciuili libros* (Gell. XIII. 20. § 9). The references in the Digest are supposed to relate to this son; D. XXI. 1. 1 10. § 1 (Ulpian) *Catonem quoque scribere lego;* XXIV. 3. 1 44. pr. (Paul) *Nerua et Cato responderunt, ut est relatum apud Sext. Pomponium digestorum ab Aristone libro quinto;* XLV. 1. 1 4 (Paul) *Cato libro quinto decimo scribit;* L. 16. 1 98. § 1 (Celsus) *Cato putat mensem intercalarem,* &c. So *Inst.* I. 11. § 12 *Apud Catonem bene scriptum refert antiquitas.* The famous *Catoniana regula* is probably the son's. It was a rule that what would not be a valid legacy, if the testator died directly his will was made, was not valid whenever he died. See D. XXXIV. 7; XXXIII. 5. 1 13; XXXV. 1. 1 86.

BRUTUS, whose full name was *M. Junius Brutus*, is mentioned by Cicero as *iuris peritissimus* (*Brut.* 34. § 130; *Off.* II. 14. § 50) and by Pomponius (D. I. 2. 1 2. § 39) as one who with P. Mucius and Manilius *fundauerunt ius ciuile.* He attained the rank of praetor. Cicero speaks of his and Cato's books as giving not only the answers of the jurisconsults to the bare point of law, but the exact details of the cases as well (*Or.* II. 33); and we hear of discussions which took place between him and other lawyers of the time. Thus the citizenship of C. Mancinus, who had been surrendered by the fetials to the Numantines but not received by them, was denied by P. Rutilius and P. Mucius, and apparently was maintained by Brutus (D. XLIX. 15. 1 4 *inter Brutum et Scaeuolam uarie tractatum est;* L. 7. 1 18 (17); Cic. *Or.* I. 40). Another discussion in which Brutus took part is named by Cic. *Fam.* VII. 22, and turned upon the use of the future tense. The lex Atinia said *Quod subreptum erit, eius rei aeterna auctoritas esto.* 'Title to a thing which has been stolen is eternal', i.e. is not affected by a stranger's having possessed it for a length of time which would otherwise have made him owner by usucapion. Did the use of the future *erit* restrict the application of the law to things stolen subsequently to the law of Atinius? What the decision was, we are not told (Gell. XVII. 7; cf. D. XLI. 3. 1 4. § 6). The truth is, the tense *erit* is properly subordinate to the imperative *esto* (*Lat. Gr.* § 2. 1481, 1495, 1603). The question whether it would apply to things stolen before the Act is rather one to be determined, in the absence of express words, by the usual practice in legislative matters. *Subreptum est* would have been wrong in strict grammar, unless, which would be most unlikely, the law were meant not to apply to future acts of stealing.

Labeo recorded a saying of Brutus that a man who had borrowed a beast of burden and used it otherwise than had been agreed on, i. e. had used it for a different journey or for a longer journey, was found guilty of theft (Gell. VI. (VII.) 15 ; cf. D. XLVII. 2. 1 77 (76) pr.). Another discussion is mentioned in Cic. *Fam.* VII. 22 (see under Trebatius). His opinions are also mentioned in D. VII. 1. 1 68 (on which see my note); IX. 2. 1 27. § 22; XVIII. 2. 1 13, *Celsus refert Mucium Brutum Labeonem, quod Sabinum, existimare*; XLI. 2. 1 3. § 3, *Brutus et Manilius.*

His work *de iure ciuili* was in three books. All the books commenced with Brutus' mentioning the presence of his son and himself in a country villa—different in each. Crassus, in defending Plancus against an accusation brought by Brutus' son, laid hold of this in order to reflect on the accuser's character, who had run through all the property left him by his father (Cic. *Clu.* 51; *Or.* II. 55). In the latter passage the words *nisi puberem te iam haberet, quartum librum composuisset, et se etiam in balneis lotum cum filio scriptum reliquisset* clearly indicate that there were only three books, and Scaevola is there reported to have said that there were only three genuine books. Hence the text of Pomponius (D. I. 2. 1 2. § 39) should be corrected by transposition of Manilius and Brutus (Maians. I. pp. 115, 128, followed by Mommsen and others). The Brutus to whom Serv. Sulpicius addressed his short exposition of the edict (D. I. 2. 1 2. § 44; XIV. 3. 1 5. § 1) must have been later.

MANILIUS, whose full name, as given in the *Fasti Capit.* (*Corp. I. L.* I. p. 438), was *M'. Manīlius P. F. P. N.* was consul with L. Marcius Censorinus in 149 B. C. (Cic. *Brut.* 15. § 61, &c.), and in that capacity commenced the siege of Carthage, the younger Scipio Africanus being tribune of the fourth legion (Cic. *Somn. Scip.* I.). Manilius was in command of the land forces (App. *Lib.* 75). He is frequently mentioned as a lawyer by the side of Sex. Aelius, Brutus, and P. Mucius (Cic. *R. P.* I. 13; III. 10; *Fam.* VII. 10; *Or.* I. 48;

Caecin. 24). He had an estate in the neighbourhood of Labicum, and lived in a small house in the Carinae (Cic. *Par.* 6. § 50), i.e. the western part of the Esquiline, where the temple of Tellus was. Crassus is made by Cicero (*Or.* III. 33) to say, in speaking of the wider studies of the men of former times, that he had himself seen Manilius strolling (*ambulantem*) across the forum, which was a sign of his being willing to advise any citizen who desired it: and that, both then and when he was sitting at home, men came to consult him, as they did Sex. Aelius, not only on points of law but on the marriage of their daughters, and the purchase of land, and any other matter of duty or business. Cicero introduces Manilius as an interlocutor in the *de Republica*, describing him as *uir prudens omnibusque illis et iucundus et carus*, the others (*illis*) being Scipio Africanus the younger, Q. Aelius Tubero the Stoic, C. Laelius (cf. Cic. *Brut.* 21, 22), P. Rutilius (see p. ci), Q. Mucius Scaevola the augur, and others. As a business speaker Cicero puts him nearly on a par with P. Mucius (*P. Scaeuola ualde prudenter et acute loqui putabatur, paulo etiam copiosius; nec multo minus prudenter M. Manilius,* where *prudenter* denotes competence to deal with the matter in hand, especially from a legal point.

He is mentioned by Gellius (XVII. 7) in the discussions about the *lex Atinia* (see under BRUTUS, p. xcv); about the heir bringing an action for theft (Cic. *Fam.* VII. 22, see p. cxix); about treasure-trove (D. XLI. 2. 1 3. § 3); about children being *fructus* (Cic. *Fin.* I. 4; D. VII. 1. l 58, see note, p. 240). Varro (*L. L.* VII. 105) quotes from him a definition of *nexum* as *omne quod per aes et libram geritur, in quo sunt mancipia.* Mucius' definition runs *quae per aes et libram fiant ut obligentur, praeter quae mancipio dentur,* Manilius thus making *nexum* the genus of which *mancipium* is a species, Mucius making them both species of the genus *quod per aes et libram geritur.* Aelius Gallus defined *nexum* as simply *quodcunque per aes et libram geritur* (*Fest.* p. 165), which would therefore agree with Manilius. It is quite possible that *mancipium* and *nexum* may have meant much the same originally, but that *mancipium* was gradually applied only to one class of cases and *nexum* to the others.

Manilius drew up several *formulae* for stipulations on the sale of slaves and animals: so Varro *R. R.* II. 3. § 5 *Stipulantur paucis exceptis uerbis: ac Manilius scriptum reliquit sic 'Illas capras hodie recte esse, et bibere posse, habereque recte licere, haec spondesne';* ib. 5. § 11; *paulo uerbosius haec, qui Manilii actiones sequuntur;*

7. § 6 (some MSS. have *mamilii*); and Cic. *Or.* I. 58 speaks of *Manilianas uenalium uendendorum leges* (where see Wilkins). Pomponius speaks of three, or rather (if we correct the reading, see p. xcvi) seven books *de iure ciuili:* and says that some of his writings were still extant.

P. Mucius Scaevola, the father of the still more celebrated lawyer Q. Mucius *pontifex,* and first cousin of Q. Mucius the augur, was tribune of the commons 141 B.C. (Cic. *Fin.* II. 16), and in that capacity got an inquiry ordered into the conduct of L. Tubulus, the praetor of the previous year, who was charged with taking bribes when trying cases of murder. L. Tubulus went into exile at once without waiting for trial. P. Mucius was praetor B.C. 136 (Cic. *Att.* XII. 5), and was consul with L. Calpurnius Piso Frugi in 133, the year of Tiberius Gracchus' famous legislation and death. Mucius was said to favour the legislation (Plut. *Tib. Gr.* 9; Cic. *Acad.* II. 5). When, on the election to the tribunate for the following year, the opponents of Gracchus proposed in the senate that he should be at once put down as a tyrant, the consul Mucius declared that he would not commence the use of violence, nor put a citizen to death untried, but that he should not regard as valid any unconstitutional measure which Gracchus might get the people to vote. Scipio Nasica exclaimed that, as the consul by clinging to the law was bringing both laws and Rome together to destruction, those who wished to save their country should follow him: and Gracchus was attacked and killed (Val. Max. III. 2. § 17; Plut. *Tib. Gr.* 19). It was afterwards proposed that Nasica's conduct should be submitted to the judgment of P. Mucius. Nasica declined, saying that he was *iniquus.* On protests being uttered against such a charge, Nasica replied that he did not mean that he was unfair to *him,* but to all; apparently intimating that Mucius had betrayed his country's interests by not acting against Gracchus (Cic. *Or.* II. 70). Mucius afterwards took part in decrees conferring honours on Nasica, and pronounced that he had in good right (*iure optimo*) taken up arms (Cic. *Planc.* 36; *Dom.* 34). His name is concerned in a question of law connected with C. Gracchus, which is recorded in the Digest (XXIV. 3. 1 66). Some property belonging to the dowry of Licinia, wife of C. Gracchus, was destroyed in the tumult in which her husband was killed. P. Mucius, uncle of the lady, held that the husband's estate was answerable, because the tumult had arisen from his fault. (The facts of the case are however somewhat difficult, as Plutarch says (*C. Grac.* 17) that the property of Gracchus and his friends was confiscated and Licinia's dowry also.)   He was judge (*iudex*) in a case of libel (*iniuriarum*) upon the poet L. Accius and condemned the defendant (*Cornif.* II. 13).

P. Mucius was *pontifex maximus* from the year 123 B.C. at latest; for in that year he gave a decision that ground dedicated by a Vestal virgin without the order of the people was not consecrated (Cic. *Dom.* 53).   Other ecclesiastical decisions of his are recorded.

In the case of a man killed on board ship and thrown into the sea, he decided that the estate (*familia*) was pure, because the face (*os*) was not above ground, but that certain sacrifices must be performed by the heir.   If the man had been drowned the sacrifices would not have been required (Cic. *Legg.* II. 22).

In Cicero's *de Legibus* II. 19—21 is an account of the ecclesiastical law on the devolution of the *sacra*.   They shew the difficulties, which arose in the maintenance of family rites and sacrifices, when a deceased's estate was divided among several heirs and legatees, or was not entered on at all, or was divided among creditors.   But these difficulties were met by rules of the priests, not by laws of the state.   The priests were familiar with civil, as well as with sacred, law, and used their knowledge of the former to discover means of evading religious obligations.   One ingenious method was for the legatee to give the heir a formal acquittance in full, but at the same time to stipulate for the payment of the same amount or thing.   The *sacra* being attached only to the devolution by death did not attach to property received in discharge of a purely civil verbal obligation.   Both Scaevolae, father and son, are mentioned by Cicero in this passage, and very likely may have each in turn developed the system of devolution to meet fresh difficulties.   Savigny has an interesting article on it, *Verm. Schr.* I. p. 151 sqq.

Augustin (*Ciu. D.* IV. 27) ascribes to 'the learned pontifex, Scaevola', who was followed by Varro, the division of gods into three classes, those of poets, of philosophers, and of statesmen, of which the first class was injurious, and the second partly injurious, partly superfluous, the line of objection taken being the same which Plato takes in the second book of the *Republic*. (See Mayor on Cic. *N. D.* I. § 61.)   Which Scaevola, father or son, is meant we do not know.

His opinions on some matters are recorded, often along with those

of his contemporaries Brutus and Manilius. For the question whether
partus ancillae in fructu sit see note below, p. 240; for that of the
possibility of theft from an inheritance not yet entered on, see
Cic. *Fam.* VII. 22 and D. XLVII. 4. 1 1. §§ 10, 15; for the *lex Atinia*
Gell. XVII. 7 and above p. xcv; for the question, whether a Roman,
given up to the enemy but not received by them, retained his Roman
citizenship, see D. XLIX. 15. 1 4; L. 7. 1 18. (71); cf. Cic. *Or.* I. 40.
Mucius held that he did not retain his citizenship. His definition of
the *ambitus* of a house is given in Cic. *Top.* 4; and of *gentiles* ib. 6.
Gentiles are such as are of the same name, freeborn, of ancestors who
have been always free, and they must not be *capite deminuto*. Pomponius (D. I. 2. 1 2. § 39) says he left ten books, and Crassus his brother
is said (Cic. *Or.* I. 56) to have referred to his *commentarii* ('note-
books'?).

He is stated by Mommsen (*Hist.* Bk. IV. Chap. 13) to have compiled the chronicles of the city in 80 books and published them.
This is an inference from Cicero's statement (*Or.* II. 12) that up to
Mucius' time the *pontifex* kept a chronicle on a slab at home, and
from the statement of a scholiast (Servius?) on Vergil *Aen.* I. 377
that such a publication in 80 books was made.

P. Mucius was a thorough jurisconsult (Cic. *Or.* I. 48) and a
good speaker; *loquebatur ualde prudenter et acute, paulo etiam
copiosius* (Cic. *Brut.* 28): and was also famed as an excellent player
both at ball and backgammon (*pila et duodecim scriptis*, Cic. *Or.* I. 50,
where see Wilkins' notes).

P. LICINIUS CRASSUS MUCIANUS was own brother of P. Mucius,
but adopted by the rich Crassus (consul 205 B.C.). He is often
named as a lawyer by Cicero (*Or.* I. 37; *Brut.* 26; &c.). Gellius
(I. 13. § 10) relates that he was renowned as having five of the greatest
advantages: he was *ditissimus, nobilissimus, eloquentissimus, iuris-
consultissimus*, and *pontifex maximus*. He was consul B.C. 131, and
sent to Asia to conduct the war against Aristonicus, son of Eumenes,
and was killed in the war in that or the next year (Cic. *Phil.* XI. 8;
Vell. II. 4. § 1). Two anecdotes of him are told in Val. Max. III. 2. § 12;
Gell. *l. c.* Pomponius (D. 1. 2. 1 2. § 35) confuses him with the
great orator, Lucius Crassus (see p. cvi), and misplaces him in the
order of jurists. He is not said to have left any writings.

Q. TUBERO, i.e. Q. Aelius Tubero the Stoic; consul B.C. 118,
is mentioned by Pomponius (*Quintus Tubero ille stoicus Pansae*

(*Panaeti ?*) *auditor* (D. I. 2. 1 2. § 40); and by Cicero as a learned lawyer (Cic. *ap. Gell.* I. 22. § 7). He is said as tribune to have decided against the evidence of his uncle P. Africanus that augurs were not exempt from service as *iudices* (*Brut.* 31).

Q. MUCIUS Q. F. Q. N. SCAEVOLA the augur, consul 117 B.C. died between 88 and 82 B.C. (Val. Max. III. 8. § 5, Cic. *Am.* 1). He is described by Cicero as not a great orator but a great lawyer *Brut.* 26. § 102 ; and a very genial man *ib.* 58. § 212 ; *Or.* I. 35, &c. see Wilkins' *Introd.* p. 91. He is not named by Pomponius.

RUTILIUS, i.e. *P. Rutilius Rufus,* was born somewhere about the year 158 B.C., being described as *adulescentulus* in B.C. 138 (Cic. *Brut.* 22). Brought up in intimacy with P. Mucius Scaevola, he was a conspicuous figure among the Romans of his time, both for know-ledge of law and still more for his upright character. In 134 B.C. he was with Scipio at Numantia as tribune of the soldiers (Cic. *R. P.* I. 11 ; App. *Iber.* 88), probably selected by Scipio. He must have been at some time an unsuccessful candidate for the tribunate of the Commons (Cic. *Planc.* 21), and hence could hardly be the P. Rutilius mentioned in Cic. *Or.* I. 40 as having turned out of the senate C. Hostilius Mancinus. He was B.C. 116 a candidate for the consul-ship against Aemilius Scaurus, and was unsuccessful. He accused Scaurus of bribery, and Scaurus was acquitted. Whereupon he retorted and accused Rutilius of bribery, producing as evidence of it Rutilius' account-books, in which the letters A F P R appeared. Scaurus interpreted them to mean *actum fide P. Rutili,* i.e. that he had guaranteed a payment by way of bribe. Rutilius said they were merely for *ante factum post relatum,* i.e. a memorandum, that the date of the entry was subsequent to the date of the transaction. (A similar form is found in Fronto, *ad Ant. Imp.* I. 5 p. 102 Naber, *ante gestum post relatum aiunt, qui tabulas sedulo conficiunt.*) Curius, who was assisting in Rutilius' defence, wittily exclaimed that neither was right : the letters really meant, *Aemilius fecit, plec-titur Rutilius.* The issue of the trial is not known. In 108 he was legate to Metellus in Africa in the campaign against Jugurtha (Sall. *Jug.* 50, 52, 86). In 105 B.C. he was consul with Cn. Mallius Maxi-mus, who was defeated by the Cimbri (Liv. *Ep.* 67). Rutilius is men-tioned by Frontinus as having let his son serve in the ranks instead of attaching him, as he was entitled, to his own person (Front.

Strat. IV. 1. 12). The campaign we do not know. In the disturbances caused by Saturninus B.C. 100 he, with Q. Scaevola the augur and others, took up arms at the call of the senate (Cic. *C. Rab.* 7). About 98 B.C. he went as legate (Pomponius says wrongly *proconsul*) to Q. Mucius Scaevola (pontifex) to Asia, of which province Scaevola was made governor. The stern and upright justice between the provincials and the Roman tax-farmers, which made this governorship so memorable, was avenged by the tax-farmers on Rutilius. He was put on his trial some time between 95 and 92 B.C. (the dates of Crassus' consulship and censorship, cf. Cic. *Brut.* 30, where Crassus is called *consularis*) for extortion, and as the *equites*, the moneyed classes, then were the *iudices*, the issue of the trial was viewed with great apprehension by his friends. Rutilius declined the aid of the powerful orators L. Crassus and M. Antonius: he would have no impassioned appeal to the feelings of the court; he would make his defence consist in the simple truth, plainly stated, without exaggeration or rhetorical art. Accordingly he spoke in his own defence, and Q. Mucius spoke for him, but the only words of real oratory were a few which Rutilius allowed his nephew Cotta to say (Cic. *Brut.* 30). Thus, says Cicero, the man who was as innocent as he was learned, than whom Rome had none more honest and more good (*neque integrior, neque sanctior*), was condemned, because oratory was not put to its proper use, and the case was pleaded as if Rome were Plato's republic (Cic. *Or.* I. 53). He went into exile, and with a fine confidence chose Asia. The towns, eager to shew the injustice of the accusation, sent deputations to greet his arrival (Val. Max. II. 10. § 5). We hear of him in Mitylene in B.C. 88 (Dio Cass. *Fr.* 97) when Mithridates came there, and orders were given to put all Romans to death (App. *Mithr.* 22, 23)[1]. Rutilius avoided the common fate by putting on Greek dress (*soccos et pallium* Cic. *Rab. Post.* 10). It was with him scarcely an evasion. He had adopted Asia as his home and country. He became a citizen of Smyrna (Cic. *Balb.* 11), and Cicero saw him there B.C. 78, and, as he says (*R. P.* I. 8; 11), heard from him then the conversation which Cicero afterwards embodied in his books *de Republica*. When some one endeavoured to console him with the thought of a civil war approaching when all exiles would be recalled,

---

[1] A story of Theophanes that Pompey found in a fort among Mithridates' papers, a speech of Rutilius urging the destruction of the Romans was disbelieved by Plutarch (*Pomp.* 37).

Rutilius answered, 'What ill have I done you that you should wish me a return worse than my departure? I would sooner my country should blush at my banishment than mourn at my return' (Sen. *Ben.* VI. 37). P. Sulla, probably the Dictator's nephew, proposed to recall him, but he declined (Quintil. XI. 1. § 13). Ovid, smarting under the dreariness of Tomi, accounts for Rutilius' patience by the fact that Smyrna was as pleasant a residence as could be found (*Pont.* I. 3. 63).

Cicero is never tired of praising the man and mourning his loss. His character and exile became a stock example cited by Seneca frequently along with Regulus, Socrates, and others (e.g. *Dial.* III. 3. § 4, &c.). He was *documentum hominibus nostris uirtutis, antiquitatis, prudentiae* (Cic. *Rab. P.* 10): he was *uir non sui saeculi sed omnis aeui optimus* (Vell. II. 13). He had attended Panaetius' lectures (at Athens?), and might be described as a thorough master of the Stoic system; he was skilled in Greek literature; by natural disposition vehement and ready to attack; much occupied as a professed jurisconsult, and yet always ready to spend time and trouble as an advocate in the courts. His style of speaking was severe and pointed, but too thin to be popular or persuasive (Cic. *Brut.* 30; D. I. 2. 1 2. § 40). Though the identity is not positively established, there is little doubt that he is the Rutilius or P. Rutilius of whom the following facts are recorded.

He made a speech *de modo aedificiorum*, which Augustus published to shew that his own plans were in accordance with those advocated by great Republicans (Suet. *Aug.* 69). It appears Augustus ordered that no one should build near the public streets to a greater height than 70 feet (Strab. v. 7, p. 235). This is no doubt what Suetonius alludes to (Maians. II. p. 16). He passed a law relating to the position of those tribunes of the soldiers who were nominated by the general instead of elected by the people. From him they were called *Rufuli* (Liv. VII. 5. § 8; Festus p. 261; cf. Marquardt, *Staatsverwalt.* II. p. 354). As praetor (we are not elsewhere informed of his holding the office) he made two important reforms. 1. The first related to the sale of the property of debtors who being insolvent or fraudulent or obstinate had not satisfied their creditors after judicial process, or who had died without leaving any legal representative (Gai. III. 78 sq.). Rutilius is said to have introduced this sale of their property as a whole, probably on the analogy of the *sectio bonorum* to which state debtors were liable; and to have improved the formula, by which the purchaser in such a case prosecuted his rights. This used to be by means of a fiction, that the *bonorum emptor* was entitled just as if he had been the former owner. Rutilius drew the formula differently. He made the statement of claim (*intentio*) run directly in the name of the former owner, and inserted the name of the purchaser in the condemnation clause as the person entitled to the judgment (ib. IV. 35 : cf. Puchta § 179, Kuntze § 274 and the references there given). 2. The second reform of Rutilius was to put a check on the excessive demands made by patrons upon their freedmen. He refused to patrons actions against their freedmen, except to enforce performance of due services (*operae*, see D. XXXVIII. 1), and to give effect to a bargain made by the patron for his admission as partner in his freedman's property (D. XXXVIII. 2. 1 1 ; ib. 1. 1 2), in default of due respect (*obsequium*, see D. XXXVII. 15).

His opinion is cited in the Digest VII. 8. 1 10. § 3 ; XXXIII. 9. 1 3. § 9 ; XLIII. 27. 1 1. § 2. From Gellius IV. 1. § 22 we may infer that the opinion, attributed to Rutilius in D. XXXIII, was reported by Sabinus, from whom Ulpian probably took it, as well as many other opinions, at second hand.

Rutilius wrote an autobiography in Latin, and also a history in Greek. The few fragments and references preserved are collected by H. Peter *Hist. Rom. Frag.* pp. 122—124 *ed. min.*

DRUSUS is quoted once in the Digest (XIX. 1. 1 38. § 1) by the side of Sextus Aelius. Possibly he is the blind jurisconsult, whose house Cicero says was filled by clients (*T. D.* v. 38 : cf. Val. Max. VIII. 7. § 4).

Of the others named by Pomponius, between Rutilius and Quintus Mucius the pontifex,

PAULUS (AULUS ?) VIRGINIUS is not otherwise known. Probably he is the same as A. Virginius mentioned along with Rutilius in Cic. *Lael.* § 101.

SEXTUS POMPEIUS was brother of Cn. Pompeius Strabo, and uncle of Cn. Pompeius Magnus. Cicero says of him *praestantissimum ingenium contulerat ad summam iuris ciuilis et ad perfectam geometriae et rerum Stoicarum scientiam* (*Brut.* 47).

CAELIUS ANTIPATER lived about the time of the Gracchi, and wrote a history of the second Punic war in seven books. The frag-

ments now remaining are collected by H. Peter, pp. 98—108. His
claims as a lawyer are simply those of Cicero's mention in *Brut.* 26
*Caelius Antipater scriptor, quemadmodum uidetis, fuit ut temporibus
illis luculentus, iuris ualde peritus, multorum etiam, ut L. Crassi,
magister.* From Cicero, doubtless, Pomponius took his name.

CHAPTER VIII.

JURISTS OF CICERO'S TIME.

Q. MUCIUS, whose full name was *Q. Mucius P.F. P.N. Scaeuola,*
commonly distinguished as Pontifex from *Q. Mucius Q.F. Q.N.
Scaeuola,* the Augur, who was his father's first cousin, is the earliest
lawyer whose writings were used in the Digest. Son of a distinguished lawyer, he maintained the family traditions as man, as statesman, and as jurist. He was tribune of the Commons in 106 B.C.
(Cic. *Brut.* 43. § 161), and curule aedile with L. Licinius Crassus the
great orator in 104 B.C., when they exhibited splendid games (Cic.
Off. II. 16. § 57). Scaevola is particularly mentioned by Pliny
(*H. N.* VIII. § 53) as having been the first to exhibit at Rome a fight
of several lions at once. About the year 98 B.C. (Mommsen *Gesch.*
II. p. 211, ed. 7) Scaevola (then praetor, στρατηγός?) was governor
of Asia. He took with him as legate P. Rutilius, and, though his
governorship lasted only nine months (C. *Att.* v. 17. § 5), its fame
was long lived. He discharged his expenses from his own means,
and administered rigorous justice between the provincials and the
tax-farmers, while declining to nominate any of his own staff as
iudices to try the cases. Those condemned were compelled to refund,
and those guilty of capital crimes were executed. In particular one
of the leaders, though offering large sums for a release, was at once
crucified (Diod. Sic. XXXVII. 6—8; Cic. *Verr.* II. 13. § 34). The
senate approved his action so as to treat it as a model for future
governors of Asia (Val. Max. VIII. 15. § 6), and the provincials kept
afterwards a festival (*Mucia*) in his honour (C. *Verr.* II. 22. § 51).
The publicans and their friends, the Equites, so bitterly resented his
conduct (cf. Cic. *Planc.* 12. § 33), that selecting Rutilius for attack
they put him on trial for extortion, and, having the constitution of

the courts, condemned him to banishment (see above, p. cii).
Scaevola defended him, as Cicero says, *more suo, nullo apparatu,
pure et dilucide*, but without the vigour and impressive eloquence
which alone could have prevailed in such a case (Cic. *Or.* I. 53. § 229;
Brut. 30. § 115). Meantime Scaevola had been consul with L.
Licinius Crassus in 95 B.C. (*Brut.* 64. § 229), and the two carried a
law which met the claims of the Italians to full Roman privileges,
not with politic concession, but with a disastrous legal pedantry.
The *lex Licinia Mucia de ciuibus regundis* (cf. *finium regundorum
iudicium*) treated the claims of Italians to Roman citizenship as a
lawyer might treat attempts at encroachments on neighbours' land.
Each was to be citizen of his own state, and forbidden to claim or
exercise the rights of another (Cic. *Corn.* 67 and Ascon. *ad loc.*; *Off.*
III. 11. § 47). The social war broke out five years afterwards.

Scaevola was made *Pontifex Maximus*, but when, we do not
know. At the funeral of C. Marius, B.C. 86, C. Flavius Fimbria,
one of his violent adherents, endeavoured to have Scaevola assassinated. He was wounded, but not fatally; whereupon Fimbria gave
him notice of trial, and the charge being asked, declared that it was
for having only half received the thrust of the dagger (Cic. *Rosc. Am.*
12. § 33). Four years later the Marians effected their object. In
B.C. 82 Damasippus, on instructions from the younger Marius then
shut up in Praeneste by Sulla, attacked and killed Scaevola (amongst
others) before the statue of Vesta, or, as some say, in or near the
Curia Hostilia (Cic. *Or.* III. 3. § 10; *N. D.* III. 32. § 80; Vell. II. 26;
App. *B. Ciu.* I. 88).

Scaevola and Crassus were often opposed to each other as advocates. Cicero (*Brut.* 42. § 155) says Scaevola readily accepted the
position, though Crassus surpassed him, while Crassus was not
willing to give opinions on law cases, knowing Scaevola to be his
superior. In one celebrated case, M. Curius *v.* M. Coponius, which
Cicero frequently mentions (*Or.* I. 39. § 180; *Brut.* 39. § 145; 52.
§ 194 sqq.; *Caecin.* 18. § 53), M. Curius was appointed heir, provided that testator's postumous child should die before he came of
age. No postumous child was born. Scaevola argued before the
centumuiri that the will must be strictly followed, and, that, the
conditions having failed, Curius had no claim. Crassus maintained
successfully that the testator must be taken to mean that Curius
should inherit, if there were no child who lived to be of age. Cicero
says the pleadings were so admirable that Scaevola was thought the

best orator of all lawyers, Crassus the best lawyer of all the orators (*Brut.* § 143). Crassus is made by Cicero in the *De Oratore* politely to give both distinctions to Scaevola. Both excelled in stating a case and explaining its legal and equitable bearings, but in some respects were contrasts to one another. No one more copious than Crassus, no one more apt and concise than Scaevola. In setting off a case with illustrations and refuting his opponent Crassus shewed the resources of a brilliant orator ; Scaevola was rather a clear expositor and formidable critic. Crassus was humorous but dignified ; Scaevola severe though not without a touch of humour (*Brut.* §§ 143—148). He left some orations behind him (ib. § 163).

Cicero was a pupil of Scaevola the augur, and on his death attended the pontifex, whom he calls the most distinguished man in the whole state for ability and uprightness (Cic. *Am.* I.). An illustration of his character is given in the *De Officiis* (III. 15. § 62). Scaevola was buying an estate and requested the seller to name his price once for all. He did so : Scaevola said the estate was worth more, and paid 100,000 sesterces (about £850) more than the price asked. Good faith in all the business of life was with him, as man and as lawyer, the main object of consideration. In his edict for the province of Asia he had a clause, which Cicero borrowed, allowing want of good faith to be pleaded against the validity of a transaction (*Habeo exceptionem ex Q. Mucii P. F. edicto Asiatico 'extra quam si ita negotium gestum est, ut eo stari non oporteat ex fide bona'* Cic. *Att.* VI. 1. § 15). Scaevola was in the habit of saying that those actions (*arbitria* cf. pp. 58—60) were of the most searching and exhaustive character in which the formula contained the words 'in good faith'; that good faith had the widest possible application : it affected the relation of guardian and ward, of partners, of trustee and *cestui que* trust, of principal and agent, of buyer and seller, letter and hirer, and that, as there might be cross suits, it required a great judge to decide the mutual obligations of the parties (Cic. *Off.* III. 17. § 70). He composed an oath to be taken by any one who adopted a *paterfamilias*. The adopter was to swear that he was too old to marry and had not in the adoption any improper design upon the property of the proposed arrogatee (Gell. V. 19. § 6, see my note, p. 165). Another result of his practical skill survived in the Justinian law. A testator gives a man something on condition of his not doing this or that. The fulfilment of the condition cannot be ascertained till he is dead, and then the legacy is of no use. Scaevola

said the legatee should be entitled to the legacy on giving to the
party entitled in default a bond to repay the legacy, if he broke the
testator's conditions.   This bond was called *Muciana cautio*, D. XXXV.
I. 1 7; 1 18; 1 72. §§ 1, 2; 1 73; &c.

Pomponius (D. I. 2. 1 2. § 41) names as Q. Mucius' pupils,
Aquilius Gallus, Balbus Lucilius, Sextus Papirius and Gaius Juventius.   Mucius was the first to write a systematic treatise on the
civil law, treating it in 18 books (*ius ciuile primus constituit
generatim in libros decem et octo redigendo*).   In the Florentine
Index he is named third (after Julian and Papinian), and the work
given is one book of definitions (ὅρων).   From this book there are in
the Digest four short extracts, D. XLI. 1. 1 64; XLIII. 20. 1 8; L. 16.
1 241; 17. 1 73.   There are also 50 citations of him (by the name of
Q. Mucius, except D. XVII. 1. 1 48; XLIX. 15. 1 4 where he is called
Scaevola), two at least being from the *Ius Ciuile*, D. XXXIII. 9. 1 3. pr.;
XXXIV. 2. 1 27 ; cf. XVII. 2. 1 30.   Some fragments are found in Gellius
and elsewhere.   They are collected in Huschke's *Ius anteiust.*   The
rules for the devolution of the *sacra* seem more properly referable to
P. Scaevola, the father of Q. Scaevola, pontifex (see above, p. xcix).

His works received commentators.   Servius Sulpicius made notes
or criticisms on them, cf. D. XVII. 2. 1 30 *Seruius in notatis Mucii
ait;* Gell. IV. 1. § 20 *Seruium Sulpicium in reprehensis Scaevolae
capitibus scripsisse.*   Gaius edited or commented on them (Gai. I.
188 *in his libris quos ex Q. Mucio fecimus*) : and Pomponius wrote
lectiones ad Q. Mucium in 39 books, to which no doubt belong
D. XLI. 1. ll 53, 54, which are now by the inscriptions assigned to
Modestin.   The extracts from this work of Pomponius are numerous,
and fill 13½ of Hommel's pages.   Quotations from Q. Mucius occur
in other extracts, e.g. XXXIII. 1. 1 7; XXXIV. 2. 1 34.   Gellius (xv. 27)
mentions also a work in several books of Laelius Felix *ad Q. Mucium.*

Of the pupils of Q. Mucius only C. Aquilius Gallus is well known
(see below).

L. LUCILIUS BALBUS had the credit, along with Aquilius, of being
the teacher of Serv. Sulpicius (Cic. *Brut.* 42 ; Pompon. D. I. 2. 1 2.
§ 43).   Cicero calls him learned and well trained, but somewhat
slow and deliberate.   See also Cic. *Quinct.* 16. § 53; 17. § 254.

SEXT. PAPIRIUS and C. JUVENTIUS are not otherwise known than
from Pomponius, who names them as among the principal pupils of
Q. Mucius.

C. AQUILIUS[1] GALLUS was a thorough lawyer, devoted to the study
and practice of his craft both by taste and ability. It is characteristic of him that the only state office which we know him to have
held, was that which became the symbol and organ of the law itself—
the praetorship, which he held at the same time as Cicero B.C. 66.
For the consulship in the next year he declined to stand, alleging ill
health and his occupation in the law courts (Cic. *Att.* I. 1 *Aquillium
non arbitrabamur competitorem fore, qui et negauit et iurauit morbum et illud suum regnum iudiciale opposuit*). He presided in
B.C. 81 at the trial of the action in which Cicero pleaded for
P. Quinctius, and is constantly addressed by Cicero. He assisted
Cicero in his defence of Caecina (27. § 77) in B.C. 69 ; he presided in
B.C. 66 as praetor in a trial for *ambitus* (Cic. *Clu.* 53. § 147), and he
is mentioned in Val. Max. VIII. 2. § 2 as judge in a case in which a
book-obligation was sought to be enforced, and the defence was that
it was granted only *mortis causa*. (See other grounds of defence in
Savigny *Verm. Schr.* I. p. 254.) But these, no doubt, are only accidental instances of the ordinary course of Aquilius' life. To the
world he was almost more distinguished by his fine house on the
Viminal than by his profession (Plin. XVII. § 2), but his own passion
was for law. Cicero describes him as devoted to the interests of the
public, skilful in advice, and always ready to give it, of a nature so clear
and straightforward that the maxims of just law were its natural
expression, so wise in law that he seemed to grow the nobler from
its study (Cic. *Caecin.* 27. § 78). He cared for and studied the law
itself and not the advocate's *rôle*. When a case turned on a question
of fact, he declined it and replied to the consulter; '*Nihil hoc ad
ius ; ad Ciceronem*'. It is 'not a point of law: Cicero is your man '
(Cic. *Top.* 12. § 51). He had a principal share in training Servius
Sulpicius (Cic. *Brut.* 42. § 154), and lived at the time, as Pomponius
states (D. I. 2. 1 2. § 43), at Cercina (see under SULPICIUS).

Three special legal improvements are attributed to him. One is
the *Stipulatio Aquiliana*, i.e. a comprehensive form of stipulation
embracing all liabilities, to be followed by a general release (D. XLVI.
4. 1 18). Another is a form of words for institution of grand-
children as heirs, who should be born after the death of testator and
whose own father should have died before the testator, leaving them
in fact *sui heredes*. The form is given in an extract from Cervidius

---

[1] The Flor. MS. spells the word with one l. Inscriptions spell it both with
one and with two.

Scaevola (D. xxviii. 2. 1 29), which is full of difficulty.   A third was
the explicit recognition of fraud as a ground for action, and was
doubtless introduced by Aquilius when praetor.   *Inde euerriculum
malitiarum omnium, iudicium de dolo malo, quod C. Aquillius fami-
liaris noster protulit; quem dolum idem Aquillius tum teneri putat,
cum aliud sit simulatum, aliud actum* (Cic. *N. D.* iii. 30. § 74; cf.
Off. iii. 14, 15. §§ 60, 61 and below p. 131).   The action took the
shape of claiming *restitutio in integrum* (D. iv. 3).

In the Digest Aquilius (either as Gallus or Gallus Aquilius) is
cited in Javolen's editions of Labeo xxxii. 1 29. § 1; xl. 7. 1 39; also
by African xxviii. 6. 1 33. § 1; by Scaevola l. c.; by Ulpian viii. 5. 1 6.
§ 2; xix. 1. 1 17. § 6 (at second hand from Mela); xxx. 1 30. § 7;
xliii. 24. 1 7. § 4; by Paul xxx. 1. 1 27; xxxiv. 2. 1 32. § 1; l. 16.
1 77; and by Licinnius Rufinus xxviii. 5. 1 75 (74).   In D. l. 16. 1 96
Celsus says that M. Tullius, in a case in which he was arbitrator,
was the first to lay down that the seashore (*litus*) extended inwards
as far as the largest wave came.   He probably learnt this from
Aquilius, who was, as Cicero tells us (*Top.* 7. § 32), in the habit of
defining the seashore *qua fluctus eluderet (alluderet?* see Mayor on
Cic. *N. D.* ii. § 100).   Mommsen suggests that in the Digest for
idque Marcum Tullium aiunt constituisse we ought to have *idque M.
Tullius Gallum Aquilium ait constituisse.*

The *lex Aquilia,* D. ix. 2, has nothing to do with C. Aquilius
Gallus.   It was of much earlier date.   See below, p. 99.

SERVIUS SULPICIUS, whose full name was Servius Sulpicius Q. F.
Lemoniā Rufus (i. e. of the Lemonian tribe), was the greatest lawyer
of the Republic, at least in the estimation of the Digest writers.
Cicero tells us he was the same, or very nearly the same, age as himself, and therefore was born about 106 B. C., son of a man of equestrian
rank, the grandfather being a person of no note (Cic. *Brut.* § 150;
Mur. § 16).   He passed through the same early training as Cicero,
and went with him to Rhodes B. C. 78, studied oratory and dialectic,
and practised as an advocate in the Courts with great distinction.
Pomponius (D. i. 2. 1 2. § 43) tells an anecdote of what determined
him to study law.   He was engaged in conducting a friend's case
and consulted Q. Mucius Scaevola on a point of law.   Not fully com-
prehending Scaevola's answer, he asked him again, and again failed to
understand.   Whereupon Scaevola reproached him with being a
patrician and noble and advocate and yet ignorant of the law with

which he was concerned.   Stung with the reproach Servius attended the best lawyers of the day, and obtained a first training from
Lucilius Balbus and more complete instruction from Aquilius
Gallus (*institutus a Balbo Lucilio, instructus autem maxime a Gallo
Aquilio*).   He went to Aquilius to Cercina for this purpose and
there he wrote several works.   Cercina, an island near the coast of
Africa, a little north of the Syrtis minor, was a place where trading
vessels often congregated (Liv. XXXIII. 48. § 3; *Bell. Afr.* 34).   Marius
was there for a time (Plut. *Mar.* 40), and Hannibal for a night
(Liv. *l. c.*).   Sempronius Gracchus, accused of adultery with Julia,
daughter of Augustus, was in exile there for 14 years, *inter extorres
et liberalium artium nescios* (Tac. *Ann.* I. 53; IV. 13).   The place
seems strangely chosen for an active jurisconsult like Aquilius.
We have no confirmation of any part of the story from other
sources.

Sulpicius was quaestor with Murena, and had the troublesome
district of Ostia assigned to him (Cic. *Mur.* 8. § 18).   He was praetor,
and presided over the trials for *peculatus* (ib. §§ 35, 42).   In 63 B.C.
he was an unsuccessful candidate for the consulship, and with Cato
accused Murena, one of the successful candidates, of *ambitus*.   Cicero
defended Murena in the brilliant and witty speech which is preserved.
He speaks of and to Sulpicius with the respect due to their strong
friendship and Sulpicius' great merits, but points out that a popular
election is much more readily carried by military glory than by a
jurisconsult's sober and technical profession, and rallies the lawyers
on their unmeaning forms.   In B.C. 51 Sulpicius was consul with
M. Marcellus.   In the civil war he took no decided side (see Cicero's
letters to him *Fam.* IV. 1, 2; *Att.* X. 14; 15, &c.), but afterwards
inclined to Caesar, and was made by him governor of Achaia B.C. 45
(Cic. *Fam.* VI. 6. § 10).   Whilst in this office he wrote two letters to
Cicero, which are preserved in the collection of Cicero's letters (*Fam.*
IV. 5; 12), one consoling Cicero in tender and beautiful language
for the loss of his daughter, the other relating with marks of
genuine feeling the murder of M. Marcellus.   In the following year
(U.C. 710 B.C. 44) Caesar was assassinated on the Ides (15th) of
March, and Sulpicius proposed on the 17th that no public notice
should be put up of any decree or grant of Caesar since the Ides of
March.   Antony and others agreed to it (Cic. *Phil.* I. 1. § 3).   When
the senate determined to send commissioners to Antony to Mutina
directing him to leave D. Brutus undisturbed in Gaul and himself to

take Macedonia, &c. the commissioners were Serv. Sulpicius, L. Philippus, and L. Piso. They left Rome early in January 43 B.C., Sulpicius being in bad health. When they got near the camp of Antony Sulpicius died. Cicero's ixth Philippic is devoted to praising his patriotic conduct and proposing a public funeral and the erection of a statue in his honour on the Rostra. This statue still remained in the time of Pomponius.

Cicero says that Sulpicius might possibly have been in the first rank of orators, if he had not preferred to be far the first in the inferior profession of lawyer. In that he surpassed Scaevola and others, because he alone was a scientific lawyer : he had studied dialectic, and thence had learnt to distribute the whole into parts, to discover the latent characteristic, to explain the obscure, to distinguish the ambiguous, to detect fallacies and to draw right inferences. He had studied literature and had an elegant style ; and, though a pupil of Balbus and Gallus, he surpassed them both, being more careful and profound than the quick and ready Gallus, more active and efficient in business than the slow and considerate Balbus (Cic. *Brut.* §§ 151—154). Quintilian says he was in the habit, by way of exercise, of turning Latin poetry into prose (x. 5. § 4) ; and that he gained marked fame by his speeches, three of which were extant in Quintilian's time, besides some notes of speeches which were so carefully made as to give him the impression of being intended for a permanent record (VII. 1. § 116 ; 7. § 30). He is named by Plin. *Ep.* v. 3 in a list of grave Romans who had written light verses. He is said to have written 180 law books, of which many were extant in Pomponius' time. Of his works, one fragment from a book *de dotibus* is given by Gellius (IV. 4), and a reference to the same book in ib. 3 ; D. XII. 4. 28 ; mention is made of a book *de sacris detestandis* (Gell. VII. (VI.) 12) ; of two books on the Edict addressed to Brutus (D. I. 2. 1 2. § 44) ; and of some criticisms on Q. Mucius (Gell. IV. 1. § 20). Several explanations of words by him are given by Varro, Festus, and others, and are collected by Huschke. He had many pupils. Namusa is said to have digested their writings in 140 books (D. ib.). There are no extracts from him in the Digest, but his opinion is frequently (about 80 times) quoted, often as given by one of his scholars, e.g. D. III. 5. 1 20 (21). pr. ; IV. 8. 1 40 ; v. 1. 1 80 ; XVII. 2. 1 65. § 8 ; XXIII. 3. 1 79 ; XXXIII. 4. 1 6 ; XXXIV. 7. 1 12 ; XXXIV. 2. 1 39 ; XXXV. 1. 1 40. § 3 ; XXXIX. 3. 1 1. § 6.

There is no evidence for referring to Serv. Sulpicius the introduction of the *Actio Seruiana* for recovery of things mortgaged by a farmer, Just. IV. 6. § 7 (Puchta *Cursus* § 251 note *f*).

CORNELIUS MAXIMUS was apparently, though the passage is corrupt, the master of Trebatius (D. I. 2. 1 2. § 45), and in that capacity is alluded to by Cicero in one of his playful letters to Trebatius (*Fam.* VII. 8). Trebatius used frequently to adduce his opinion as an authority (ib. 17). Whether he is also meant by Cn. Cornelius in ib. 9 is doubtful. He is apparently mentioned by the side of Tubero in Gai. I. 136; and his opinion is quoted by Alfenus against that of Serv. Sulpicius in D. XXXIII. 7. 1 16. § 1.

ALFENUS UARUS, one of Servius Sulpicius' scholars, and coupled by Pomponius (D. I. 2. 1 2. § 44) with Ofilius, as the two scholars that had most authority. He attained the dignity of consul, and wrote, according to the Florentine Index, *Digesta* in 40 books, of which however the 7th is the highest-numbered book from which an extract is made in the Digest, but the 39th is referred to in D. III. 5. 1 20 (21). Paul made an epitome of it, extracts from which are also found in the Digest. Those from the *Digesta* itself are 29 and fill $5\frac{1}{2}$ of Hommel's pages; those from Paul's *Epitome* are 25 and fill $3\frac{1}{2}$ pages. Gellius VII. (VI.) 5. § 2 quotes from the 34th book of the *Digest*, 2nd of the *Collectanea*, a double reference, which some connect with Namusa's collection of the writings of Servius' scholars. Alfenus was *consul suffectus* with Cocceius in B.C. 39 U.C. 715; and, if it was his son that was the consul of A.D. 2, we learn that the father's praenomen was Publius (Henzen on Fast. Biond. *Corp. I. L.* I. p. 467, who refers to Dion's *Index* under lib. LV. for the son). The agnomen *Catus* which is given him by Rudorff and others is simply a conjecture of Huschke's for the mysterious 'Gaius', which follows Alfen's name in Pomponius (*Z. G. R.* XV. 187). If it had really been his agnomen, would Horace (see below) have substituted *uafer?*

There is a romantic story told of Alfenus by Porphyrio the Commentator on Horace, and alluded to apparently by Horace himself in the lines where, illustrating the Stoical view, that the wise man knows all arts implicitly, he says *ut Alfenus uafer omni obiecto instrumento artis clausaque taberna sutor erat* (*Sat.* I. 3. 130; some MSS. have *tonsor*). Porphyrio says Varus was a cobbler of Cremona, who gave up his business, went to Rome and profited so much by the instruction of Sulpicius, that he gained the consulship and re-

ceived a public funeral.   *Uafer* is an epithet which naturally applies
to a lawyer.

The lawyer is by some identified with the Alfenus to whom Catullus
addresses his 30th epigram, and possibly with the Varus of epigrams
10 and 22.   This latter however is much more likely Quintilius
Varus the poet.   Further he is on the authority of Servius and the
scholiasts on Vergil identified with the Varus who with Vergil
attended the lectures of Siron, the Epicurean philosopher (Schol.
Veron. to Verg. *Ecl.* v. 9 ; Ribbeck *Praef. ad Verg. ed. min.* p. x,
but this seems by no means certain : Quintilian speaks of a L. Varus
as an Epicurean and friend of Caesar), and to. whom Vergil addressed his 6th *Eclogue* and also some verses in *Ecl.* IX. 27 sqq.   The
Bernese scholiast (on *Ecl.* VIII. 6) states that Varus was one of
Augustus' commissioners for settling lands in the neighbourhood of
Cremona on veteran soldiers B.C. 40, and that in revenge for a
Mantuan (Octavius Musa) having taken some of his cattle in pledge
and starved them to death, Varus distributed to the veterans some of
the Mantuan lands.   Others make Musa to have been the spoiler, and
Varus to have succeeded Pollio as legate and to have been sent with
instructions to restore some of the land, instructions which he very
imperfectly carried out (see Teuffel-Schwabe § 208. 3 ; Forbiger *ad
Verg.* ll. cc. ; Ribbeck *Praef. cit.* pp. xviii—xx).

Of the extracts in the Digest the following are most noticeable : v. 1. l 76, where he refers to the opinion of philosophers that
the particles of the human body are continually being replaced by
others ; IX. 2. 1 52 ; XXXV. 1. 1 27 ; XXXIX. 2. l 43 ; L. 16. l 203 ;
and others from Paul's abstract, XIX. 2. l 30 ; l 31 ; XXXII. l 60 ;
XXXIX. 3. l 24 ; XLI. 1. l 38.   They contain some interesting cases
well expressed.   He is cited 17 times, usually as Alfenus, but once
(D. XXXIII. 4. l 6) as Alfenus Varus, and thrice as Varus, viz. VI. 1.
l 5. § 3 ; XL. 12. l 10 ; L. 16. l 39. § 6.

OFILIUS[1], one of Servius' pupils, who with Alfenus had the most
weight as a lawyer.   Aulus Ofilius was of equestrian rank and did
not rise above it.   Cicero twice at least mentions him in his letters,
once B.C. 45 to Atticus (XIII. 37), once B.C. 44 to Trebatius (*Fam.*
VII. 21 ; and cf. XVI. 24. § 1), in both cases respecting some law
business.   Pomponius says he was more learned than either Cascel-

---

[1] In Cicero the name is spelt Offilius.   In inscriptions it appears to be most
frequently Ofillius, frequently Ofilius, rarely Offilius.   (*Indices* to *Corp. I. L.* iii.
ix. x.)

lius or Trebatius : that Capito 'followed' him, and that he was one
of those whose instruction Labeo attended. 'He was very intimate
with Julius Caesar and wrote many books on civil law, which laid
a basis ·in all parts of the subject'. Huschke (*Z. G. R.* xv. 189)
aptly remarks that Caesar amongst other plans formed the idea of
making a digest of the law, *Ius ciuile ad certum modum redigere
atque ex immensa diffusaque legum copia optima quaeque et necessaria
in paucissimos conferre libros* (Suet. *Iul.* 44).   It would seem probable that Ofilius was his agent for this purpose, as Varro was for
forming a library.   This 'Tribonian of the Republic' (Huschke, p.
202) left, whether as part of Caesar's scheme or not, works which
appear to have dealt with all the great branches of law.   The
words of Pomponius are probably corrupt ; *nam de legibus uicensimae
primis conscribit : de iurisdictione idem edictum praetoris primus
diligenter composuit,* D. I. 2. 1 2. § 44.   Sanio has suggested *uiginti
libros* for *uicensimae,* and Huschke and Rudorff support this.   After
de iurisdictione Huschke supposes a number (e.g. x. *libros*) to have
fallen out, but it is possible to take the sentence as it stands, *de iur.*
denoting the branch of the subject on which Ofilius worked in drawing up the Edict.   Then in D. XXXII. 1 55. §§ 1, 4, 7 *Ofilius libro
quinto iuris partiti* is quoted ; in XXXIII. 9. 1 5. §§ 5, 8 *Ofilius libro
sexto decimo actionum.*   Whether *Ofilius ad Atticum ait* (D. L. 16.
1 234) refers to a separate work, addressed possibly to T. Pomponius
Atticus, we do not know.   But we shall not be far wrong, if we
infer from these notices that Ofilius wrote on the statute law (*de
legibus*), on the relations of some parts of the civil law (*ius partitum*),
on the *ius honorarium* (*edictum Praet.*), and on *Actiones* (cf. D. I. 2.
1 2. §§ 5, 12).

What Ofilius did with the Edict is difficult to say.   Pomponius'
words are that 'he was the first to draw up the Edict with care'.
This would naturally apply to a good lawyer in the office of praetor.
But Ofilius did not leave the equestrian rank and consequently
never was praetor.   Pomponius probably meant that Ofilius was
the first to deal with the traditional edict in a thorough and
systematic manner : he rearranged and revised it for the benefit of
the praetor at the time or a future one.   Such assistance by experts
must often have been given.   If he did it at Caesar's instigation, its
general adoption would be pretty certain ; (see below under JULIAN).
But Pomponius is not a writer who inspires confidence in the precise
historical correctness of his expressions.

h 2

There are no extracts from Ofilius' works in the Digest, but Ofilius is cited often (about 50 times), e. g. D. II. 1. 1 11. § 2; 7. 1 1. § 2; 9. 1 1; IV. 1. 1 16. § 1; 8. 1 21. § 1; XIV. 2. 1 2. § 3; XXI. 1. 1 17. pr.; XXIV. 3. 1 18. § 1; XXXII. 1 29. § 1; XXXIII. 4. 1 6. § 1; XXXIX. 3. 1 1. § 5; § 21; 1 2. § 10; 1 3; XLIII. 20. 1 1. § 17; 21. 1 3. § 10; XLVII. 2. 1 21. pr. &c.; Gai. III. 140.

Besides Alfenus Varus and A. Ofilius, Pomponius (§ 44) mentions as scholars of Servius and writers, Gaius, Titus Caesius, Aufidius Tucca, Aufidius Namusa, Flavius Priscus, Gaius Ateius, Pacuvius Labeo, Antistius, Labeonis Antistii pater, Cinna, Publicius Gellius.

Mommsen proposes either to strike out Gaius or to transpose the word so as to give Cinna a praenomen. Asher (*Z. R. G.* v. 91) suggests that the commentator Gaius was meant, Justinian's compilers thinking him to be an ancient authority like Q. Mucius. For Huschke's conjecture, see above under ALFENUS. Schulin (*ad Pand. tit. de origine iuris*, 1876) thinks that this law (D. I. 2. 1 2) was not one continuous extract, but consisted originally of several extracts, which have been run together by the copyists; and that *Gaius* in §§ 37, 42 and 44 is the remains of the inscription of extracts from Gaius *ad* XII. *tab.*

Of T. Caesius, Aufidius Tucca (see however below), and Fl. Priscus nothing more is known. For Pacuvius Labeo see under his son's name, p. cxxiv.

AUFIDIUS NAMUSA is said by Pomponius to have arranged all the writings of these scholars of Servius into 140 books (*quorum omnes qui fuerunt libri digesti sunt ab Aufidio Namusa*, &c.). Namusa is cited by Javolen *ex posterioribus Labeonis*, D. XXXV. 1. 1 40. § 3; and Labeo probably refers to him in D. XXXIII. 5. 1 20, *Apud Aufidium libro primo rescriptum est;* and Ulpian in D. XVII. 2. 1 52. § 18, unless Tucca be meant. Namusa is cited by Ulpian D. XIII. 6. 1 5. § 7: and by Paul D. XXXIX. 3. 1 2. § 6. Possibly this work of Namusa's is the source of the references to *Seruii auditores* (D. XXXIII. 4. 1 6. § 1; 7. 1 12. pr.; § 6; XXXIX. 3. 1 1. § 6). A juridical fragment is quoted from P. Aufidius by Priscian, VIII. 4. § 18 (Huschke *Iur. Antei.* p. 99[4]).

C. ATEIUS is probably the writer meant by Labeo, D. XXIII. 3. 1 79. § 1 *Ateius scribit Seruium respondisse;* XXXII. 1 30. § 6; XXXIV.

2. 1 39. § 2; by Paul XXXIX. 3. 1 2. § 4; and XXXIX. 3. 1 14. pr.; where Flor. has *Antaeus*, the inferior MSS. *Ateius*.

It has been suggested that he was father of C. Ateius Capito, the rival of Labeo, and the same as the C. Ateius Capito whom Cicero speaks of as a close friend of his own and a warm supporter of Julius Caesar (Cic. *Fam.* XIII. 29, B.C. 46). This C. Ateius was tribune with Aquilius Gallus (the coincidence of names is curious) in B.C. 55, when Pompey and Crassus were consuls. He violently opposed the assignment of provinces to the consuls, and especially Crassus' departure for Syria (Plut. *Crass.* 16; Dio. XXXIX. 32 sqq.), and was afterwards 'noted' by Appius for having made a false report of the conspiracy (Cic. *Diu.* I. 16). If he was father of the famous Capito, he obtained the rank of praetor, and was son of one of Sulla's centurions (Tac. *An.* III. 75).

There was a grammarian Ateius also. He may have been a freedman of the Capitos. See Suet. *Gr.* 10; Teuffel-Schwabe, § 211. 1.

CINNA is cited by Ulpian in D. XXIII. 2. 1 6; XXXV. 1. 1 40. § 1.

PUBLICIUS GELLIUS. A jurist called Publicius is cited by Marcellus, D. XXXI. 1 50. § 2; by Modestin XXXV. 1. 1 51. § 1; by Ulpian XXXVIII. 17. 1 2. § 8 (*Africanus et Publicius temptant dicere*), but neither the authors by whom he is cited, nor the company in which his name appears, seem to suit a pupil of Servius.

There is nothing to connect this man with the *Actio Publiciana* (D. VI. 2; *Inst.* IV. 6. § 4).

TREBATIUS, whose full name was *C. Trebatius Testa*, was of a family settled at Velia in Lucania (Cic. *Top.* 1. § 5; *Fam.* VII. 20). He was of the equestrian rank (Porph. ad Hor. *Sat.* II. 1. 1); and was a pupil in civil law of Cornelius Maximus. Cicero was much attached to him and desirous of promoting his interests. In B.C. 54 he had intended taking him with him on some journey (cf. *Fam.* VII. 17. § 2), but his plans were altered, and, when discussing with Balbus whether he should send Trebatius to Caesar, he received a letter from Caesar, suggesting Cicero's sending him some one whose career he might assist. Cicero sent him Trebatius, saying there was no better man or more upright and modest character: besides which he was a leader in civil law, from his remarkable historical and legal knowledge (*Accedit etiam quod familiam ducit in iure ciuili singu-*

lari[1] *memoria, summa scientia* Cic. *Fam.* VII. 5). It was in this
year Cicero wrote his books *de republica.* Possibly Trebatius may
have been made useful in connexion with them. Caesar offered him
the position of a tribune without the military work (ib. 8. § 1) but
he refused; apparently did not go to Britain with Caesar (ib. 17.
§ 3); and, though kindly and considerately treated, did not much
relish life in the army (ib. 18. § 1). Cicero's letters to him at this
time are written as to a congenial spirit and are very pleasant: he
rallies him in a lively tone with plenty of puns and chaff. ' You
' that have learnt to draw up securities for others, keep yourself
' secure from those British charioteers (ib. 6), unless you can catch
' a chariot and drive home in it (ib. 7). I thought you had learnt
' wisdom from Cornelius : it tells greatly against him that you are so
' unwise as to decline Caesar's offers (ib. 8). So Caesar thinks you
' quite a lawyer. You must be glad to have found a place where
' some one thinks you have wits (*aliquid sapere*). If you had gone
' to Britain, I will answer for it there would have been no better
' lawyer (*peritior*) there. Mind you use a stove to keep off the cold :
' I can quote Mucius and Manilius' opinion on its propriety (ib. 10).
' I wish you were here to meet me in a contest of wit or argument :
' it would be a deal better than you will get from our enemies or even
' from our friends the Aedui (ib. § 4). You write that Caesar con-
' sults you : I would rather he should consult your interests. If there
' is no chance of that, come back to us. You will get more from a
' single talk with me than from all put together at Samarobriva.
' If you stay much longer, our playwriters will have you on the stage
' in the character of a British lawyer (ib. 11). Pansa tells me you
' have turned Epicurean! What havoc that will make with your
' law ! How can you draw any more formulae with *ut inter bonos*
' *bene agier oportet ?* For no good man is selfish. How can you say
' what should be done ' for partition of common property' ? If every
' man looks after himself only, what can there be in common ?
' And then what becomes of your studies of religious oaths ? How
' can you swear by the stone Jove (*Iouem lapidem iurare*[2]), if you

----

[1] So Wesenberg and Baiter. The Cod. Med. has *singularis*, which Zimmern
I. p. 298 with others translates, ' he has also what in civil law is the chief point,
a singular memory and great knowledge'. Compare the use of *fam. duc.* in
Cic. *Fin.* IV. 16. § 45. But what the context wants is the statement that Trebatius was a good lawyer, not a comparative estimation of the qualities which
make a lawyer. Of course *fam. duc.* should not be pressed, as some have pressed
it, to mean that Trebatius was the head of a special school of law.
[2] An obscure phrase explained by Polyb. III. 25; Paul. Fest. p. 115 of a

'know that there is no Jove to be angry with any one? (ib. 12).
'I am afraid you have little scope for your profession there: they
'don't join issue (*manum conserere*), but cross swords. However you
'are not a very forward fighter, and so you need not fear that any
'one in an interdict will use against you, the plea 'provided you have
'not been first to use armed force'. But I do advise you to keep
'clear of the Treviri' (Caesar marched against them in B.C. 53): 'I am
'told they are very *Tresviri Capitales* (cf. D. I. 2. 1 2. § 30): I wish
'they had been only the *Tresviri* of the mint (ib. 13). Balbus
'assured me you would be quite a rich man. Did he mean, what we
'Romans mean by riches, a good supply of coin in your pocket? or
'what the Stoics call riches, the sky above you and the earth below?
'I am told you are so haughty, as to give no answers to those who
'question you. I can at least congratulate you on there being no better
'jurisconsult at Samarobriva (ib. 16). You are very economical in
'using palimpsests for your letters: I hope you have not destroyed
'mine for the purpose: I don't blame you if it is only your legal
'drafts' (ib. 18). Subsequently Trebatius is found on Caesar's side in
the civil war, and writing to Cicero to say that Caesar wished Cicero
either to join him or at least to go to Greece out of the way (Plut.
Cic. 37). He was at Caesar's side on one occasion, when Caesar
incurred great odium by not rising to receive an address from the
senate. Trebatius hinted to him to rise, but Caesar only replied by
an unfriendly look (Suet. *Iul.* 78). After Caesar's death, B.C. 44,
Cicero while voyaging to Greece (as he intended, though he afterwards altered his mind) called at Velia, saw Trebatius' home, paternal
estate and friends, and was reminded thereby that Trebatius once,
having referred to Aristotle's *Topica* at Cicero's Tusculan Villa, had
asked Cicero to translate them for him. Accordingly on his voyage
from Velia to Vibo, Cicero wrote from memory an account of the
Topica, illustrated it with legal examples, and addressed it to Trebatius (Cic. *Top.* 1; *Fam.* VII. 19, 20). From Tusculum, in the
summer of the same year, he sends C. Silius to Trebatius to consult
him professionally (ib. 21). Another letter of uncertain date relates
how Cicero over his wine with Trebatius had told him that it was a
disputed point, whether an heir could sue for theft committed before
he became heir. Trebatius said no one ever thought that. Cicero
drank freely and went home late, but found the passage, wrote it out,

prayer to Jove to cast them away, if they break faith, as they throw away a
stone. But?

and sent it to Trebatius, *ut scires, id quod tu neminem sensisse dicebas, Sex. Aelium, M'. Manilium, M. Brutum sensisse: ego tamen Scaeuolae et Testae assentior* (ib. 22). Horace addresses to Trebatius the 1st Satire of his second book (cir. 30 B.C.), which is framed as a dialogue between them. Trebatius recommends Horace to sing (Octavius) Caesar's praises. Horace says he is not fit for so high a theme, and prefers satirical writings. Trebatius reminds him of the penalties for 'bad poems' against persons (*mala carmina* i.e. libels), to which Horace retorts by a pun, 'What if the poems be *good*, and Caesar praise them ? '

Of his legal career we are told but little. He had the early training of Labeo (*institutus est a Trebatio* D. I. 2. 1 2. § 47), who however attended other teachers as well. Pomponius says he was less eloquent but a better lawyer than Cascellius, and that Ofilius was more learned than either. On the important question whether codicils should be sanctioned, Trebatius had the decisive voice. L. Lentulus died in Africa and left a codicil confirmed by his will imposing a trust on Augustus amongst others. Augustus performed the trust, whereupon others did the same, and Lentulus' daughter paid some legacies which were not strictly due. Augustus summoned the lawyers to advise him whether codicils should be allowed. Trebatius advised in their favour, as a convenient form for persons on a journey. His authority was at that time the highest; and, Labeo afterwards leaving a codicil, their validity was fully established (Just. II. 25).

He wrote books, several of which were extant but not much used in Pomponius' time (D. I. 2. 1 2. § 45). Some were *de iure ciuili*, nine books were *de religionibus*. This last work is quoted by Gell. VII. (VI.) 12, and Macrob. *Sat.* I. 16. § 28; III. 3. §§ 2, 5 (where a tenth book is quoted); 7. § 8. It is also quoted by the scholiasts on Vergil and by Arnobius; see the passages in Huschke *Iurispr. Anteiust.* On one point, in which, according to Gellius IV. 2, he gave a contrary opinion to Labeo, the Digest has followed Trebatius (XXI. 1. 1 14. § 3).

He is often (almost 80 times) quoted in the Digest, chiefly by Javolen and (probably at second hand through Javolen's editions of Labeo) by Ulpian and Paul (D. XXXII. 1 29. pr.; 1 30. § 5; 1 100. §§ 2—4) and others. Cf. IV. 3. 1 8. §§ 3, 4; 8. 1 21. § 1; XI. 7. 1 14. § 11; XVI. 3. 1 1. § 41; XVIII. 6. 1 1. § 2; XXI. 1. 1 6. § 1; 1 12. § 4; 1 14. § 3; XXX. 1 5. § 1; 1 30. § 5; XXXIX. 3. 1 1. § 3; XL. 7.

1 3. § 11;   XLI. 1. 1 16; 1 19; 2. 1 3. § 5; XLIII. 23. 1 2; 24. 1 1. § 7;
1 22. § 3.

AULUS CASCELLIUS was a contemporary of Trebatius.   The words
of Pomponius relating to his legal instructor are evidently corrupt.
He could hardly have been a pupil of Q. Mucius (as that would
imply his being born before 100 B.C.), but may well have been a
pupil of one of those who learnt from Mucius.   Pomponius seems
to name Volusius.   Pliny names Volcatius, a noble, as his master
(*H. N.* VIII. 144).   He attained the rank of quaestor, and was
offered the consulship by Augustus, but declined it (D. I. 2. 1 2. § 45).
The cause was probably the same as Labeo's (see below).   He was a
firm republican and free in expressing his thoughts.

He positively declined to draw a formula (pleadings in an action)
on behalf of any of the grantees of land seized by the triumvirs
(Octavius, Antonius and Lepidus), and, when fully expressing his
thoughts on the empire and warned by his friends of the danger of
doing so, answered that what men in general found evils he found a
protection—old age and childlessness (Val. Max. VI. 2. § 12).   He is
named by Horace as a living type of a learned jurisconsult.   This is
in the *Ars Poetica* 37, the date of which is uncertain, but according to
the latest opinions between 24 and 20 B.C. (Nettleship *Journ. of Phil.*
XII. 44) or somewhat later (Mommsen *Hermes* XV. 114).   Ammianus
refers to him with Trebatius and Alfenus as types of old-world
lawyers (XXX. 4. § 12).   He selected a grandson of Q. Mucius for
his heir (D. I. 2. 1 2. § 45).

He was more eloquent than Trebatius but not so good a lawyer.
His wit is celebrated.   When Vatinius (Cicero's old enemy) was
pelted with stones by the people on account of the poor games he
had given, he got a law passed that no one should throw into the
arena anything but *poma*.   A man came to Cascellius to consult him
on some matter of his own, and asked whether *nuces pineae* (fir cones?)
came under the head of *poma* (cf. D. L. 16. 1 205).   Cascellius at once
had a hit at Vatinius: 'Yes, if you want to pelt Vatinius with
them', was the reply (Macrob. *Sat.* II. 6).   Another man came
to consult him about a division of property.   'I want to divide
a ship'.   Cascellius took 'divide[1]' literally, and answered, 'You'll
ruin it, if you do' (Quint. VI. 3. § 87; Macrobius puts it *nauem
si diuidis, nec tu nec socius habebitis*).   Only one book of his was

---

[1] Dirksen (*Der Rechtsgelehrte A. Cascellius*) takes the answer as a play on
nauis. This is a mistake. See the initial words of the chapter of Macrob.

extant in the time of Pomponius.   It was a book *bene dictorum*, which is ambiguous, and may mean a book of good sayings, i.e. witticisms, or of well-expressed opinions.

In Gai. IV. 166 we read of a *Cascellianum* or *secutorium iudicium*, employed to obtain possession of the thing in dispute, after an action on a wager (*sponsio*) has been decided in favour of the suitor not in possession.   Whether this was named after Aulus Cascellius, we do not know.   It would, one would think, be introduced by a praetor, and Cascellius was not praetor, so far as Pomponius knew.

He is cited with others of his time in the Digest, chiefly by Labeo (as edited by Javolen) XXVIII. 6. 1 39. § 2 ; XXXII. 1 29. pr.; 1 100. pr.; XXXIII. 4. 1 6. § 1; 6. 1 7; 7. 1 4; 1 26. § 1; 10. 1 10; XXXIV. 2. 1 39. § 1 ; XXXV. 1. 1 40. § 1 ; once by Celsus L. 16. 1 158 ; twice by Ulpian XXXIX. 3. 1 1. § 17 ; XLIII. 24. 1 1. § 7, both of which citations were very likely taken from Labeo.

In Cic. *Balb.* 20 we are told that Q. Mucius, the augur, when consulted on a point of the law of *praediatores* (i.e. purchasers of lands forfeited to the state from failure of the parties who had taken contracts, cf. Gai. II. 61), used to refer the client to Furius or Cascellius, who were themselves *praediatores* and familiar with the matter. Mommsen suggests that this Cascellius was the lawyer's father (*Hermes* XV. p. 114).

TUBERO, whose full name was *Q. Aelius Tubero* (Cic. *Lig.* 1 ; Gell. XIV. 2. § 20), was a patrician who studied under Ofilius, and was first an advocate and afterwards became a lawyer.   His father, L. Aelius Tubero, was an intimate friend of Cicero ; they had been *domi una eruditi, militiae contubernales, post affines, in omni denique uita familiares* (Cic. *Lig.* 7. § 21).   He was legate to Q. Cicero, when the latter was governor of Asia B.C. 61 (Cic. *ad Q. Fr.* I. 1. § 10). When the civil war broke out between Caesar and Pompey, L. Tubero was sent by the senate to take the government of Africa. The son accompanied him, but they were not allowed to land—as Tubero said, by Ligarius, who as legate of Considius, had been left there in charge of the government, or, as Cicero said, by the praetor Varus, who had succeeded Considius.   On this repulse they went to Macedonia to Pompey's camp (Cic. *Lig.* 7—9) and the son was in Pompey's ranks at the battle of Pharsalus (ib. 3).   In B.C. 46 he prosecuted C. Ligarius, as an opponent of Caesar, for not allowing him to land or even to take water.   His speech was quoted by

Quintilian (XI. 80) and extant in Pomponius' time. Cicero defended
Ligarius in a speech now extant, and Caesar, who heard the case
himself, acquitted Ligarius, being, according to Plutarch (*Cic.* 39),
much affected by Cicero's pathetic and flattering address. Tubero
was so much chagrined at his failure, that he was partly thereby
induced to give up advocacy (D. I. 2. 1 2. § 46). He married a
daughter of Serv. Sulpicius, and his own daughter was the mother of
the lawyer and statesman, C. Cassius Longinus (ib. § 51). He is said
to have been considered *doctissimus iuris publici et priuati.* He
wrote several books on both subjects, but his antique style of writing
(cf. Gell. VI. 9. § 11) made the books not popular. Gellius mentions
a work of his *de officio iudicis* (XIV. 2. § 20), and says (ib. 7. § 13)
Ateius Capito quoted an opinion of Tubero's that a decree of the
senate was always made by an actual division (*per discessionem*),
and Capito agreed that this was so. The same on another point
(ib. § 8).

He is cited in the Digest by Labeo D. XVIII. 1. 1 77; XXXII. 1 29.
§ 4 ; XXXIII. 6. 1 7 ; 7. 1 25 ; by Celsus either directly or as reported
by Ulpian VII. 8. 1 2 ; XV. 1. 1 5. § 4 ; 1 6 ; XXXII. 1 43 ; XXXIII. 10. 1 7.
§ 2 (*magnopere me Tuberonis et ratio et auctoritas mouet*); XLV. 1.
1 72. pr.; and so probably VII. 8. 1 2. § 1; and by Paul XXXIV. 2.
1 32. § 1.

A history of Rome by Tubero is often cited, and as the father
wrote history (Cic. *Q. Fr.* I. 1. § 10) it seems natural to refer the quotations to his work. See them collected in Peter's *Hist. Rom. Fr.*
p. 199 *ed. min.* He is however called Q. Tubero in Liv. IV. 23 ;
Suet. *Iul.* 83, and, hence presumably, the jurist is considered to be
historian as well, perhaps however editing or using his father's notes
(Teuffel-Schwabe, § 172. 8; 208. 1).

C. AELIUS GALLUS, from whom one passage of a line and a half
appears in the Digest (L. 16. 1 157), probably taken second hand from
some one, wrote a work *de significatione uerborum quae ad ius ciuile
pertinent* (Gell. XVI. 5. § 3), apparently in two books. Festus quotes
it twenty times. The passages, with three others from Gellius, Servius and Priscian, are collected in Huschke's *Iurispr. Antei.* p. 94.
Those most interesting relate to *reus* (see below p. 46), *nexum, possessio, religiosum.* His definitions are cited in the Digest XXII. 1.
1 19. pr.; L. 16. 1 77 (*Gallum*).

His name is not mentioned in the Florentine Index.

BLAESUS is quoted by Labeo : *Blaesus ait Trebatium respondisse* (D. XXXIII. 2. 1 31).

GRANIUS FLACCUS is quoted by Paul D. L. 16. 1 144 (*Granius Flaccus in libro de iure Papiriano scribit, &c.*). For the *ius Papirianum* see D. I. 2. 1 2. §§ 2, 36 (above p. xci). Granius Flaccus is also quoted by Censor. *de die natali* 3 (*Granius Flaccus in libro quem ad Caesarem de indigitamentis scriptum reliquit*); and by Macrob. *Sat.* I. 18. § 4 (*quod cum Uarr. et Granius Flaccus adfirment*). Other quotations of Granius and Granius Licinianus are referred to the same by Huschke *Iur. Anteiust.* p. 107 ed. 4. But see Teuffel-Schwabe §§ 199. 7 ; 359. 4, 5.

JUNIUS GRACCHANUS wrote a work *de potestatibus*, the 7th book of which is quoted by Ulpian in his work *de officio quaestoris* (D. I. 13).

FENESTELLA is quoted in the same place and classed with Junius and Trebatius. He lived from about 52 B.C. to 19 p. Chr. and wrote on legal and other antiquities, perhaps in the course of his *Annales*. See fragments in Peter *Hist. Rom. Fragment.* p. 272 sqq.; Teuffel-Schwabe § 259. 2, 3.

UITELLIUS. Of this jurist we only know that Sabinus wrote some books *ad Uitellium* (D. XXXII. 1 45 ; XXXIII. 7. 1 12. § 27 ; 9. 1 3. pr.); Cassius some notes (XXXIII. 7. 1. c.); and Paul four books *ad Uitellium* (see under PAUL). Some have supposed him to be the grandfather of the emperor Vitellius, and therefore *procurator rerum Augusti* (Suet. *Uit.* 2).

CHAPTER IX.

LABEO AND THE TWO SCHOOLS OF JURISTS.

LABEO was the son of a lawyer. The father was a friend of Brutus, joined in the conspiracy against Julius Caesar, and after the battle of Philippi dug himself a grave in his tent, and with the help of a slave killed himself (App. *B. Ciu.* IV. 135 ; Plut. *Brut.* 12, 51). Appian describes him as famous for wisdom (i. e. legal skill?). His name was apparently Pacuvius Antistius Labeo (D. I. 2. 1 2. § 44).

The still more famous son, whose full name *M. Antistius Labeo* is given us by Porphyrio (ad Hor. *Sat.* I. 3. 82), was born about 50—60 B.C., and died about 12—20 A.D. He attended the lectures or consultations of Alf. Varus, Cascellius, Ofilius, Tubero, and especially Trebatius, who trained him. *Omnes hos audiuit, institutus est autem a Trebatio* (Pompon. D. ib. § 47). But his education was general as well as special: Gellius (XIII. 10) mentions especially his study of grammar and dialectic and the older Latin literature. In politics, as might be expected, he was a stern republican, a stickler for old constitutional rights, and ever ready to shew his animosity to the imperial government. His great rival as a contemporary lawyer, C. Ateius Capito, described him as eminently skilled in the laws and customs of the Roman people and in the civil law, but fanatically opposed to the slightest concession to the imperial rule. *Sed agitabat hominem libertas quaedam nimia atque uecors, tamquam...diuo Augusto iam principe et rempublicam obtinente ratum tamen pensumque nihil haberet, nisi quod iustum sanctumque esse in Romanis antiquitatibus legisset.* Capito gave an instance: a woman brought a complaint against Labeo to the tribunes of the commons; they sent to summon him to appear and reply to the complaint. Labeo refused, saying that the tribunes might come and arrest him, but to summon him was not within their competence (Gell. XIII. 12). His opposition to Augustus was shewn on the occasion of the Emperor's filling up the number of the senate (B.C. 18). Augustus took an oath to select the best men and nominated thirty, each of whom were, after taking the same oath, to name five others, the lot deciding among each set of five who should be enrolled as senator. These thirty, so chosen by lot, were each to name five in the same way. After this process had continued for some days, Augustus interfered, and himself selected the remainder up to the number of 600 (Dio Cass. LIV. 13). Labeo was one who had to choose and he named Lepidus, the former triumvir, whose son had conspired against Augustus. Augustus declared Labeo had violated his oath, and threatened to punish him. Labeo replied that there could not be anything very bad in naming Lepidus, as Augustus allowed him still to remain pontifex. Augustus asked if there were none worthier to name. Labeo replied, 'each must judge for himself'. On another occasion when the senators talked of taking it in turns to guard Caesar, Labeo said he snored, and therefore was not fit to act as guard in an antechamber (ῥέγκω καὶ οὐ δύναμαι αὐτοῦ προκοιτῆσαι, Dio Cass. ib. 15; Suet. *Aug.* 54).

The emperor rewarded the more obsequious disposition of Ateius
Capito by advancing him to the consulship out of his turn, on purpose that he might so far have precedence of Labeo. The latter he
offered to make *consul suffectus*, but Labeo declined, gaining additional popular favour from the indignity which his incorruptible
republicanism had caused him. (Tac. *An.* III. 75 *Illa aetas duo
pacis decora simul tulit, sed Labeo incorrupta libertate et ob id fama
celebratior, Capitonis obsequium dominantibus magis probabatur.
Illi, quod praeturam intra stetit, commendatio ex iniuria, huic, quod
consulatum adeptus est, odium ex inuidia oriebatur.*) Porphyrio (on
Hor. l. c.) thought Horace referred to the great lawyer, when he
used the expression *Labeone insanior*, but as Labeo would not be
more than 20 years old when this Satire was written, it is more
likely that some one else was intended.

The time saved from political office was given by Labeo to law.
He divided the year into halves, and spent six months at Rome,
giving answers in public on cases submitted to him, and also some
more direct instruction to students : *Iuris ciuilis disciplinam prin-
cipali studio exercuit, et consulentibus de iure publice responsitauit*
(Gell. XIII. 10); *Romae sex mensibus cum studiosis erat* (Pomp. D. I.
2. 1 2. § 47). The other six months he spent in the country, occupied in writing law treatises. Pomponius gives the number of
volumes written by him as 400, and says many of them were still in
use. The Florentine Index names only two works, *Pithana* (Probabilities) in 8 books, and 10 *Posteriores libri*. The *Pithana* were
abridged and commented on by Paulus, and probably only in
this form known to Tribonian. There are 34 extracts in the Digest,
the longest of which are D. XIV. 2. 1 10; XIX. 1. 1 53; 1 54; XLI. 1.
1 65. The *Posteriores* were published after his death. Gellius says
that the 38th, 39th, and 40th were full of explanations and etymologies of Latin words. Ulpian quotes the 37th book (D. IV. 3. 1 9.
§ 3); and Paul the 38th (D. XLVIII. 13. 1 11. (9.) § 2). It was
abridged by Javolenus and used by the compilers in two forms (see
under JAVOLENUS). The one is rather an account of Labeo's opinions
criticized by Javolen. From this there are 47 extracts (see e. g. D.
XXIV. 3. 1 66; XXXV. 1. 1 40; XL. 7. 1 39). In the other Labeo as
a rule speaks directly. From this there are 27 extracts, the longest
of which are D. XXXII. 1 29 (perhaps really an extract from the former
work); 1 30; XIX. 2. 1 60. Labeo wrote also on the law of the Pontifices, extracts from which work are found in Festus : and on the

XII. tables, from which work extracts are given by Gellius.   One extract from some books on the Praetor's edict is also given by Gellius. (All these fragments are in Huschke.) The citations of Labeo in the Digest are very numerous (540), but the work or book is rarely named. Pernice supposes most of them to be taken from the work on the Edict (Labeo, I. p. 55).   It is referred to in D. IV. 3. 1 9. § 4; L. 16. 1 19.   Books of *Epistulae* are mentioned in XLI. 3. 1 30. § 1.

If D. XXXIV. 2. 1 32 *Labeo testamento suo Neratiae uxori suae nominatim legauit uestem* &c. speaks of our Labeo, we have an extract from his will and learn the name of his wife. (But Labeo, is a name occurring of others than the jurist, e. g. D. XXVIII. 1. 1 27; XXXIX. 5. 1 35. § 2.) That he left codicils is certain, and his practice in this respect removed all doubts as to the validity of such a quasi-testamentary disposition (*Inst.* II. 25).

Labeo and Capito are stated by Pomponius to have for the first time created opposing parties or schools of lawyers. His words are *Hi duo primum ueluti diuersas sectas fecerunt; nam Ateius Capito in his quae ei tradita fuerant perseuerabat; Labeo ingenii qualitate et fiducia doctrinae, qui et ceteris operis sapientiae operam dederat, plurima innouare instituit.   Et ita Ateio Capitoni Massurius Sabinus successit, Labeoni Nerua, qui adhuc eas dissensiones auxerunt... Massurius Sabinus primus publice respondit* (D. I. 2. 1 2. §§ 47, 48). He proceeds to mention Gaius Cassius Longinus as succeeding Sabinus, and Proculus as succeeding Nerva.   At the same time as Nerva were Nerva *filius* and another Longinus.   *Sed Proculi auctoritas maior fuit, nam etiam plurimum potuit; appellatique sunt partim Cassiani, partim Proculiani (Proculeiani* F.), *quae origo a Capitone et Labeone coeperat* (ib. § 52).   The successors of Cassius were, in chronological order, Caelius Sabinus, Priscus Javolenus, Aburnius Valens and Tuscianus; also Salvius Julianus.   The successors of Proculus were Pegasus, Celsus *pater*, Celsus *filius* and Priscus Neratius (§ 53).   The succession is often taken to be succession in a general sense as heads of the school or party for the time, but a more precise meaning has been suggested and is certainly possible.   Gellius speaks of there being in his time (?160—170 A.D.) many stations in Rome where lawyers regularly taught and advised on cases (*Quaesitum esse memini in plerisque Romae stationibus ius publice docentium aut respondentium, an* &c. XIII. 13).   It is reasonable to suppose that there were two such stations in the earlier time, at one of which Labeo habitually appeared, and at the other Capito. Any difference in principle or method between the two lawyers would naturally become emphasized by such a definite public position and would be encouraged and propagated by their pupils. The meaning of Pomponius' expression (*successit*) and of the series of successors becomes clear. The heads of parties were in fact on this theory successive occupants of rival professorial chairs. (Bremer, *Die Rechtslehrer*, &c. p. 68, who refers to Schrader as suggesting this notion.) The only other information which we have on this subject is Pliny's expression (*Ep.* vii. 24. § 8), *domus G. Cassi, huius qui Cassianae scholae princeps et parens fuit*, and the mention in Gaius and other lawyers of various controversies in which the two schools took different sides. But from the statement of Pomponius and the facts of Labeo's life, we may form a probable idea of the nature of the difference between these schools.

Labeo was a great student of Roman legal antiquities and a lover of the old constitution. On a superficial view one might have expected him to be a conservative lawyer. On the other hand, if one imported into Roman history the notions which naturally arise under monarchical governments, we should find in his republican politics a ground for the character of an innovator which Pomponius gives him. But there was in the position of Labeo no opposition between these tendencies. He saw the old republican freedom superseded by a monarchical rule, and the forms of the constitution employed to give the unconstitutional despotism a legal appearance. The proconsular *imperium* was exercised within the city, and the tribunicial power which had been created as a check upon the *imperium*, was combined with it in the person of the Princeps, and exercised for life instead of for a year. Nor could the old dictatorship serve as a just precedent. It was one thing on a great emergency to entrust extraordinary powers to a single officer for a time. It was a very different thing to perpetuate such a power, to establish it as a system, and attach it to one family. A constitutional lawyer may not be curious to inquire how far the form and substance are in their ancient relation to one another, if the forms are observed and the institution is undergoing a moderate and gradual development suited to the changes of the nation and of circumstances. But when a monarchy becomes aggressive, lovers of constitutional rights and precedents become alarmed, and a Pym and a Hampden raise the standard of revolt. And if a monarchy comes into being and grows irresistibly under the forms of a republic, a Labeo will find a natural

vent for his faith and knowledge in shewing the difference between
the spirit and the letter of the law.   The questioning spirit, once
quickened and active, scrutinizes all matters in turn.   What is the
origin and purpose of the form?   What is the meaning of the
language used?   Is the rule really based on a principle, or is it a
mere temporary expedient which is no longer fitted to the circumstances?   Has it not been extended to cases which were not
within the original purview, or restricted in a way which makes it
worthless or harmful?

Further Labeo was a man of varied culture and philosophical
training (Gell. XIII. 10).   Hence criticism would naturally take a
scientific as well as a practical direction, and harmony of underlying
principles would become a guide and object in his legal studies.   The
law must be not a mere bundle of rules, but a consistent whole.

The precise result of such a disposition in a mind of power is not
easily calculable.   It might vary considerably in different persons
and circumstances, and assume a different aspect on one legal issue
from what it would on another.   The 'reason of the thing' might be
found in rigor or in flexibility, in consistency of theory or in practical
convenience, in strictness of logic or in the equity of the facts.   If
the professor was timid or comfortable, he might find in the excess of
scepticism a ground for practical acquiescence : if self-confident or
discontented, he would be eager to innovate.   But in neither case
would his method as a lawyer be wooden and mechanical.   Labeo
was bold and bitter, and the 'divine rage in his soul', which had its
source or its fuel in politics, gave a restless life and vigour to his legal
studies and made him stir the dry bones of law.

Labeo's questionings would meet with a certain and steady re-
sistance from the numerous party who from one cause or another
dislike change.   There would be the mass of limited and slow-
moving intellects, who could not understand the discussion ; and of
lawyers who having acquired the knowledge requisite for the routine
of business were not disposed to go to school again, and to alter the
practice to which they were accustomed.   But these would not be
all.   Men of real capacity, whose caution was in excess of their
scientific tendency, would find much reason in what was traditional
and established, and be more willing to 'bear the ills they have, than
fly to others that they know not of'.   And politics would naturally
play its part in the matter.   Those who acquiesced, or even found their
advantage in the new government, would inevitably look with sus-

picion on the opinions of Labeo, and be impelled by natural dislike, or prudential considerations, or worship of the powers that be, to oppose the innovator in law, as they would oppose the uncompromising republican in politics. As the hopes of republicans faded before the steady consolidation of the monarchy, the impetus given by Labeo would be confined to matters of private law and dissipate itself in a number of subordinate points. The stream would be lost in the sands and shallows. Both schools were represented by writers and teachers of conspicuous ability. We know of no special cause which would persistently make the followers of one school band together against those of the other, or elevate into great principles the divergencies of view on particular points or cases. Temporary enthusiasm for a teacher, temporary partisanship for a special opinion there probably was, but the points of view would be sometimes exchanged, the successor in the one school would sometimes agree with a predecessor in the other, and dissent from a predecessor in his own : some questions might come up for decision by an imperial rescript on a case; others would be modified by the progress of legislation and the discussion of other parts of the law ; so that eventually—there is a century and a half between Labeo and Gaius—the remains of the active controversies of the first century would be the vigorous discipline of legal intellects, the purification and better grounding of legal doctrine, and the ticketing of opposing views on some particular questions with the names of the rival parties. A number of such questions are mentioned by Gaius in his Commentaries, and some others survive even in the Digest. It is not difficult to find arguments on each which might justify the idea that the one side favoured principle and the other convenience, or the one strictness and the other equity ; only it is difficult to confine such arguments to one side only. Either in turn might sometimes take either position. If we did not find the views ticketed, we might have attributed them to the wrong authors[1].

[1] Dirksen in his elaborate and sensible dissertation ' on the Schools of the Roman Jurists ' (*Beiträge*, Leipzig 1825), rejecting the notions of earlier writers that the one school regarded equity and the other *strictum ius*, comes to the conclusion that the Sabinians drew their opinions chiefly from experience, and clung to the letter of the rule or resorted to some analogy from the civil law, and paid only a subsidiary regard to equity; while the Proculians looked to the inner meaning and object of the law and to systematic consistency (p. 46). Kuntze (*Excurse*, p. 323) finds the contrast of the schools in *utilitas* opposed to *subtilitas*, or, in still more general language, in naturalism opposed to idealism, on which he discourses in a somewhat romantic fashion. I have taken some references from Dirksen.

The following is a brief statement of the various questions which we know were debated between the schools. I give first those mentioned by Gaius, who often speaks of the Sabinians as *nostri praeceptores* or the like, and of the Proculiani as *diuersae scholae auctores* or the like; sometimes of *Sabinus et Cassius* for the one, and *Labeo et Proculus* for the other. There is no reason to suppose that all controversies became party questions, or that all lawyers were members of one party or the other. It is therefore desirable to confine the enumeration to those which it is tolerably clear were controversies between these schools of lawyers.

1. Gai. I. 196; Ulp. XI. 28. A male arrived at puberty was freed from being under a guardian. When was a person *pubes?* (Women being always under guardians were not concerned with this question.) Sabinus and Cassius &c. (*Cassiani* as Ulpian calls them) said it depended on the constitution of the particular individual, and for *spadones* the usual age must be taken. The Proculians (*Proculeiani*, Ulp.) fixed one period for all, viz. the completion of the 14th year. Ulpian says that Priscus (Neratius? Javolenus?) contended for both conditions. One may fancy that the Proculians would say the bodily development is not the essential point, the mental development is; and for mental development age is a better and more convenient test. However that was, Justinian adopted the Proculian view (*Inst.* I. 22. pr.).

2. Gai. II. 15. The Sabinians thought animals were *mancipi* from their birth: Nerva and Proculus &c. held that they were *mancipi* only when they were tamed; if they proved untameable, they must be ranked as *mancipi* at the usual age of taming. As only those animals were *mancipi, quae collo dorsoue domari solent* (cf. Vat. Fr. 259) i.e. oxen horses asses mules, it was natural to regard taming as of the essence of the distinction. And it is possible that the taming was looked at also as the domestication, in fact the inclusion of the animals in the family, and thus rendering them fit for the more solemn conveyance applicable to children and slaves. This controversy was obsolete in Justinian's time.

3. Gai. II. 37 and III. 87. A surrender in court of an inheritance had very different effects in different cases. It was effective, so as to make the surrenderee heir in place of the surrenderor in one case only, viz. if the surrenderor was statutable heir *ab intestato* and had not entered. It was nugatory, if the surrenderor was heir by the

will and had not entered. If however either of these persons surrendered after entering, he remained bound to the creditors, the
debts perished altogether, and the tangible assets passed to the surrenderee. But how was it in the case of a necessary heir, i.e. a slave
made free and heir by the will? He had no choice to accept or not;
he was heir at once, and required no entry to perfect his heirship.
A surrender in such a case, the Sabinians said, was nugatory. The
Proculians held that it had the same effect in this as in other cases
after entry. Evidently the Sabinians argued, he is necessary heir,
therefore he cannot divest himself of the position. The Proculians
would reply, Yes, but having become heir, he can by his own act
transfer the tangible assets to another just as he can convey any single
article. The necessity is only that there may be some one to be
responsible to the creditors, and responsible he remains after surrender just as before. This controversy was obsolete in Justinian's
time.

4. Gai. II. 79; D. XLI. 1. 1 7. § 7. *A* manufactures an article out
of *B*'s material, e.g. wine out of *B*'s grapes, a ship out of *B*'s planks,
a dress out of *B*'s wool, a plaster out of *B*'s drugs, a bowl out of *B*'s
silver. Whose property is the manufactured article? Sabinus and
Cassius said it follows the material and therefore is *B*'s; Nerva and
Proculus (*diuersae scholae auctores*) said it was *A*'s, but *B* has a
right of action against *A* for the unlawful use of his material, both
the *actio furti* and a *condictio* (see p. 93). Justinian adopted a
middle course, though leaning to the Proculians: *B* was to retain the
property if the article could be reduced to its former condition (e.g.
by melting down the vessel); if it could not, the manufacturer is the
owner (*Inst.* II. 1. § 25).

5. Gai. II. 123. If a son in his father's power is neither made heir
nor expressly disinherited but is passed over in his will, the will is
invalid. But how if the son dies in his father's lifetime? It makes
no difference, said the Sabinians: the will is invalid *ab initio*. On
the contrary, said the Proculians, the death of the son removes the
only obstacle to the father's will. The will takes effect only on the
death of the testator: if there is no *suus heres* then, the testator's
will is effectual. Justinian decided for the Sabinian view (*Inst.* II.
13. pr.).

6. Gai. II. 195. A thing bequeathed *per uindicationem* became,
according to Sabinus and Cassius, &c., the property of the legatee

immediately the inheritance was entered on, whether he knew it or not: but if he repudiated, the legacy became null altogether. Nerva and Proculus &c. held that the legatee acquires no property till he accepts. A constitution of Antoninus Pius was considered to decide the point for the Proculian view. Cf. D. xxx. 1 44. § 1; Paul. *Sent.* III. 6. § 7.

7. Gai. II. 200. A thing bequeathed *per uindicationem* but conditionally—whose property is it, pending the condition? The Sabinians compared the case of a *statuliber*, and just as the slave remains the property of the heir, pending the condition of his freedom (cf. D. XL. 9. 1 29. § 1), so, according to them, the thing bequeathed remained the property of the heir. The Proculians held that the thing meantime belongs to no one (cf. Gai. II. 9), and that the same applies to an unconditional legacy, before the legatee accepts it. Presumably the Proculians would argue that a legacy by *do lego* is evidently left away from the heir, and he can therefore have no right, till the legatee has refused it. The Sabinian view prevailed. See D. x. 2. 1 12. § 2 and notes p. 95.

8. Gai. II. 216—222. *Per praeceptionem hoc modo legamus: Lucius Titius hominem Stichum praecipito.* This form of legacy was viewed differently by the two parties. If *capito* were substituted for *praecipito*, the legacy would be *per uindicationem*. Does *praecipito* practically differ from *capito?* The Sabinians said, Yes: it confines the legacy to heirs; only what is part of the inheritance, and consequently only what is the testator's own, can be so left; and the mode of claiming it is by a suit *familiae erciscundae*. A legacy in this form to an outsider is null. Sabinus himself thought that the *S. consultum Neronianum* even did not cure the defect, but that was refuted by Julianus and Sextus (Africanus? see ch. XII.). The Proculians held that '*prae*', was not important, and that the legacy would be governed by the rules applicable to a direct bequest (*per uindicationem*), with the enlargement due to the *S.C. Neronianum*. The distinction among forms of legacies was abolished by Justinian (Cod. I. 43. 1 1; *Inst.* II. 20. § 2).

9. Gai. II. 231. A legacy or gift of freedom in a will, preceding the appointment of heir, counted for nothing. This was undoubted. Did the like rule apply to the appointment of a guardian? Yes, said the Sabinians. No, said Labeo and Proculus: the appointment of a guardian is valid, though it precede the words of institution of heir.

Nothing is thereby taken out of the inheritance. Justinian (*Inst.*
II. 20. § 34; Cod. VI. 23. 1 24) went further than the Proculians, and
allowed legacies and freedoms to be valid, whatever part of the will
they occupied. The order of writing was unimportant.

10. Gai. II. 244. Is a legacy to one who is in *potestate heredis*
good? Servius said it was, and that too whether it was conditional
or unconditional; but that it became invalid, if, when the legacy
vested, the legatee was still in the power of the heir. Sabinus and
Cassius thought a conditional legacy only was good; an unconditional
legacy was bad; for if the testator died at once after making his will,
the legacy could have no effect, and it was absurd to hold that the
extension of the testator's life should have any effect on the validity
of the will. The Proculians held that even a conditional legacy was
bad, because no one, heir or not, can legally owe anything, conditionally or unconditionally, to those who are in his power. The
Sabinian view prevailed, as we see from Ulpian XXIV. 23 *Ei, qui in
potestate manu mancipioue est scripti heredis, sub conditione legari
potest, ut requiratur*[1] *quo tempore dies legati cedit, in potestate heredis
non sit;* Just. *Inst.* II. 20. § 32.

11. Gai. III. 98. Legacy under an impossible condition (e.g. if
the legatee touch the sky with his finger). The Sabinians held that
the condition counted for nothing and the legacy was due unconditionally. The Proculians held that the legacy was as invalid as a
stipulation on a like condition was. Gaius adds that in truth there
is no good distinction in this matter between a legacy and a stipulation. Justinian adopted the Proculian view (*Inst.* III. 19. § 11).

12. Gai. III. 103. A man stipulates for himself *and* for an outsider (i.e. one in whose power he is not). All agreed that nothing
was due to the outsider; but the Sabinians held that the whole, the
Proculians that only half, was due to the stipulator. Justinian
adopted the Proculian view (*Inst.* III. 19. § 4).

13. Gai. III. 141. Must price be in money? Sabinus and
Cassius thought not, and appealed to Homer (*Il.* VI. 472—475) to
shew that barter was the earliest form of purchase and sale. The

---

[1] This expression appears to have been misunderstood by Dirksen p. 73.
He says the Sabinians held that a legacy to one in *potestate heredis* was valid,
only if the express condition was attached to the legacy, that it should stand
good if at the moment of vesting the legatee was no longer in *pot. hered.* I take
ut requiratur to be the requirement of the law, not an express requirement of the
testator.

Proculians thought it must; else no one could say which was the thing sold and which was the price, and it was absurd that both should be sold and both should be price. Caelius Sabinus (successor of Cassius) apparently replied to this argument, that the decision which was the thing sold and which was the price depended on which was offered for sale (*uenalis*). The Proculian view prevailed. Justinian said it was supported by other lines of Homer, and by stronger arguments, and had been admitted by previous emperors (*Inst.* III. 23. § 2).

Paul (D. XIX. 4. 1 1) explains the reason why such stress is laid on distinguishing the thing sold from the price. The buyer is liable on the contract if he does not make the seller owner of the purchase-money; the seller is only bound to guarantee the purchaser against fraud on his own part and against eviction. And sale differs from barter in that the contract of sale is complete on agreement being arrived at between the parties; barter is not complete till delivery is made on the one part. In other words purchase is a consensual contract, barter is a real contract. What the precise drift of the dispute in this case was is not clear, because the position of the law at the time is not known. Some hold that purchase was at that time confused with barter, and that the Proculians were desirous of separating it, so that mere agreement should be sufficient to make it a valid obligation (Pernice *Labeo* I. p. 465). Others hold that purchase was already a valid contract, and that the Sabinians were desirous to make barter into a consensual contract also (Bechmann *Kauf* I. p. 7).

14. Gai. III. 167. A slave, the common property of two persons, makes a stipulation, or receives by mancipation some object. If he does so expressly in the name of one of his masters, he acquires for that master only: if otherwise, he acquires for both in the proportion of their respective shares. If however he is acting at the order of one of his masters (without naming him), for whom does he then acquire? The Sabinians said the order was tantamount to his expressly naming that master (cf. D. VII. 1. 1 25. § 6), and consequently the slave acquired for that master only. The Proculians said, the order made no difference: both masters were entitled to the benefit of the slave's acquisitions. Justinian decided in favour of the Sabinian view (*Inst.* III. 28. § 3; Cod. IV. 27. 1 2 (3). § 2).

15. Gai. III. 168. Is an obligation dissolved by the payment, with the creditor's consent, of a thing different from that which was

agreed on? The Sabinians said it was dissolved *ipso iure*. The Proculians said it was not dissolved: *ipso iure* the debtor remained bound, but he could resist any action by the plea of fraud (*dolus malus*). Justinian adopted the Sabinian view (*Inst.* III. 29. pr.; cf. D. XIII. 5. 1 1. § 5).

16. Gai. III. 177, 178. Novation requires a different person or a different condition or a different time of payment, in fact some clear difference between the old and the new obligation. The Sabinians maintained that it was enough, if there was a security (*sponsor*) less or more. The Proculians said the addition or removal of a security had no effect. Justinian adopted the Sabinian view. Probably the Proculians argued that the change must be in the obligation itself, not in the number of persons who were to be liable on it.

17. Gai. IV. 78. A son or slave of another is liable to me on a tort: he comes by some means (e.g. by adoption or purchase) into my power. Is the claim, which I have for him to be surrendered to me *noxae*, finally merged and destroyed? The Cassians said, Yes, it is brought into a position in which it could not have originally existed. There could and can be no right of action between a master or father and slave or son in power. The Proculians thought that the claim to the noxal surrender lies dormant while the child or slave is in the offended man's power, but revives on his passing out of the power. Justinian approved of the Sabinian or Cassian view (D. XLVII. 2. 1 18; *Inst.* IV. 8. § 6). It is difficult to see how the Proculians could defend their position, at least on equitable grounds. But probably they took the same line as on No. 15. They would maintain that in strict law the claim was not affected. That followed the slave where-ever he was until it was duly satisfied: but the purchaser or other alienor would in ordinary circumstances have a plea of *dolus malus* to protect him against the alienor's noxal claim.

18. Gai. IV. 79. In order to effect a noxal surrender of a son mancipation was required. Sabinus and Cassius held that one mancipation was sufficient; for the clause of the XII. tables, which spoke of three in the case of a son (see p. 167), applied only to voluntary mancipations. The Proculians held that the three manci-pations were requisite in this case as in others; for the XII. tables said a son did not pass out of his father's power, except he be manci-

pated thrice. The form of mancipation in this as in other cases was obsolete in Justinian's time.

19. Gai. IV. 114. After suit has been accepted but before judgment the defendant satisfies the plaintiff. Ought the judge to acquit? Yes, said Sabinus and Cassius: all suits admit of acquittal, presumably at all stages. The Proculians agreed as regards *bonae fidei* actions, because the judge is there free: they agreed also as regards *in rem actiones*, because the right of acquittal is expressed in the formula. Here the MS. is mutilated. Kruger and Studemund suggest that Gaius proceeded to say that in the case of condictions the satisfaction came too late. Huschke makes other distinctions. Justinian adopted the Sabinian view (*Inst.* IV. 12. § 2).

Dirksen connects with this controversy the references to Sabinus, Cassius, &c. in D. XXII. 1. 1 38. § 7; v. 3. 1 40. pr.; x. 2. 1 12. pr.

20. Gai. IV. 170. The MS. is so mutilated that the fact only of a controversy is clear.

21. Fr. Vat. 266 (Ulpian). A person bound in contravention of the *lex Cincia* (which forbad gifts of an immoderate amount, except to near relations) discharges the obligation by payment to a person not within the exceptions of that law. He can reclaim the money at any time by a *condictio indebiti;* for that is *indebitum*, against which the debtor has a standing plea, *perpetuo exceptione tutus.* The Proculians maintained that any one could use this plea, *quasi popularis sit exceptio.* The Sabinians denied this. In later times the heir certainly could reclaim it, unless it was shewn that the donor died without repenting of having made the gift. So much was declared by a constitution of Alexander Severus. The provisions of the *lex Cincia* are imperfectly known. It appears not to have voided gifts made in contravention of its provisions, nor to have inflicted a penalty for breach. See the opening words (mutilated) of Ulpian's *Regulae.* Some have thought the *condictio indebiti* was only applicable in this case as in others, where money had been paid in some mistake &c. (Savigny *System* IV. § 165; Keller *Pand.* II. p. 580). The law appears never to have been repealed, but to have gone out of use, other regulations for the control and ascertainment of gifts being made by imperial constitutions (cf. Cod. VIII. 53; *Inst.* II. 7; Keller *Pand.* I. p. 159). In accordance with this, part only of this passage of Ulpian has been retained in the Digest (XII. 6. 1 26. § 3). See Puchta *Cursus* § 206; Keller *Pand.* II. p 576 sqq.

22. Just. *Inst.* iii. 26. § 8. A man, who has a commission to buy a thing with a limit of price, buys it at a higher price. Can he compel his principal to take the purchase at the price limited? No, said the Sabinians. Yes, said the Proculians. Gaius (iii. 161) states the Sabinian view without any mention of the other school. But in an extract from his *Rer. Cott.* given as D. xvii. 1. 1 3 we find, *sed Proculus recte eum usque ad pretium statutum acturum existimat, quae sententia sane benignior est.* The last words are adopted by Justinian in the *Institutes.* Probably the word *recte* is an insertion by Tribonian.

23. D. xxiv. 1. 1 11. § 3 (Ulp.). Gifts between husband and wife were invalid, but gifts in view of death were effective. Until the death the ownership remained with the donor. Marcellus says that if a husband makes a gift to his wife, being still in her father's power, and delivers the thing to her, the Sabinians considered that, if she was emancipated before her husband's death, the gift with all its accessories (e. g. interest, &c.) became hers on her husband's death. Julian approved this. The opinion of the Proculians is not stated. Probably they held that it became her father's directly due delivery was made.

24. D. xxix. 7. 1 14 (Scaev.). A man makes a will with heirs instituted and others substituted in default. The instituted heirs die in his lifetime. After their death he makes a codicil revoking or adding legacies. Is the revocation or addition valid? Sabinus and Cassius were reported to have said yes, on the ground that codicils are to be taken as part of the will, and to take effect if that is good. Proculus dissented, and Scaevola approved of the dissent. A legacy given by a codicil to a man, alive when the will was made, but not alive when the codicil was made, is good for nothing. The same principle applies here : a bequest is addressed to the heir, and, if the heir is dead, the address is nugatory. So much when the instituted heir or heirs are dead. But suppose two instituted heirs, and one only dead. The one alive, when the codicil was made, will have to pay the entire legacy, the substitutes will have nothing to do with it. This presumes the legacy imposed in general words '*quisquis mihi heres erit*'.

25. D. xxx. 1 26. § 2 (Pompon.). If a testator bequeaths part of his goods (*bonorum pars*), Sabinus and Cassius held that this was a bequest of the named share of the value of the estate (less the debts,

I presume, cf. D. L. 16. 1 39. § 1 and notes p. 188). Proculus and Nerva held that it was a bequest of the named share of the things themselves. Pomponius (whose opinion is accepted by Justinian) gave the heir the option to do which he liked, but with this restriction that the share of the value must be paid in the case of things absolutely incapable of being divided, or at least incapable of being divided without loss.

26.   D. XXXIX. 6. 1 35 (Paul.). A gift made in view of death (*mortis causa*) is revocable by the donor during life. If the property was not intended to pass till the donor's death, then the donor could bring vindication. If it was conveyed with the condition of being reconveyed, if the donor got well or revoked the gift, then the proper action was a condiction, the ground on which the gift was made having given way (ib. 1 29). This last proposition is said to have been confidently maintained by the Cassians. What the view of the Proculians was is not told us. Possibly they held that an *actio in factum* was the proper remedy (cf. ib. 1 30 *uel utilem*). The dispute mentioned and decided by Justinian (Cod. VIII. 56. (57.) 1 4) probably was of later times, and related to the particular formalities required for a valid gift.

27.   D. XLI. 1. 1 11 (Marcell.). A ward can alienate nothing without the presence and authority of his guardian (D. XXVI. 8. 1 9. § 1; § 5). He cannot even part with (*alienare*) natural possession according to the Sabinians. Justinian, through Marcellus, approves this view. What was the Proculian view? Probably that the authority of the guardian was a creation of the civil law, and had nothing to do with natural possession. Compare the language of Labeo (D. XLIII. 26. 1 22. § 1) *quo magis naturaliter possideretur, nullum locum esse tutoris auctoritati.* Much seems to depend on what is meant by *alienare*. There is no doubt a ward could lose possession *corpore*, but whether he could legally transfer the possession is quite another matter. Cf. D. XLI. 2. 1 29 (Ulp.) *Possessionem pupillum sine tutoris auctoritate amittere posse constat, non ut animo sed ut corpore desinat possidere; quod est enim facti, potest amittere. Alia causa est, si forte animo possessionem uelit amittere, hoc enim non potest.*

28.   D. XLI. 7. 1 2 (Paul.); XLVII. 2. 1 43. § 5 (Ulp.). A thing abandoned by its owner, according to Sabinus and Cassius, ceased at once to be his. Proculus held that it continued his, until it was seized by some one else. The Sabinian view prevailed.

29. D. XLV. 1. 1 138. pr. (Venul.).   A man stipulates for something to be paid on the days of a specified market (*certarum nundinarum diebus dari*). When may he claim it? Sabinus said on the first day of the market. Proculus and the other authorities of the opposing school thought the claim could not be made, till the market was entirely over. Ulpian agreed with them, and Justinian adopts this in the Digest. (On the reading see Mommsen *ad loc.* The *non* is evidently required by the sense.)

Dirksen (p. 113) points to the connexion of this dispute with that mentioned in D. XLV. 1. 1 115. § 2, where Sabinus maintains that a stipulated penalty for non-performance may be sued for as soon as the performance is possible. Pegasus maintains that the plaintiff must wait till performance is impossible. Papinian approves of Sabinus' view, provided that there is an express stipulation for the performance, and not merely for the penalty in case of non-performance.

30. Cod. VI. 29. 1 3. A similar point to that in No. 5 was the case of a child *en ventre sa mère* at the death of the testator, who, if he were born and there were none preceding him, would be *suus heres* (e.g. the testator's grandchild by a son in *potestate*). The testator passes him over in his will. If the child is born alive, even though he die without uttering a cry, the Sabinians held the will is broken. We are not told what the Proculians held, but presumably their view was that a cry was necessary as a proof of life. In the old German law a similar requirement (*das Beschreien der Wände*) was made. Cf. Pernice *Labeo* p. 24; Gerber *Deutsches Privatrecht* § 34). Justinian decided in favour of the Sabinian view.

The above seem to be the only cases in which the existence of a controversy between the schools is clearly shewn either by express statement, or by the use of the name of the party *Sabiniani*, &c., or by opposing views being represented by leading members of the two parties. But there are a considerable number of other cases where such a controversy may be reasonably supposed, though it is also possible that there may have been no definite controversy at all, or one only between individual lawyers. Such cases, many of which are treated as controversies of the schools by Dirksen, are where an opinion is said to have been maintained by *Sabinus et Cassius*, or where some leading members of the schools are named.

In the following places *Sabinus et Cassius* are named, but we rarely know the opposite view or its supporters : Gai. III. 133 (Nerva opposes); D. v. 1. 1 28. § 5; IX. 4. 1 15; xv. 1. 1 3. § 9; 1 42; xvi. 3. 1 14. § 1; XVIII. 1. 1 35. § 5; xxvi. 7. 1 37 (*bis*); xl. 4. 1 57 (opposed to *alii quidam*); xli. 2. 1 1. § 5 (*Sabino et Cassio et Iuliano placuit*); xli. 3. 1 4. § 16; 1 10; xlii. 3. 1 4. § 1; xliii. 16. 1 1. § 14.

Leading members are named in Gai. II. 178 *Sabinus*)(*alii ;* D. II. 4. 1 8. § 2 *Celsus*)(*Iulianus,* cf. D. xxxvii. 14. 1 15; III. 5. 1 17. (18.) *Proculus et Pegasus,* also *Neratius ;* xv. 1. 1 30 *Proculus et Pegasus ;* xviii. 2. 1 14. § 1 *Labeo et Nerua ;* xx. 4. 1 13 *Nerua, Proculus ;* xxvi. 2. 1 33 *Trebatius* and *Iauolenus*)(*Labeo* and *Proculus ;* xxxi. 1 20 *et Proculo placuit et a (Celso) patre accepi ;* xxxiii. 7. 1 12. § 3 *et Labeo et Pegasus ;* xxxiv. 2. 1 15 *Labeo*)(*Cassius ;* xxxix. 2. 1 15. § 32 *Labeo*)(*Sabinus ;* xli. 1. 1 27. § 2 *Cassius*)(*Proculus et Pegasus ;* xli. 2. 1 1. § 14 *Nerua filius*)(*Cassius et Iulianus ;* xlv. 1. 1 115. § 2 *Pegasus*)(*Sabinus ;* 3. 1 28. § 4 *Proculus*)(*Cassius ;* xlvi. 3. 1 93. § 3 *Sabinus*)(*Proculus ;* 1 95. § 7 *Labeo et Pegasus.* And no doubt there are other instances of the like kind.

On the other hand, on some points there was cross voting among the leaders, e. g. Gai. III. 140, Labeo and Cassius agree against Ofilius (Capito's teacher) and Proculus; Vat. Fr. 1 Proculus and Celsus differ from Labeo; similarly Vat. Fr. 71 a; D. VII. 5. 1 3 Nerva differs from Cassius and Proculus; 8. 1 12. § 1 Nerva differs from *Sabinus et Cassius et Labeo et Proculus ;* &c.

CHAPTER X.

JURISTS OF FIRST HALF OF FIRST CENTURY.

C. Ateius Capito is named by Pomponius as the leader of a school opposed to Labeo. He was a pupil or follower of Ofilius, and was contrasted with Labeo in two special ways; he was devoted to the new imperial system, and he adhered closely to the old paths in law (D. I. 2. 1 2. § 47). His grandfather was one of Sulla's centurions, his father had been praetor (Tac. *A.* III. 75). If this praetor was C. Ateius, the tribune of b.c. 46, *qui Caesarem semper coluit et dilexit* (Cic. *Fam.* XIII. 29. § 6; see above, p. cxvii), Capito's politics were hereditary; and there seems to be nothing against this view[1]. In A.D. 5 he was made consul, receiving that dignity earlier than he would have done, because Augustus was desirous to prefer him to his great rival Labeo, whose republican independence was in marked contrast to Capito's obsequious flattery of the ruling power. Tacitus tells how, when a Roman knight, L. Ennius, was accused of treason, because he had melted down a silver statue of the emperor for some ordinary purpose, and Tiberius put a veto on the charge, Capito interfered and claimed for the senate the right of deciding what action should be taken against such a wrong, done not only to the emperor but to the state (Tac. *A.* III. 70). Again Tiberius used in a decree respecting new year's gifts a word, which as it occurred to him in the night, was not good Latin, and the next day sent for the philologers to advise him. M. Pomponius Marcellus, a purist in Latin, found fault with it. Capito said it was Latin, and that, if it had not been before, it would be for the future; to which Marcellus replied that Capito told a lie, 'For, Caesar, you can give citizenship to men but not to words' (Suet. *Gram.* 22; Dio LVII. 17).

Capito was, with L. Arruntius, charged with relieving the city from the inundations of the Tiber A.D. 15, but their proposal to divert some of the rivers which supplied it was energetically opposed, and nothing was done (Tac. *A.* I. 76, 79). He was appointed *curator aquarum* A.D. 16, and apparently held office till his death (Frontin. *Aq.* 102), which occurred A.D. 22. His fame as a lawyer was great. Tacitus classes him and Labeo together as the two ornaments of peace ib.), and speaks of his having, by his flattery to the emperor, cast a slur upon his high public position and his good private reputation (ib. 70). He is called by Tacitus *diuini humanique iuris sciens;* by Gellius (x. 20. § 12) *publici priuatique iuris peritissimus ;* by Macrobius (*Sat.* VII. 13. § 11) *pontificii iuris inter primos peritus.*

Some fragments, preserved in Gellius and elsewhere, are from his works called *Coniectanea, libri de pontificio iure* and *liber de officio senatorio.* The *de iure sacrificiorum* is taken to be a part of the second. The fragments preserved contain historical anecdotes,

---

[1] There were however others of the name. In one of the senate's decrees which preceded the rupture between Pompey and Caesar the name of *L. Ateius L. f. An(iensi tribu) Capito* appears among those concerned with the drafting of the decree, and presumably on the side opposed to Caesar. Curio, afterwards Caesar's active supporter, is in the same position. What relation Lucius was to Caius we know not. An inscription naming *L. Ateius M. F. Capito* is also found in *Corp. I. Lat.* I. 1341.

etymologies, definitions, distinctions of words, and bits of antiquarian lore. They are collected in Huschke's *Iurispr. anteiustiniana.*

He is quoted in the Digest by Proculus (VIII. 2. 1 13. § 1); and by Ulpian (XXIII. 2. 1 29). For citations of 'Ateius' see above, p. cxvi. Some, probably all, refer not to this Capito, but to the pupil of Servius, who may have been this Capito's father.

MASURIUS SABINUS succeeded Capito as head of his school, but gave its doctrines additional point, and gained for himself a permanent reputation by his systematic treatment of the civil law. He was the first who gave opinions on legal points publicly, this privilege being granted to him unasked by Tiberius, as Pomponius says (D. I. 2. 1 2. §§ 48, 50), though precisely what is meant thereby is not clear. Probably his opinions so given obtained legal authority in the courts. His means were small, and in fact he was largely dependent on contributions from his scholars. At about the age of 50 he was enrolled among the Equites. He lived long enough to comment on the *S.C. Neronianum.* An inscription at Verona contains among the names of the *fanorum curatores* that of *C. Masurius C. F. Sabinus (C. I. L.* v. 3924). Borghesi has suggested that this refers to the lawyer, and that he was a native of Verona (Teuffel-Schw. § 281. 1).

He is named in the Florentine Index as the author of three books on the Civil Law, but no extract from this famous work is found in the Digest. Three jurists of the first rank wrote commentaries on it, Pomponius in 35 books, Ulpian in 51 books, and Paul in 16 books (though a 17th book, a 20th book, a 32nd book and even a 47th book are named, doubtless by copyists' mistakes, in the Digest XXXIX. 5. 1 4; XII. 5. 1 1; XLI. 3. 1 31; LIV. 7. 1 10; see Mommsen's large ed.); and extracts from these commentaries form nearly a seventh of the whole Digest. From a comparison of the extracts from these commentaries (Leist. *Versuch einer Gesch. d. röm. Rechtssysteme* and Rudorff *R. G.* I. p. 168) we may infer the principal matters and order of Sabinus' work to have been something as follows. 1. Wills and intestate succession; legacy, freedmen's services and *statuliberi.* 2. Alienation *inter uiuos,* e.g. sale, partnership, partition, gifts between husband and wife, dowry. 3. Guardianship. 4. Theft, Aquilian damage, *damnum infectum* and *operis noui nuntiatio.* 5. Condictions, *actio de peculio,* actions on the aediles' edict; stipulations, securities, payment. 6. Protection of property, e. g. *rei uindicatio, iuramentum in litem, interdicta de ui, quod ui aut clam* and *de precario;* acquisition of property, possession and usu-capion; servitudes; pledge; *postliminium.* The last division (6) was apparently not treated by Ulpian.

Other works of Sabinus are mentioned, *Commentarii de indigenis, Fasti* (at least 2 books), *Memorialia* (at least 11 books), fragments from which are collected in Huschke's book. The second book of *Responsa* is named in D. xiv. 2. 1 4. pr.; the 5th book *ad Edictum praetoris urbani* in D. xxxviii. 1. 1 18; and books *ad Uitellium* in D. xxxii. 1 45; xxxiii. 7. 1 12. § 27; 9. 1 3. pr. References to Sabinus in the Digest and Vat. Fr. are frequent—between 200 and 300. Persius no doubt referred to him in the lines *Cur mihi non liceat, iussit quodcunque uoluntas, excepto si quid Masuri rubrica uetauit (Sat.* v. 90). His name was applied to denote the school op-posed to Proculus. See above, p. cxxxi &c.

On the Masurius Sabinus of Ulpian's time see below, ch. xiv.

NERUA, i.e. *M. Cocceius Nerua,* is named by Pomponius as the successor of Labeo in his school. The family was distinguished. L. Cocceius (Nerva) was consul *suffectus* with P. Alfenus Varus B.C. 39 (*Corp. I. L.* i. p. 467). M. Cocceius Nerva was consul B.C. 36 (ib. pp. 449, 467). He himself was consul *suffectus* with C. Vibius Rufinus in some year before A.D. 24 (Nipperdey on Tac. *An.* iv. 58). In the year 24 he was *curator aquarum* and held the office till his death. In A.D. 26 he accompanied Tiberius in his retirement from the city, being the only senator of consular rank who formed one of Tiberius' small retinue (Tac. *An.* iv. 58). In A.D. 33, while in good health and reputation, he determined to die. Tiberius went to him, asked for the reason, and implored him to change his mind: ' it would be a severe trial for his own feelings and fame, if so constant a follower, the nearest of his friends, abandoned life without reason for death'. Nerva declined discussion and starved himself to death. Those who knew him well said, that in fear and indignation at the woes impend-ing on the state he preferred an honourable end, while his character was unsullied (Tac. *An.* vi. 26). He was grandfather of the Emperor Nerva. Frontinus speaks of his being *scientia iuris illustris;* Tacitus says *omnis diuini humanique iuris sciens.* His opinions are quoted over 30 times in the Digest, e.g. vi. 1. 1 5. § 3 *Uarus et Nerua;* vii. 5. 1 3; 6. 1 1 *Labeonis et Neruae;* 8. 1 12. § 1; x. 3. 1 6. § 4; xii. 4. 1 7 *Nerua Atilicinus responderunt;* xv. 1. 1 4. § 3 *et Nera-tius et Nerua;* xvi. 3. 1 32; xviii. 1. 1 1. § 1; xxiii. 3. 1 56. § 3;

xxx. 1 26. § 2; xLIII. 8. 1 2. § 28, &c.; Gai. II. 15; 195; III. 133.
One opinion is specially noticeable. Property belonging to a tenant
and on the premises was held to be tacitly pledged for rent (D. xx. 2.
1 4; 1 6). On the rent being in arrears it appears to have been
usual for the landlord to take an inventory and close the doors.
Slaves were of course included in the property, but could be manumitted before the doors were closed. Nerva appears to have held
that a slave could still be manumitted, if the master could perform
the essential act of personal manumission, and shewed that if the
slave appeared at a window this could be done. The opinion was
however rejected with scorn by other lawyers (*derisus Nerua iuris
consultus qui per fenestram monstrauerat seruos detentos ob pensionem
liberari posse* D. xx. 2. 1 9). The closing of the doors must therefore
be taken as rather a conventional mark of a change of legal circumstances, than the interposition of a mere physical difficulty. Cf.
Cujac. *Obs.* xvii. 39.

CASSIUS, i.e. C. Cassius Longinus, succeeded Sabinus. He was
of the Cassian family well known in Roman history, from which
came the conspirator against Caesar. His mother was daughter of
the jurist Tubero and granddaughter of Servius Sulpicius, whom he
was in the habit of calling his great grandfather (*proauus* Pompon.
D. I. 2. 1 2. § 51). There has been some confusion between him and
L. Cassius Longinus[1], whom Tiberius selected as the husband of
Drusilla (Tac. *A.* vi. 15). Both were consuls in the same year
A.D. 30, M. Vinicius and L. Cassius being the regular consuls, and
L. Naevius Surdinus and C. Cassius being *suffecti* (*Corp. I. L.* x.
1233). Pomponius gives his colleague the name of Quartinus (a
mistake for Surdinus). C. Cassius was legate propraetor of Syria in
A.D. 49 and, though there was no war, kept the legions in a state of
active preparation for it (Tac. *An.* xii. 12). Amongst other things
he directed the Jews to transfer the high priest's robe into the tower
of Antonia in order that it might be under the control of the
Romans. But the Jews procured from Rome permission to retain it
(Joseph. *Arch.* xv. 11. § 4, cf. xx. 1. § 1). In A.D. 58 the senate, in

---

[1] L. Cassius was proconsul in Asia in A.D. 41, and fetched back to Rome as a
prisoner and executed by Caligula, who had been warned by an oracle to beware
of 'Cassius'. Cassius Chaereas was the name of the tribune of the praetorians
who afterwards killed Caligula (Suet. *Calig.*57; Dio LIX. 29 who confuses Lucius
with Gaius Cassius). Another L. Cassius Longinus was consul *suffectus* A.D. 11
(Wilmanns 104).

delight at Corbulo's defeat of Tiridates and destruction of Artaxata, proposed the permanent celebration of it by keeping as festivals the day of the victory, the day of the news reaching Rome, and the day of that meeting of the senate. C. Cassius agreed to other proposals, but with grave irony objected that, if thanks to the gods were to equal this happy stroke of fortune, the whole year would not be sufficient; and reminded them that while it was right to devote some days to religious observances, others must be kept for human needs (Tac. *An.* XIII. 41). Later in the year he was chosen to calm a civic disturbance at Puteoli, but his stern character was not acceptable to the deputations from the place, and at his own request the charge was transferred to some brothers *Scribonii* (ib. 48). Soon after Piso's conspiracy Nero's suspicions fell on Cassius and on his wife's nephew Silanus, who had been brought up by Cassius (ib. xv. 52). The dignified character and ancestral wealth of the one, and the youth and nobility of the other were their real offence. Nero gave the first indication of his displeasure by forbidding Cassius to attend the funeral of Poppaea. Soon afterwards he sent a letter to the senate requesting the removal of both Cassius and Silanus from the state. He charged Cassius with having among the images of his house one of C. Cassius, inscribed '*Duci partium*', and with having sought to renew his ancestor's conspiracy by putting forward Silanus as an aspirant to the throne. Cassius was banished to Sardinia, Silanus was banished and killed. Cassius' wife, Lepida, the aunt of Silanus was charged with incest and awful sacrifices, but her fate is not told us (ib. xvi. 8, 9). Suetonius, who mentions that Cassius was blind, says or implies that he was ordered to put himself to death within three hours, and did so (*Nero* 37). This appears to be a mistake. For Pomponius, agreeing with Tacitus in the sentence of banishment, says that he was recalled by Vespasian and died afterwards.

Cassius' fame as lawyer was great. *Ea tempestate Cassius ceteros praeminebat peritia legum* (Tac. *An.* XII. 12). Hyginus (Grom. p. 124) calls him *prudentissimus uir, iuris auctor* on occasion of mentioning a decision he gave relative to changes wrought by the winter current of the Po. The decision was this. If the stream gradually carried away part of a man's land, he had no right to claim any accretions there might be on other land; it was his own fault not to have better secured the bank (Grom. pp. 49, 50 and my notes below, p. 72). But sudden and violent action of the stream might estab-

lish a new course instead of the old one, or might make an island.
In such cases the ownership was not affected : the owner might
follow his land, and if the land of several owners was affected, they
would be proportionately intitled to the land in its new form.   On
another matter, one of the policy of the criminal law, Cassius is
said by Tacitus to have taken a leading part in the discussion in the
senate.   Old custom, sanctioned and regulated by various decrees of
the senate, of which the first called *Silanianum* is referred to A.D.
10, another to the following year (D. xxix. 5. 1 13 ; Cujac. *Observ.*
i. 18), another under Claudius, another under Nero called *S. C. Neronianum* or *Pisonianum* from the consuls of the year A.D. 57 (Paul.
Sent. iii. 5. § 5 ; D. l. c. 1 8 ; Tac. *An.* xiii. 32), had required that,
when a man was killed, all his slaves, under the same roof and not
proved to have assisted him, should be put to question and death.
In A.D. 61 the city praefect, Pedanius Secundus, was murdered by
one of his slaves.   The people were disposed to resist the execution
of this extreme measure upon four hundred slaves.   Cassius, as
reported by Tacitus, strenuously opposed any relaxation as dangerous
to the safety of every master.   'The old laws were right, and change
' was always for the worse.   It was impossible for the murderer to
'have accomplished his object, if he had not profited by the con-
'nivance of his fellows.   These large bands of slaves of foreign
'nations, uninfluenced by the religious rites and scruples of Romans,
'could be ruled only by fear.   And if there were some innocent
'among so many guilty, their fate cannot be weighed against the
'public good ; it was only what was impossible to avoid when a
'great example has to be made.'   The slaves were executed (Tac.
An. xiv. 42—45).

But the best evidence of his reputation as a lawyer is the fact
that the school which was headed by Capito and Sabinus in succession was frequently called by Cassius' name.   Cf. Plin. *Ep.* vii. 24.
§ 8 *Laetor quod domus aliquando C. Cassi, huius qui Cassianae
scholae princeps et parens fuit, seruiet domino non minori.   Implebit
enim illam Quadratus meus ;* whom Pliny thought as great an orator
as Cassius was a lawyer.   This school was apparently called indif-
ferently either by the names of Cassius and his master (D. iv. 8.
1 19. § 2) Sabinus, e.g. *Sabinus et Cassius ceterique nostri praeceptores* (Gai. i. 196 ; ii. 195, &c.), *Sabino et Cassio uisum est* (ib. iii.
133, &c.), *et ueteres putant et Sabinus et Cassius scribunt* (Vat. Fr. 1) ;
or by that of *Sabiniani* (D. xxiv. 1. 1 11. § 3 ; xli. 1. 1 11, &c.), or

k 2

Cassiani (Ulp. XI. 28; D. I. 2. 1 2. § 52; XXXIX. 6. 1 35. § 3; XLVII. 2. 1 18). See above, p. cxli.

He wrote a work on *Ius ciuile*, the 8th book of which is cited in D. VII. 1. 1 7. § 3; 1 9. § 5; 1 70. § 2; and the 10th book in ib. 1 70. pr. Aristo wrote notes on it, ib. 1 7. § 3; 1 17. § 1 *Aristo apud Cassium notat;* XXXIX. 2. 1 28; cf. IV. 8. 1 40. Javolen wrote a work in 15 books from which there are a considerable number of extracts in the Digest, where it is called simply *Iauolenus ex Cassio* (e.g. D. VIII. 2. 1 12). Cassius himself wrote notes on Vitellius (*et Sabinus definit et Cassius apud Uitellium notat* D. XXXIII. 7. 1 12. § 27), and on Urseius Ferox (*Cassius apud Urseium scribit* D. VII. 4. 1 10. § 5; but cf. XXIV. 3. 1 59; XLIV. 5. 1 1. § 2). His opinions are frequently referred to (between 100 and 200 times) by other lawyers; e.g. D. I. 9. 1 2 (*Cassius Longinus*); II. 1. 1 11. § 2 (*Cassio et Pegaso*); 4. 1 4. § 2 (*Gaius Cassius*); IV. 6. 1 26. § 7 (*edicebat Gaius Cassius*), &c.

FULCINIUS, once called *Priscus Fulcinius* (D. XXXI. 1 49. § 2), lived after Labeo and apparently before Proculus (ib. and XXV. 2. 1 3. § 1 where he is joined with Mela), certainly before Neratius, who reports an opinion of Fulcinius with a note of his own (XXXIX. 6. 1 43). Further he is quoted by Pomponius (XXIV. 1. 1 29. pr.), by Gaius (XI. 7. 1 29. § 2), by Paul (XIII. 1. 1 13; XXV. 2. 1 6. pr.; XLIII. 16. 1 8; L. 16. 1 79), and by Ulpian (XXV. 1. 1 3; XLII. 4. 1 7. pr.).

MELA, called *Fabius Mela* in D. XLIII. 23. 1 1. § 12, is quoted 34 times in the Digest, often on points on which Labeo's opinion is also given. He appears to have written before Proculus (cf. IX. 2. 1 11. pr.; XXV. 2. 1 3. § 1). He is quoted once by Venuleius (XLII. 8. 1 25. § 8); twice by Africanus (XLVI. 3. 1 39; L. 16. 1 207); six times by Paul (e.g. XVII. 1. 1 22. §§ 9, 11; XXV. 2. 1 3. § 4 *Mela Fulcinius aiunt*); otherwise only by Ulpian (V. 1. 1 2. § 6; XV. 3. 1 7. § 2; XIX. 1. 1 17. § 6 *Gallus Aquilius, cuius Mela refert opinionem;* 2. 1 13. § 8; 5. 1 20. § 1; XXIV. 3. 1 24. § 2; XXVII. 3. 1 1. § 6; XXXIII. 1. 1 14; XLIII. 14. § 8; XLVI. 3. 1 39 *Mela libro decimo scribit;* XLVII. 2. 1 52. § 18, &c.). There are no extracts in the Digest.

CARTILIUS is mentioned twice in the Digest: viz. by Proculus XXVIII. 5. 1 70 (69), where Proculus is asked to decide between the opinions of Trebatius and Cartilius, and by Ulpian XIII. 6. 1 5. § 13.

ARRIANUS is quoted by Ulpian (D. v. 3. 1 11 *Arrianus libro secundo de interdictis putat teneri, quo iure nos uti Proculus scribit,* from which it may be inferred that he was earlier than Proculus; XXVIII. 5. 1 19 *ex facto agitatum Pomponius et Arrianus deferunt... Et Pegasus quidem existimat ad eam partem admitti, Aristo contra putat, quia &c., quam sententiam et Iauolenus probat et Pomponius et Arrianus, et hoc iure utimur ;* XLIII. 3. 1 1. § 4 *bellissime Arrianus scribit*); and by Paul *ad Plautium* (XXXVIII. 10. 1. 5; XLIV. 7. 1 47). Some have identified him with Arrianus Maturus, whom Pliny describes *Ep.* III. 2, and to whom he writes several letters (I. 2; II. 11; 12; IV. 8; 12; VI. 2; VIII. 21). But Pliny's Arrianus does not appear to have been a lawyer. Another, Arrianus Seuerus, is mentioned as *praefectus aerarii* in or after Trajan's time (D. XLIX. 14. 1 42). The identification of either with our Arrianus would conflict with the natural, though not necessary, inference from D. v. 3. 1 11.

PROCULUS.   All we really know of Proculus is what Pomponius tells us. *Neruae successit Proculus. Fuit eodem tempore et Nerua filius : fuit et alius Longinus ex equestri quidem ordine, qui postea ad praeturam usque peruenit. Sed Proculi auctoritas maior fuit, nam etiam plurimum potuit : appellatique sunt partim Cassiani, partim Proculiani (Proculeiani* Flor.)*, quae origo a Capitone et Labeone coeperat. Cassio Caelius Sabinus successit, qui plurimum temporibus Uespasiani potuit : Proculo Pegasus, qui temporibus Uespasiani praefectus urbi fuit. Caelio Sabino Priscus Iauolenus.* As Nerva died A.D. 34, Proculus probably flourished in the reign of Tiberius and the following Caesars. His name is supposed to have been Sempronius on the strength of D. XXXI. 1 47 (where however Mommsen proposes to read *Sempronius Nepos Proculo suo salutem,* which accords with the subsequent *Proculus respondit*), and of an inscription (Gruter p. 560) which may or may not refer to the jurisconsult. The cognomen Proculus was common enough, as may be seen from Wilmanns' *Inscriptions* (*Indices* p. 393). A jurisconsult of the name is mentioned in the *Testam. Dasumii* (Bruns[4] p. 229) which is of the date of 109 A.D.; and Rudorff inferring from D. XXIX. 2. 1 60; 1 62; XXXV. 1. 1 40. § 5 *et ego (Iauol.) et Proculus probamus,* that Proculus the well-known jurist was a contemporary of Javolen, thinks the mention in Dasumius' will to relate to him, and his succession to Nerva not to have referred to any definite post, but to a gradual recognition of his preeminence in the school of Labeo (*Z. G. R.* XII. 338).

But Pomponius evidently makes Proculus to belong to a generation before Vespasian, and Javolen's *probamus* need not at all imply that the two were contemporary.

The Florentine Index names one work of Proculus, Epistles in 8 books. They contained opinions on special cases submitted to him. From this work there are 37 extracts in the Digest occupying 6 of Hommel's pages. Three extracts are from the 11th book, which does not accord with the Flor. Index. He wrote notes on Labeo (D. III. 5. 1 9. (10.) § 1; xxxv. 1. 1 69). An extract in the Digest (xxxiii. 6. 1 16), following an extract from Proculus' Epistles, is inscribed as *Idem libro tertio ex posterioribus Labeonis*. Either this is from the notes to Labeo (cf. XVII. 2. 1 65. § 5) or more probably *Idem* is a mistake for Javolenus (so Mommsen *ad loc.*). Proculus is also cited 134 times in the Digest and several times in Gaius and the Vatican Fragments. In a rescript of Marcus Anton. and Verus his opinion is referred to with respect: *Proculum, sane non leuem iuris auctorem* (D. xxxvii. 14. 1 17. pr.). His eminence is shewn by such expressions as *Nerua et Proculus et ceteri diuersae scholae auctores* (Gai. II. 15; 195); and *Proculeiani* (Ulp. xi. 28; Vat. Fr. 266; Just. II. 1. 25).

Some of the most noticeable extracts from Proculus are D. VIII. 6. 1 16; XVII. 2. 11 76—80; XVIII. 1. 1 68; XLI. 1. 11 55, 56; XLV. 1. 1 113; XLIX. 15. 1 7; L. 16. 11 124—126.

NERUA *filius*, as he was called to distinguish him from his father M. Cocceius Nerva, was a leader of the school of Labeo at the same time as Proculus, but of inferior authority. At the age of 17 or a little more, he acted publicly as a jurisconsult (D. III. 1. 1 1. § 3). He was a favourite of Nero's, who assigned to him (A.D. 65), along with Petronius Turpilianus and Tigellinus, triumphal ornaments to commemorate his victory over Piso's conspiracy. Nerva was praetor designate at the time (Tac. *An.* xv. 72). He is supposed to have been the father of the emperor Nerva.

He wrote a work *de usucapionibus* which is cited by Papinian (D. XLI. 2. 1 47); and his opinions are often quoted in the Digest, e.g. III. 2. 1 2. § 5; VII. 1. 1 13. § 7; xv. 1. 1 3. § 8; XL. 2. 1 25; XLI. 2. 1 1. pr.; § 3; § 22; 1 3. §§ 13, 17; XLVI. 4. 1 21.

CHAPTER XI.

JURISTS OF SECOND HALF OF FIRST CENTURY.

PEGASUS, according to Pomponius, succeeded Proculus in the school started by Labeo, and was himself succeeded by Celsus the father. Pomponius says also that he was praefect of the city in the time of Vespasian. Juvenal (IV. 77) speaking of an event in Domitian's reign mentions the presence of Pegasus ; *attonitae positus modo uillicus urbi interpres legum sanctissimus, omnia quamquam temporibus diris tractanda putabat inermi iustitia.* On this the scholiast remarks that he was the son of a trierarch, that his name was taken from the figurehead of his father's vessel, that he was governor of several provinces, and afterwards *praefectus urbi*, and was so famed for his knowledge of law that the people called him a book rather than a man, and that the *S.C. Pegasianum* was named from him. Some difficulty has been found in *positus modo.* But the reigns of Domitian and Vespasian were separated by only two years, and, if he was appointed praefect just before Vespasian's death, the expression seems quite intelligible. Two alterations of the law are referred by Gaius to senate's decrees passed in the consulship of Pegasus and Pusio, one removing the maximum limit of age imposed by the *lex Aelia Sentia* on Latins, who by marrying and having children were allowed to claim Roman citizenship (Gai. I. 31); and the other giving an heir, who was charged with a trust to restore the inheritance, a right to retain one-fourth (II. 254), and, in case the heir refused to enter at all from doubts of the solvency of the inheritance, empowering him to do so, at the request of the *cestui que trust*, without incurring liability (ib. 258). Justinian amended the *S.C. Trebellianum* so as to render the *S.C. Pegasianum* no longer necessary (*Inst.* II. 23. § 7). The *Institutes* refer this *S.C. Pegasianum* to the time of Vespasian (ib. § 5).

No extract from any work of his is given in the Digest, but he is cited 28 times : e.g. D. II. 1. 1 11. § 2; III. 2. 1 2. § 5; 5. 1 17 (18); IV. 8. 1 21. § 10; V. 4. 1 1. § 3; VII. 1. 1 9. § 3; 1 12. § 2; 1 25. § 7; IX. 2. 1 5. § 2; XV. 1. 1 30. pr.; XXVIII. 5. 1 19; XXXII. 1 12; XXXIII. 7. 1 12. § 3; XXXIX. 5. 1 19. § 6 ; &c.

CAELIUS SABINUS is named by Pomponius as of most influence in the time of Vespasian. He succeeded Cassius in the school formed by

Capito, and was succeeded by Javolenus.   He was (with Flavius
Sabinus) *consul suffectus* A.D. 69, having been appointed by Otho, and
confirmed by Vitellius (Tac. *H.* I. 77).   His full name is given in the
Act. Arual. of that year as *Cn. Arulenus Caelius Sabinus*.   He wrote
a work *de edicto aedilium curulium* from which one short extract is
given by Gellius (IV. 2. §§ 3—5), and probably another (ib. VI. (VII.)
4. §§ 1—3).   He is cited by Gaius III. 70 ; 141 ; and by Ulpian and
others in several places on the Aediles' edict, XXI. 1. ll 14, 17, 20, 38,
65 ; also XXXV. 1. l 72. § 7.

URSEIUS FEROX is chiefly known from the title of a work attributed to Julian in the Florentine Index, from which there are 43
extracts in the Digest, filling five of Hommel's pages.   The precise
nature of Julian's four books *ad Urseium Ferocem* is not certain.
In three extracts (XXIII. 3. l 48; XXX. l 104; XLVI. 3. l 36) after a
certain amount of matter come the words *Iulianus notat*.   So Ulpian
D. X. 3. l 6. § 12 has *Urseius ait*, &c. followed by *Iulianus autem
recte notat*.   In an extract from this work which forms XVI. 1. l 16.
§ 1 we have *Gaius Cassius respondit*, &c. followed by *Iulianus autem
recte putat*.   This last has probably been altered by Tribonian.   But the
other passages seem to shew that the work was really not a commentary of Julian's on a work of Urseius Ferox, but the work of
Urseius edited with notes by Julian (so also Mommsen *Z. R. G.*
VII. 483), and therefore probably the language generally in these
extracts is that of Urseius, not of Julian.   Hence *Cassius apud Urseium
notat* (D. VII. 4. 1 10. § 5) probably refers either to some notes
written by Cassius on this work, and retained by Julian, or to some
notes of Cassius quoted by Urseius.   And the like may be said of
Cassius existimasse Urseium refert (D. XLIV. 5. l 1. § 10), where
Mommsen inclines to correct it to *Cassium...Urseius*.   Several of the
extracts contain answers given by Sabinus, e.g. D. VII. 1. l 35; XXX.
l 104. § 7, &c.; *Collat.* XII. 7. § 9; or Proculus e.g. D. IX. 2. l 27. § 1;
X. 3. l 5; &c.: one at least contains an answer of Gaius Cassius (D.
XVI. 1. l 16. § 1), and so probably D. XXIV. 3. l 59, where 'Gaius' is
named.   In another (D. XXXIX. 6. l 21) we have *plerique, in quibus
Priscus quoque, responderunt*.   Priscus is probably Javolen.

Perhaps the easiest explanation of the facts is that Urseius lived
about the time of Nero, that Cassius wrote some notes on his work,
and Julian incorporated them with his own; and that the passages
in which Cassius and Priscus are referred to are part, not of the

work of Urseius, but of Julian's notes to it.   Paul was doubtless
referring to the same work, when he says *apud Ferocem Proculus
ait* (D. XXXIX. 3. 1 11. § 2).   In the *Collatio* l.c. the 10th book of
Urseius is mentioned.   Probably this is a mistake.

ATILICINUS is often (27 times) mentioned in the Digest as an
authority, frequently beside Proculus or Nerva, e.g. D. II. 14. 1 27.
pr. *Neratius Atilicinus Proculus ;* IV. 8. 1 21. § 9 *Proculus et Atilicinus;* VIII. 3. 1 5 *Neratius hoc Proculum et Atilicinum existimasse
ait ;* X. 3. 1 6. § 3 *Sabinus et Atilicinus responderunt ;* XII. 4. 1 7
Nerua Atilicinus responderunt ; XVII. 1. 1 45. § 7 *Nerua Atilicinus
aiunt ;* XXXII. 1 19 ; XXXIV. 3. 1 16 ; XXXV. 2. 1 49. pr. *Atilicinus
Nerua Sabinus;* XLIV. 4. 1 4. § 8; XLV. 2. 1 17 *Atilicinus Sabinus
Cassius ;* but also by himself, e.g. D. XX. 6. 1 6. § 2.   He is cited by
Julian *Dig.* XVI. (D. XII. 4. 1 7) and Pomponius VI. *ad Sab.* (D. XXX.
1 48) and Neratius (above).   See also Vat. Fr. 77.   In XXIII. 4. 1 17
we have an answer by Proculus to a case put by Atilicinus.   There
is no reason for refusing to identify the questioner with our jurist,
so that we may well consider him to have been somewhat younger
than Proculus.

An opinion of his is reported by Aufidius (*Anfidius* MS.) Chius
in the Vat. Fr. 77.   Aufid. Ch. is alluded to in Mart. v. 61.

PLAUTIUS must have been an important writer, as Neratius wrote
on him in several books (*Neratius libris ex Plautio ait* D. VIII. 3. 1 5),
Javolenus in five books, Pomponius in seven books, and Paulus in
18 books.   In the Florentine Index the three last works are mentioned and are all called *ad Plautium ;* but in the inscriptions to the
extracts themselves Javolen and Pomponius' works are called, like
that of Neratius, *ex Plautio.* (The sole exceptions D. VII. 1. 1 49 *Pompon. ad Plautium* and XXV. 3. 1 34 *Iauolenus ad Plautio* (so F) are
clearly mistakes.)   The extracts from Paul's work are always inscribed *ad Plautium.*   What this difference in title indicates is not
certain : but, as Paul's work was so much more voluminous than the
others, it is natural to suppose that he edited and commented on the
whole of Plautius, and that the others commented on selections only.
The number of extracts from Javolen's work are 18, occupying one-
and-a-half of Hommel's pages ; from Pomponius' are 37 occupying
four pages ; from Paul's are 190 occupying 22 pages, this work of
Paul's being one of the larger components of the Digest.   The various
treatises on Plautius were dealt with together by the Edictal Com-

mittee immediately after the works on the Edicts, Paul's being taken
first as the latest and largest.   In some extracts from it (D. III. 3. 1
61; xx. 4. 1 13; xxxiv. 2. 1 8; xxxv. 1. 1 43; 1 44; 2. 1 49) part is
stated to be Plautius' text, part to be Paul's note; and as Plautius
refers to Cassius, Nerva, Proculus, and Atilicinus we get a superior
limit for the time of his writing, Javolen and Neratius giving the
inferior limit.   His time will be about Vespasian, or at any rate
towards the end of the first century *p. Chr.*   Ulpian in his 17th book
ad Sabinum uses the expression *omnes auctores apud Plautium de hoc
consenserunt* (Vat. Fr. 77) which points to the work having been so
edited as to make it a collection of various opinions.

CELSUS *pater* is mentioned by Pomponius as the successor of
Pegasus in the leadership of the school started by Labeo, and as himself
succeeded by his more distinguished son.   His opinions are quoted
by his son D. XII. 4. 1 3. § 7 ; xxxi. 1 20; 1 29.   Neratius says *et
Aristoni et Celso patri placuit*, &c. (D. XVII. 1. 1 39).   Where Celsus
is named without the addition of *pater* it is generally assumed that
the son is meant.   The last quarter of the 1st century is the time to
which the father must be assigned.   In xxxi. 1 29 he is said to have
been in the council of the consul *Ducennius Uerus*, but this consulship is wholly unknown.   (C. Ducenius Proculus was *consul suffectus* A.D. 87, as we learn from the *Acta Arualia*.)

PEDIUS, whose name is given as *Sextus Pedius* (D. IV. 8. 1 32. § 20;
IX. 2. 1 33; xxxix. 1 5. § 9), was later than Ofilius and Sabinus
(D. XIV. 1. 1 1. § 9 ; L. 16. 1 13. § 1), but apparently earlier than
Pomponius (D. IV. 3. 1 1. § 4) ; the inference commonly taken from III.
5. 1 6 that he was earlier than Julian being displaced by Mommsen's
making 1 6 continuous with 1 5).   He wrote on the Edict in at least
25 books (D. xxxvii. 1. 1 6 § 2), and on Stipulations in more than
one book (D. XII. 1. 1 6).   He is often (54 times) quoted by Paul and
Ulpian and by them only (see above and VI. 1. 1 6; xxi. 1. 1 4. § 4 ;
1 23. § 9 ; xliii. 17. 1 1. § 4 ; 19. 1 1. § 7 ; 24. 1 1. § 6 ; cf. Vat. Fr.
93).   There are no extracts in the Digest.   In the abbreviations given
in *Cod. Einsidl.* (Keil's *Gram.* IV. p. 328 ; Huschke *Iur. Anteiust.* p.
143, ed. 4) *S. P. M.* is interpreted *Sextii Pedii Mediuani*.   (I see
however no other jurist so denoted in these notes by initials.)

UIUIANUS is cited 16 times in the Digest, but there are no extracts from his writings.   He reported opinions of Sabinus, Cassius,

and Proculus (D. XXIX. 7. 1 14); and his opinion was referred to by
Pomponius (D. XIII. 6. 1 17. § 4); but there is no further indication
of the time at which he wrote.   His opinions are cited by Scaevola
XXIX. 7. 1 14; by Ulpian in his works on the Edicts D. IV. 2. 1 14. § 5;
8. 1 21. § 11; IX. 2. 1 27. § 24; XIX. 5. 1 17; XXI. 1. 1 1. §§ 9, 10;
1 17. §§ 3, 5; XXXIX. 2. 1 24. § 9; XLIII. 16. 1 1. §§ 41—46; 19. 1 1. § 6;
by Paulus, D. IV. 9. 1 4. § 2; XIII. *l. c.*; XIX. 4. 1 1. § 3.   In *Collat.*
XII. 7. § 8 we have *Item libro* VI. *ex Uiuiano relatum est, si furnus,*
&c., which reference is omitted in transferring the passage to D. IX.
2. 1 27. § 10 (see above p. lxx).

FUFIDIUS wrote *Quaestiones*, from the second book of which African
quotes in D. XXXIV. 2. 1 15.   Fufidius there reports an opinion of
Atilicinus.   Gaius (D. XL. 2. 1 25) contrasts the opinions of Fufidius
and Nerva the younger.   Paul refers to Fufidius in D. XLII. 5. 1 29.
(Cujas suggested his identification with L. Fufidius, an advocate
mentioned by Cic. *Brut.* 29. § 112; Plin. *H. N.* XXXIII. § 21; others
of the name are mentioned Cic. *Pis.* 35; *Fam.* XIII. 11, 12; *Q. Fr.* III.
1, 2; Hor. *Sat.* I. 2. 12, but they are all inconsistent with the Digest.)

CAMPANUS is twice mentioned, in both cases by writers on trusts,
viz. by Valens D. XXXVIII. 1. 1 47; by Pomponius XL. 5. 1 34. § 1.

PUTEOLANUS *libro primo adsessoriorum scribit* D. II. 14. 1 12
(Ulp.).   Nothing more is known of him or his work.

OCTAUENUS is quoted by Valens (D. XXXVI. 1. 1 69. (67.) pr.); by
Terentius Clemens (XL. 9. 1 32), by Pomponius (XIX. 1. 1 55; XXX. 19;
XL. 1. 1 13; 4. 1 61. § 2; 5. 1 20 *bellissime Aristo et Octauenus puta-
bant*); by Marcian (XX. 3. 1 1. § 2); often by Paulus (e.g. VI. 1. 1 6;
XVIII. 6. 1 8 *Proculus et Octauenus aiunt*); and Ulpian (e.g. V. 2. 1 16;
1. 18; VII. 8. 1 12. § 6).   He wrote after the *lex Iunia Norbana*, which
was passed 19 *p. Chr.* (Dosith. 2).   There are no extracts from him
in the Digest.

UARIUS LUCULLUS is referred to by Aristo in an extract from
Pomponius (D. XLI. 1. 1 19).   Mommsen conjectures *Uarius* to be a mistake for *Uarro;* and for *Lucullus* refers to C. *Tull.* 4. § 8 *M. Lucullus,
qui summa aequitate et sapientia ius dixit primus hoc iudicium,
composuit.*   If this was the Lucullus meant, one would have expected
Pomponius (who wrote on Aristo) to have named him in his list of
the lawyers.

SERUILIUS is stated by Terentius Clemens (D. XXXVII. 14. 1 10) to have reported an opinion of Proculus.

ARISTO, often quoted (80 times) in the Digest, is no doubt the same as Titius Aristo, a friend of Pliny the younger, who addresses two letters to him (v. 3; VIII. 14). He attended Cassius' lectures (D. IV. 8. 1 10); was with Neratius Priscus in the Council of Trajan (D. XXXVII. 12. 1 5); and was so ill A.D. 97, that he requested Pliny and other friends to ascertain from the physicians whether his disease was incurable, in order that he might in that case adopt a voluntary death (Plin. *Ep.* I. 22). The doctors gave a favourable prognostic; and Aristo was still alive in the consulship of Afranius Dexter, i.e. A.D. 105 (ib. VIII. 14. § 12). Pliny speaks of him in terms of warm praise: *Nihil illo grauius, sanctius, doctius, ut mihi non unus homo sed literae ipsae omnesque bonae artes in uno homine summum periculum adire uideantur. Quam peritus ille et priuati iuris et publici! Quantum rerum, quantum exemplorum, quantum antiquitatis tenet! Nihil est quod discere uelis, quod ille docere non possit.... In toga negotiisque uersatur, multos aduocatione plures consilio iuuat. Nemini tamen istorum* (i. e. philosophers) *casti-tate, pietate, iustitia, fortitudine etiam primo loco cesserit* (ib. I. 22). There are no extracts from him in the Digest, but he is frequently referred to. He often gave answers on points of law. Thus answers to Celsus are named (D. II. 14. 17. § 2; XL. 7. 1 29. § 1); to Neratius Priscus (XX. 3. 1 3; cf. XL. 4. 1 46); and also of Neratius to him (XIX. 2. 1 19. § 2); and of Aristo to others (VIII. 5. 1 8. § 5; XXXVI. 1. 1 3. § 2). He wrote notes on Labeo's *posteriores* (D. XXVIII. 5. 1 17. § 5); on Sabinus (VII. 8. 1 6); on Sabinus' books *ad Uitellium* (XXXIII. 9. 1 3. § 1); on Cassius (VII. 1. 1 7. § 3; 1 17. § 1; XXXIX. 2. 1 28); and apparently made a collection of decisions (*Aristo in decretis Frontianis ita refert*, D. XXIX. 2. 1 99, which Rudorff (*R. G.* I. p. 184) and Mommsen suppose to refer to decisions on appeal given by Frontinus, who was several times consul). Gellius says that he read in a book of Aristo the jurisconsult *haudquaquam indocti uiri*, that the Egyptians regarded thefts as lawful and did not punish them. Neratius in his *Membranae* often reports Aristo's opinions (D. II. 14. 1 58; XIII. 1. 1 12. § 2; XVII. 1. 1 39; XVIII. 3. 1 5; XXXVI. 3. 1 13); and hence probably it comes that their two opinions are so often cited together (e.g. VII. 2. 1 3. § 2 (= Vat. Fr. 83); XVII. 2. 1 62; XXIII. 3. 1 20; &c.). Further Pomponius frequently refers to Aristo, and as

Mommsen thinks from the words of Paul (D. XXIV. 3. 1 44. pr. *ut est relatum apud Sextum Pomponium digestorum ab Aristone libro quinto*) collected and edited Aristo's writings and opinions.   The words however seem more naturally to denote a work by Aristo which Pomponius quoted.   Vat. Fr. 88, 199 also refer to Aristo.   The letter from Salvius Aristo to Julian (D. XXXVII. 5. 1 6) can hardly refer to our Aristo, who must have been old when Julian was a youth.   See Mommsen *Z. R. G.* VII. 474 sqq. and his Index to Keil's Pliny s. v.

AULUS, named beside Aristo in D. XXVIII. 5. 1 17. § 5, is not otherwise known.

CHAPTER XII.

JURISTS OF FIRST HALF OF SECOND CENTURY.

MINICIUS wrote some work which Julian edited and annotated in six books.   In the Florentine Index Julian's six books *ad Minicium* are named.   The inscriptions of the extracts, of which there are 40 in the Digest, occupying $3\frac{1}{2}$ of Hommel's pages, have *ex Minicio*, except III. 3. 1 70, which has *ad Minicium*.   In two places, VI. 1. 1 61; XXXIII. 3. 1 1, Julian's note is expressly distinguished: and so in a citation in XIX. 1. 1 11. § 15, where *libro decimo apud Minicium* is probably a mistake for some other book (X. for V.?).   In two extracts we have *Iulianus respondit* (III. 3. 1 76; XLVI. 8. 1 23). Minicius is referred to D. XIX. 1. 1 6. § 4.

He is generally identified with the Minicius Natalis to whom Trajan addressed a rescript, allowing matters affecting military discipline, and among them the hearing of prisoners (*custodiarum cognitio*), to be dealt with on holidays.   The rescript is given in an extract from Ulpian's 7th book *de officio proconsulis* (D. II. 12. 1 9). This Minicius Natalis is no doubt the elder of the two mentioned in several inscriptions, from which it is seen that he was consul A.D. 107 and proconsul of Africa, with his son serving under him as legate (*C. I. L.* II. 4509, Wilmanns 1172; VIII. 2478; 4676; X. 5670. For the son see II. 4510, 4511; VIII. 4643; Wilmanns 1179.) Minicius Natalis is also mentioned in inscriptions *Eph. Epig.* I. p. 251; IV. p. 271.   The full name of both was *L. Minicius L. F. Gal(lus) Natalis Quadronius Uerus.*

A letter of Pliny *Minicio suo* (VII. 12) is by some supposed to be addressed to the lawyer.

LAELIUS. A jurist of this name is mentioned by Paul twice, D. v. 3. 1 43; and 4. 1 3. In the latter place Laelius is said to have mentioned his being present when a woman of Alexandria was brought to Hadrian, who had been delivered of four children at once and a fifth forty days after; cf. D. xxxv. 4. 1 7 (Gai.). Gellius (xv. 27) gives three extracts from the first book of Laelius Felix *ad Q. Mucium* relating to the *comitia* and in one referring to Labeo. Macrob. (*Sat.* I. 6. § 13) gives a quotation from M. Laelius Augur which Huschke doubtfully refers to Laelius Felix. In Plin. (*H. N.* XIV. 93) the editors read *L. Aelius.*

UALERIUS SEUERUS is quoted by Julian (D. III. 5. 1 29. (30.) *respondit U. S.*) and by Ulpian III. 3. 1 8. pr.; XLIII. 20. 1 1. § 21 ; and probably II. 4. 1 4. § 3 (*ut Seuerus dicebat*). A *C. Ualerius Seuerus* was *consul suffectus* A.D. 124 (*Corp. I. L.* III. p. 873).

NERATIUS PRISCUS lived in the reigns of Trajan and Hadrian. He was consul with Annius Verus, when a senate's decree was passed imposing the forfeiture of half his property on any one who castrated his slave (D. XLVIII. 8. 1 6). The consulship is put in A.D. 83 by Borghesi, in 98 by Asbach (see Teuffel p. 794 n. 4). He was one of Trajan's council with Aristo, when he decided that a father, who had on account of his illtreatment of his son been compelled to emancipate him, could not claim as manumissor the succession (*bonor. poss.*) of his son (D. XXXVII. 12. 1 5); and he was with Celsus and Julian one of Hadrian's council (Spart. *Hadr.* 18). His position was so high that many thought Trajan intended to leave him, and not Hadrian, as his successor ; and friends so strongly recommended him that one day Trajan said to Priscus *commendo tibi prouincias, si quid mihi fatale contigerit* (ib. 4. § 8). The offices which he held are enumerated in an inscription found at Saepinum, a municipal town in Samnium : *L. Neratio L. f. Uol. Prisco, Praef. Aer. Sat. Cos. Leg. Pr. Pr. in prou. Pannonia scribae quaestori et munere functi patrono* (Wilm. No. 1152) ; i e. 'erected by the quaestorial clerks, present and past, to their patron, Lucius Neratius Priscus, son of Lucius, of the Voltinian tribe, praefect of the treasury of Saturn' (see note on *fisco*, p. 184), 'consul, legate, pro-praetor[1] in the province of Pannonia'. Mommsen (Index to Keil's *Pliny*) identifies him also with the Priscus to whom A.D. 98 Pliny writes (*Ep.* II. 13)

---

[1] This is the official title of the governor of one of the minor imperial provinces.

and addresses as ruling a large army; and perhaps with the Priscus of *Ep.* VI. 8; VII. 8; 19; and VII. 15. (His brother Neratius Marcellus (D. XXXIII. 7. 1 12. § 43) was also consul, and, in Trajan's reign, legate in Britain. Hadrian forced him to kill himself, Spart. *Hadr.* 15.)

His works named in the Florentine Index are *Regulae* in 15 books; *Membranae* in 7 books, and *Responsa* in 3 books. From these there are in the Digest 64 extracts, usually short, so that they do not occupy more than 7½ of Hommel's pages, out of which the extracts from the *membranae* fill 6. His *libri ex Plautio* are mentioned in the Digest (XXXIII. 7. 1 12. § 35). He is frequently cited, both in the Digest (128 times) and elsewhere (Vat. Fr. 54; 71; 75; 79—85; *Collat.* XII. 7. § 7). A letter to Aristo is referred to in D. XIX. 2. 1 19. § 2. Some extracts in the Digest are made either from an edition of some of his writings or from a commentary by Paul (4 books). See D. VII. 8. 1 23; XV. 1. 1 56; XVII. 1. 1 61; XXIV. 1. 1 63, &c. Gellius (IV. 4) speaks of a book *de Nuptiis* which may have been part of one of his more general works.

IAUOLENUS PRISCUS. Little is known of the life of this lawyer. A statement by Pomponius, one extract in the Digest, and one letter of Pliny contains all our direct information. Julian (D. XL. 2. 1 5) tells us that he remembered his teacher Javolenus both in Africa and Syria, when holding a council to approve manumissions (cf. Ulp. I. § 12 sq.), setting some of his own slaves free, and that he himself when praetor and consul followed the precedent (D. XL. 2. 1 5). What magistracy Javolen held is not told us. Pliny (A.D. 106 or 107) tells a good story of Passennus Paulus, who, having collected some friends to hear him read some elegiac verses, began by addressing Javolenus Priscus, *Prisce iubes*. Whereupon Javolen who probably had little taste for recitations, and as a lawyer was not going to take the responsibility thus thrown on him (cf. *fideiubere, actio quod iussu*, &c.) could not resist saying, *Ego uero non iubeo*. The reply was received with general laughter and joking, partly we may suppose at the poet, and partly at the candid and facetious lawyer. The courteous Pliny was shocked, and apologises for Javolen. 'He was 'no doubt somewhat cracked, but still he took part in social duties, 'was a member of councils, and even acted publicly as a legal ad-'viser.' (*Est omnino Priscus dubiae sanitatis, interest tamen officiis, adhibetur consiliis atque etiam ius ciuile publice respondet.* Plin. *Ep.*

VI. 15.) It is not necessary to think Javolen was more than a humourist. Pomponius (D. I. 2. 1 2. § 53) classes him with the Sabinians and says that he succeeded Caelius Sabinus, who flourished in the time of Vespasian, and was himself followed by Aburnius Valens, Tuscianus and Salvius Julianus : so that he evidently belonged to the reigns of Domitian and Trajan. Capitolinus (*Ant. P.* 12) speaks of Diavolenus or Javolenus, along with Vindius, Valens, Maecianus and Ulpius Marcellus, as one of Antoninus' counsellors, but this is discredited by Zimmern, Mommsen (Index to Keil's *Pliny*), and others, the lateness of the time and the fact that he is not named as one of Hadrian's councillors making it improbable.

In the Digest there are 206 extracts, occupying 23 of Hommel's pages. Three works are named in the Florentine Index. 15 books *Ex Cassio* (5½ pages of Hommel); 14 books of Epistles (9 pages of Hommel); and 5 books *ad Plautium* (1½ pages of Hommel). Besides these there are a number of extracts (occupying 7 of Hommel's pages) from a book called *Ex posterioribus Labeonis*, which is classed by Bluhme as the last in the Sabinian series, whereas Javolen's other works are in the Edictal series. The precise relation of this work to *Labeonis libri* x *posteriorum a Iauoleno epitomatorum*, which is named in the Florentine Index and is one of the books in the Appendix to the Papinian series, is a riddle. Notice especially that extracts from these works alternate in D. XVIII. 1. ll 77—80, XIX. 2. ll 57—60, and that the same case is differently reported in D. XXIII. 3. l 80 and l 83. (See Pernice's discussion *Labeo* I. pp. 69 —81. He holds the two works to be different and not, as some have suggested, the same work differently named.) Javolen is not often cited by other writers. Where *Priscus* is cited in the Digest, it is generally thought that Javolen, and not Neratius, is meant. One of the supports of this conclusion is however removed by Mommsen's reading *Proculus et Neratius* instead of *Priscus et N.* in D. VII. 8. l 10. § 2.

Javolen's style may be seen in the longer extracts such as D. XVII. 1. l 36; XXXV. 1. l 40; XL. 7. l 39; XLI. 3. l 23; XLII. 5. l 28. He, or rather Labeo, frequently quotes the opinions of the earlier lawyers Q. Mucius, Gallus (Aquilius), Servius, Ofilius, Trebatius, Tubero, Cascellius, Namusa.

CELSUS, i.e. P. IUUENTIUS CELSUS, son of another lawyer of the same name, is often called Celsus *filius*, but is also the lawyer meant

when Celsus only is named. His full name is given in a *S. Cons.*
quoted in D. v. 3. 1 20. § 6 as *P. Iuuentius Celsus Titius Aufidius
Oenus Seuerianus* (where Borghesi reads *Titus* and *Hoenius*). Little
is known of his life. He was A.D. 94 engaged in a conspiracy against
Domitian, and to avoid conviction requested a private interview with
the Emperor, in which he knelt to him, called him master and god[1],
and proceeded to deny the charge, and to promise that if he were let
off he would turn informer against others. He was set free, but
accused no one, excusing himself on one pretext after another, until
Domitian was killed (Dio Cass. LXVII. 13). In 106—107 he was
praetor and (according to Plin. *Ep.* VI. 5; cf. v. 20) took a leading
part in an angry discussion in the senate. Varenus a defendant on
a charge of extortion had obtained by Pliny's advocacy the consent
of the senate to his witnesses being formally summoned (*euocari*),
as well as those of the prosecutors. · At a subsequent meeting of the
senate, Licinius Nepos reopened the matter, blamed the senate, and
demanded or ironically suggested that this should be made a standing
order for all defendants on a charge of extortion. Celsus defended
the senate's action, and with angry invective rebuked Nepos. Both
disputants had come prepared for the contest and spoke from written
notes. Celsus was consul first with L. Neratius Marcellus and
afterwards with Q. Julius Balbus in A.D. 129 (*Corp. I. L.* VI. Nos.
527; 10299; III. pp. 875, 876; D. v. 3. 1 20. § 6) and this is called
his second consulship (Cod. VII. 9. 1 3), though nothing is known of
his first consulship. An important decree of the senate on Hadrian's
proposal was made in this year relative to the sale of the assets of an
inheritance (D. l.c.). He is mentioned as being one of Hadrian's
legal advisers with Salvius Julianus, Neratius Priscus, and others
(Spart. *Hadr.* 18; where the MSS. have *Iulium Celsum*). Pomponius
names him with Neratius Priscus, as succeeding to his father in the
headship of Proculus' school. (D. I. 1. 1 2. § 53.) An inscription
in which *Iuuentius Celsus* as pontifex occurs in A.D. 155 can hardly
refer to the lawyer (Wilmanns No. 312).

He is considered to have been a man of sharp temper and vigorous
expression. His answer when consulted by Domitius Labeo is
famous, and *quaestio Domitiana* was used in the middle ages almost
proverbially for a foolish question and *responsum Celsinum* for a rude
answer. The question was whether one who had been summoned to
write a will, and had written and put his seal to it, could be counted

[1] Cf. Suet. *Dom.* 13.

R.   *l*

as one of the necessary seven witnesses. To which Celsus replied 'Either I do not understand what it is you consult me about or your 'question is very foolish. For it is something more than ridiculous 'to doubt whether a man is a good witness when he has written the 'will itself' (D. XXVIII. 1. 1 27 an extract from Celsus' own Digest). Possibly Dom. Labeo's doubt may have arisen from the fact that the witness was not summoned as such but as writer of the will (cf. ib. 1 21. § 2; Cod. VI. 23. 1 31. § 2 *septem testes, quos ad testimonium uocari necesse est*, &c., and Puchta *Curs.* § 99 *n*). Some other instances of sharp language by Celsus have been noted e.g. *quod totum et ineptum et uitiosum est* D. XXVIII. 5. 1 60 (59). § 1 ; *Quid tam ridiculum est quam?* &c. (D. XLVII. 2. 1 68 (67). § 2); *Celsus adulescens scribit...esse hanc quaestionem de bono et aequo; in quo genere plerumque sub auctoritate iuris scientiae perniciose, inquit, erratur* (Paul. D. XLV. 1. 1 91. § 3), where *adulescens* is noticeable. Again Ulpian D. III. 5. 1 9 (10). § 1 speaking of an opinion of Antist. Labeo's says *istam sententiam eleganter deridet Celsus.* See also D. XVIII. 2. 1 13. pr. and Vat. Fr. 75. § 5 (where however the MS. is somewhat corrupt). But one can hardly lay much stress on a few expressions of this kind. From the way in which his opinion is quoted by subsequent jurists it is clear that he was very highly thought of and in D. IV. 4. 1 3. § 1 we read of his being consulted by a praetor. In D. XXXIII. 10. 1 7 a considerable extract is found, in which Celsus quotes the older jurists Tubero and Servius, and discusses their opinions with deference, while at the same time expressing his own with that almost epigrammatic neatness which the Roman lawyers often called *elegantia*. Many of his views exhibit a reasonable regard to natural circumstances rather than to the precise letter, which is eminently characteristic of the best Roman lawyers, and is quite consistent with sharp logical insight. See e.g. D. VIII. 6. 1 6 ; XII. 6. 1 26. § 12 ; XXIV. 1. 1 5. § 15 ; XXVIII. 2. 1 13 pr. ; XXXI. 1 22 ; 1 30 ; &c. A curious statement is quoted from him, that no one is so deaf as not to be able to hear at all, if a person speaks *supra cerebrum illius* (Cod. VI. 22. 1 10. § 3). The only work from which extracts occur in the Digest is his *Digesta* in 39 books. These extracts are 141 in number: they occupy 14 of Hommel's pages. See also Vat. Fr. 75—80 (where he is often referred to) and ib. 1. Besides this work there are cited also his *Epistolae*, at least 11 books (D. IV. 4. 1 3. § 1); his *Quaestiones*, at least 19 books (D. XXXIV. 2. 1 19. § 3) and his *Commentarii*, at least 7 books, which however may have been part of the *Digesta*

(*Celsus libro nono decimo digestorum, commentariorum septimo,* D. XXXIV. 2. 1 19. § 6). There are 54 citations from the *Digesta* and 121 citations from this or other works. Of the citations Pomponius makes 8, Marcianus 4, Paul 4 and Maecianus 1, and Ulpian all the rest.

IULIANUS, i.e. P. SALUIUS IULIANUS, the last name in Pomponius' list of lawyers, was one of those who succeeded Javolenus as leaders of the Sabinian school. He himself calls Javolenus his praeceptor (D. XL. 2. 1 5). He was probably from the colony of Hadrumetum in Africa (at least his son is so described Spart. *Iul.* 1); and was praetor and twice consul. One of these consulships fell in A.D. 148 when C. Bellicius Torquatus is named as his colleague (*Corp. I. L.* VI. No. 375 ; 3885). Mommsen however attributes this consulship to Julian's son (*Z. R. G.* IX. 88 n. sq.). Julian was *curator aedium sacrarum* in A.D. 150 (*Corp. I. L.* VI. 855), and at one time Prefect of the city (Spart. *Did. Iul.* 1). He was in Hadrian's council (Spart. *Hadr.* 18) and is called *amicus noster* in a rescript of M. Antonius and Verus which, speaking of his opinion in the past tense, seems to imply that he was then dead (D. XXXVII. 14. 1 17). The letters of Fronto and M. Antoninus (pp. 59, 60 ed. Naber) speak of him as in bad health. He was buried five miles from Rome on the *Uia Labicana* (Spart. *Did. Iul.* 8. § 10).

His son was put to death by Commodus on a charge of conspiracy (Lampr. *Com.* 4 ; cf. 3). His granddaughter is said by Spartianus (*Did. Iul.* 1.) to have been mother of Didius Julianus, who was made emperor in succession to Pertinax. Didius was killed in A.D. 193, at the age of 60 according to Dio, or 56 according to Spartianus. If the lawyer was his great grandfather, he must have been born say 65 years before Didius, i.e. about A.D. 70.

His authority as a lawyer was great. In the reign of Hadrian (A.D. 131 according to Euseb. *Chron.*) he arranged and revised the praetor's edict (*perpetuum composuit edictum* Eutrop. VIII. 17 ; *primus edictum quod uarie inconditeque a praetoribus promebatur in ordinem composuit,* Aurel. Victor *Caes.* 19). A rescript of Leo and Anthemius A.D. 473 says *in praesenti negotio aequitati conuenientem Iuliani tantae existimationis uiri atque disertissimi iuris periti opinionem sequi* (Cod. VI. 61. 1 5). Similarly Justinian A.D. 530 *Papinianus huiusmodi sententiae sublimissimum testem adducit Sabinum Iulianum summae auctoritatis hominem et praetorii edicti ordinatorem* (Cod. IV. 5. 1 10); and again in the Const. *Tanta* (§ 18) confirming the Digest, *Iulianus legum et edicti perpetui suptilissimus conditor*, for which the Greek constitution Δέδωκεν § 18 has ὁ πάντων τῶν ἐν νομοθεσίαις εὐδοκιμηκότων σοφώτατος ᾿Ιουλίανος, and, immediately after, speaks of Hadrian having by means of Julian compressed the annual edicts of the praetors into a small book (ἐν βραχεῖ τινὶ συνῆγε βιβλίῳ). His name is put first of all in the Florentine Index.

Before discussing Julian's revision the general nature of the edict demands attention. An edict is simply a public notice, and a praetor's edict is such a notice issued in his capacity as praetor. Such edicts would often deal merely with the particular matters which happened to require the praetor's action. As the equitable jurisdiction of the praetor grew, it became customary for the praetor on entering into office to give public notice of the rules which he should follow in the administration of justice. Such a general notice was called *edictum perpetuum*, ‘a standing notice’[1], being one not intended for a special case but for the whole course of his year of office. To a great extent it would be taken from his predecessors, and so far it was called *translaticium*[2] traditional; but some parts might be recast by the praetor, or new clauses might be added. The issue of such an edict would not exhaust the praetor's authority: additional action or edict might be required by circumstances (cf. D. II. 1. 1 7. pr.), but it is obvious that the very purpose of such a notice would be annulled or impaired, if the praetor did not observe his own edict in the cases to which it applied in principle. Cicero speaks at some length on this subject (B.C. 70) in Act. II. Lib. 1 against Verres, Capp. 40—48, and again in reference to his own edict issued as governor of Cilicia. A provincial edict was partly similar to the urban edict, and often taken from it, though some rules would be required by the special circumstances or customs of the particular province. But the principle was the same. A few passages may be cited. *Posteaquam ius praetorium constitutum est, semper hoc iure usi sumus: si tabulae testamenti non proferrentur, tum uti quemque potissimum heredem esse oporteret, si is intestatus mortuus esset, ita secundum eum possessio daretur. Quare hoc sit*

---

[1] See a fuller discussion in Prof. Clark's *Practical Jurisprudence*, pp. 203 sqq., 347 sqq.

[2] It was *translatum* so far as actually copied from a predecessor; *translaticium* is a secondary formation describing the character thus acquired. So *editi iudices* are judges nominated; *editicii* ‘nominative’ and were judges taken from *editae tribus* (cf. Cic. *Planc.* 15. § 36).

aequissimum, facile est dicere, sed in re tam usitata satis est ostendere, omnes antea ita ius dixisse, et hoc uetus edictum translaticiumque esse (Cic. *Uerr.* Lib. I. 44. § 114). Then speaking of a change made for a particular case Cicero proceeds : *In Sicilia de possessionibus dandis edixit idem quod omnes Romae praeter istum…Quaero cur ea capita in edictum prouinciale transferre nolueris…Non enim hoc potest hoc loco dici, multa esse in prouinciis aliter edicenda : non de hereditatum quidem possessionibus, non de mulierum hereditatibus.` Nam utroque genere uideo non modo ceteros sed te ipsum totidem uerbis edixisse, quot uerbis edici Romae solet* (Ib. 45, 46. §§ 117, 118). Speaking of his own edict B.C. 51 Cicero says that he copied many clauses from Q. Mucius Scaevola's edict for the province of Asia, and then proceeds, *Breue autem edictum est propter hanc meam* διαίρεσιν, *quod de duobus generibus edicendum putaui, quorum unum est prouinciale, in quo est de rationibus ciuitatum, de aere alieno, de usura, de syngraphis, in eodem omnia de publicanis ; alterum quod sine edicto satis commode transigi non potest, de hereditatum possessionibus, de bonis possidendis uendendis, magistris faciendis, quae ex edicto et postulari et fieri solent ; tertium de reliquo iure dicundo* ἄγραφον *reliqui : dixi me de eo genere mea decreta ad edicta urbana accommodaturum* (*Att.* VI. 1. § 15). *Romae composui edictum : nihil addidi, nisi quod publicani me rogarunt, cum Samum ad me uenissent, ut de tuo* (i.e. his predecessor Appius) *edicto totidem uerbis transferrem in meum. Diligentissime scriptum caput est quod pertinet ad minuendos sumptus ciuitatum : quo in capite sunt quaedam noua, salutaria ciuitatibus… hoc uero, ex quo suspicio nata est, tralaticium est* (*Fam.* III. 8. § 4). C. Cornelius in B.C. 67 carried a law, *ut praetores ex edictis suis perpetuis ius dicerent* (Ascon. *in Corn.* p. 58), possibly in consequence of Verres' practices.

What precisely Julian did, when he *edictum perpetuum composuit,* we are not told. *Componere* was used by Cicero to describe drawing up his own edict. Pomponius (D. I. 2. 1 2. § 44), in speaking of Ofilius' numerous legal works, says *de iurisdictione edictum praetoris primus diligenter composuit* (see above, p. cxv). Ofilius was not praetor, but the word describes the ordinary work of the praetor. As such we may fairly suppose Julian's work to have been, though very likely more thorough, and under the imperial auspices certainly more permanent. The predominance of the imperial power would naturally throw the praetor's initiative into the shade, and inferior importance would bring about neglect. So that in course of time

some remodelling would be very desirable. Julian may have improved
the form, rearranged the matter and incorporated some amendments,
but substantially the rules of law would not be altered. One inno-
vation is mentioned by Marcellus (D. xxxvii. 8. 1 3, cf. 9. 1 1. § 13).
By a new clause introduced by Julian an emancipated son passed
over by his father's will does not on obtaining *bonorum possessio*
exclude sons of his own still in their grandfather's power, but shares
it with them, bringing his own property into hotchpot. Other
amendments of Julian's are supposed to be referred to in D. iv. 2.
1 1; xliii. 19. 1 4. The great difference however between Julian's
edict and those of preceding praetors was in the authority which it
obtained. Their's lasted for their year of office and no more. *Qui
plurimum tribuunt edicto praetoris, edictum legem annuam dicunt esse*
(Cic. *Verr.* Lib. ii. 42. § 109). Julian's was confirmed by a *S. Consultum* (Const. *Tanta* § 18), introduced by a speech from Hadrian
(Const. Δέδωκεν § 18)[1] who declared that any point which should
arise, not provided for in the edict, should be decided in analogy
with it. After this the standing edict (*edictum perpetuum*) referred
to was Julian's (D. xxxi. 1 77. § 29; xlix. 14. 1 1. § 1; Vat. Fr.
§ 317; Cod. ii. 1. 1 3; iv. 26. 1 2, &c.). Sometimes it is called
praetoris edictum (D. xxiii. 2. 1 58), or simply *edictum* (D. xxxvi. 3
1 5. § 1). See Rudorff *Z. R. G.* iii. pp. 28, 29; *Rechts-Gesch.* i. § 97.

We read of the Edict of the *Praetor urbanus*, of the Edict of the
Praetor Peregrinus (cf. *Lex Rubria* 20), of the Edict of the Province
of Asia, of Sicily, of Cilicia, &c., and of the Edict of the Curule
Aediles, all in the sense of standing codes of rules promulgated for
the several magistrates' period of office. (*Ius edicendi habent magistratus populi Romani, sed amplissimum ius est in edictis duorum
praetorum urbani et peregrini, quorum in prouinciis iurisdictionem
praesides earum habent; item in edictis aedium curulium, quorum
iurisdictionem in prouinciis populi Romani quaestores habent; nam
in prouincias Caesaris omnino quaestores non mittuntur et ob id hoc
edictum in his prouinciis non proponitur*, Gai. i. 6.) Whether
Julian made one edict out of all these edicts (Rudorff *Z. R. G.* iii.
p. 21), or revised separately the city, foreign, provincial and aediles'

---

[1] One would have liked earlier authority. It is curious that the one constitution speaks only of the speech, the other only of the *S. C.* A notice in a
Greek Epitome, a.d. 920 (appended to Zachariae *Proch. Nom.* p. 292), that the
revision of the edict was intrusted to Julian and Servius Cornelius is, I think
with others, of no historical value (Rudorff accepts it, *Rechts-Gesch.* i. p. 268).
The 'Servius' is from D. i. 2. 1 2. § 44; for 'Cornelius' see perhaps above, p. cxiii.

edicts, or dealt only with the city praetor's edict, which was as it were the leading authority, we do not know, but the last seems improbable, and the two first suppositions may be only formally different. Gaius commented on the *edictum urbicum* and *edictum prouinciale* (see below, p. clxxviii); Ulpian and Paulus on the *edictum* (simply), and also on the *edictum aedilium curulium*. No fragments remain of the *edictum praetoris peregrini* (Mommsen *Staatsrecht* II. p. 212, ed. 2 ; cf. Clark *Pract. Jur.* p. 350).

There is no need to suppose that the praetors after Julian issued no edicts of their own. Gaius' words speak of the power as in operation. But subsequent praetors would act rather by way of interpretation and prescribing subordinate details, than in the quasi-legislative capacity which was the attribute of their office before (cf. Walter *Rechts-Gesch.* II. § 440). Imperial rescripts filled the place of the praetors' previous action.

The principal work of Julian, from which extracts have been taken into the Digest, is called by the same name *Digesta*. This work is the first of all named in the Florentine Index. Fitting (*Alter der röm. Juristen*, p. 6) shews that the sixth book was written before the *Sc. Iuuentianum* (14 March, 129 pr. Chr.) : else Julian would have been cited in reference to it (D. v. 3. 1 20); and that the 64th book contained a reference to a rescript of Antoninus Pius (D. IV. 2. 1 18); so that the bulk of the work was written in the reigns of Hadrian and the first Antonine. Mommsen (*Z. R. G.* IX. 94) from the character and phraseology (*respondi, respondit,* &c.) of the extracts infers that the *Digesta* was an orderly arrangement under certain heads of a number of questions with detailed explanations as given in lectures. The order of the edict appears to have been followed (see however Lenel *Ed. Perp.* p. 7) as far as the 58th book. After that the matter appears miscellaneous. Marcellus wrote notes on it, which are often given with the text in the extract in the Digest e.g. IV. 6. 1 41; v. 1. 1 75; xv. 1. 1 16; xxiii. 3. 1 44. § 1 ; xxx. 1 82. § 3 ; 1 92. pr.; xxxvi. 1. 1 28. (27). Notes of Scaevola (e.g. II. 14. 1 54; xviii. 6. 1 10. § 1); and of Paulus (e.g. IV. 2. 1 11 ; xviii. 5. 1 4) are found as separate extracts. Ulpian (but no one else before his time) quotes Julian's Digest profusely. The extracts from it in Justinian's Digest are stated to be 376 in number : they occupy 58 of Hommel's pages. Citations (in extracts from other writers) occupy about 17 pages more. Besides these there are no less than 620 other citations of Julian where the work is not expressly named. No doubt these are, at least mainly, from the *Digesta*.

Three other works of Julian are named in the Florentine Index, viz. 6 books *ad Minicium* (or *ex Minicio*), 4 books *ad Urseium Ferocem* (which were probably annotated editions of those authors), and one book *de ambiguitatibus*. Extracts from these occupy 9 or 10 pages.

The total number of extracts from works bearing Julian's name is 456, occupying 68 of Hommel's pages. Some extracts of considerable length form D. xxx. 1 81—1 104 (with some interruptions); xxxvi. 1. 1 28. (27); xli. 3. 1 33; 4. 1 7; xlvi. 3. 1 34; 8. 1 22; &c. In D. xxxiv. 5. 1 13. (14) we have a discussion of the ambiguities in the use of disjunctives.

UALENS, whose full name is given as *Aburnius Ualens* D. i. 2. 1 2. § 53; and iv. 4. 1 33; and xxxii. 1 78. § 6, is named by Pomponius as successor with Tuscianus, a jurist otherwise unknown, to Javolen. One work of his *de fideicommissis* in 7 books is named in the Florentine Index, and furnishes 19 extracts to the Digest. He cites answers of Javolen (D. xxxiii. 1. 1 15) and Julian (D. iv. 4. 1 33). He is quoted three times by Paul D. xxxi. 1 82. § 2; xxxii. 1 78. § 6; xl. 5. 1 25. Hence he probably wrote under Hadrian or Anton. Pius. A lawyer named Salvius Valens is said by Capitolinus (*Pius* 12) to have been in the council of Ant. Pius with Vindius Verus, Volusius Maecianus, Ulpius Marcellus and Diavolenus. A rescript of Pius to him is mentioned in D. xlviii. 2. 1 7. § 2. It is possible this may be the same as Aburnius Valens. Mommsen reads Fulvius for Salvius on the strength of an inscription (Orelli 3153) which at Viertel's suggestion (*de uitis iurisconsultorum* p. 30) he refers to our jurist. Mommsen gives it as follows: *L. Fulvio C. fil. Popin.* (write *Pupinia*) *Aburnio Ualenti pontifici praefect(o) urbi feriarum Latinar(um) facto ab Hadriano* ii *cos.* (i. e. 118 p. Chr.) iii *uiro a(uro) a(rgento) a(ere) f(lando) f(eriundo) quaest(ori) Aug(usti) tribuno plebis designato candidato Aug(usti) eq(uo) publ(ico)*[1] *c(larissimo) i(uueni) d(ecreto) d(ecurionum).* This nominal praefecture of the city was often given to young men of rank, and hence we may infer that Valens was born in A.D. 100 (Mommsen *Z. R. G.* ix. p. 90).

---

[1] *Equo publico*, as abl. of description, is common in imperial inscriptions (see Wilmanns ii. p. 540) to denote a member of the six *turmae* instituted by Augustus (cf. Madvig *Verfass.* i. p. 177; Hirschfeld *Untersuch.* p. 244: etc.).

A short extract from the '7th book *Actionum*' is given in D. XXXVI. 4. 1 15 inscribed with Valens' name. Krüger suggests that this is a mistake for Venuleius.

The extracts fill about 3 of Hommel's pages. Of the longer extracts are XXXIV. 1. 1 22; XXXV. 1. 1 89; XXXVI. 1. 1 69. (67).

UINDIUS is mentioned only a few times in the Digest, viz. by Paul (D. II. 9. 1 2 *Uindius putat* and *ut Pomponius et Uindius scribunt*); by Ulpian (II. 14. 1 7. § 18 *Uindius scribit;* v. 1. 1 5 *ut et Pomponius et Uindius scripserunt*); and by Maecianus (XXXV. 2. 1 32. § 4 *Uindius noster ait*). In Vat. Fr. 77 we find him contemporary with Julian, *Uindius (Uenidius* MS.) *tamen, dum consulit Iulianum, in ea opinione est*, &c. He is no doubt the Vindius Verus who was in the council of T. Antoninus Pius, and the M. Vindius Verus who was consul with Pactumeius Clemens 16 June 138 p. Chr. (*C. I. L.* III. p. 879).

PACTUMEIUS CLEMENS is mentioned once in the Digest by Pomponius (D. XL. 7. 1 21. § 1) *Pactumeius Clemens aiebat...imperatorem Antoninum constituisse.* Antoninus Pius no doubt was meant, for Pactumeius was consul with Vindius in the year 138 p. Chr. (*Corp. I. L.* III. p. 879 where he is called *C. Pactumeius Clemens*). An inscription at Cirta (the modern Constantine in Algiers) calls him a jurisconsult and gives a full list of the official positions he had held (Wilmanns 1180) *P.*[1] *Pactumeio P. F. Quir. Clémenti* x *uirum stlitibus iudicand. quaest. leg. Rosiani Gemini soceri sui procos. in Achaia trib. pleb. fetiali legato Diui Hadriani Athenis Thespiis Plateis item in Thessalia praetori urbano legato Diui Hadriani ad rationes ciuitatium Syriae putandas legato eiusdem in Cilicia consuli legato in Cilicia Imp. Antonini Aug. leg. Rosiani Gemini procos. in Africa iuris consulto patrono* IIII *coloniarum DD. PP.*[2] 'Erected by a decree of the decemvirs at public cost to P. Pactumeius 'Clemens, son of Publius, of the Quirinian tribe, one of the ten com-'missioners for deciding suits, quaestor, legate of Rosianus Geminus '(cf. D. XLVIII. 5. 1 6. § 2; 6. 1 6) his father-in-law when proconsul 'in Achaia, tribune of the commons, fetial, legate of the divine 'Hadrian at Athens, Thespiae, Platea and likewise in Thessaly, 'praetor of the city, legate of the divine Hadrian to settle the

---

[1] Probably P is a mistake for C. Klein (*Fast. Cons.* p. 67) corrects C in the other inscription.

[2] *decurionum decreto pecunia publica.*

'finances of the towns of Syria (cf. Spart. *Hadr.* 11), legate of the 'same (Hadrian) in Cilicia, consul, legate in Cilicia of the Emperor 'Antoninus (Pius) Augustus, legate of Rosianus Geminus when 'proconsul in Africa, jurisconsult, patron of four colonies'. He was evidently made consul just at the time of Hadrian's death, perhaps in his absence on the duty in Cilicia, to which he was first appointed by Hadrian, afterwards reappointed or continued by Antonine (cf. Mommsen *Mon. Ancyr.* p. 179, ed. 2).

AFRICANUS, whom we can hardly be wrong in identifying with the *Sextus Caecilius Africanus* mentioned in D. xxv. 3. 1 3. § 4 as consulting Julian, is named in the Florentine Index as the author of *Quaestiones* in 9 books. He is quoted by Paul (D. XIX. 1. 1 45. pr. *idque et Iulianum agitasse Africanus refert*), and by Ulpian (xxx. 1 39. pr. *Africanus libro uicesimo epistularum apud Iulianum quaesit*, and xxxviii. 17. 1 2. § 8 *Africanus et Publicius temptant*). There are in the Digest 131 extracts from the *Quaestiones*. They fill 23½ of Hommel's pages. Fitting concludes that the work was written at the end of Hadrian's or beginning of Ant. Pius' reign. The difficulty of many of the extracts has made *Africani lex* a synonym for a difficult passage. Cujas commented on the whole of them (Tom. IV. ed. 1837 Prati).

Gellius (xx. 1) speaks of Sextus Caecilius as holding a discussion in his presence with Favorinus on the law of the Twelve Tables. He is described as *in disciplina iuris atque in legibus populi Romani noscendis interpretandisque scientia usus auctoritateque inlustris*, and Gellius gives us his defence of the early procedure authorised by the Twelve Tables, especially of the famous law *si plus minusue secuerunt, se fraude esto.*

Justinian (Cod. VII. 7. § 1 a) calls Sex. Caecilius *iuris antiqui conditor.* And Sex. Caecilius is referred to in several places in the Digest, viz. xxi. 1. 1 2; xxxiii. 9. 1 3. § 9; xxxv. 1. 1 71. pr.; xi. 9. 1 12. § 2; xlviii. 5. 1 14. (13). § 1. Further the Digest in not a few places contains mention of the opinion of *Caecilius;* xv. 2. 1 1. § 7; xxi. 1. 1 14. § 10; xxiv. 1. 1 64; xxxv. 2. 1 36. § 4; xlviii. 5. 1 28. (27). § 5.

On the whole there seems no reason to doubt that the Sex. Caecilius of Gellius and the Sex Caecilius and Caecilius of the Code and Digest are the same as Africanus : but in two of these passages the text is almost certainly wrong (Mommsen l. c.). Thus *Caelius*

should be written in XXI. 1. 1 14. § 10 (cf. 1 14. § 3; 1 17 *passim;*
1 38. § 7; § 11; 1 65. § 2); and *Sex. Aelius* should be written in
XXXIII. 9. 1 3. § 9 (cf. Gell. IV. 1. § 20). In XXIV. 1. 1 64 Javolen
cites an opinion of Proculus and Caecilius which cannot refer to
Africanus, who was much later than Javolen. Probably *Caecilius* is
a corruption for *Caelius.*

Possibly Africanus is meant by Gaius II. 218 *Iuliano et Sexto
placuit* (see p. clxxii). That African stood in close relation to Julian
is tolerably clear. The Greek scholiasts in several places refer to
Julian's opinions, given in the extracts from African by the simple
word *respondit* (cf. *Aegid. Menagii Præf. ad Cuiac. in Africanum;*
Mommsen *Z. R. G.* IX. 93). Mommsen suggests that probably
African's *Quaestiones* was an account of Julian's opinions and discussions with his pupils. A similar view is taken by H. Buhl *Z. R. G.*
XV. pp. 191 sqq. See also Schulin *ad Pomp. de origine iuris,* p. 15.

Some of the longer extracts from African are XV. 1. 1 38; XVI. 1.
1 19; XXX. 1 108; XXXV. 2. 1 88; XLVI. 1. 1 21; 3. 1 38; XLVII. 2. 1 61.

POMPONIUS, i. e. SEXTUS POMPONIUS, is a lawyer of whom we
know nothing except what may be gathered from the extracts in
the Digest, and from references to him by later jurists. From the
expressions which he uses he is supposed to have been a pupil of
Pegasus (D. XXXI. 43. § 2 *Pegasus solitus fuerat distinguere*), of
Aristo (e.g. D. XXXVI. 1. 1 74. (72) *Aristo aiebat;* XL. 5. 20) and
of Octavenus (ib. &c.). Fitting gives the following times for the
composition of his various works. His Commentary on Sabinus in
35 books, and perhaps his *Fideicommissa* in 5 books were written in
Hadrian's reign and before Julian. The Handbook (*Enchiridion* in
one book or according to the Florentine Index in two books), from
which the long historical extract which forms D. I. 2. 1 2 was taken,
ends with the name of Julian, and was therefore written about the
same time. To the reign of Ant. Pius belong his commentary on Q.
Mucius in 39 books, his 5 books of *Senatus Consulta* (though they
may be earlier), his book of Rules (*Regularum*), his Commentary on
the Edict, from which we have no extract but of which the 79th
book is cited in D. XXXVII. 6. 1 1. § 9; 10. 1 1. § 8. Marcellus wrote
notes on the *Regulae,* D. XXVIII. 1. 1 16; XLIX. 17. 1 10. To this or
the next reign belongs his Commentary on Plautius in 7 books. To
the reign of Marcus Antoninus belong his *Epistulae* and *Uariae Lectiones,* which are named separately in the Florentine Index as having

respectively 20 and 15 books, but which are treated as one work in the inscriptions of D. IV. 4. 1 50; L. 12. 1 15. The 40th and 41st book of the *Lectiones* is cited in D. VIII. 5. 1 8. § 6; XX. 2. 1 2. The eighth book of a work *de stipulationibus* is quoted in D. VII. 4. 1 5. § 2; and his notes to Aristo are frequently mentioned. Julian appears to have used Pomponius' books *ad Sabinum* (Vat. Fr. 88; D. XVII. 2. 1 63. § 9) and Pomponius used at least the earlier books of Julian's *Digesta*.

Some writers have thought there were two lawyers called Sex. Pomponius, but there appears to be no necessity for this, in itself very improbable, conclusion. In D. XXVIII. 5. 1 42 (41) the last words *'ut refert Sextus Pomponius'* may be part of the extract from Julian, which ought to have been struck out by the compilers, when they inserted the extract from Pomponius instead of Julian's account of it. In D. XXX. 1 32 *tam Sextus quam Pomponius*, in XXIX. 5. 1 1. § 27 and Gai. II. 218 where Sextus is also mentioned, Mommsen (*Z. R. G.* VII. p. 479) and others suppose Sex. Pedius or Sex. Caecilius Africanus to be probably meant, though such a view is only necessary in the first passage. (Vat. Fr. § 88 is emended by Mommsen.) An extract in D. XL. 5. 1 20 has led some to infer that Pomponius lived to the age of 78, but Pomponius is there relating a question put to him, not speaking in his own person.

There are 578 extracts from Pomponius in the Digest: they occupy more than 70 of Hommel's pages. Rather more than half (37 pages) are from the *Libri ad Sabinum;* and a fifth (13½ pages) from the *Libri ad Q. Mucium.* But the citations of him by Ulpian and others are very numerous—more than 400 (in addition to the extracts). Some of the longer extracts are D. XVI. 1. 1 32; XIX. 1. 1 6; XXXIII. 1. 1 7; XXXIV. 2. 1 34; XLI. 1. 1 30.

TERENTIUS CLEMENS wrote a work in 20 books *ad leges*, i. e. on the Julian and Papian Poppaean laws, from which there are 35 extracts, mostly short, in the Digest. They fill 3½ of Hommel's pages. The longer extracts are D. XXIII. 3. 1 61; XXXI. 1 53; XXXV. 1. 1 62. He calls Julian *noster* (XXVIII. 6. 1 6) and frequently quotes him. Twice he seems to refer to the XLIVth book of Julian's Digest. The expression *Iulianus aiebat* perhaps indicates that it was written after Julian's death (XXXV. 1. 1 64). Hence Terentius' work was probably written towards the end of Antoninus Pius' reign (Fitting).

IUNIUS MAURICIANUS is named in the Florentine Index as author of one work in 6 books *ad leges* (see above). From this there are three extracts in the Digest, XXXI. 1 57; XXXIII. 2. 1 3; XLIX. 14. 1 15. Another work *de poenis* has supplied one extract, II. 13. 1 3. His opinions are quoted by Ulpian five times in the Digest (II. 14. 1 7. § 2; VI. 1. 1 35. § 1; VII. 1. 1 25. § 1; XXVIII. 2. 1 3. § 5; XLI. 10. 1 1. § 1), and also in Vat. Fr. 75; once by Paul (D. V. 3. 1 36. pr.). In two of these he remarks on Julian. He probably wrote under Ant. Pius (Fitting).

CHAPTER XIII.

JURISTS OF SECOND HALF OF SECOND CENTURY.

MAECIANUS, i.e. L. UOLUSIUS MAECIANUS, was instructor in law of Marcus Antoninus (Capit. *Marc. Ant.* 3) and afterwards one of his council (Capit. *Ant. P.* 12). He was governor of Alexandria, and was killed by the army, without the knowledge of Marcus, because he favoured the assumption of the imperial purple by Avidius Cassius A.D. 175 (Capit. *M. Ant.* 25, where '*filium Cassii*' must be corrupt; *Avid. Cass.* 7). In a rescript of Marcus and Verus, Maecianus is called *amicus noster ut et iuris ciuilis praeter ueterem et bene fundatam peritiam anxie diligens* (D. XXXVII. 14. 1 17). He thrice speaks of Julian as *noster* (e.g. D. XXXV. 2. 1 30. § 7).

In the Florentine Index he appears as author of *Fideicommissa* in 16 books (written in Ant. Pius' reign) and *Publica* (*iudicia*) in 14 books. From the first there are 40 extracts in the Digest; from the second only three. There is also a Greek extract from '*Uolusius Maecianus ex lege Rhodia*' (D. XIV. 2. 1 9), containing a rescript of Antonine's declaring the Rhodian law in matters of shipwreck to be valid, so far as it was not contrary to any Roman law. Maecianus is cited 17 times in the Digest. The extracts fill more than seven of Hommel's pages. Some are of considerable length, e g. XXXV. 2. 1 30; 1 32; XXXVI. 1. 1 66 (64); 67 (65); XLIX. 17. 1 18.

A short treatise by him is preserved to us independently and is found in the collections of ante-Justinian law books. It is addressed to Caesar (doubtless to his pupil Marcus Antoninus), and contains a description of the various parts of the *as* (i.e. the fractions which were used in dividing an inheritance; see D. XXVIII. 5 *passim*), and of the modes of noting and naming the odd pence or fractions (*aes excurrens*), when the reckoning is made in *denarii* or *sestertii*. That is to say, he first describes and names the various fractions which have 12 for a denominator ($\frac{1}{12}$, $\frac{2}{12}$, &c.), then shews how to express six-teenths (the *denarius* of 16 *asses* being taken as the unit) by twelfths, half-twelfths, &c.; and finally how to express eighths (the *sestertius* of 4 *asses* being taken as the unit) by tenths, twentieths, &c. (See my *Lat. Gr.* vol. I. app. D.) Some weights and measures close the treatise.

GAIUS is a writer of whom we literally know nothing except that he was the author of several books of Roman law, which internal evidence shews to have been written about the time of the earlier Antonines. One of the extracts from his works records an incident which happened to Hadrian in his time (*nostra aetate* D. XXXIV. 5. 1 7. pr.). The earliest certain mention of him is the law of Theodo-sius II. and Valentinian III. A.D. 426, which put his writings in the same authoritative position as those of Papinian, Paul, Ulpian and Modestin (see above, p. lxxxiv). About this time, whether before the law (Huschke *Z. R. G.* XIII. 9), or after (as others suppose, see Rudorff *R. G.* I. p. 286), an extract from his Institutes (III. 1—17) is given in the comparison of Mosaic and Roman laws, which is called *lex Dei*, or *Collatio Mos. et Rom. Legum* XVI. 2. The grammarian Priscian (*Inst.* VI. 96), who wrote at Constantinople somewhere about 500 A.D., quotes two lines from the Institutes (I. 113). The *lex Romana Uisigothorum*, prepared by a commission of Bishops and provincial nobles at Aire in Gascony, under the authority of King Alarich II. A.D. 506, as law for the subject Romans of that kingdom, contains, along with *Pauli Sententiae*, part of the Theodosian Code and other fragments, an epitome[1] in two books of the first three books of Gaius' Institutes. Justinian names Gaius three times. He describes his own Institutes to be put together from other institutes and treatises, but especially from the Institutes and *Res Cottidianae* of 'our Gaius' (*Praef. Inst.* § 6): in the Institutes themselves (IV. 18. § 5) he quotes from the work of 'our Gaius' on the Twelve Tables;

---

[1] Fitting argues that it was made between A.D. 384 and 428, or at latest 438. It disallows marriage of first cousins, hence is later than Theodosius' law pro-hibiting it (Jac. Gothof. *Cod. Th.* i. p. 332 and iii. p. 1021). It treats *dictio dotis* as still in force; hence before *Cod. Th.* iii. 13. 1 4.

and, in describing the old course of legal study, he mentions that the first year's course consisted of six books of 'our Gaius', viz. the Institutes and four separate treatises on wife's property, guardianships, wills and legacies (Const. *Omnem* § 1). '*Noster Gaius*' probably denotes only familiarity with Gaius' books. The use of these books in the Digest will be mentioned below.

There are some other references to 'Gaius', but it is disputed whether Gaius Cassius Longinus, the chief of the Sabinian school, or the writer of the Institutes (also a Sabinian), is meant. One is by Julian (D. xxiv. 3. 1 59) who speaks of Gaius' giving the same opinion as Sabinus; another by Javolen, *libro secundo ex Cassio* (D. xxxv. 1. 1 54), where he says an opinion *in commentariis Gaii scriptum est;* a third by the same writer, '*libro undecimo ex Cassio*' (D. xlvi. 3. 1 78), who says of an opinion '*in libris Gaii scriptum est*'; a fourth by Pomponius, '*libro uicensimo secundo ad Q. Mucium*' (D. xlv. 3. 1 39), who approves '*quod Gaius noster dixit*' on a cognate question to that treated by Javolen. The age of the writers, especially of Javolen, makes it unlikely that it was the author of the Institutes that is meant in any of these cases, though, as he wrote on Q. Mucius, he was an author not unlikely to have been referred to by Pomponius. Asher (*Z. R. G.* v. 85) however makes it probable that *noster* was used by pupils of their teachers, as it was used by a slave of his master. Hence Pomponius could not have called the Institution-writer *noster*. Servius, the Commentator on Vergil (*Georg.* iii. 306), says *apud maiores omne mercimonium in permutatione constabat, quod et Gaius Homerico confirmat exemplo.* This would fit Gaius *Inst.* iii. 141 very well; but it is clear from this very passage and from D. xviii. 1. 1 1. § 1, that these lines of Homer were a stock quotation used by Sabinus and his school. Still it must be remembered that the Institutes were certainly in circulation in Servius' time (in 400 A.D.), and we know of no book of Cassius' that was.

Mommsen has put forward the ingenious suggestion that Gaius was a law professor, not at Rome but at Troas in the province of Asia. He bases this theory on the following facts taken together[1]. (*a*) Only his *praenomen* is known, and for a man to be called by that only is in conformity with the usage of Greek districts only. (*b*) He

---

[1] Mommsen's essay is in Bekker and Muther's *Jahrb. des gem. Rechts* iii. (1859) p. 1 sqq. I only know it at second hand, e.g. through Kuntze *Excurs.* p. 337; Bremer *Die Rechtslehrer* p. 77, and other books.

is familiar with Greek ordinary language, as well as with Greek writers (D. XIX. 2. 1 25. § 6 ; L. 16. 1 30. § 2 ; 1 233. § 2 ; 1 236) ; and quotes the laws of Solon (D. X. I. 1 13 ; XLVII. 22. 1 4).   (c) He gave special attention to the law of the provinces.   He wrote on the *edictum prouinciale*, that is to say on 'the edict of the province', whatever it was, in which he resided (see below).   (d) Further he mentions laws of foreigners parallel to or divergent from those of Rome, e. g. *Inst.* I. 55 that of the Galatians ; ib. 193 that of the Bithynians ; III. 96 ; 134 foreigners in general.   (e) He wrote on antiquarian matters, e. g. he is the only post-Augustan jurist that wrote on the XII tables, and yet he ignores laws, e. g. *S. C. Tertullianum*[1] (cf. Gai. III. 24), which no jurist in Rome could be ignorant of. (f) He was a voluminous writer, and yet evidently had not the *ius respondendi*, for he does not allude to his having such a position (e. g. in I. 7), and no *responsa* of his are anywhere given or quoted in the Digest or elsewhere.   Nor was he busied with practical cases, for no *quaestiones* are mentioned.   (g) His writings are not noticed as authorities until the beginning of the 5th century, therefore about 250 years after they were written.   (h) Gaius mentions three towns as having the *ius Italicum*, Troas, Berytus, Dyrrachium.   The first of these was one of the most important towns of the province of Asia, and, since Augustus, a Roman colony, with Latin as the official language, as is proved by coins and inscriptions.   The province was one to which the edict of Q. Mucius Scaevola applied, and this appears to have been regarded as a model provincial edict (Val. Max. VIII. 15. § 6 ; Cic. *Att.* VI. 1. § 15 ; see above p. cv), and Q. Mucius was one of the writers on whom Gaius commented (*Inst.* I. 188).

To this argument Huschke (*Praef.* to Gaius) replies that other instances of Romans being known by their *praenomen* occur, e. g. Servius (Sulpicius) and Sextus (Pomponius) ; that the edict of the province of Asia would have been called not *prouinciale*, but *Asiaticum*, as Verres' edict was called *edictum Siciliense;* and that no jurisconsult would have thought of writing a work in thirty books on the edict of a single province ; consequently the *edictum prouinciale* must have meant an edict applicable to any province, on the analogy of *prouinciale solum, prouincialis senator*, &c.; that the references

---

[1] The date of this *S. C.* is uncertain.   Most refer it to the time of Hadrian on the authority of Just. iii. 3 § 2 ; others to that of Ant. Pius on the authority of Zonaras XII. 1 p. 593 c, and on the fact that a Tertullus was consul A.D. 158. See Schirmer *Erbrecht* I. n. 87.

to the law of the Bithynians and Galatians were really made by
Hadrian, and Gaius merely reports them ; and in any case other jurisconsults inquired into the law of the provinces (Gell. xx. 1. § 4 ;
Dosith. 12) ; that the examples used by Gaius shew that he lived at
Rome, not in Asia, e.g. *si nauis ex Asia uenerit* (D. XXVIII. 5. 1 33) ;
*si inter eos qui Romae sunt, talis fiat stipulatio 'Hodie Carthagine
dare spondes?'* (D. XLV. 1. 1 141. § 4 ; &c.) ; *si is qui ita stipulatus
fuerit 'x milia Ephesi dare spondes?'...Romae pure sic intenderit*
(*Inst.* IV. 53) &c.; and that even in the extracts from the books *ad
edict. prou.* he speaks of *fundus Tusculanus, uinum Campanum,
triticum Africum* (D. XLV. 1.   34) &c.; speaks of the praetor instead
of the proconsul (D. XXXV. 3. 1 11) ; names as the day for prayers
for the emperor the third day after *Kal. Jan.*, which applied to
Rome and not to the provinces ; &c.   Gaius (says Huschke) may
have been a Greek born in some Roman colony in the East,
and certainly shews the open mind and theoretical training and
bent which you would expect from a Greek intellect.

Dernburg (*Die Institutionen des Gaius*, pp. 89, 90) points to the
mention of the praetor, not the proconsul, &c. in such places as III.
224; II. 163; III. 57; IV. 165; &c. as evidence of the writer's
familiarity with the practice of the Roman courts rather than of the
provincial governors.   Kuntze (*Der Provincialjurist Gaius*, 1883,
p. 5) refers to such expressions as *apud peregrinos non similiter ut
apud nos, in tutela sunt feminae* (Gai. I. 193), *qualem nos habemus*
(ib. 55), *quod nos telum appellamus, illi* βέλος *appellant* (D. L. 16.
1 233; cf. 1 236) as implying a contrast between Gaius' position and
that of foreigners, but suggests that though a Greek by birth (e.g.
freedman or freedman's son) he was a Roman citizen.   Bremer suggests that Berytus was a famous law school, and that if we suppose
Gaius to have been born in Troas but to have lectured at Berytus,
we meet Huschke's difficulties.

I cannot see that there is sufficient to convince one on either
side.   The combination is certainly attractive for Mommsen's hypothesis ; and it would to some extent perhaps account for Gaius
being apparently so long unknown, or at least, unquoted.   That
Gaius was a professor and not a consulting lawyer is very probable ; and that he was a Greek, as Ulpian was a Tyrian, is likely
enough.   As professor there is nothing very strange in his com-
menting on the XII tables, or on the stores of old civil law contained in Q. Mucius Scaevola's work, and it requires no special

explanation how a man of a literary and antiquarian turn came to quote Solon's laws or give odd pieces of information about the laws of foreign nations. Indeed it would be strange if a writer on the *edictum prouinciale* did not pick up such matters. The entire absence of any other name than Gaius is certainly remarkable, but this must be taken in connexion with the fact that he is never mentioned till the 5th or 6th centuries, and then only as the writer of certain books. These books no doubt bore only the name of Gaius: why, remains a mystery. Other Greek writers were not content with only a Roman praenomen. Moreover the facts that he was first recognized as an authority in the Western provinces, and that none of his writings are in Greek, as some of Modestin's and one of Papinian's were, do not seem to favour Mommsen's hypothesis. That Troas was not very far from Constantinople can scarcely have had any influence on Justinian's recognition of him. Justinian followed Theodosius, and the law of Theodosius and Valentinian was issued at Ravenna. Troas was not a law school then, or at any time, so far as we know. Gaius' supposed ignorance of the *S. C. Tertullianum* is probably a wrong inference from the silence of the MS. There is a gap in the MS. in its present condition in the very place where the *S. C.* would be mentioned (III. 33) and, besides the incompleteness of the MS., Gaius' plan, whatever it was, certainly led to some other omissions, which can hardly be attributed to ignorance, e. g. the *S. Consulta Uelleianum* and *Macedonianum* are not mentioned (see below, p. clxxxi). The question of what is meant by the *edictum prouinciale* is interesting and requires a few words.

Mommsen denies absolutely that there was or could be any generally applicable provincial edict. The substance no doubt of the edict in various provinces was to a large extent the same, because it included a great deal of the city edict (see above, p. clxiv), but formally each province had its own edict, issued by its own governor, and binding only within his jurisdiction. No other meaning occurs to Mommsen for Gaius' naming it *edictum prouinciale*, than that it was the edict of the province in which Gaius lived. A general provincial edict is as unreal as a general man (*Z. R. G.* IX. p. 96; *Staatsrecht*, II². 213). As an authority on such a point there is none greater than Mommsen. Yet I cannot think this either an adequate interpretation of the words or the easiest hypothesis on the subject. It is very improbable that in Gaius' time, after Julian had revised or 'composed' the edict, whatever may have been the import of that term, the governors in all the different provinces continued to exercise the same power of promulgating a fresh legislative code which they did exercise in the days of Cicero. For nearly two hundred years the legislative and controlling power had ceased to be dispersed among a variety of offices, and exercised with a quasi-independent authority in the various isolated countries subject to the Roman power : it had been gathered up in the person of the Emperor, and administered in his name or under his influence in what were now parts of one consolidated empire. Subordinate details may have been still variable and varied, but the recognition and enforcement of contracts, wills, and inheritances of provincials must have been regulated on the same general principles, though modified according to the customs of the country, in Asia and Syria, in Macedonia and Africa, in Spain and Gaul. These general principles would have a common shape, which would not indeed be identical with the city edict but partly identical, partly modified, partly perhaps differently conceived. Whether Julian did to this what he did to the similar body of law, which composed the main part of each city-praetor's edict, we do not know, but there is nothing to shew that he did not. Our knowledge of his work and procedure is meagre at best : and it seems improbable that there should not have been felt the same necessity for revising the one as the other. The provinces were more important relatively to Rome in the time of Hadrian than they were in the time of Cicero, and the more completely they were incorporated as members of one empire, the more desirable it would be that the common basis of their ordinary legal business should be revised. The fact, that Gaius' work was handled by Tribonian and his colleagues *pari passu* with Ulpian and Paul's works on the edict, shews (and this Mommsen agrees to) that materially they coincided to a considerable extent. But they would probably coincide still more largely when viewed under the light of Justinian's own changes of the law and his confirmations of the changes already wrought by previous legislation or by practice. For these changes assimilated the law of Rome to the law of the world[1]. The extension by Caracalla of Roman citizenship to the whole world, the decay and omission of the old conveyances by *mancipatio* and *in iure cessio*, the development of *usucapio* into *longi temporis praescriptio*, the practical substitution of written acknowledgments of debt or

---

[1] On *ius gentium* see the careful examination in Clark's *Pract. Jur.* ch. xiv.

promissory notes for the old *litterarum obligatio* (Gai. III. 133, 134), the cessation of marriage with *conuentio in manum*, the abolition of the differences of the four forms of legacy, and other changes would have been already long before acted on in the edicts for the provinces, though in what shape, whether by aid of fictions (cf. Gai. IV. 37, 38), or by direct and simple forms, we do not know. Nor is it possible to say whether what Gaius commented on was the traditional common part of the provincial edicts, or a revision by Julian, sanctioned by Hadrian. But that the name *edictum prouinciale* should have been given to such a usual and common part of provincial edicts seems to me natural enough. And I doubt whether each provincial governor actually on entering office during the empire would formally promulgate *in extenso* such usual and common part. A general reference would probably suffice. That the edict of a single province would be commented on in thirty books by Gaius, that such a book would survive till Justinian's time, and be used by him along with the great books on the Praetor's Edict, and that the name of such a work would be not *Asiaticum* but *prouinciale*, I do not believe[1].

Turning now to the list of Gaius' works, the Florentine Index mentions thirteen, viz. 32 books on the Provincial Edict (no doubt, including two on the Aediles' Edict), a work on the urban edict of which it states 10 books only were found, 15 books *ad leges*, six books on the XII Tables, seven books *aureorum*, four books of Institutes, three books *de uerborum obligationibus*, three books *de manumissionibus*, two books on Trusts, and four single books on Cases, Rules, Dowry and Hypothec.

Of these the Institutes only is preserved to us independently of the Digest. Niebuhr's discovery of it (A.D. 1816) in the library of the Chapter at Verona, and the first notices of it will be found in Savigny's *Verm. Schr.* III. p. 155 sqq. Since the first decipherment of it by Goeschen and Bethmann-Hollweg, it has been reexamined by Bluhme, and finally by Studemund, who has issued both an exact copy of it page by page and line by line (*Apographum* 1874) and, in conjunction with P. Krüger, a handy edition of it. Ed. Böcking's editions and *Apographum* are (except for the notes) superseded by these. Huschke's edition is remarkable for learning and ingenuity,

---

[1] Mommsen expressly says that Gaius commented on the edict of his province, i.e. Asia, and yet he agrees that it is an absurdity to suppose him to have written in thirty books on the edict of a single province (see *Z. R. G.* l. c. and *Staatsrecht* l. c.). I cannot reconcile these statements.

but is too conjectural to be safely used, except as checked by others. Dubois has in the most painstaking way reprinted the Studemund text, and given the most exact account of the readings of all the editors (Paris, 1881). Those who have not Studemund's *Apographum* will find this edition largely to supply the place. He has also made a list of the more important passages where Studemund's new reading of the palimpsest throws new light. Of English works (at present) only Prof. Muirhead's scholarly edition is based on Studemund's collation, but this objection to other editions will doubtless be soon removed.

The Institutes were written according to Dernburg in A.D. 161, part, viz. Book I. and the greater part of Book II., at least as far as § 151, before the death of Anton. Pius, the rest including II. 195 after his death, and published at once. Ant. Pius died 6 or 7 March. Mommsen refers the second book entirely to the time of Marcus Antoninus (*Z. R. G.* IX. 107). Huschke agrees with Dernburg as to the second book, but thinks the books were published separately. This seems to have been the first institutional treatise in the history of Roman law. Its style, its omission of some important matters (*dos, commodatum, depositum, pignus, obligationes quasi ex contractu,* and *quasi ex delicto,* several important *senatus consulta, peculium castrense,* the *querela inofficiosi test.* (Dernburg *Gaius* p. 37), its unequal treatment of some matters compared with others, its repetitions (comp. I. 22 with III. 56 ; I. 156 with III. 10; II. 35—37 with III. 85—87; II. 86—96 with III. 163—166; III. 181 with IV. 106—108) have been adduced by Dernburg as evidence that the work was notes for lectures, and, if so, was probably written for the session January to July of 161 A.D. and published by himself.

Fitting refers to the reign of Ant. Pius the commentaries on the provincial and urban edicts, and perhaps the books on verbal obligations and on the XII tables. After the death of Pius come the books on the Julian and Pap. Poppaean law and on trusts. After 178 A.D. comes the treatise on the *S. C. Orfitianum.* In the Institutes Gaius speaks of having previously written on the Edict and also of two other works not named in the Florentine Index, *Libri ex Q. Mucio* (I. 185) and *de bonorum successione* (III. 33, 54).

The commentary on the provincial edict contributes numerous extracts to the Digest. The extracts occupy 33 of Hommel's pages. Some of the longer extracts are D. XIII. 6. 1 18 ; XV. 1. 1 27 ; XVIII. 1. 1 35 ; XIX. 2. 1 25 ; XXXV. 2. 1 73. There are a few extracts from a work on the Curule Edict in 2 books, which added to the 30 books, *ad ed. prou.*, from which extracts are found, make up the 32 books attributed to the latter by the Index.

Of the commentary *ad edictum urbicum*, or, as named in the Digest *ad ed. praetoris urbani* the Index says the compilers found only 10 books. The treatises referred to in the Digest, as part of this, are quoted not by the number of the particular book of the commentary but by the subject-matter: viz. *de testamentis*, in 2 books (e.g. D. xxviii. 5. 1 32; 1 33); *de legatis* in 3 books (D. xxx. 1 65; 1 69; 1 73); or by a particular title, viz. the first four titles of D. xxxix. (1 19; 1 28; 1 19; ix. 4. 1 30; xxxix. 3. 1 13; 4. 1 5; xix. 1. 1 19); *de liberali causa* (D. xl. 12. 1 2; 1 9); *de re iudicata* (D. xlii. 1. 1 7); *de praediatoribus* (D. xxiii. 3. 1 54) and *qui neque sequantur neque ducantur* (D. l. 16. 1 48). One extract from a work *de tacitis fideicommissis* (D. xxxiv. 9. 1 23), and one from a work *de S.C. Tertulliano* (D. xxxviii. 17. 1 8), are also found. The work *ad leges* in 15 books is doubtless represented in the Digest by a number of extracts *ad legem Iuliam et Papiam*. A '*lex Glicia*', from a work on which one extract is taken (D. v. 2. 1 4), is otherwise unknown. The four *libri singulares* named by Justinian (Const. *Omnem*, § 1 above p. xxvi) as then forming part of the regular instruction, may be identified respectively with the treatise called *Dotalicion* in the Flor. Index (from which there is no extract) and the parts of the commentary on the city praetor's edict on guardianship (Gai. i. 185), testaments and legacies.

The treatise called '*aureorum*' in the Index is that named in Justinian's preface to the Institutes as *Res cottidianae*. Both names are given in the Digest, in xli. 1. Long extracts of an institutional character are found in that title and in xliv. 7 and xvii. 1. 1 2. Much of them has passed also into Justinian's *Institutes*. The work *de casibus*, from which there are several short extracts, did not relate apparently to actual, but only to hypothetical, cases or points.

The total number of extracts from Gaius in the Digest are 535. They occupy 63 of Hommel's pages. Gaius is never quoted by other lawyers unless any of the four passages named above (p. clxxv) refer to him.

The style of Gaius is that of an accomplished teacher. It shews clear analysis of the subject-matter, neat division definitely expressed, with ease and precision. There are no superfluous words, and the

words are well adapted to give the meaning.   The Latin is easy and
good.   Lachmann (*Kl. Schr.* p. 229) speaks of the 'noble elegance' of
his style.   The almost uniform current of praise which had prevailed
has been somewhat broken of late, especially by Kuntze (*Excurs.*
p. 338, ed. 2) who considers him to have second-rate ability, and
talks of his want of precise thought, of his errors in legal history,
and his trivialities and awkwardnesses.   And quite recently he has
enlarged upon this in a pamphlet called *Der Provinzial-jurist Gaius
wissenschaftlich abgeschätzt*, Leipzig, 1883.   This criticism is well and
clearly expressed, but the perspective is unhistorical and therefore
wrong.   Gaius cannot be judged as if he lived in the days of historical
criticism, or had been trained in a German school of scientific law.
There is no doubt a certain *naiveté* about his explanations of the
origin of laws, which reminds us of our own Blackstone.   Like
Blackstone too he wrote *ad populum*, at least in his Institutes.   And
Gaius certainly hit the right mean between pedantic precision and
loose generality of statement.   It is more difficult to criticise the
extracts in the Digest, because one can never be sure they have come
to us as Gaius wrote them.   As for errors in legal history, how many
lawyers, not specially schooled to it, write without them? and what
ancient writer is better than Gaius?   Kuntze however, after all,
calls Gaius a clever and accomplished teacher, though without creative
force or a creator's conscious independence.   The praise at least we
may accept, and perhaps suspend the blame, until we have some other
work of Gaius, continuous and authentic, of a character better adapted
to shew creative power than a first book for students.

UENULEIUS SATURNINUS is named in the Florentine Index (immediately after Gaius) as the author of five works: *Stipulationes* in 19
books; *Actiones* in 10 books; *de officio proconsulis* four books; three
books of *Publica* (*iudicia*), and one book *de poenis paganorum*.

There are in the Digest 71 extracts from the works of Venuleius
filling 10 of Hommel's pages.   Of these the *Stipulationes* occupy
four; the rest are from the *Actiones*, the *de officio proconsulis*, the
Publica iudicia and another work (perhaps part of the *Actiones*, but)
called in the inscriptions of the extracts *Interdicta*.   One of the four
extracts from the *de officio proconsulis* (XL. 14. 1 2) is inscribed simply
Saturninus (not *Uenuleius Sat.*).   These works were written after
the death of Hadrian and refer to no one later than Julian.   There
is no extract from a work of Venuleius *de poenis paganorum*.   (In

D. XLVI. 7. 1 18 *disputationum* seems to be a mistake for *stipulationum*.)

But in D. XLVIII. 19. 1 16 immediately following an extract from Venul. Saturn. *de off. procons.* is an extract from Claudius Saturninus *libro singulari de poenis paganorum.* And rescripts of Pius to Claudius Saturninus are mentioned in D. XX. 3. 1 1. § 2 ; L. 7. 1 5. (4.) pr. In D. XVII. 1. 1 6. § 7 a Claudius Saturninus is mentioned as praetor. Tertullian (*Cor. Mil.* 7) speaks in high terms of a treatise by Claudius Saturninus respecting chaplets (*de coronis liber*). See Teuffel-Schwabe[4], *Nachtr.* p. 1211.

Some (e.g. Fitting) consider these to be the same person, Claudius Venuleius Saturninus. Teuffel-Schwabe objects that there is nothing in the extracts from Venuleius, which is at all similar to quotations from Demosthenes and Homer, such as we find in Cl. Saturninus. The matter is further complicated by D. XII. 2. 1 13. § 5, which speaks of Quintus Saturninus agreeing with Marcellus, and XXXIV. 2. 1 19. § 7 in which Q. Saturninus' tenth book *ad edictum* is mentioned. But, except the name Saturninus, there is nothing to connect him with the other jurists or jurist so named. Ulpian in three places (D. I. 9. 1 1. § 1 ; XLVII. 14. 1 1. § 4 ; 18. 1 1. pr.) and Modestin in XLVIII. 3. 1 14. § 7 quote Saturninus.

Cod. VII. 35. 1 1 ; V. 65. 1 1 seem to have nothing to do with the jurist.

Of the longer extracts from Venuleius are D. XLII. 8. 1 25 ; XLIII. 24. 1 22 ; XLIV. 3. 1 15 ; XLV. 1. 1 137 ; XLVI. 8. 1 8 ; XLVIII. 2. 1 12. Huschke conjecturally attributes to Venuleius Vat. Fr. 90—93.

MARCELLUS, i.e. L. ULPIUS MARCELLUS was in the legal council of Antoninus Pius, and also, as we know from his own words, in that of Marcus Antoninus (Spart. *Ant. P.* 12 ; D. XXVIII. 4. 1 3). He was also imperial legate *pro praetore* in Lower Pannonia, as we learn from an inscription found at Sopianae, now Fünfkirchen, in Hungary. It records the performance of a vow to Virtue and Honour. *Uirtuti et Honori L. Ulpius Marcellus Leg. Aug. pr. pr. Pannon. inf. u. s.* (i.e. *uotum soluit, Corp. I. L.* III. no. 3307 ; cf. 3306).

The Epitomator of Dio Cass. LXXII. 8 speaks of an Ulpius Marcellus as sent by Commodus against the Britons, who had crossed the wall. He is described as very moderate and economical, of lofty spirit, superior to bribes, but not pleasant or sociable. Sleepless himself, he used to send written messages at different hours of the night to the several officers. He had his bread from Rome, not because he preferred it to the bread of the country but that from its staleness and hardness it might not tempt him to eat too much. His success against the Britons was sufficient to excite against him the jealousy of Commodus. Mommsen (note on above inscr.) treats Dio's Marcellus as different from the lawyer : others think the legate in Pannonia and commander in Britain was son of the jurist (Teuffel Schwabe⁴, § 360. 8). Most writers identify them ; but there is some difficulty in supposing him to have been sent to Britain for such a task, at least 25 years after he had a seat in the imperial council.

According to the Florentine Index Marcellus wrote *Digesta* in 31 books, six books *ad leges* (*Iuliam et Pap. Poppaeam?*), and one book of *responsa*. He also appears in the Digest as an annotator on Julian (see above) and on Pomponius (D. XXVIII. 1. 1 16 ; XXIX. 2. 1 63 ; XLIX. 17. 1 10) : and the fifth book of a work *de officio consulis* is also quoted by Marcian (D. XL. 15. 1 1. §4). In two extracts from a book *de officio praesidis* (D. XL. 15. 1 1. § 4) and from another called *Publica* (D. III. 2. 1 22) the name of Marcellus is generally considered to be a mistake for that of Macer, who is known to have written such works. One expression of Ulpian's has become almost proverbial, as if a thing must be very plainly true for Marcellus to abandon criticism and agree with Julian : *et ait Iulianus teneri, et est uerissimum, cum et Marcellus sentit* (D. IX. 2. 1 27. § 3) ; cf. Cujac. *Observ.* XIV. 35. It is quite possible that Ulpian only meant to emphasize the weight due to the consentient opinions of two lawyers of such high authority, without implying any over-captiousness on the part of Marcellus. Ulpian wrote notes on Marcellus (D. XX. 1. 1 27 ; XXVI. 7. 1 28 ; XXIX. 7. 1 9).

There are in the Digest 161 extracts from Marcellus, including the two supposed to be really from Macer. All but a few are from the *Digesta*, which, according to Fitting, was written under the *Diui fratres* A.D. 161—167. The extracts from Marcellus are mostly short and therefore occupy only 21 of Hommel's pages. But there are 253 citations of Marcellus. See also Vat. Fr. 75, 82, 84. The following extracts are of fair length : XXIII. 3. 1 39 ; XXIV. 3. 1 57 ; XXVIII. 4. 1 3 ; XXXV. 2. 1 56 ; XXXVI. 1. 1 44 ; XL. 5. 1 56 ; XLVI. 3. 1 72. That from the 28th book is specially noticeable, as giving in some detail an account of the argument in a case where a testator had run his pen through the names of the heirs, and the crown claimed the property as escheated.   Hadrian after some doubt upheld the legacies and freedoms as still valid.   Marcellus was acting as an assessor to the emperor (*in cognitione principis*).

TARRUNTENUS PATERNUS, called by Dio Πάτερνος Ταρρουτήνιος, was Latin secretary to Marcus Antoninus, and was appointed by him to command a band of Cotini in an expedition against the Marcomanni (Bohemia).   He was ill treated by them, and the Cotini were destroyed (Dio LXXI. 12).   Under Commodus we find him Captain of the Guard.   He was apparently confederate with Quadratus in his conspiracy against Commodus, and, on Quadratus and others being put to death, he with the other *praefecti praetorio* caused Saoterus, a disgraceful favourite of Commodus, to be killed. Paternus was removed from his office and made a senator, but in a few days after was charged with conspiracy to make Salvius Julianus emperor and give him his daughter in marriage.   Both Paternus and Julianus were put to death A.D. 183 (Dio LXXII. 5; Lamprid. *Com.* 4; 14).   Paternus wrote a work in four books *de re militari*, from which two extracts are found in the Digest XLIX. 16. 1 7; L. 6. 1 6.   He is also quoted by Macer, D. XLIX. 16. 1 12. Vegetius made use of this work in writing his own, and calls Paternus *diligentissimus iuris militaris adsertor* (Veget. *Mil.* I. 8).

SCAEUOLA i.e. Q. CERUIDIUS SCAEUOLA.   The full name occurs in D. XXVIII. 6. 1 38. § 3.   This jurist was M. Antoninus's chief legal adviser (Capit. *M. Ant.* II).   One case decided by the emperor is related by Scaevola himself, as Ulpian informs us D. XXXVI. 1. 1 23. (22.) pr. Papinian and Severus, afterwards the emperor Septimius Severus, were among his pupils (Spart. *Carac.* 8).   Nothing more is known of his life.   His writings mentioned in the Florentine Index were *Digesta* in 40 books, written, according to Fitting, during the reign of Marc. Antoninus and probably after the death of Verus, i.e. after A.D. 169 : *Quaestiones* in 20 books, written under Commodus or later : *Responsa* in 6 books, written not earlier than Sept. Severus, as O. Hirschfeld infers from the use of the word *praefectus legionis* (D. XXVI. 7. 1 47. § 4) instead of *praefectus castrorum* (*Hermes* XII. p. 142) : *Regulae* in four books : one book *de quaestione familiae* and one of *Quaestiones publice tractatae*.   Some notes of his on Julian and Marcellus are also cited (D. II. 14. 1 54; XVIII. 6. 1 11; XXIV. 1. 1 11. § 6; XXXV. 2. 1 56. § 2).   Claudius Tryphoninus (D. XVIII.

7. 1 10; xxxiv. 1. 1 15. § 1; 1 16. § 2, &c.) and Paulus (D. v. 2.
1 13; xl. 9. 1 26) wrote notes on his writings.   Both call him *noster*,
Tryphonin twice, Paul nine times.   Modestin speaks of him together
with Paulus and Ulpian as οἱ κορυφαῖοι τῶν νομικῶν, and in a constitution of the emperors Arcadius and Theodosius he is called
auctor prudentissimus iurisconsultorum (Cod. Theod. iv. 4. 1 5).   One
of the notes of Claud. Tryphoninus is often quoted as a tribute to his
great ability: but in truth Tryphoninus (D. xxxv. 1. 1 109) is merely
sarcastic.   The case was this.   A testator appointed two heirs and
requested one *ut acceptis centum nummis restitueret hereditatem Titiae
coheredi suae*.   Both heir and heiress enter on the inheritance, and
die before the 100 sesterces are given.   Titia's heir, desirous of getting
the trust-inheritance, offers 100 sesterces.   Can he claim to have this
inheritance (or share of the inheritance)?   Scaevola answered 'The
heir cannot obey the condition', meaning apparently that, if it was
a condition of the trust that Titia should give the 100 sesterces, Titia
being now dead, the condition cannot be fulfilled (cf. D. xxx. 1 104.
§ 1).   Tryphoninus on this remarks that it was clever of Scaevola to
confine his answer to a plain point of law, though there was room
for doubt whether there was any condition at all (*magno ingenio
de iure aperto respondit, cum potest dubitari an in proposito condicio
esset*).   Tryphonin means that *acceptis centum nummis* may be interpreted 'My will is that you take 100 sesterces (out of the inheritance I leave you) and restore the rest to Titia' (cf. D. xxxv.
2. 1 93).   It seems to be simply a harmless ironical compliment to
Scaevola for avoiding the real difficulty and merely repeating what
every one knew.   See Cujac. *ad D.* xxxii. 41 (Vol. viii. p. 99).

Scaevola is an important contributor to the Digest.   There are
306 extracts; and many of these are of considerable length, so that
they fill 74½ of Hommel's pages, 44 of which are extracts from the
Digesta, and 20 from the *Responsa*.   Besides these there are 61
citations.   In the books of the Digest, treating of legacies, the
extracts from Scaevola's *Digesta* and *Responsa*, are especially long and
important.   See xxxi. 11 88, 89; xxxii. 1 32—1 42; xxxiii. titles
1. 2. 7; xxxiv. titles 1 and 3; xxxvi. 1. 1 77 (75)—82 (80); xl. 5.
1 41; 7. 1 40.   Some interesting cases are given in D. xlv. 1. 1 122.
The general character of the extracts from Scaevola's *Digesta* and
Responsa is that of a string of cases, the facts being stated with
neatness and precision, and the opinion or decision of Scaevola added
in very brief terms, sometimes with reasons, often with none.   The

Quaestiones contained more discussions. See e.g. D. III. 5. 1 8 (9);
1 34 (35); XXI. 2. 1 69; XXIX. 7. 1 14. The extract given in XXVIII.
2. 1 29 is notorious for its difficulty.

It is not unusual to find passages from Scaevola twice over in
the Digest and even in the same book. Fitting points out that the
cases are given with a fuller statement of the facts in the extracts
from Scaevola's *Digesta*, and that in those from the *Responsa* they
are either abridged or have general names (e.g. *Titius, Maeuius*) substituted for the actual names. Hence he concludes that the *Responsa*
was subsequent to the *Digesta*. Mommsen, holding that *Digesta*
was a term applied to an orderly arrangement of the collected works
of a lawyer, puts the *Digesta* as late as after the time of Alexander
Severus (*Z. R. G.* VII. p. 484). But Tryphoninus, who lived under
Sept. Severus, commented on the *Digesta*, and Paulus refers to a
case which is also found quoted from Scaevola's *Digesta*. It is possible that Tryphoninus' notes may have been made on the separate
treatises and republished in the *Digesta;* and that Paul may have
got the case from the *Responsa*. But Fitting's arrangement seems
the simpler. That *Digesta* may have meant 'collected works' is possible enough, but it may have also meant 'collected cases', and been
used in that sense by Scaevola.

The following comparisons are interesting.

D. XXXII. 1 93. pr. (Scaev. *Resp.*) abridged from 1 38. § 4 (Scaev.
Digest).

D. ib. § 1 (Scaev. *Resp.*) abridged from XXXIV. 3. 1 28. §§ 13,
14 (Scaev. *Digest*).

D. ib. § 5 (Scaev. *Resp.*) nearly same as 1 38. § 8. (Scaev.
Digest).

D. XXXVI. 2. 1 28 (Scaev. *Resp.*) abridged from XXXIII. 7. 1 28.
(Scaev. *Digest*).

D. XXXIV. 3. 1 31. §§ 2, 3 (Scaev. *Resp.*) has general names for the
historical names given in 1 26. § 4 (Scaev. *Digest*): but § 3 of the
former is omitted in the latter.

D. XLIX. 1. 1 24. pr. (Sc. *Resp.*) is made more general, by the addition of the cases of a *tutor* and *curator*, than XLII. 2. 1 64 (Sc. *Dig.*).

Paul in his *libri ad Uitellium* has apparently copied Scaevola
(Mommsen *ad D.* XXXII. 1 78): thus

D. VII. 1. 1 50 (Paul.) quotes with name a case given D. XXXIII. 2.
1 32. § 5 (Scaev. *Digest*).

D. XXXII. 1 78. pr. (Paul.) abridged from XXXIII. 7. 1 20. § 6 (Scaev. *Resp.*).

D. XXXII. 1 78. § 2 same as XXXII. 1 93. § 2 (Scaev. *Digesta*).

D. XXXII. 1 78. § 3 more specific than XXXII. 1 101. § 1 (Scaev. *Digest*).

And compare XXVIII. 2. 1 19; XXXIII. 4. 1 16. esp. § 4 sqq.; 7. 1 18; XXXIV. 2. 1 32.

PAPIRIUS JUSTUS is named (as Justus) in the Florentine Index, immediately before Ulpian, as author of *Constitutiones* in 20 books. In the Digest there are 18 extracts, eight of which are taken from the first book, nine from the second book, and one from the eighth book. This last is a rescript of *Imperator* Antoninus addressed to Avidius Cassius. The others are all rescripts from *Imperatores* Antoninus and Verus. Fitting refers the work to the time of Commodus. The extracts occupy two of Hommel's pages. Of the longer are XLIX. 1. 1 21; L. 1. 1 38; 8. ll 10—12 (1 9).

PAPIRIUS FRONTO is cited four times in the Digest, viz. twice by Callistratus, D. XIV. 2. 1 4; L. 16. 1 220. § 1 (*Papirius Fronto libro tertio Responsorum ait*); twice by Marcianus, XV. 1. 1 40; XXX. 1 114. § 7 (*Scaeuola notat et Papirius Fronto scribit*).

TERTULLIANUS is named in the Florentine Index (between Gaius and Ulpian) as the author of two works: *Quaestiones* in eight books, and a single book *de castrensi peculio.* From this last there are three short extracts in the Digest XXIX. 1. 1 23; 1 33; XLIX. 17. 1 4. The Code v. 70. 1 7. § 1 *a* refers to the same book, and calls him *iuris antiqui interpres.* From the *Quaestiones* there are two extracts, D. I. 3. 1 27; XLI. 1. 1 28. These five extracts occupy one page of Hommel. Ulpian cites him in the third book *ad Sabin.* D. XXVIII. 5. 1 3. § 2 *et sane et Iuliano et Tertulliano hoc uidetur :* in the eighth book *ad Sabin.* D. XXIX. 2. 1 30. § 6 *quod et Sextum Pomponium opinatum Tertullianus libro quarto quaestionum refert ;* and in his 13th book *ad Sabin.* D. XXXVIII. 17. 1 2. § 44 *quod et in magistratibus municipalibus tractatur apud Tertullianum, et putat dandam in eos actionem.*

It is clear that he wrote after Pomponius and before Ulpian's *Libri ad Sabinum,* i. e. before Caracalla's sole reign. More than this is only conjectural. There seems to be no reason for connecting him with the *S. C. Tertullianum* (see p. clxxvi n.). But it is an interesting question whether, as is generally thought, the jurist is the same person as the great ecclesiastical writer, Q. Septimius Florens Tertullianus, who is said by Hieronymus (*de Uit. illustr.* 53) to have flourished under Severus and Caracalla, to have been from Carthage, and the son of a 'proconsular' centurion (a description which Dessau, *Hermes* xv. p. 473, suggests is due to Jerome's misunderstanding Tert. *Apolog.* 9). Eusebius (*Hist. Eccl.* II. 2) describes the ecclesiastic as τοὺς Ῥωμαίων νόμους ἠκριβηκὼς ἀνὴρ τά τε ἄλλα εὔδοξος καὶ τῶν μάλιστα ἐπὶ Ῥώμης λαμπρῶν. Neander (*Antignosticus* p. 202 Bohn's transl.) thinks there is sufficient in the method of argument and controversial tactics of the ecclesiastic to enable us to recognize a trained advocate, and in the juridical cast of his language and in his comparisons borrowed from law to find palpable evidence of his early studies. But Neander still hesitates to identify the two in consequence of the frequent occurrence of the name. The extracts in the Digest are few, and we have no other knowledge of the jurist, so that there is really no sufficient evidence for a decision. Mommsen (*Z. R. G.* VII. 485) notices that the word *Digesta* is hardly used except in juristic literature ; but that Tertullian uses it of the Gospels (*adv. Marc.* IV. 3 ; ib. 5) and (*ad Nat.* 1) of Varro's sources (*ex omnibus retro digestis*).

Messius is once quoted by Paul (*libro tertio decretorum*) in D. XLIX. 14. 1 50 *Papinianus et Messius nouam sententiam induxerunt.*

Paconius is once quoted by Paul (*libro octauo ad Plautum*) in D. XXXVII. 12. 1 3. There is in Cod. v. 37. 1 6 a rescript addressed by Alex. Severus to A. Paconius, who may or may not be the same man. Mommsen reads *Paconius* in XIII. 6. 11. § 1 where Flor. and others have *Pacunius*, and others again *Pacuuius.*

Claudius Tryphoninus was a contemporary of Papinian, and was perhaps in the council of the emperor, see D. XLIX. 14. 1 50. He wrote notes on Scaevola's *Digest*, which are often (20 times) given in the Digest appended to extracts from Scaevola. Sometimes they have been treated as separate extracts, e.g. XXXII. 1 36 ; XXXIV. 9. 1 26 Mommsen ; XL. 5. 1 17. His notes are generally given under the name of Claudius ; but Claudius Tryphoninus is found in XXVI. 7. 1 58. He calls Scaevola '*noster*' (D. XX. 5. 1 12. § 1 ; XLIX. 17. 1 19. pr.). A rescript is addressed to him under his full name by

Antoninus (Caracalla) A.D. 213 (Cod. I. 9. 1 1). The only work named in the Florentine Index is his *Disputationes* in 21 books. The date of its composition is about the time of Caracalla. In the 10th book (D. XLVIII. 19. 1 39) he speaks of a rescript *ab optimis imperatoribus nostris*, which Fitting refers to Caracalla and Geta, for in the earlier books (D. XXVII. 1. 1 44; XLIX. 15. 1 12. § 17; cf. III. 1. 1 11) he speaks of Severus as dead.

The Digest contains 80 extracts from his *Disputationes*. They fill 18 to 19 of Hommel's pages. Some of the longer extracts are XVI. 3. 1 31; XXIII. 2. 1 67; 3. 1 78; XXVI. 7. 1 55; XXXVII. 4. 1 20; XLI. 1. 1 63; XLIX. 15. 1 12; 17. 1 19. A good extract is L. 16. 1 225. In XLVIII. 19. 1 39 he refers to Cicero's speech for Cluentius.

CHAPTER XIV.

PAPINIAN, ULPIAN, PAUL.

AEMILIUS PAPINIANUS was said by some to be a relative of Severus' second wife, Julia Domna. As she was from Emessa in Syria (Capit. *Macrin.* 9), it is possible that Papinian was also from that province (Bremer p. 88). The first we hear of him is, that he with Severus adopted the legal profession at Rome under Scaevola (*cum Seuero professum*[1] *sub Scaeuola*), that is to say after attending Scaevola's lectures and public consultations, he commenced advising and teaching, while retaining in some way the advantage of Scaevola's assistance. He succeeded Severus in the office of Counsel to the Treasury (*Advocatus fisci* Spart. *Car.* 8) and afterwards was Master of Petitions and thus framed the imperial rescripts (*rescriptum ab imperatore libellos agente Papiniano* D. XX. 5. 1 12. pr.). He was probably an assessor in the court of the *praefecti praetorio* (D. XXII. 1. 1 3. § 3). Under Severus his great friend we find him A.D. 204 Captain of the Guard (*praefectus praetorio*,

---

[1] *Profiteri* 'to declare oneself as teacher, jurisconsult, &c.' is used of a teacher of rhetoric in Plin. *Ep.* II. 18; IV. 11 *passim;* of lawyers, D. I. 2. 1 2. § 35; of mathematicians (Lampr. *Alex.* 27). Hence 'professor'. On the subject generally see Puchta *Cursus* § 103; Bremer *Die Rechtslehrer* &c. p. 16, who take *profiteri* to mean a declaration before a public authority (*magister census*), so as to found a claim for exemption from public burdens. Cf. Vat. Fr. § 204; D. XXVII. 1. 1 6 § 12; Cod. x. 53 (52).

ὁ ἔπαρχος Dio Cass. LXXVI. 10), an office which combined military power with the highest criminal and civil jurisdiction (cf. Mommsen *Staats-Recht* II. pp. 828, 932, 1058). There were usually two or three in this office (ib. p. 831 n.). He attended the emperor in Britain (Dio ib. 14), probably up to the time of the death of Severus at York in A.D. 211. Dio mentions an attempt made there by Caracalla to murder his father ; the attempt was seen and frustrated. Severus summoned Caracalla and Papinian to his tent, put a sword in the midst and told Caracalla to ʻslay him if he wished, or, if he chose, to tell Papinian to do it, as he would of course execute at once a command from Caracalla' (who was emperor with Severus). I take this as merely the language of natural excitement and bitter grief, and not justifying any inference whatever as to Papinian's loyalty to Severus. Before his death Severus specially commended his two sons Bassianus (Caracalla) and Geta (Spart. *Car.* 8) to him. Caracalla dismissed Papinian from office (Dio LXXVII. 1), very probably on his dissuading him from killing his brother Geta. Caracalla persevered, and the death of Geta was followed in a day or two by that of Papinian (A.D. 212), whom he regarded as one of Geta's party (cf. Zosim. I. 9). The emperor dissembled his intention, and leaning on Papinian's shoulder was coming from the Capitol to the Palatium, when the soldiers seized Papinian and hurried him to his death. He is said to have warned them that his successor would certainly be a great fool if he did not avenge such a cruel outrage on the office of praefect,—a prophecy supposed to be fulfilled when Macrinus holding the office planned the death of Caracalla (Spart. ib.). This story seems inconsistent with Dio's statement of Papinian's having been dismissed from office before ; and it would have had more point, if the vengeance had fallen on praetorians who killed their own commander. A soldier killed Papinian with an axe. He was reproved by Caracalla for not having done his bidding with a sword (Dio LXXVII. 4 ; Spart. *Car.* 4), that being the proper instrument for putting criminals to death (D. XLVIII. 19. 1 8. § 1 : hence the expression *ius gladii habere* D. I. 18. 1 6. § 8 ; cf. 16. 1 6. pr.). The precise cause of his murder was variously reported. The more general account was that, on the emperor's requiring him to address the Senate and the people in excuse for the murder of Geta, Papinian replied that ʻparricide was not so easy to defend as to commit.' Another version was that being requested to compose for the emperor a speech justifying the murder by invective against Geta he declined, saying that to accuse an innocent man who had been slain was to repeat the parricide.   Both accounts may have been true, notwithstanding Spartian's stupid objection that the prefect could not *dictare orationem (Carac.* 8. cf. Hirschfeld *Untersuch.* I. p. 213. n.). Papinian's son, a quaestor, was killed also (ib. 4).

The court over which Papinian presided included at some time Ulpian and Paul as assessors (Spart. *Pescen.* 7 ; Lampr. *Alex. Sev.* 26 ; cf. D. XII. 1. 1 40).   No Roman law-court could have been stronger. Papinian's own reputation has received loud and constant recognition from that time to this.   Spartian (*Sever.* 21) calls him *iuris asylum et doctrinae legalis thesaurum.*   Not to mention such epithets as *consultissimus, disertissimus,* &c. the constitution of Constantine, by which the criticisms even of Ulpian and Paul on Papinian's legal opinions were to be disallowed, is clear proof of his high authority (Cod. Theod. I. 4. 1 1. quoted above, p. lxxxiv.).   This direction was confirmed by the well-known 'Law of citations' (ib. 1 3, also quoted) of Theodosius II. and Valentinianus III., which in disputed questions gave a casting vote to the opinion of Papinian.   *Ubi diuersae sententiae proferuntur, potior numerus uincat auctorum, uel, si numerus aequalis sit, eius partis praecedat auctoritas, in qua excellentis ingenii uir Papinianus emineat, qui ut singulos uincit, ita cedit duobus.* Zosimus (5th century) calls him a most just man, and one who surpassed all Roman lawgivers before and after in knowledge and interpretation of the laws (I. 9).   The third year students were called after him *Papinianistae,* his *Responsa* forming one of the chief subjects of instruction at that period of legal study.   The first lecture on Papinian was celebrated by a feast.   Justinian confirmed this practice and name and feast, and is loud in his praises of Papinian.   He is *splendidissimus, summi ingenii* (Const. *Deo* § 6), *sublimissimus, acutissimus, pulcherrimus, maximus* (Const. *Omnem* §§ 1, 4).   The students were to have a taste of the other works of Papinian besides the *Responsa;* and in one of the books of the Digest (xx.) which was to be lectured on in the third year, Justinian has dislocated the proper order of extracts in order to get Papinian at the commencement of all the titles in which his works are quoted.   *Uobis ipse pulcherrimus Papinianus non solum ex responsis, quae in decem et nouem libros composita fuerant, sed etiam ex libris septem et triginta quaestionum et gemino uolumine definitionum nec non de adulteris et paene omni eius expositione in omni*

R.   *n*

nostrorum digestorum ordinatione praefulgens, propriis partibus prae-
clarus sui recitationem praebebit. Ne autem tertii anni auditores,
quos Papinianistas uocant, nomen et festiuitatem eius amittere ui-
deantur, ipse iterum in tertium annum per bellissimam machina-
tionem introductus est; librum enim hypothecariae ex primordiis
plenum eiusdem maximi Papiniani fecimus lectione, ut et nomen ex
eo habeant et Papinianistae uocentur et eius reminiscentes et laeti-
ficentur et festum diem, quem, cum primum leges eius accipiebant,
celebrare solebant, peragant, et maneat uiri sublimissimi praefectorii
Papiniani et per hoc in aeternum memoria hocque termine tertii anni
doctrina concludatur (ib. 4). Cujas commented on the whole of the
extracts from Papinian which appear in the Digest, and these commentaries, published after his death, fill a thick folio, or 1150 double-
columned pages of the Prati edition in quarto. He calls Papinian 'the
greatest lawyer that has been or will be: he occupies the same
single preeminence among jurisconsults that Homer does among
poets' (*Praef.* to Comment. IV. p. 558 Prati). Puchta justifies the
admiration of ages for Papinian by his long political services, his
high office, his greatness as practical jurist and writer, in which last
respect very few can be compared with him, and above all by the
integrity of his character and the moral force, which gave nobility to
the whole of an active life and made him the model of a true jurist
(*Cursus* § 100). Similarly Rudorff *R. G.* I. § 73. Mommsen speaks
of him as without doubt the first of Roman jurists in juristic geniality
and living sense of right and morality, but at the same time perhaps
the least Roman in his thoughts and language (*Z. R. G.* IX. p. 100).
Kuntze echoes the praise (*Cursus* § 321).

The style of Papinian is generally very close, the intention being
to give the case or the opinion in as few words as possible. Esmarch
is rapturous in admiration: 'clear and deep thought, with completely adequate expression; no word too much or too little; every
word exactly in the right place; worthy of the best days of the
Romans, &c.' (*Röm. R. G.* § 133, ed. 2). I agree with Mommsen in
thinking the style not characteristically Roman. The construction is
sometimes strained, and the words used in meanings not those of
classical writers.

There is in many passages (cited by Kuntze *Cursus* § 321) a very
noticeable sense of the dignity and worth of family relations and of
ethical propriety. Some instances may be given. Thus where the
vendor of a slave has bargained (below p. 186) that he should not

be kept in Italy, and the purchaser has broken the condition, Papinian held that a pecuniary interest must be shewn in order to entitle the vendor to claim satisfaction. The standard was *quod uir bonus arbitratur*, and it was not conformable to the character of a good man to believe that the mere gratification of spiteful feeling should found a claim for damages. On the other hand if the vendor bargained that the slave should not be shipped to foreign parts, the purchaser might be liable in damages for the breach, even if there were no pecuniary loss to the vendor, provided that the condition had been imposed from kindly feeling towards the slave. The law might fitly recognise human affection as an interest, while it refused to recognise vengeance (*beneficio adfici hominem interest hominis*) D. xviii. 7. 1 6. § 1 ; 1 7. Similarly xvii. 1. 1 54. pr. *placuit prudentioribus affectus rationem in bonae fidei iudiciis habendam.*

A father institutes his unemancipated son as heir, but only on a condition which the laws disapprove. Such a condition, said Papinian, must be regarded as one which it is not in the son's power to perform : for any acts which offend against due affection, reputation or modesty, must be considered as acts which we not only ought not, but cannot, do. *Quae facta laedunt pietatem existimationem uerecundiam nostram et, ut generaliter dixerim, contra bonos mores fiunt, nec facere nos posse credendum est* (D. xxviii. 7. 1 15).

A testator used no words of express trust, but contented himself by declaring that he had no doubt that whatever his wife took under the will she would restore to their children. Marcus Antoninus ruled that it should be enforced as a trust. Papinian commends the rescript on the ground that otherwise the father would be deceived in shewing due respect to a wedded life well past and trust in their common children (D. xxxi. 1 67. § 10).

See also xiii. 5. 1 25. § 1 ; xxviii. 2. 1 23. pr.; xxxv. 1. 1 72. § 1 ; xxxix. 5. 1 31. § 1.

He mentions in one place a change of opinion; the compilers have subjoined the old opinion in the next extract (D. xviii. 7. 1 6. § 1 ; 1 7. Cf. Cod. vi. 2. 1 22. § 3a). This is an instance of what was perhaps a not uncommon practice of the compilers, viz. when they came to a reference or citation of some other book or author to add or substitute the original. See e. g. D. i. 6. 1 2 quoted above, p. lxiv : and the suggestions made (p. lvi.) in reference to D. vii. 1. 1 33.

The Florentine Index enumerates his works used in the Digest (and we know of no others) as *Quaestiones* in 37 books; *Responsa* in 19 books; *Definitiones* in two books, *de Adulteriis* in two books, and also in one book, and a treatise in one book called ἀστυνομικὸς. Papinian's name occurs second in this Index, Julian's alone being put before him. Only two of his works bear indications of the date of composition. The greater part of the *Quaestiones* (Book XVII. onwards) was, according to Fitting, written in the reign of Sept. Severus. Of the *Responsa* the fourth book was written after A.D. 206, for it contained a discussion of the terms of a constitution of that year (cf. D. XXIV. 1. 1 32. § 16 ; 1 53). Very probably the whole work was subsequent to that date and was perhaps Papinian's last work. It is noticeable that, while with one exception the title of consecration (*divus*) is regularly given to deceased emperors in the *Responsa*, in the *Quaestiones* on the other hand it is omitted 20 times, against 13 that it is added. So Mommsen, who suggests that Papinian had at first not thoroughly learnt the official style. The treatise ἀστυνομικὸς was written in Greek. We have an extract in D. XLIII. 10. 1 1. The corresponding Latin title would be *de officio aedilium*. Bremer arguing from this, as well as from his reported relationship to Julia Domna, and from some references to provincial matters which occur in his writings, thinks that he for a time lectured at Berytus. Thibaut (*Civ. Abh.* p. 140) also points out that a Greek treatise on aedile's duties would probably be intended for aediles in Greek towns.

The number of extracts from Papinian in the Digest is 601. They occupy 92 pages of Hommel, of which the *Quaestiones* supply 45 pages, the *Responsa* 40. There are 153 citations besides. The Vatican Fragments have about 50 extracts (almost all from the *Responsa*), some of which also appear in the Digest. A few passages are contained in the *Collatio* (II. 3 ; IV. 7—11 ; VI. 6), one passage of two lines (*de pactis*) is given at the end of the *lex Uisigothorum*. A few mutilated bits of the *Responsa* have been lately discovered. See Krüger *Z. R. G.* XIV. 93 ; XV. 83 ; Huschke *Die jüngst aufgefundenen Bruchstücke* &c. The following parts of the Digest have series of extracts from Papinian, some extracts being of considerable length (XXVI. 7. ll 35—42 ; XXXI. ll 64—80 ; XXXV. 2. ll 7—15 ; XLVI. 3. ll 94—97). In book XX. he commences all the titles save one. Notes of Paul are found in D. I. 21. 1 1. § 1 ; XVIII. 1. 1 72 ; XXII. 1. 1 1. § 2 ; and of Ulpian in D. III. 5. 1 30 (31). § 2.

DOMITIUS ULPIANUS was born at Tyre, or at least of a Tyrian family, as he tells us himself in recounting the colonies which had the *ius Italicum.* (*In Syria Phoenice splendidissima Tyriorum colonia, unde mihi origo est.* The right was conferred by Severus and Caracalla. D. L. 15. 1 1. pr.). From his occasional mention of the Punic language (D. XXXII. 1 11. pr.; XLV. 1. 1 1. § 6) and references to Egypt, Asia and Syria, Bremer suggests that he was resident for a time in those parts, probably as professor at Berytus (*Die Rechtschulen*, p. 87). But the first we hear of him is as assessor, apparently with Paul, to Papinian, and afterwards as either *ad memoriam* i.e. master of the records, or *ad libellos* i.e. master of petitions, Paul holding the other office (Spart. *Pescen.* 7). Some said he was *praefectus praetorio* under Heliogabalus; at any rate he was, with the senate and others, removed by that emperor from the city, and was ordered to be slain, but the order was not carried out (Lampr. *Heliog.* 16; *Alex.* 26). Under Alexander Severus we find him *praefectus annonae* (commissioner of corn supply) on 31 March, 222 (Cod. VIII. 37. (38) 1 4), and captain of the guard 1 Dec., of the same year (Cod. IV. 65. 1 4). Alexander was only 16 years old when he came to the throne (Lampr. *Alex.* 60 ; Gibbon ch. vi. n. 47) and obviously required guidance. Lampridius tells us that he made, or again made, Ulpian and Paulus captains of the guard, and therefore senators; that Ulpian was one of his councillors and master of a portfolio (*scrinii ad libellos*?); further that he acted as his guardian, though against the wish of Alexander's mother, who however was afterwards thankful for it; that he was the only person who had private interviews with the emperor and was always summoned when anyone else had an interview, was present at his private dinners, and was in fact a constant companion and chief minister (*Alex.* 21; 26; 31; 34; 51; 67). Dio confirms this, saying that Ulpian was made *praef. praet.* immediately on Alexander's succession, and administered the affairs of the Empire (LXXX. 1). Probably the Tyrian origin of Ulpian may have contributed to his selection, Alexander's parents being from Emessa, also in the district of Phoenician Syria. Zosimus (I. 11) makes his appointment directly due to Alexander's mother, Mamaea. Alexander calls him *parens meus* and *amicus* (Cod. *l. c.*). He is said to have been exposed to danger from the soldiers on several occasions, and to have been protected only by the emperor's throwing his purple over him (Lampr. *Alex.* 51). A three days' tumult between the soldiers and populace, in which the former attempted to burn the city down, was apparently connected with Ulpian, who is said amongst other reforms to have displaced Flavianus and Chrestus (captains of the guard?) in order to succeed them. Soon afterwards the Praetorians set on him in the night, and, though he fled for refuge to the emperor and the empress-mother, at the palace, killed him (Dio LXXX. 2). It is likely enough that he fell in an effort to reduce the military under the civil power. Epagathus, who was the instigator of the attack, was sent off to Egypt under the pretext of being made governor, and from thence was taken to Crete and executed. It was not safe to attempt to punish him in Rome (ib.).

One specific recommendation on the part of Ulpian and Paul is recorded. Alexander thought of ordering a distinct dress for all offices, for all positions of dignity, and for all slaves. The jurists dissuaded him on the ground that it would lead to quarrels if men were thus marked out for insults. The emperor contented himself with distinguishing knights from senators by the character of the band on the *toga* (*claui qualitate*, Lampr. *Alex.* 27).

Athenaeus in his 'Learned diners' introduces, as one of the guests and talkers, Ulpian of Tyre, who went by the name of Κειτούκειτος, because he was perpetually asking people in the streets, promenades, bookshops and baths whether this or that word was found in a particular use or sense κεῖται ἢ οὐ κεῖται; 'Does it or does it not occur?' (I. 1). He is called a rhetorician, gives (xv. 20—33) an account of a number of special names for crowns or chaplets (στέφανοι), and ending his discourse with an expression subsequently taken as an omen, died easily (ἀπέθανεν εὐτυχῶς οὐδένα καιρὸν νόσῳ παραδούς) a few days after to the great grief of his friends. Athenaeus wrote this somewhere about the time of Ulpian the jurisconsult, and he introduces among the other personages at least one well-known philosopher of the time, Galen of Pergamos, the great physician who died after A.D. 199. Another personage is Masurius, a jurist (Athen. I. 2). Now Lampridius (*Heliog.* 16) after mentioning the removal of the senate from Rome, says *Sabinum consularem uirum, ad quem libros Ulpianus scripsit, quod in urbe remansisset, uocato centurione mollioribus uerbis (Heliogabalus) iussit occidi.* The centurion however was happily deaf. Lampridius goes on *Remouit et Ulpianum iuris consultum ut bonum uirum.* Ulpian as we know wrote a long treatise *ad Sabinum*, and Sabinus' name was Masurius (D. I. 2. 1 2. §§ 48—50). Doubtless Lampridius confused the great lawyer of Tiberius' reign with a descendant who was a contemporary of Ulpian and may have been a lawyer. The coincidences of 'Ulpian of Tyre' with Masurius a lawyer in Athenaeus, of Ulpian the lawyer with Sabinus, 'on' or 'to whom Ulpian wrote,' in Lampridius, and the fact that Ulpian wrote a long treatise on the lawyer Masurius Sabinus are certainly very curious. But it can hardly be (as some have thought) that Athenaeus meant to place our Ulpian among his banqueters. Neither profession, nor character, nor death agree. It may be that the rhetorician Ulpian was the father of the lawyer.

Ulpian never names Paul: Paul once only (D. xix. 1. 1 43) names Ulpian. Ulpian speaks of Modestin as his admirer (*quod et Herennio Modestino studioso meo de Dalmatia consulenti rescripsi* D. xlvii. 2. 1 52. § 20) i.e. probably a pupil. There are so few lawyers after Ulpian, of whom we have extracts, that he is rarely quoted. Macer refers to him (l. 5. 1 5), and Modestin calls him ὁ κράτιστος (xxvi. 6. 1 2. § 5; xxvii. 1. 1 2. § 9; 1 4. § 1) and speaks of Cervidius Scaevola, Paulus and Domitius Ulpianus as οἱ κορυφαῖοι τῶν νομικῶν (1 13. § 2). Of the historians Lampridius calls him *iuris peritissimus* (*Alex.* 68), and Zosimus (i. 11) describes him as an excellent lawgiver (νομοθέτης), able to deal with circumstances of the time, and to forecast the future, an inspector (ἐπιγνώμων) of, and almost a partner in, the imperial power. Diocletian (Cod. ix. 41. 1 11) gives him the ordinary epithet of *prudentissimus;* Justinian (Cod. vi. 51. § 9) calls him *summi ingenii uir* and (Nov. 97. § 6) τὸν σοφώτατον. But the greatest tribute to him is the use made of his writings in the Digest. They form the core, and more than a third in quantity, of the whole work.

In the Florentine Index 23 of his works are mentioned; two of which are very important, the Commentary on the Edict in 81 books, to which two books on the Edict of Curule Aediles are appended, making 83 in all; and 51 books *ad Sabinum*. Fitting (not regarding the use of *imperator* as any indication of the emperor being alive at the time of the book being written, p. 3) puts Books i.—viii. of the Commentary on the Edict before a.d. 211; ix.—l. in the reign of Caracalla (a.d. 211—217); then the Commentary on Sabinus, as far as xxxiii., during the same reign; and the rest of this commentary, and finally Books li. to end of the Commentary on the Edict, after Caracalla's death (p. 43). Apart from the question of the use of *imperator*, this view throws an enormous amount of work on the few years of Caracalla's sole reign. Mommsen with greater probability holds that the greater part of the Edict-Commentary was written before the death of Severus, but was partly revised, completed and published about A. D. 212 (*Z. R. G.* IX. 102, 114). Under Caracalla were written the 10 books *ad leges* (*Iul. et Pap. Pop.*); 10 books of *Disputationes*; 10 books *de omnibus tribunalibus*; 10 books *de officio Proconsulis*; six books on *Fideicommissa*; six books *de censibus*; three books *de officio Consulis*; 2 books of *Institutiones*, and one book *de officio praetoris tutelaris* which Mommsen (Vat. Fr. 4to edit. p. 395) thinks to be a second edition of a work *de excusationibus*, not named in the Index but probably written and published in Severus's reign. Later than Caracalla are the five books *de adulteriis*. In or after Caracalla's reign come the four books *de appellationibus* and the single books *de off. praefecti Urbi*, *Regulae* and *Pandectae*. The last-named is quoted from in the Digest, but a Πανδέκτον in 10 books is named in the Index. A work in four books *ad leg. Ael. Sentiam* and *de off. consularum* (one book) are similarly not named, but furnish extracts. Some notes to Papinian (see p. cxcvi) and Marcellus (p. clxxxv) are also given in the Digest.

Independently of the Digest we have preserved to us 29 titles from an abridgement of Ulpian's single book of *Regulae*; and a few fragments from his *Institutiones*. The *Regulae* follow to a considerable extent the order of Gaius' Institutes but are more concise. The author evidently was familiar with Gaius' work. They have been edited by Böcking 1855 (with a discussion by Mommsen), by Huschke, and by Krüger. The fragments of the *Institutiones* have been edited with supplements from the Digest and *Collatio* by Böcking, and also by Krüger in his *Kritische Versuche* 1870. The *Collatio* has 13 extracts from the *de officio Proconsulis*, five from the *Institutiones*, three from the *Regulae*, and three from the Edict Commentary. The Vatican Fragments have over 100 extracts from treatises *de excusationibus* and *de officio praet. tutelaris*, 24 extracts from the XVIIth book of the Commentary on Sabinus (this book relates to usufruct) and some others. Many of these extracts are however badly mutilated.

The treatise *de officio Proconsulis* has been made the subject of a special dissertation by Rudorff, who has collected and arranged all the fragments preserved to us (Berlin 1860). The seventh book contained an account of the legislation against the Christians, which excited Lactantius' (*Inst.* v. 11, 12) vigorous criticism. Ulpian is there called *Domitius*.

In the Digest there are 2464 extracts from Ulpian. They occupy

590 of Hommel's pages. Of these pages the extracts from the Edict-Commentary fill 342, besides 10 on the Edict of the Curule Aediles; from that on Sabinus 130; from the Disputations 25; *Fideicommissa* 17; *de off. Proconsulis* 15; and the *opiniones* about 9; *ad leges Iul. et Pap.* 8, and from the treatises *de adulteriis* and *de omnibus tribunalibus* 6 or 7 pages each.

Ulpian's style is easy and good. There is often a good deal of discussion of the reasons, and quotation of others' opinions. Originally it contained still more discussion and quotation, as we can see from comparing some passages in the Vatican Fragments with their counterparts in the Digest. (See above p. lxxiii foll.)

JULIUS PAULUS was a contemporary of Ulpian's, and the few facts known of his life have been already mentioned in the account of Papinian and of Ulpian. He was an assessor to Papinian in the reign of Severus, and apparently master of the records (Spart. *Pescen.* 7). By Heliogabalus or Alexander he was made one of the captains of the guard (*praef. praetorio*) and, probably as such one of Alexander's council, and agreed with Ulpian in dissuading that emperor from his proposal to have officials, dignities and slaves marked each by a special dress (Lampr. *Alex.* 26; 27; 68). He refers to his presence in the emperor's council on certain law questions in D. IV. 4. 1 38; XXIX. 2. 1 97; XLIX. 15. 1 50, and in Papinian's court D. XII. 1. 1 40. A case in which he appeared as advocate before the *Praetor fideicommissarius* is mentioned in D. XXXII. 1 78. § 6.

Artemidorus (*Oneirocr.* IV. 80) tells us that 'Paulus the lawyer' dreamt when engaged in a suit before the emperor that Νίκων (*Victor ?*) was counsel with him, and hence felt sure, from the significance of the name, that he would win. But Nicon had failed once before in a suit before the emperor; the dream was really ominous of failure, and failure accordingly ensued to Paulus. It seems probable that this is a story of our Paulus (Tzschirner *Z. R. G.* XII. 150 sqq.). In another case in which he was consulted we hear of an opinion of Ulpian's being adduced (D. XIX. 1. 1 43). He speaks frequently of '*Scaeuola noster*', which probably implies that Scaevola was his teacher (cf. above pp. clxxv, clxxxvii). Epithets like *iuris peritissimus* (Lampr. *Alex.* 68) and *prudentissimus* (Gordian in Cod. v. 4. 1 6, Diocletian in Cod. IX. 22. 1 11) are of course applied to him.

As a writer he was exceedingly prolific. No less than 70 works of his are named in the Florentine Index, many of them with similar titles to those of Ulpian. (One is named twice over.) His chief works were a commentary on the Edict in 80 books; *Quaestiones* in 26 books, *Responsa* in 23 books; *Brevia* in 23 books; and commentaries on Sabinus in 16 books, and on Plautius in 18 books. He also wrote four books on Vitellius (which Mommsen (*ad* D. XXXII. 2. 1 78) holds to have been in great part compiled by direct copying from Scaevola's *Responsa*, comparing D. VII. 1. 1 50; XXVIII. 2. 1 19; XXXII. 1 78. §§ 1, 2, 3; XXXIII. 4. 1 16; 7. 1 18; XXXIV. 2. 1 32 with the passage of Scaevola referred to in his notes) and four books on Neratius, probably an edition of Neratius with notes. Some short notes of his on Papinian and Scaevola are found in the Digest (above pp. clxxxvii, cxcvi), and one note on Marcellus' notes on Julian (D. XV. 3. 1 14). Further, he epitomized Alfenus Varus' Digest and Labeo's 'Probabilities,' neither of which abridgements are named in the Florentine Index. He also wrote 10 books *ad leges* (*Iul. et Pap. Popp.*), three *ad leg. Ael. Sentiam*, three on Trusts; *de censibus* (two books) *de iure fisci* (two books); *de officio Proconsulis* (two books) *de adulteriis* (three books); *Decreta* (three books), several manuals viz. *Regulae* in seven books, and also in one book; *Sententiae* six books and also five books; Institutes (two books) *Manualia* (three books). His 48 monographs are on all parts of the law, wills, codicils, inheritance, degrees of relationship and affinity, secret trusts, patronage, gifts of freedom, gifts between husband and wife, guardianships; several important statutes (*leges Cincia, Vellaea, Falcidia*) and senate's decrees (*Orfitianum, Tertullianum, Silanianum,* &c.); on interest and hypothec; on the duties of the captain of the watch, captain of the city, *praetor tutelaris;* on crimes and punishments, on public trials, on appeals, on actions, and on concurrent actions, on ignorance of fact and law, on unusual law (*de iure singulari*); &c.

There is little evidence as to the date of the composition. But of the more important treatises the *Decreta* were written under Severus and Caracalla's joint reign (A.D. 198—211) the *Sententiae* soon after Severus' death, the *Quaestiones* also under Caracalla, the earlier books of the *Responsa* under Elagabalus or Alexander and from the XIVth book under Alexander. The commentaries on the Edict and on Sabinus offer few indications of date. Fitting thinks they were probably written before A.D. 206, as the extracts in D. XXIV. 1 shew no knowledge of the *Oratio Severi et Antonini* named by Ulpian in 1 32. The 70th book of the Edict-Commentary contains a mention of Marcianus (D. VII. 9. 18), who also was apparently not an author till after Caracalla's death. So that unless we read *Maecianus*, as Fitting suggests, the work could not have been completed till much later. (See Mommsen *Z. R. G.* IX. p. 115, who also dissents from Fitting's notion (p. 25) that *noster* was used only of living persons.) He is cited in the Digest by Modestin v. 2. 1 9; XXVII. 1. 1 13. § 2 (who classes him with Papinian and Ulpian as a κορυφαῖος τῶν νομικῶν); and XXIX. 5. 1 18; and by Macer XXXVIII. 12. 1. 1; XLIX. 4. 1 2. § 3; 16. 1 13. § 5.

A considerable part of the *Sententiae* has come down to us in the code of the Visigoths (see p. clxxiv), and other parts of it have been preserved in the *Collatio*, which has 28 extracts from it, besides 11 from other works of Paul. The *Consultatio* has also a few extracts. The Vatican Fragments have 70 or more extracts from Paul, chiefly from the *Responsa*, the *Manualia*, and ·the part of the commentary on the Edict relating to the *lex Cincia*. The recognition of the *Sententiae* by Constantine and Theodosius has been already mentioned, p. lxxxiv.

There are 2081 extracts from Paul in the Digest. These occupy about 268 pages of Hommel, or more than a sixth of the whole Digest. Only Ulpian was a larger contributor. No one else occupies 100 pages. The extracts from the commentary on the Edict occupy 92 or (with the commentary on that of the Curule Aediles) 94 pages; the Sabinus commentary 31 pages; the *Quaestiones* 29, and the *Responsa* over 19; the books *ad Plautium* 22 pages, and the *Sententiae* 15. Of the others none fills seven pages.

Although the number of extracts from Paul is not much less than from Ulpian, the quantity of matter is less than half. The fact is, Ulpian was generally taken as the basis and interpolated with short additions from Paul and Gaius. But long extracts from Paul are found e.g. D. II. 14. 1 27; IV. 8. 1 32; X. 2. 1 25; XVII. 1. 1 22; 2. 1 65, XXXV. 2. 1 11; XXXIX. 2. 1 18; XLI. 2. 1 1; 1 3; 3. 1 4; 4. 1 2; XLV. 1. 1 83; 1 91.

CHAPTER XV.

LATEST JURISTS.

CALLISTRATUS was the author of five works named in the Florentine Index: *de cognitionibus* in six books; *edictum monitorium* (six books); *de iure fisci* (four books); *Instituta* in three books, and *Quaestiones* in two books. The *de iure fisci* and *Quaestiones* may have been written under Severus; the *de cognitionibus* was written under Severus and Caracalla (Fitting).

The Digest contains 101 extracts from Callistratus. They fill 15 of Hommel's pages. All the works are represented, but there are nine pages from the *de cognitionibus* and three from the *Quaestiones*. Some of the longer extracts are D. XIV. 2. 1 4; XXII. 5. 1 3; XXVII. 1. 1 17; XLVIII. 10. 1 15; 19. 1 28; XLIX. 14. 11 1– 3; L. 6. 1 6 (5).

Bremer infers from his frequent mention of the provinces that Callistratus wrote in some Greek town (*Die Rechtslehrer*, p. 97 sq.).

ARRIUS MENANDER is mentioned by Ulpian (Book XI. *ad edict.* D. IV. 4. 1 11. § 2) as being excused from a guardianship, because as councillor he was in attendance on the emperor (*circa principem occupatus*), probably the emperor Severus. The Florentine Index names one work *de re militari* in four books. The Digest has six extracts from it, viz. XL. 12. 1 29; XLIX. 16. 11 2, 4, 5, 6; 18. 1 1. They occupy about two of Hommel's pages. He is also cited by Macer in D. XXXVIII. 12. 1 1; XLVIII. 19. 1 14; XLIX. 16. 1 13. §§ 5, 6. The work was apparently written under Severus and Caracalla.

MARCIANUS (called in Just. IV. 3. § 1 *Aelius Marcianus*) is named in the Florentine Index as author of Institutes in 16 books, Rules in five books, two books on Appeals, two on *Publica* i.e. criminal trials, and single books on Informers (*de delatoribus*) and the action of Hypothec. The work on *Publica* is referred by Fitting to the time of Caracalla's sole reign; the Appeals were written after Severus' death; the others after Caracalla's death. A single book *ad S. Consultum Turpilianum* is not named in the Index, but a long extract occurs in D. XLVIII. 16. 1 1. There are 283 extracts from Marcian in the Digest. They fill more than 36 of Hommel's pages, those from the Institutes filling 16, and the Rules and Hypothec about six each. The Institutes have been used also by Tribonian in compiling Justinian's Institutes, some of the passages being the same as extracts in the Digest. His notes on Papinian's work *de adulteriis* are twice given as separate extracts : D. xxiii. 2. 1 57 a; xlviii. 5. 1 8.

Most of the extracts are short : but the work on hypothec has been extensively used in D. xx. e.g. 1. ll 5, 13, 16; 4. 1 12; 6. ll 5, 8. From the other works some of the longer passages are D. xxx. 1 114 ; xxxix. 4. 1 16 (which names a number of Eastern products liable to customs duties); xlviii. 10. 1 1; 16. 1 1; 21. 1 3 ; xlix. 14. 1 18 ; 1 22.

An *Aelius Marcianus* (hence perhaps the name given by the Institutes to our Marcian) is named as proconsul of Baetica in the time of Ant. Pius D. i. 6. 1 2 (called *Aurelius Marcianus* in *Collat.* iii. 3. § 1): a *Marcianus* is named as contemporary of M. Antoninus in D. iv. 2. 1 13 ; and rescripts are addressed *Marciano* in A.D. 223 (Cod. ii. 12 (13). 1 6), in 228 (Cod. vii. 21. 1 4) and 239 (Cod. iv. 21. 1 4). Possibly the last three were addressed to the jurist.

Macer (called *Aemilius Macer* in three places only, D. ii. 15. 1 13 ; xxviii. 1. 1 7; xxxv. 2. 1 68) appears in the Florentine Index as author of five works each in two books: *de re militari ; publica iudicia ; de officio praesidis ; ad legem uicensimam hereditatum ; de appellationibus.* The first four may have been written in Caracalla's time : the last belongs to that of Alexander Severus. There are 65 extracts in the Digest, they occupy 10 of Hommel's pages, most being from the *publica iudicia* and the *de appellationibus.* Of the longer passages are xxxv. 2. 1 68 ; xlii. 1. 1 63; xlix. 1. 1 4 ; 8. 1 1; 13; 16. 1 12 ; 1 13. Of these the first is especially interesting, because it gives the Roman rules for calculating the value of annuities (see below pp. 188—191).

Florentinus, author, according to the Florentine Index, of Institutes in 12 books. The only clue to his time is that he refers to a constitution of Divus Pius (D. xli. 1. 1 16), and is said not to be quoted by any other jurist. In Cod. iii. 28. 1 8, vi. 30. 1 2 are constitutions of A.D. 223 addressed to Florentinus, but as in the second he is called *miles*, there seems no ground for connecting him with the author of the Institutes.

Florentin's Institutes furnish 42 extracts to the Digest, all short. The longest are xxix. 1. 1 24 containing a rescript of Trajan;

XXX. 1 116; XLVI. 4. 1 18, containing the form devised by Gallus Aquilius for a comprehensive release. A few extracts have been used for Justinian's Institutes also.

JULIUS AQUILA, called in the Florentine Index *Gallus Aquila*, probably from a confusion with Gallus Aquilius. He wrote a book of *Responsa*, from which two extracts of three lines each are given in the Digest, XXVI. 7. 1 34; 10. 1 12, both of which very possibly relate to the same case, and decide that a ward's slaves may be questioned where the ward's curator is suspected. A decree of Severus on this matter (D. XXVII. 3. 1 1. § 3) is by some taken as probably subsequent (Zimmern), by others as prior, to this decision (Rudorff). He is placed in the Florentine Index between Marcian and Modestin; and the Index is roughly chronological. A Julius Aquila *qui de Etrusca disciplina scripsit* is named by Pliny among his authorities for the second and eleventh books, but that is probably much too early an author to be the jurist.

LICINNIUS RUFINUS was according to the Florentine Index author of Rules in 12 books. An extract from the 13th book is however given in the Digest (XLII. 1. 1 34). There are 16 other short extracts. He quotes Julian D. XXIII. 2. 1 51, and refers to Gallus Aquilius D. XXVIII. 5. 1 75 (74). But his date is fixed by an extract from Paul's book XII of *Quaestiones* (D. XL. 13. 1 4), in which his question to Paul and Paul's answer is given. Fitting holds the imperator Antoninus named in XXIV. 1. 1 41 to be Ant. Pius; Rudorff and Mommsen (*Z. R. G.* IX. 102) to be Caracalla.

HERENNIUS MODESTINUS was a pupil, or at least an admirer, of Ulpian, whom he wrote from Dalmatia to consult (above p. cxcix). He with others took part in the instruction of the younger Maximin (Capit. *Max.* 27) who was killed in A.D. 238. A constitution of Gordian's (Cod. III 42. 1 5) in A.D. 239 mentions a *responsum* given by Modestin '*non contemnendae auctoritatis iurisconsultus :*' and an inscription (*Corp. I. L.* VI. p. 50, No. 266, Bruns p. 259) gives an account of a suit against the Fullers' Company, in which they claimed immunity from rates. The suit was decided in their favour by the *Praefecti Uigilum* at Rome, among whom Herennius Modestinus is mentioned. It was begun in A.D. 226 and decided A.D. 244. Modestin is mentioned by Arcadius Charisius in D. L. 1 18. § 26, who agrees that the character of certain municipal functions was *ut Herennius Modestinus et notando et disputando bene et optime ratione decreuit.*

Fifteen works by Modestin are named in the Florentine Index, of which the principal are *Responsa* in 19 books; *Pandekton* in 12 books; *Regulae* in 10 books; *Differentiae* in 9 books; *Excusationes* in 6 books, and Punishments in 4 books. The others are all single books, and relate to marriage, dowry, wills, legacies and trusts, manumissions and other subjects of less defined character. According to Fitting the *Differentiae, Pandekton,* and *Excusationes* were written after the death of Caracalla A.D. 218, the Rules and Punishments (except the last book of the Punishments) probably in Caracalla's time. The *Excusationes* (i.e. grounds for excusing guardians from the duty) was written in Greek but with quotations from other writers and laws in their original Latin. It forms an important part of one title in the Digest (XXVII. 1). The commencement of the work is preserved (l 1). Although the Vatican Fragments contain a chapter on this subject, Modestin is not quoted: perhaps because he wrote in Greek, and the work of which we have fragments was intended for the western empire (cf. Huschke *Iur. Antiq.* p. 698). Two short passages from Modestin's Rules and Differences are preserved independently of the Digest (Huschke l.c. p. 626). On D. XLI. 1. ll 53, 54, see under Q. MUCIUS (p. cviii).

In the Digest there are 344 extracts from Modestin. They occupy 40 of Hommel's pages, of which the *Responsa* fill 11, the *Excusationes* 8, the *Regulae* $6\frac{1}{2}$, the *Pandekton* $5\frac{1}{2}$, and the *Differentiae* $3\frac{1}{2}$. All Modestin's works were dealt with by the Edictal Committee, and the extracts occur together, only Ulpian's work or works *de excusationibus* and *de off. praet. tutel.* being interspersed with Modestin's treatise on the same subject. The Latin extracts are generally short. The longer ones are XXVI. 7. 1 32; XXXI. 1 34; XXXVIII. 10. 1 4; XLIX. 16. 1 3; L. 1. 1 36.

ANTHUS or FURIUS ANTHIANUS, so called in the Florentine Index (where he stands last but two), wrote a work on the Edict, of which a part containing five books was handled by Justinian's Commissioners. From the first book three extracts, containing about 14 lines together, appear in the Digest II. 14. 1 62; IV. 4. 1 40; VI. 1. 1 80. All stand last in their respective titles. There is nothing to shew the time of his writing.

RUTILIUS MAXIMUS is named in the Florentine Index as author of one book on the Falcidian law. One extract of four lines is all that appears in the Digest (xxx. 1 125). Rudorff suggests that he is the same as the Maximus who is named in a mutilated Imperial rescript in Vat. Fr. § 113. In the Florentine Index he comes last but one.

HERMOGENIANUS, the last in the Florentine Index, was the author of *Iuris Epitomae* in six books. There are 107 extracts in the Digest. Being mostly short, they fill only $9\frac{1}{2}$ of Hommel's pages. Of the longer are xxxvii. 14. 1 21; xxxix. 5. 1 33; xlix. 14. 1 46; l. 4. 1 1 (xxxvi. 1. 1 15 is by Cujas and Mommsen given to Ulpian). He is generally held to have written about A.D. 339 (Mommsen Vat. Frag. larger edit. p. 399; Fitting *Z. G. R.* xi. 450) from his extracts, as they stand, shewing an acquaintance with changes made by Constantine (e.g. compare D. iv. 4. 1 17 with Cod. Theod. xi. 30. 1 16; &c.).

Whether he was the author of the *Codex Hermogenianus*, a collection of rescripts apparently intended as an appendix to the *Codex Gregorianus*, is doubtful. It is said there were several persons of the name about that time.

ARCADIUS, called in the inscription to D. i. 11. 1 1 *Aurelius Arcadius Charisius, magister libellorum*, is named in the Florentine Index as author of three single books on Witnesses, on the office of the *Praefecti praetorio*, and on civil functions (*muneribus*). From the last is one long extract in D. l. 4. 1 18; from the second one extract forming D. i. 11; from the first are four extracts D. xxii. 5. 1 1; 1 21; 1 25; xlviii. 18. 1 10. Together they fill $2\frac{1}{2}$ of Hommel's pages. He appears to be of the same age as Hermogenianus, and for the same reason: comp. D. i. 11. 1 1 with Cod. Theodos. l.c. He refers to Modestin in l. 4. 1 18. § 26.

CHAPTER XVI.

OF LAWYERS' LATIN[1].

SOME notice has been taken, in the course of the commentary on the title *de usufructu*, of certain usages and expressions which occurred in the text, but lawyers' Latin requires more general treatment. The subject has of course three sides, grammatical, lexicographical and rhetorical, and a full discussion would include careful distinction between the several lawyers as well as comparison with the lay writers of the period. The remarks which I shall make have no pretence to completeness, and deal only with some points, chiefly grammatical, which have caught my attention as at least unusual in classical Latin. The writers whom I regard here are mainly those used for the Digest. Neither the Theodosian nor the Justinian Codes come within my range.

The general style of lawyers' Latin before the middle of the third century *p. Chr.* is not studied and rhetorical, but rather the ordinary language of daily life and business among educated persons, loose in some respects, but from the requirements of the subject-matter brief and precise in others. On the whole it is simple, straightforward and pleasant; with numerous technical expressions, but free from pedantic tautology or circumlocution; frequently neat and compressed, but readily intelligible when the method and subject-matter are fairly familiar. The difficulties and obscurities, which we find, are due mainly at least to two causes. First, we seek to know more than the writer intended to say : we want answers on further points of law than were in contemplation either in the particular passages or even in the Digest at all; and doubt always arises when

---

[1] The only discussions of this subject that I am aware of are three. 1. Duker's *Opuscula uaria de Latinitate Jurisconsultorum*, 1773. This book consists mainly of some criticisms by Valla with replies and comments by others. They relate chiefly to the distinction between so-called synonyms ; and to the use of words by the lawyers for which there is little or no classical authority. I have scarcely found anything suitable for my purpose. 2. Brisson's *Parerga*, appended to his lexicon. This is a very painstaking collection of instances in the Florentine Digest of noticeable spellings, forms, words and phrases. Some of the instances are treated in Mommsen's edition as mere copyists' errors ; others are now recognised as correct forms or spellings : of the remainder I have found some useful. 3. An interesting abridgment of a forthcoming paper by W. Kalb on the Latin of Gaius, contained in Wölfflin's *Archiv für latein. Lexicographie* i. 1. 1884. I have named Kalb on the points where I have been indebted to this paper.

R.　　　　　　　　　　　　　　　　　　　　　　　　　　*o*

interpretation is made the means of development. Secondly, to the character of the Digest as a hasty compilation, made in the manner described above (chapp. iv. v.), may reasonably be attributed much of the obscurity and uncertainty that is found.

The latter point has an especial bearing on the grammatical side of the matter. The only pure sources of law Latin are inscriptions and reported *formulae* on the one hand, and Gaius, the Vatican Fragments and some few other fragments on the other. The former are most important and interesting as specimens of the ' Curial style', i.e. the style of conveyancers, pleaders and Parliamentary draftsmen, but of course are stiff and meagre. The latter are juristic literature, and therefore more freely written and more suited to our purpose. But neither of Gaius nor of the Vatican Fragments have we more than one MS to rest on, though, fortunately, that is, in each case, an earlier, and so far a purer, source than we have in the case of most classical authors. The *lex Dei*, or *Collatio Mosaicarum ac Roman-arum legum* rests on three MSS, but they are not good. Both Paul's *Sententiae* and Ulpian's *Regulae* are generally considered to have come to us only as abridged by some one of a much later age. The Digest, which alone is various enough to form a good basis for a study of juristic Latin, is difficult to trust in this matter. The combination of the copyist and corrector of the Florentine MS (see chap. xvii.) is fortunate as regards the text of Justinian's work, but this text itself is open to suspicion and something more. The writings of the Jurists have undergone manipulation, often of a rough and hasty character, from Greeks in a Greek-speaking country in the sixth century of our era, men who cared for law but not for the exactitude of their repre-sentation of the original authors, or for the niceties of style. The inference we should thence draw is supported by a comparison of Gaius' Institutes, and of the Jurists in the Vatican Fragments with the Digest. There is certainly more regularity of style about both the former than about many parts of the latter, while other parts leave little or nothing to desire. It is almost certain indeed that some *anacolutha* and the like are due to the scissors of the compilers, and accordingly I pass them over here (see notes on pp. 173, 192, 202, 249, &c.). Nor do I notice what are probably mere mistakes [1] of the copyists (noticed in Mommsen's edition).

---

[1] E.g. I do not believe that any Latin writer of this age would deliberately write *uix est ut legatarium uoluit dare* (D. xxx. 1 114. § 4), *uti exigeret et ea con-tentus erit* (xxxii. 1 37. § 4), *nemo dubitat quin non solet* (D. xxix, 2. 1 72); &c.

As compared with the language of Cicero and Quintilian the jurist Latin shews a development, in some respects reasonable enough, in others not unnatural but scarcely commendable. Of the uses of some forms and words we find previous instances in Plautus, Cato and Varro, who give us the language of common life, more than can be expected in the works of orators and rhetoricians. But the distinctive use of the indicative and subjunctive moods has somewhat lost its sharpness, and there is some vacillation in the use of primary and secondary tenses.

Moods and Conjunctions.

1. Nothing shews this more clearly than the use of moods and tenses in the hypothetical cases which occur in infinite numbers in the Digest. Cicero in the *de Officiis* III. 23 (Lat. Gr. §§ 1532, 1533) puts a number of such cases and uses the future indicative and present, &c. subjunctive indiscriminately, but whichever he selects he adheres to in that sentence. In the Digest it is different: there is a greater range of variety, and these varieties are found jostling one another in the same sentence. This may be best shewn by the comparison of another chapter of Cicero, which in some respects resembles the cases put in the Digest.

Cic. *Off.* III. 24. §§ 92, 93. *Si quis medicamentum cuipiam dederit ad aquam intercutem pepigeritque, si eo medicamento sanus factus esset, ne illo medicamento umquam postea uteretur, si eo medicamento sanus factus sit et annis aliquot post inciderit in eundem morbum nec ab eo, quicum pepigerat, impetret ut iterum eo liceat uti, quid faciendum sit? Cum sit is inhumanus, qui non concedat, nec ei quicquam fiat iniuriae, uitae et saluti consulendum. Quid? si qui sapiens rogatus sit ab eo, qui eum heredem faciat, 'cum ei testamento sestertium milies relinquatur, ut ante quam hereditatem adeat, luce palam in foro saltet,' idque se facturum promiserit, quod aliter heredem eum scripturus ille non esset, faciat quod promiserit necne? Promisisse nollem et id arbitror fuisse gravitatis. Quoniam promisit, si saltare in foro turpe ducet, honestius mentietur, si ex hereditate nihil ceperit, quam si ceperit, nisi forte eam pecuniam in rei publicae magnum aliquod tempus contulerit, ut uel saltare, quum patriae consulturus sit, turpe non sit.*

Here in the first sentence we have the subjunctive selected for the hypothesis, but it is used consistently in the apodosis *faciendum sit* as well as in the protasis *si dederit, pepigeritque…si factus sit… et inciderit nec impetret* (Cf. Lat. Gr. § 1532). The same is true of the third sentence. In the fifth sentence we have the future indicative selected, but it also is used consistently in the apodosis *mentietur* as well as in the protasis *si…ducet*. *Ceperit* and *contulerit* must here be taken as completed futures indicative (cf. Lat. Gr. § 1533).

Further the perfect subjunctives in the first and third sentences relate to time prior to the presents *impetret* and *faciat*. *Pepigerat* is pluperfect as relating to a time prior to *inciderit*, and indicative because it is in a relative clause defining the person already referred to as *quis*.

There is a difference in these two sentences in that the first has the imperfect *ne uteretur* following *pepigerit ;* the third has the present *ut adeat* following the like tense *rogatus sit*. Both are allowable : the choice of the imperfect in the first sentence is due to the desire to distinguish between the time of the covenant and the time when the covenanted event occurs. The covenant was past: hence *si factus esset, ne uteretur :* the occurrence is subsequent and regarded only as prior to *impetret*. The third sentence is somewhat differently framed and the distinction is unnecessary.

(*a*) Now in the Digest the consistency, or, as I may call it, the uniformity of key, is often not preserved, e.g.,

Si de me petisses, ut triclinium tibi sternerem et argentum ad ministerium praeberem, et fecero, deinde petisses ut idem sequenti die facerem, et, cum commode argentum domi referre non possem, ibi hoc reliquero et perierit, qua actione agi possit et cuius esset periculum ? (D. XIII. 6. 1 5. § 14 Ulp.)

Here *petisses* and *fecero, petisses* and *reliquero*, are not consistent : and *possit* as apodosis is not well adjusted to the diverse protases.

Si rem tuam, cum bona fide possiderem, pignori tibi dem ignoranti tuam esse, desino usucapere…Si rem pignori datam creditoris seruus subripuerit, cum eam creditor possideret, non interpellabitur usucapio debitoris (D. XLI. 3. 1 33. §§ 5, 6 Jul.).

Here *possiderem* does not suit with *dem* in time, nor *dem* with *desino* in mood. *Subripuerit*, if taken as perf. subj., does not suit with *interpellabitur*, nor, if taken as completed future, with *possideret*.

Si seruum hereditarium heres, qui coactus adierit, iussisset adire hereditatem ab alio eidem seruo relictam, et tunc hereditatem, quam suspectam sibi esse dixerat, restituerit, an etiam eam hereditatem quae

per seruum adquisita esset restituere deberet, quaesitum est (D. XXXVI. 1. 1 28. § 1 Jul.)

Here *iussisset* is subsequent in time to *adierit*, and *restituerit* is subsequent in time to, but coordinate in construction with, *iussisset*. *Dixerat* is similar to *pepigerat* in the passage of Cicero, and defines the inheritance as that first-named which he entered only by the prætor's order. The pluperfect subj. *iussisset* may perhaps, here and often, have been originally conceived as dependent on *quaesitum est*, but such a justification is also often absent.

Almost any page of the Digest will supply instances of harmony and disharmony in tenses and moods of these hypothetical cases.

(*b*)   One special cause for a disharmony, real or apparent, is the fact that the apodosis is usually in the present or future indicative, whatever be the tense and mood of the protasis. The cases are regarded as merely subjects for a judgment of the law or for a prediction of the result of an action, and whether the supposed facts are regarded as occurring in the past, present, or future makes no difference: variety and fluctuation in statement are therefore not unnatural. The real grammatical protasis to such apodoses as *tenetur, tenebitur, dicendum est, erit, ualet, uidebitur, cessat, liberabor*, &c. may be conceived to be a summary of the facts, in the form *si ita ut dixi res habet* or *habebit*.

(*c*)   The variety of tenses and moods is very great. *Si mandat, si mandet, si mandabit, si mandauerit, si mandauit, si mandabat, si mandaret, si mandauerat, si mandasset* are all found without any practical difference in meaning[1]. The subjunctive is not specially employed to denote that the hypothesis is unreal, nor the indicative that it is real, nor do the imperfect and pluperfect subjunctives 'imply impossibility' (cf. Lat. Gr. § 1497), though there are cases where their use is normal. The tenses most frequently used are the forms in *-eri-* and the corresponding passives. Next to these come the present and pluperfect subjunctive and the perfect indicative. The imperfects indic. and subj. and the pluperfect indicative are, I think, the rarest.

(*d*)   I fail to detect any difference in meaning or use in these sentences between *mandauero* and *mandauerim*, or between *mandatum sit* and *mandatum fuerit*. Compare D. XLVI. 1. 1 42 (Jav.) *si*

---

[1] In English many in putting hypothetical cases would use *if he is, if he be, if he shall, if he should, if he was, if he were, if he has, if he had*, &c., without substantial difference of meaning.

ita fideiussorem accepero...non obligatur fideiussor; 1 43 (Pomp.) *si fideiussorem te acceperim...confideiussores non erunt:* x. 3. 1 4. § 4 (Ulp.). *Eapropter scribit Iulianus, si missi in possessionem damni infecti simus et ante, quam possidere iuberemur, ego insulam fulsero, sumptum istum...consequi me non posse;* &c. The first person most frequently ends in *-ero* (e.g. *mandauero, stipulatus,* or *prohibitus fuero*).

(*e*) This tense or set of tenses usually seems to bear a future character, but it is qualified in subordinate clauses frequently by a past tense, less frequently by a present: viz.

Contemporaneous acts dependent on a sentence with *-eri-* are regularly, though not invariably, in the imperfect, preceding acts in the pluperfect.

A purpose with *ut,* and subsequent act with *antequam,* are usually expressed by the imperfect, though the present is not uncommon.

As illustrations may be taken :

Si, cum decem mihi deberes, pepigero, ne a te uiginti...petam, in decem prodesse tibi pacti conuenti uel doli exceptionem placet. Item si, cum uiginti deberes, pepigerim ne decem petam, efficeretur per exceptionem mihi opponendam, ut tantum reliqua decem exigere debeam (D. ii. 14. 1 27. § 5 Paul.).

Si liber homo, cum bona fide seruiret, mandauerit Titio ut redimeretur et...eam pecuniam dederit, quae erat ex peculio...ad bonae fidei emptorem pertinente, nullae ei mandari actiones possunt (D. xvii. 1. 1 8. § 5 Ulp.).

Si ei, cui damnatus ex causa fideiussoria fueram, heres postea exstitero, habebo mandati actionem (ib. 1 11 Pompon.).

Si ex pluribus heredibus unus, antequam ceteri adirent hereditatem, pecuniam quae sub poena debebatur a testatore omnem soluerit et hereditatem uendiderit nec a coheredibus suis propter egestatem eorum quicquam seruare poterit, cum emptore hereditatis recte experietur (D. xviii. 4. 1 18. pr. Jul.).

Si quis, cum falso sibi legatum adscribi curasset, decesserit, id heredi quoque extorquendum est (D. xlviii. 10. 1 4 Ulp.).

Si domino heres exstitero, qui non esset soluendo, cuius fundum tu mihi dare iussus esses, manebit tua obligatio (D. xxx. 1 108. § 6 Afric.).

2. The indicative is found (of non-existent hypothetical cases), in sentences of comparison (Lat. Gr. § 1580) where in classical Latin we

should have the subjunctive, e.g. *perinde ex his causis atque si erant falsarii puniuntur* (D. XLVIII. 10. 1 1. § 4 Marcian.); *pro eo habebitur atque si aditus est qui adiri debuit* (XLIX. 5. 1 5. § 3 Ulp.); *non uideor ui deiectus, qui deici non expectaui sed profugi. Aliter atque si, posteaquam armati ingressi sunt, tunc decessi* (IV. 2. 1 9. pr. Ulp.). (*Atque si* with subjunctive is frequent. Cf. Gai. III. 181 *unde fit ut, si legitimo iudicio debitum petiero, postea de eo ipso iure agere non possim...Aliter atque si imperio continente iudicio egerim.*)

3. *Cum* is frequently used both with indicative and subjunctive to introduce an hypothesis, and is practically the same as *si*.

Cum mandatu alieno pro te fideiusserim, non possum aduersus te habere actionem mandati : sed si utriusque mandatum intuitus id fecerim, habebo mandati actionem (D. XVII. 1. 1 21 Ulp.).

Cum seruus extero se mandat emendum, nullum mandatum est (ib. 1 54. pr. Pap.)

Cum extaret impubes qui se filium defuncti diceret, debitoresque negent eum filium esse defuncti, et intestati hereditatem ad adgnatum qui forte trans mare aberit pertinere, necessarium erit puero Carbonianum edictum (D. XXXVII. 10. 1 3. § 12 Ulp.).

4. *Cum* meaning 'since', is found in the Digest with the indicative, where classical Latin would have the subjunctive.

Tutores, cum iudicatum persequi non potuerunt, periculo culpae non subiciuntur (D. XXVI. 7. 1 39. § 12 Pap.) where a particular case is referred to, not a general proposition affirmed.

Inter bonorum uentrisque curatorem et curatorem furiosi itemque prodigi pupilliue magna est differentia, quippe cum illis quidem rerum administratio, duobus autem superioribus sola custodia committitur (ib. 1 48 Herm.); D. XLVIII. 10. 1 22. pr. (Paul); X. 1 5. 1 24. § 6 Ulp.

5. In dependent questions the indicative (as in other writers of the time) is often left; e.g. *Labeo distinguit cuius gratia uel heres instituitur uel legatum acceperit* (D. VII. 1. 1 21 Ulp.); *nec distinguimus unde cognitum eum habuit* (ib. 1 22); *quis ergo statuet qui potius manumittitur* (XL. 5. 1 24. § 17 Ulp.); *an autem illa repudianda est, considerandum est* (XXIV. 3. 1 22. § 7 Ulp.); XXXVII. 11. 1 10.

The use of the indicative after *forsitan* (e.g. D. III. 3. 1 43. pr. *forsitan et ipsi dantur*) is found in earlier lay writers. (Cf. Lat. Gr. § 17 67.)

6. With *licet* both indicative and subjunctive are found, e.g. *licet immineat* (D. vii. 1. 1 12. § 1); *licet sit* (ib. § 3); *licet amittatur* (§ 4); but *licet solebat* (1 9. § 7) all from the same book of Ulpian: *licet... datus est* (D. xxvii. 1. 1 21. § 2 Marcian); *licet fugitiua erat* (D. xxx. 1 84. § 10 Julian). So in other writers of the time and later. Koffmane *Gesch. d. Kirchenlat.* i. p. 132.

Quamuis with indic. e.g. D. xvi. 3. 1 1. § 18 Ulp., xxxviii. 2. 1 41. § 1 Paul. Cf. Lat. Gr. § 1627; Dräger *Hist. Synt.* § 566.

7. In subordinate clauses, where in classical Latin the subjunctive would be used to shew that the clause is part of a report or of a hypothetical case or of an infinitive sentence, the indicative is often found in the Digest. In many cases the indicative might be justified as subordinate to the principal verb and not to the infinitive or other clause, but there are so many instances where such an explanation would not hold, that we are forced to consider the use of the indicative as due to a neglect of the finer shades and distinctions of the language : e.g.

Quod ideo placuisse Seruius scribit, quia spem reuertendi ciuibus in uirtute bellica magis quam in pace Romani esse uoluerunt (D. xlix. 15. 1 12 Tryph.).

Ait enim se propterea non teneri, quod pater eius dotem pro se dedit, cui heres non exstitit (Vat. Fr. 94 Paul. The Digest xxiv. 3. 1 49. § 1 has *exstiterit* but retains *dedit*).

Ipsa lege Papia significatur ut collegatarius coniunctus, si liberos habeat, potior sit heredibus, etiam si liberos habebunt (Gai. ii. 207).

The present indicative is always found in the *Priuileg. ueteran.* (*Corp. I. L.* iii. pp. 844 sqq. i. ; instances in Bruns p. 196) e.g. *ueteranis ciuitatem dedit et conubium cum uxoribus, quas tunc habuissent cum est ciuitas eis data.* It will be observed in extenuation, that the time denoted by *cum est* is the time of *dedit*, though the clause is grammatically referable to *habuissent*.

8. Relative clauses, which might have either subjunctive or indicative, sometimes exhibit both coordinately, e.g. *excepto eo, qui... datus est, uel qui...persequatur uel suscipit* (D. iii. 3. 18. § 2). *Adiuuantur in primis hi qui metus causa cepissent :...succurritur etiam ei qui in uinculis fuisset : ei quoque succurritur qui in seruitute fuerit... item ei succurritur qui in potestate hostium fuit* (D. iv. 6. 11 2, 9, 11. 14 Callistr.).

9. The future passive infinitive is written in the Digest from the Florentine MS e.g. *restitutu iri* (XVIII. 4. 1 10) ; *praestatu iri* (ib. 1. 1 66 pr.) ; *defensu iri* (XXXIII. 1 4. §§ 9, 10), &c.   This form is not noted in Neue's *Formenlehre* II. p. 383 ed. 2.   It appears to have arisen from forgetfulness of the fact, that the form in *-um* is a supine governing the supposed subject, *iri* being impersonal (Lat. Gr. § 1380).   The passive meaning has suggested the use of what some Grammarians have called the passive supine.   Moreover the concurrent use of such expressions as *optimum factum, optimum factu est* (cf. Kühner *Ausführ. Gr.* II. p. 538) might help towards the notion that *factum* and *factu* were much the same.   The regular form in *-tum* (*-sum*) is also found, e.g. D. XIX. 1. 1 11. § 18 *praestatum iri*. But, as abbreviations were forbidden by Justinian and are not found in the Florentine MS, we cannot consider these forms in *-tu* to be merely abbreviations for forms in *-tum*.

10.   An infinitive is sometimes found dependent on a gerund or gerundive : e.g. *Sabinus nullas praetoris partes esse ad compellendum defendere* (D. III. 3. 1 45 pr. Paul.); *quae supra diximus in procuratore non compellendo suscipere iudicium* (ib. 1 17. § 2 Ulp.).

11.   The verb of 'saying', 'thinking', &c., on which an infinitive clause depends is frequently omitted.   This omission is probably sometimes due to the compilers, but it is not confined to the law writers, and in any case is too natural to require special justification in such writings.   See D. VII. 1. 1 73; III. 3. 1 14; 1 45. pr.

12.   *Quod* with a finite verb is sometimes used instead of an infinitive clause ; e.g. *Pater filio ita scripsit : scio quod...inuigilabis hereditati Lucii Titii* (D. XXIX. 2. 1 25. § 8 Ulp.); *potest dicere sperasse quod in testamento quoque gratus circa eum fieret* (D. XXXVIII. 2. 1 8. § 3 Ulp.); *si putat, quod utiliter actionem daturus sit, decernat* (XXXIX. 2. 1 15. § 28 Ulp.).

13.   *Cur* for *quod* is sometimes found, e.g. *domini persona spectatur, qui sibi debebit imputare, cur minori rem commisit* (D. IV. 4. 1 3. § 11 Ulp.); *neque imputare ei possumus, cur non deseruit accusationem uel cur abolitionem non petierit* (XXXVIII. 2. 1 14. § 2 Ulp.); *Nam, et si mandassent, tenerentur tutelae, cur seruum pupillo necessarium non comparauerunt* (D. XVII. 1. 1 8. § 4 Ulp.).

There are some instances of this in Cicero (after *accusare*) and in others.   See Mayor on Plin. *Ep.* III. 5. § 16; Dräger *Hist. Synt.* II. p. 481 ed. 2.

Quare is similarly used D. XL. 5. 1 55 Marcian.

14.   *Quatenus* = *ut*, 'so that', e.g. *Pro eo qui in fuga esse dicitur, cautio ab eo extorquenda est, quatenus et persequatur et omnimodo eum restituat* (D. IV. 2. 1 14. § 11 Ulp.); *licentiam habeat curator furiosae adire iudicem competentem, quatenus necessitas imponatur marito mulieris sustentationem sufferre* (XXIV. 3. 1 22. § 8 Ulp.)

15.   *Quam* is sometimes used without *magis* or *potius* or *tam* preceding, e.g. *pro herede autem gerere non esse facti quam animi* (D. XXIX. 2. 1 10. pr. Ulp.); *haec enim actio poenam et uindictam quam rei persecutionem continet* (ib. § 5); *cum posset non suscipere talem causam quam decipere* (D. XVI. 3. 1 17. pr. Ulp.); XXX. 1 49. § 5 Ulp.

This omission is also found in classical writers occasionally.   See Dräger *Hist. Synt.* § 519. 2. *d.*

Use of Cases.

16.   *Prouoco* is used with accusative of the judge to whom an appeal is made, e.g. *si multi sint debitores aut iudicem prouocent* (D. XXVIII. 8. 1 6 Gai.).   So in the passive, e.g. *stultum est illud admonere, a principe appellare fas non esse, cum ipse sit, qui prouocatur* (D. XLIX. 2. 1 1. § 1 Ulp.)   So also 3. 1 1; 4. 1 1. § 4, &c.   Evidently the use of *appellare* has been transferred to *prouocare.*

On *condemnare aliquem aliquid* see Lat. Gr. § 1199.

17.   *Contineri* is used with a dative; e.g. *utrum filii obligatio promissioni contineatur* (D. XXIII. 3. 1 57 Jav.); *respondit rationum reddendarum condicioni contineri omne quod*, &c. (XL. 5. 1 41. § 11 Scaev.)

Contrahere, e.g. *cum essem tibi contracturus* (D. XVI. 1. 1 8. § 14 Ulp.).

I have denied (pp. 192, 202) the use of *obscurare* and *impedire* with datives, contrary to their habit.   But in such matters it is difficult to decide whether the fault is Tribonian's or the copyist's. In D. XLVIII. 2. 1 3 fin. (quoted by Schrader *ad Inst.* I. 7) we have *ei impedierit*, where either *eum* or the omission of *ei* is an easy correction.   In *Inst* I. 7 the better MSS. have the dative; but comp. I. 6 init.

18.   *Iubere* with dative and infinitive active is found, e.g. *si iussero filio uel seruo adire* (D. XXIX. 2. 1 26 Paul.); *si per epistulam*

seruo pupilli tutor hereditatem adire iusserit (ib. 1 50 Mod.); though
the accusative is more common. The dative with infin. is found in the
Cod. Med. of Cic. *Att.* IX. 12. § 2, and in MSS of Curt. V. 6. § 8, but is
now corrected by the editors. In Liv. XXVII. 16. § 8 (according to the
MSS) we have *interroganti scribae...deos iratos Tarentinis relinqui
iussit*, but, even if the text is right and there is no anacoluthon, as if
respondens or *respondit* were intended, the passive infinitive with a
subject different from *scribae* gives ground for a different construction
(cf. Lat. Gr. §§ 1348, 1349 and note).   Neither are Tacitus *Ann.* IV.
72 *tributum iis iusserat modicum*; XIII. 15 *Britannico iussit exsurgeret;*
ib. 40 *quibus iusserat ut resisterent*, parallel to our instances.   (In
Liv. XLII. 28. § 1 *iussum* is due to conjecture; in Caes. *B. Civ.* III. 98
the texts, which I have, all give accusative.)

19.   On *noxae dedere* see p. 132;

his rebus recte praestari, p. 69;

accepto ferre, p. 154, and Lat. Gr. II. Praef. p. XXXVII;

doti (predicative dative 'as a dowry') *esse* or *dare ; hypothecae
esse* or *dare, pigneri esse, accipere, dare* &c , Lat. Gr. pp. xlii, xlv, l.

20.   The use of genitives to denote the 'matter charged' or the like
is common in earlier writers as well as in the Digest.   It has probably
arisen from the ellipse of *nomine, crimine, iudicio*, &c. (Lat. Gr. §§
1324—1327).

Hence *qui damni infecti caueri sibi postulat* (D. XXXIX. 2. 1 13. § 3
Ulp.); *damni infecti utiliter stipulari* (ib. § 8); *quamuis promisisset
damni infecti uicino* (ib. 1 26); *damni infecti stipulatio* (1 18. pr.
Paul.); *d. inf. actio* (1 33 Ulp.); &c.

So *aquae pluuiae arcendae agere, conueniri, teneri* (D. XXXIX. 3.
1 1. §§ 18, 20, 21 Ulp.).

Si pater filii nemini iniuriarum agat (D. III. 3. 1 39. § 4 Ulp.).

21.   The action created by the *lex Aquilia* (see p. 99) is called in
Cic. *Rosc. Com.* 11. § 32 *iudicium damni iniuria constitutum.*   So ib.
18. § 54 *cum lis contestata cum Flauio damni iniuria esset.*   The full
phrase was no doubt *damni iniuria dati.*   In Gaius III. 210; IV. 76
we have *damni iniuriae actio.*   In the Digest both phrases are used,
e.g. *damni iniuria tenearis* (IX. 2. 1 27. § 10; § 11; § 29; 1 29. § 1);
damnum iniuria dare (ib. 1 27. § 17; 1 29. § 7, &c.): but *damni iniuriae
actio* (ib. 1 27. pr.; 1 41. pr.).   It is possible that *damni iniuriae* may
be an instance of the specification of a general notion by the addition

of another word, as *datus adsignatus* p. 34 ; or of the combination of
the loss and the wrong, without a conjunction, like *uti frui*, &c. p. 27 ;
but even if it was so understood, it is likely that the genitive arose
from misunderstanding *iniuria* when *dati* was omitted. Cf. Cic. *Tull.*
17 § 41.

22. It is common to put a bare numeral, though indeclinable, to
denote a sum of money, e.g. *si uiginti dederit ; si iurauerit se decem
daturum* (D. xxxv. 1. 1 26) ; even as price or value with verb or
substantive, e.g. *seruus quinque ualens, cum uicarius ualeret decem* (xv.
1. 1 11. §§ 4, 5 Ulp.); *Stichus habet in peculio Pamphilum, qui est
decem* (ib. 1 38. § 2 Ulp.); *faber mandatu amici sui emit seruum decem
et fabricam docuit, deinde uendidit eum uiginti* (xvii. 1. 1 26. § 8
Paul.); *ex duabus stipulationibus una quindecim sub usuris maioribus,
altera uiginti*, &c. (D. xlvi. 3. 1 89. § 2 Scaev.)

The money meant by the old lawyers was *sestertia* or *milia sester-
tiûm* (cf. Lat. Gr. i. p. 446). Cf. *si seruus decem milibus emptus,
quinque milibus sit* (D. xxi. 2. 1 57 Paul.); *decem legata sunt ;
cogendus tota decem praestare* (xl. 5. 1 6 Paul.); *si cui legata sint
centum* (ib. 1 7 Ulp.); *de fisco numerari decies centena dotis nomine
iussit* (xxii. 1. 1 6 Pap.), for which sum we have the simple *decies* in
xxxv. 1. 1 77. § 3 Pap. (*filiae decies restituere*). But Justinian may
be supposed usually to understand *aureos*. For in transferring Gai.
iii. 102 *si sestertia* x *a te dari stipuler et tu sestertia* v *promittas* to
his own Institutes he writes (iii. 19. § 5) *si decem aureos a te dari
stipulatur, tu quinque promittas :* and in amending the *lex Papia* he
says (Inst. iii. 7. § 3; Cod. vi. 4. 1 4, § 9) that he shall put one *aureus*
for 1000 sesterces in estimating the property of a deceased freedman
(*si minores centenariis sint, id est, minus centum aureis habeant sub-
stantiam ; sic enim legis Papiae summam interpretati sumus, ut pro
mille sestertiis unus aureus computetur*). This was of course not
merely a change of expression, but a large reduction of the amount,
the *aureus* since Constantine's time being worth about 12*s*. 6*d*., and
1000 sesterces in the days of the Jurists being worth (say) £10
(taking a mean between the silver value, given by Marquardt *Staats-
verw.* ii. p. 71, as 175 m. 41 pf., and the gold value given as 217 m.
52 pf.).

In D. xlviii. 14. § 1 (Mod.) *centum aureis cum infamia punitur ;*
l. 16. 1 88 (Cels.) *sic dicimus centies aureorum habere, qui tantum in
praediis ceterisque similibus habeat,* the compilers have probably substi-

tuted *aureorum* for *HS.*   Cf. Cujac. *Observ.* XIX. 31 = Vol. I. p. 869 ed. Prati.

23.   The expressions *duumuir, duumuiri* (plur.), *triumuir, triumuiri, decemuir,* &c. are found in other Latin as much as in the lawyers, but they have a publicist character and are therefore not out of place here.

Prof. Nettleship (*Journal of Philology,* VI. p. 97, anno 1875) has suggested that *duum* and *trium* are neuter substantives, used as numerals and corresponding in form to Sanskrit *dvayám* and *trayám,* which he says are used at the end of compounds, as we might say *a pipe dozen* for *a dozen pipes.*   According to this *duumuiri* would be 'couple men', *triumuiri* 'trio-men', and in the singular 'a couple-man; a trio-man'.   I know of no such compound in Latin, and think there is a much simpler explanation of the phrase nearer home.

The origin of the expression is found in such sentences as these: *quod decemuirum sine prouocatione esset* (Cic. *R. P.* II. 36. § 71), 'because he was (one) of the ten men without appeal'; *alterum collegam tuum,* XXuirum *qui fuit ad agros diuidendos Campanos, uideo huc uenire* (Varr. *R. R.* I. 2. § 10); *cuius pater flamen aut augur aut quindecemuirum sacris faciundis aut septemuirum epulonum aut Salius est* (Gell. I. 12. § 6 apparently quoting Labeo; cf. ib. III. 9. § 4; XIII. 12. § 6).

So in inscriptions : *C. Lucilius C. f. trium uirum cap.* i.e. 'one of the *tresuiri capitales*' (*Corp. I. L.* v. 872); *P. Babrinius M. f. duom uirum* (ib. 971); *P. Pactumeio P. f. Quir. Clementi* X *uirorum stlitibus iudicand.,* i.e. 'one of the decemviri for deciding suits' (ib. VIII. 7059).   So in the *Mon. Ancyr.* I. 45 where the Latin is mutilated, but the Greek is quite decisive.

In these inscriptions the partitive genitive is used as descriptive of the office.   It differs from the use in Cicero, &c., in being attributed instead of predicated.   The like use of oblique cases is found in the frequent *pro consule, pro quaestore,* &c.; *trib. pot.* or *tribunic. potestat.* for *tribuniciae potestatis,* or *tribunicia potestate;* and in *eq. pub.* on which see above, p. clxviii, note.

The next stage in the development is shewn in the numerous inscriptions which among other contractions omit the termination of the genitive plural, e.g. *neue quis* IIuir. IIIIuir. *esto* (*lex Iul. munic.* 140); 'no one is to be (one) of the *duouiri* or *quattuoruiri';* *Cn.*

Cornelius Cn. f. Scipio Hispanus, tr. mil. II. x*uir. sl. iudik.* x*uir. sacr. fac.* i.e. 'twice tribune of the soldiers, one of the *decemuiri litibus iudicandis,* one of the *decemuiri sacris faciundis'* (*Corp. I. L.* I. 38); *L. Ateius M. f. Capito duomuir. quinq.* (ib. 1341). There is no reason for taking x*uir.* &c. of the former inscription as in any respect different from the *duomuir.* of the latter. All are abbreviations, for *duomuirum, decemuirum,* &c., but it is easy to see that a nominative (*duomuir, decemuir*) might be supposed to be found in each place : and there is no internal absurdity in supposing one member of a commission of two to be called *duomuir,* 'a man of two', whereas *duouir* would look like a contradiction in terms.

The third stage of the development is reached when these abbreviated forms are used, leaving the reader to supply any termination which suits the construction. Thus in *ni quis eorum...*II*uir.* IIII*uir. aliamue quam potestatem...petito* (*Lex Iul. Mun.* 135) it is natural to read the words as *duomuiratum, triumuiratum.* Again *ex decreto* II*uir.* IIII*uir. praefect. ue Mutinensis* (*Lex. Rubr.* 20) we understand genitives *duomuiri, quattuoruiri, praefectiue* (the *quattuor* being really a genitive plural just as much as the *duum*).

Hence it was taken that a commissioner was not described as *decemuirum,* but as *decemuir,* and Cicero writes *ut sibi iam decemuir designatus esse uideatur* (*Rull.* II. 19. § 53), whereas an inscription would have put x*uir. designat.,* meaning, at least originally, *decemuirum designatorum.* Thus compounds were supposed, and were used in any case required; e.g. *duumuir, duumuiro, duumuiri* (nom. pl. e.g. D. III. 4. 1 6; XLIV. 7. 1 35. § 1) *seuir, octouir,* &c. Cf. Hor. *Sat.* II. 5. 56 *recoctus scriba ex quinqueuiro.* (See Neue *Formenlehre* I. pp. 440, 441.)

Corssen (*Ausspr.* I. p. 268) takes *duum* as a genitive dual, and explains *duumuiri* as formed on the analogy of *duumuir,* but misses what seem to me the main elements of the formation of *duumuir* as well as *duumuiri,* the attributive use of the genitive plural and the inscriptional contraction.

24. *Hoc amplius* 'besides', 'moreover', 'more than this' is a very common phrase in the Digest. What is *hoc?* Is it (*a*) nominative and accusative? (*β*) or ablative of measure, 'by this the more'? (*γ*) or ablative of standard of comparison, 'more than this'? In the case of (*a*) and (*β*) *hoc* would refer to what follows, in the case of (*γ*) to what precedes.

The phrase is found also in other than legal writers, e.g. Cic. *Phil.* XIII. 21. § 50 *Quae cum ita sint, de mandatis litterisque M. Lepidi uiri clarissimi Seruilio assentior, et hoc amplius censeo, Magnum Pompeium...fecisse, &c.*; *Verr.* II. 50. § 123 *Agrigentini de senatu cooptando Scipionis leges antiquas habent, in quibus et illa eadem sancta sunt, et hoc amplius;* '*cum Agrigentinorum,*' &c.; *Tull.* 19. § 44 *Fuit illud interdictum apud maiores nostros de ui, quod hodie quoque est;* '*Unde tu,*' &c. *Deinde additur illius iam hoc causa, quicum agitur,* '*cum ille possideret*', *et hoc amplius,* '*quod nec ui nec clam nec precario possideret*' (cf. ib. § 24 *nihil amplius...Quid ergo addit amplius?*). *Nat. Deor.* II. 12. § 34 *Bestiis natura sensum et motum dedit et cum quodam appetitu accessum ad res salutares, a pestiferis recessum; hoc homini amplius, quod addidit rationem;* (and comp. § 33 *quibus natura nihil tribuit amplius quam ut, &c.*) *Caecin.* 10. § 27; *Fin.* v. 4. § 11; *Fam.* IX. 25. § 1; *Brut.* I. 5. § 1 *Cui quum essem assensus, decreui hoc amplius*[1], *ut tu, &c.*

Cato has the phrase several times; *R. R.* 57 *ubi uindemia facta erit, loram bibant menses tres; mense quarto heminas in dies, &c.; hoc amplius Saturnalibus et Compitalibus in singulos homines congios;* ib. 94 *Fici uti grossos teneant, facito omnia quo modo oleae, et hoc amplius, cum uer adpetet, terram adaggerato bene;* ib. 142; 157. § 10.

Nepos *Alc.* 11. § 2 *Namque ea, quae supra scripsimus, de eo praedicarunt atque hoc amplius: cum Athenis, &c.*, which is clear for *a*.

Sen. *N. Q.* III. 15. § 1 *Quaedam ex istis sunt quibus adsentire possumus, sed hoc amplius censeo: placet, &c.* So also *Dial.* VII. 3. § 2.

Quint. I. 1. § 8 *De pueris, inter quos educabitur ille huic spei destinatus, idem quod de nutricibus dictum sit; de paedagogis hoc amplius, ut aut sint eruditi plene, &c.*

Plin. *Ep.* II. 11. § 19 *Consul censuit Mario urbe Italiaque interdicendum, Marciano hoc amplius Africa.*

Suet. *Claud.* 11 *Parentibus inferias publicas et hoc amplius patri circenses annuos natali die; Jul.* 38 *Populo trecenos nummos quos pollicitus olim erat, uiritim diuisit, et hoc amplius centenos pro mora.*

Compare the use of *eo amplius; Calig.* 15 *inferias is annua religione publice instituit et eo amplius matri Circenses carpentumque;*

---

[1] Brisson (*de Formulis* II. 58, p. 168) quotes Dion. Hal. XIII. (?) μετὰ τοῦτον ἀναστὰς ἕτερος εἶπεν, ἐμοὶ δέ, ὦ βουλή, δοκεῖ καὶ τοῦτο ἔτι προσθῆναι τῇ γνώμῃ.

Sall. *Jug.* 80. § 6 *Denas uxores alii, alii plures habent, sed reges eo amplius.*

In the lawyers we have *hoc amplius, eo amplius; hoc minus, eo minus.* Instances of *hoc amplius* are numerous; e. g.

Gai. III. 127 *In eo quoque par omnium causa est, quod, si quid pro reo soluerint, eius reciperandi causa habent cum eo mandati iudicium; et hoc amplius sponsores ex lege Publilia propriam habent actionem depensi;* IV. 167 *fructus licitationis summam poenae nomine soluere et praeterea possessionem restituere iubetur, et hoc amplius fructus, quos interea percepit, reddit;* ib. 166 a.

Ulp. *Reg.* 15 *Hoc amplius mulier, praeter decimam, dotem capere potest legatam sibi.*

D. I. 7. 1 15. pr. Ulp. *si pater familias adoptatus sit, omnia quae eius fuerunt et adquiri possunt, tacito iure ad eum transeunt qui adoptauit: hoc amplius liberi eius qui in potestate sunt eum sequuntur;* III. 2. 1 2. pr.; 3. 1 8. pr.; VII. 8. 1 12. § 1 Ulp. *Nerua adicit stramentis et sarmentis etiam usurum, sed neque foliis neque oleo neque frumento neque frugibus usurum. Sed Sabinus et Cassius et Labeo et Proculus hoc amplius etiam ex his quae in fundo nascuntur, quod ad uictum sibi suisque sufficiat, sumpturum et ex his quae Nerua negauit;* ib. § 2; *Edict.* ap. D. XXI. 1. 1 1. § 1 *ex his enim causis iudicium dabimus. Hoc amplius si quis aduersus ea sciens dolo malo uendidisse dicetur, iudicium dabimus;* XXX. 1 19. pr.; 1 108. §§ 7, 8; XXXI. 1 32. § 2 *cum ita legatur 'illi hoc amplius fundum illum cum omnibus rebus quae in eodem fundo erunt', mancipia quoque continentur;* XXXII. 1 27. pr.; 1 29. § 3; 1 30. § 1 *respondi heredem teneri sinere frui; hoc amplius heredem mercedem quoque hortorum reipublicae praestaturum;* 1 54; 1 67; XXXIX. 2. 1 9. pr.; 1 15. § 31; XLI. 1. 1 9. § 7; 3. 1 33. § 1; XLII. 1. 1 15. § 11; § 12; XLVI. 8. 1 22. pr.; &c.

The following two instances are somewhat different; D. XXXII. 1 39. pr. *Pamphilo liberto hoc amplius, quam codicillis reliqui, dari uolo centum;* XLVII. 2. 1 62. § 5 *et quidem hoc amplius quam in superioribus causis seruandum.*

Eo amplius is used by the lawyers; Gai. II. 179 (referable to γ); III. 212; Vat. Fr. 301 (γ, if *quod* be struck out as Mommsen proposes); D. XXVIII. 5. 1 86 (β); XXXII. 1 8. § 2 *petiit testator ut quidquid ex bonis eius ad patrem peruenisset, filiae suae ita restitueret, ut eo amplius* (β) *haberet, quam ex bonis patris habitura esset;* XXXIII. 1. 1 21. § 5 (γ); XXXIV. 1. 1 18. § 3 (γ).

Hoc minus ' so much less ' (β) is found D. XV. 1. 1 9. § 4; XXIV.

3. 1 15. § 1; 1 31. § 3; xxxvi. 1. 1 28. § 7; xxxvii. 6. 1 1. § 20; 10. 1 5. § 3; *Eo minus* in same sense in xxxvi. 1. 1 65. § 12.

It seems to me that in all the passages of Cicero (except perhaps *Fam.* ix. 25. § 1) *hoc* is (a) i.e. the nominative or accusative referring to the clause or fact following: and the same applies to Nepos, Seneca and Quintilian. In Cato, Pliny and Suetonius the expression wears a somewhat stereotyped air, meaning simply 'in addition', 'besides', and may have grown either from (a) or (γ).

The same applies to the use of *hoc amplius* in the lawyers, who seem sometimes to have one notion in their mind and sometimes the other. Not unfrequently e.g. D. iii. 3. 1 8. pr., 1 10 there is a climax ('more than this one'), but this may be due to the *et si* following. In the two passages where it is followed by *quam, hoc* seems clearly to be the accusative or nominative.

On the legal import of the phrase in some cases of bequest the lawyers were apparently not quite agreed. Compare Maecianus D. xxxii. 1 12, and Pomponius, ib. 1 54 with Africanus xxx. 1 108. § 7; and Cujas' note on the last passage (iv. p. 144, ed. Prati).

25. The use of *in* with accusative and ablative is sometimes reversed. Thus *manent in adoptionem* (Gai. ii. 136), *in libertatem tueri* (iii. 56); *in potestatem parentum liberos esse* (i. 55; &c. all which places Studemund corrects by omitting *m*); *in libertatis esse possessionem* (D. xl. 12. 1 41. Paul.) and many other places. A long list of passages is given by Böcking, Gaius p. 342, ed. 4 = 1st Excurs. ed. 5; also by Brisson *Lex. Parerg.* lxxii. p. 1387, ed. 1743; Sittl *Die local. Verschiedenheiten d. lat. Spr.* p. 128. Originally it was a mere blunder from the faint sound of the final *m,* but it grew into an idiom (it is found in Cic. and Liv.) and hence should not be altered by Studemund. Cf. Lat. Gr. § 1962, note.

The reverse mistake is seen in D. xxviii. 1. 1 12 Iul. *in hostium potestate non peruenissent* (where Mommsen reads *potestatem*); ib. 3. 1 6. § 7 *in carcere recipi* (where Mommsen suggests the like correction); *se in concubinatu alterius tradere* (D. xxiii. 2. 1 11. Marcell.), and in other places given by Brisson l.c. lxxiii.

Omission of verb.   *Genera uerbi.*

26. *Attinet* or *pertinet* is omitted sometimes in classical Latin in such expressions as *Uerum hoc nihil ad me* (Cic. *Or.* ii. 32. § 140). In the Digest it is often omitted after *quantum,* e.g. D. iii. 3. 1 33.

pr., Ulp. *Seruum quoque et filium familias procuratorem posse habere aiunt; et quantum ad filium familias* ('as far as regards a son'), *uerum est;* XXVIII. 3. 1 6. § 13. Ulp.; XXIX. 2. 1 30. § 1. Ulp.; XLI. 1. 1 11. Marcell.; XLII. 5. 1 4. Paul.; L. 1. 1 23. Hermog. and others quoted on VII. 1. 1 12. pr. (p. 80). So also with *quod,* e.g. D. XXVII. 3. 1 1. § 21. Ulp. *tutelae actio, quod ad speciem istam, perempta est;* XLVII. 2. 1 46. Ulp.; XLVIII. 10. 1 22. § 4.

27. Some deponent verbs are used as if passive : e.g. *arbitrari* D. XI. 7. 1 2. § 4. Ulp., and probably IV. 8. 1 27. § 4 bis; cf. note on VII. 1. 1 13. § 1. (p. 98); *contestari* D. II. 12. 1 1. § 2. Ulp.; *mentiri* D. XLVIII. 10. 1 28. Mod.; *complexus* D. XLIX. 1. 1 3. § 1; *tueri* D. XXVII. 10. 1 7. pr. Jul.

On the other hand *abstentus* is used as a past participle of *abstinere se* (e.g. D. XXXVI. 4. 1 1. § 4. Ulp.) as well as passively of *abstinere* (D. XXVI. 8. 1. 21. Scaev.).

For *lauat* impers. and passive, see p. 115.

28. Böcking distinguishes between the use of *possidere* to denote a state of possession and to denote the act of taking possession. He considers the former to be *possĭdēre*, the latter to be *possīdĕre*. Thus in D. XLI. 2. 1 1. § 22 ; 1 2 he writes *municipes per se nih.l possīdĕre possunt, quia uniuersi consentire non possunt : sed hoc iure utimur ut et possĭdēre et usucapere municipes possint.* He has however doubts whether the first is *possĭdĕre*. *Pand.* § 123, note 8. See also § 124 n. 25 ; § 132 n. 8, in which last place he seems to imply that *possīdĕre iussus* is the proper phrase. But in D. XLII. 4. 1 2. § 1 ; 1 7. § 1 we have *bona iubet possideri*, never, I think, *possidi*. Cf. §§ 5, 15, 17 ; 5. 1 12. § 2 ; 1 13 &c. Böcking refers to the Schneeberg edition of Forcellini's *Lexicon :* but all the instances of *possido* there given, chiefly perfect tenses, are so far as the form goes, capable of being instances of *possideo*, except Lucr. I. 386 which Munro treats as a ἅπαξ λεγόμενον. One instance indeed (*Bell. Alex.* 34 *possideri uastarique*) must be referred to *possideo*. The direct evidence appears to be strongly on the side of *possideo* against *possido;* and I see no theoretical difficulty in supposing *possideo* to be used of the first act of being in possession as well as of the subsequent state.

29. Gaius tells us (IV. 184) that after a summons into court, if the business could not be finished on that day, the defendant had to make an engagement for trial, i.e. to promise his appearance on a fixed

day. To make such an engagement was *uadimonium facere* (cf. Cic.
Quinct. § 57). A formal promise was sometimes sufficient: sometimes
sureties had to be given also. In Cicero *pro Quinct.* the plaintiff requiring such an engagement is said *uadari*: the defendant making it
uadimonium promittere (§ 23; *Tull.* § 20); to put off the engagement
for trial is *uadimonium differre* (*Quinct.* § 22); to keep the engagement
ad uadimonium uenire (§§ 22, 48, 67); *uadimonium obire* (§ 53);
to fail to keep the engagement *ad uadimonium non uenire, uadimonium deserere, non obire* §§ 52—57. *Uadimonium* is not named
in the Digest: the like procedure remains, but this term is not used.
The defendant *promisit se sisti*, i.e. promised for his own appearance
(D. II. 11. 1 2. § 3; 1 8; 1 9); a person promising for another's
appearance *promisit aliquem sisti* (ib. 1 7; 1 10. pr.; 1 11); the person
thus making an appearance *se sistit* (ib. 1 2. § 3; 1 4. pr.), or *stat* (1 11.
fin.), or in the past tense *stetit* (ib. 10. 1 1. § 3; 11. 1 2. § 1;
1 4. § 1. bis; § 3; 1 6; 1 11. bis); the surety who produces his
principal, *sistit reum* (10. 1 2; 11. 1 11; 1 14); the person thus produced is said *sisti* (ib. 10. 1 3. pr. §§ 1, 2; 11. 1 11); or in the past tense
status esse (ib. 5. 1 3; 11. 1 9; 1 14). The engagement for appearance is spoken of according to circumstances, as *cautio, stipulatio,
promissio, iudicio sistendi causā* (e.g. 11. rubr.; 1 4. § 4; 5. § 1; 1 10.
§ 2) where *sistendi*, as is not uncommon with gerunds[1], is used
abstractly, so as to fit either an active or neuter sense (cf. Lat. Gr.
II. Praef. pp. lxiv. sqq.). This is seen in D. II. 11. 1 6. Gai. *Si is qui
fideiussorem dedit ideo non steterit, quod rei publicae causa absit,
iniquum est fideiussorem ob alium necessitate sistendi obligatum esse,
cum ipsi liberum esset non sistere*, i.e. if the defendant has a good
reason for not making an appearance, the surety is excused from
.making him appear. *Sistere* is found in this neuter sense in 10. 1 3.
pr. *quo minus quis in iudicium uocatus sistat*, unless it be a mistake
for *sistatur*, which occurs in §§ 1 and 2 of the same law.

The use of *steti* of the defendant making an appearance has been
strangely missed by the editors in Cic. *Quinct.* § 25. All the MSS.
have *Testificatur iste P. Quinctium non stetisse et stetisse se.* Hotoman
suggested *stitisse:* Keller (*Semestr.* p. 218) approved, and Baiter,
Kayser and Müller have naturally followed. As proof is quoted
Gell. II. 14, where it is said that *uadimonium sistere*, not *stare*, is the
right phrase, and that consequently in Cato *Quid si uadimonium*

---

[1] E.g. *abstinendi se* and *abstinendi* are found in D. XXIX. 2. 1 57. pr. (Gai.);
XL. 5. 1 30. §§ 10, 11 (Ulp.).

capite obuoluto stitisses? is right, and a proposed emendation *stetisses* is wrong. It certainly is odd that none of these scholars noticed that *uadimonium* occurs in Gellius and of course requires the active verb *sistere*, perf. *stitisse*, whereas *uadimonium* is not in the passage of Cicero, and the middle or neuter is required, viz. *sisti* (or rarely *stare*), perf. *stetisse* (or *status esse*). If further instances are wanted besides those given above, see Gai. IV. 185 *ut qui non steterit, is protinus a recuperatoribus in summam uadimonii condemnetur;* D. XXXIV. 5. 1 13. (14) § 2. Jul. *Ita stipulamur, ueluti Stichum et Damam et Erotem sisti: si quis eorum non steterit, decem dari? necesse est enim omnes· esse sistendos ut stipulationi satisfiat. Uel fingamus ita stipulationem factam si Stichum et Damam et Erotem non sisteris* (read with Haloander *stiteris*) *decem dari? neque enim dubitabimus quin aeque omnes sisti oporteat;* XLV. 1. 1 126. § 3. Paul. *si ita stipulatus fuero te sisti, et nisi steteris, aliquid dari,* &c.

Technical phrases, Order of words, Pleonasm, &c.

30. A number of technical phrases were used so often that they became almost compounds, and from those used with verbs corresponding substantives were formed, e.g.

(a) *fide iubere, fide iussor, fideiussorius, fide iussio, confideiussio* (D. XLVI. 1. 1 39); *fide promissor,* &c. (Lat. Gr. § 1243); *fidei committere, fidei commissum, fidei commissarius ; bona fide seruire, possidere, possideri, emere, bona fide possessor, emptor, seruiens,* also *bonae (malae) fidei possessor, emptor* (D. XLI. 1. 1 40; 1 48), *bonae fidei iudicium; manu mittere, manu missor ; mortis causa capere,* but *mortis causa capio* (subst.) is only in the rubric of D. XXXIX. 6 ; *usu capere, usu capio* (subst.): *longo tempore capere, per longum tempus capio,* subst. (D. XLI. 1. 1 48) ; *noxae dedere, noxae deditio* (e. g. *ex causa noxae deditionis* D. VI. 2. 1 5); *satis dare, satis datio ; satis facere, satis factio ; satis accipere, satis acceptio* (D. XLV. 1. 1 5. § 2).

(b) *proconsulatus* (Plin. Tac.) from *pro consule* is more of a regular compound: on this analogy we have *protutela* in Digest corresponding to *pro tutore,* as *tutela* does to *tutor.* From *decem primi* is formed *decemprimatus.*

(c) *quasi* is very frequently used to form a half compound ; e.g. *quasi-dominus* (D. XLIII. 17. 1 3. § 7) ; *longa quasi-possessio ; quasi-dos* (D. v. 3. 1 13. § 1) ; *quasi-senatoris-filius, quasi-nepos-senatoris*

(D. I. 9. 1 7); *quasi-tutela* (D. XV. 1. 1 52. pr.); &c.   See notes pp. 104, 113.

(d)   *non* is similarly used : e.g. *idem est et si superficiariam insulam a non-domino bona fide emero* (D. VI. 2. 1 12. § 3. Paul.); *a diuersis non-dominis* (ib. 1 9. § 4. Ulp.); *neque igitur fratres consortes plurium loco habendi sunt neque non-fratres* (D. XXVII. 1. 1 31. § 4. Paul.); *interdum tamen et non-procuratori recte soluitur* (D. XLVI. 3. 1 12. § 1. Ulp.); &c.

31.   Some phrases are used adjectivally or semi-adjectivally :

(a) prepositional phrases, e.g. *postulata est cognitio de in integrum restitutione* (D. III. 3. 1 39. § 6. Ulp.); *per in iure cessionem* (Vat. Fr. § 47. Paul.); *per in rem actionem* (D. V. 3. 1 16. fin.) : *in per uindicationem legato* (Gai. II. 206) ; *per in manum conuentionem* (ib. III. 14) ; *sine in manum conuentione* (Ulp. XXVI. § 7); *locus est de rato cautioni* (D. III. 3. 1 39. § 1); *Carbonianum edictum aptatum est ad contra tabulas bonorum possessionem et intestati, cum et in secundum tabulas (possessione) in quibusdam casibus possit uideri necessarium edictum* (D. XXXVII. 10. 1 3. pr.); *de in rem uerso actio* (D. XV. 3).

Similarly *propter naturam metus-causa-actionis* (D. IV. 2. 1 12. § 2).

(b)   Some phrases are used as little more than catch words :

So *do lego*, e.g. *ususfructus.* ' *do lego* ' *seruo legatus*, ' bequeathed in the words *do lego* ' (see note p. 146).   The interdicts are often denoted by the initial words, e.g. *tenetur interdicto* ' *quod ui aut clam* ' (see note p. 100) ; *In interdicto* '*unde ui*' (D. XLIII. 16. 1 6); *competere interdictum* ' *uti possidetis* ' *placuit* (ib. 17. 1 3. § 3); so also ' *iudicatum solui* ' *stipulatione pro suo procuratore data* (D. III. 3. 1 15) ; *ex* ' *iudicatum solui* ' *stipulatione* (XLVI. 7. 1 16. Nerat.); *stipulatio* ' *ratam rem* ' *interponi solet* (ib. 8. 1 10. Ulp.), the full phrase being *dominum ratam rem habiturum.*

So grants of possession : *nam et institutus secundum tabulas et ab intestato unde cognati et multo magis unde legitimi bonorum possessionem petere potuit* (D. XXXVIII. 17. 1 1. § 5) where the spaced words all qualify *bonor. poss.*   Actions, e.g. *sed an pater ex hac causa quod iussu teneatur uideamus: et puto ad omnes contractus quod iussu etiam referri* (D. XLVI. 1. 1 10. § 2) where *quod iussu* is short for the action so called ; cf. D. XV. 4. 1 1. § 6 *quod iussu actio in eos datur*, &c.

Ad communi diuidundo iudicium (D. iii. 3. 1 16. § 1); *per familiae erciscundae iudicium* (x. 2. 1 2. pr.; see also notes pp. 48, 49) are scarcely removed from ordinary language.

32.   For many technical phrases a particular order of the words was, if not invariably, at least usually, observed, e.g. *bonorum possessio, capitis deminutio, castrense peculium, dictio dotis, aduenticia dos, profecticia dos, in integrum restituere, in manum conuenire, legitima hereditas, legitima tutela, operis noui nuntiatio, patria potestas, pupillaris substitutio, suus heres.*   Schilling, confirming this observation of Hugo's, shews that there are some instances of the reverse order (*Bemerkungen* p. 406).   For a similar fixity of order in lay writers see Lat. Gr. § 1042 : and the same in half-compounds, as *pater familias,* &c., §§ 979, 983.   So *accepti latio, rati habitio,* &c.

33.   *Causā* used prepositionally 'on account of', 'for the sake of', 'with a view to', is in all writers put after the genitive : as an ordinary substantive it is usually prefixed, e.g. *recepta est alia causa donationis quam dicimus honoris causā* (D. xxiv. 1. 1 42. Gai.). In D. vii. 1. 1 7. § 1 (see my note p. 56), *causā* is prefixed, perhaps because it does not mean ' with a view to apprehended damage', i.e. to the prevention of it, but 'on the ground of apprehended damage'.

Kalb points out that, when *ex* is used, Gaius puts the genitive between the preposition and *causa,* Ulpian persistently puts the genitive after *causa,* e.g. *ex uenditionis causa* (Gai. ii. 20), *ex causa uenditionis* (Ulp. D. vi. 2. 1 14); *ex fideicommissi causa* (Gai. ii. 253, 254), *ex causa fideicommissi* (Ulp. D. xxv. 3. 1 5. § 22 ; &c.).

34.   The omission of a copulative particle is common in such phrases as *usus fructus, actiones empti uenditi,* &c., though it is not invariable (see note p. 27).   And this omission is also found in naming authorities, even though only two are named, e.g. *Sabinus Cassius* (D. v. 1. 1 28 ; xii. 1. 1 31) ; *Nerua Atilicinus* (xvii. 1. 1 45); *Nerua Sabinus Cassius* (xviii. 1. 1 57) ; *Nerua Proculus* (xx. 4. 1 13); *Mela Fulcinius* (xxv. 2. 1 3. § 4); *Proculus Cassius* (xxxv. 1. 1 43) ; *Labeo Ofilius* (xl. 7. 1 39. § 1); &c.

In laws a similar omission in the combination of tenses is frequent, e.g. *nisi quod...oportet oportebit* (*Lex Anton.* 5 = Bruns p. 87); *quae uiae propius urbem Romam sunt erunt* (*lex Iul. mun.*

7 = Bruns p. 96); *quod aduersus eam legem fecit fecerit, condemnatus est erit* (ib. 25); *quiue in senatu dixit dixerit* (*Lex Cornel.* ap. Cic. *Clu.* 54. § 148); *qui heredem fecit fecerit* (cf. Cic. *Uerr.* i. 41—43); *quo ea uia idue iter deterius sit fiat* (*Ed. Praet.* ap. D. xliii. 8. 1 2. § 20); *quam pecuniam L. Titius L. Baianio dedit dederit, credidit crediderit, expensum tulit tulerit,* &c. (Agreement ap. Bruns p. 200.)

Similarly *suos heredes accipere debemus filios filias, siue naturales siue adoptiuos* (D. xxxviii. 16. 1 1. § 2. Ulp.); *libertis libertabus,* oftener *libertis libertabusque* (Wilmanns' Index p. 684); *in libertos libertasue suos suas paternos paternas, qui quae in ciuitatem Romanam non uenerint* (*Lex Salpens.* xxiii. = Bruns p. 131). But we have also *quos quasue manumisi manumiseroue…filios filiasue,* &c. (D. xxxii. 1 37. § 7.)

Similarly *quae praedia donationis causa tradidi, cessi,…per te non fieri, quominus reddantur, restituantur* (D. xxxii. 1 37. § 3).

35. Repetition of the substantive in relative and demonstrative clauses is found in lay writers, but perhaps there is an imitation of the legal style. In Gaius we have *eam aetatam esse spectandam, cuius aetatis puberes fiunt* (i. 196); *bona uero Latinorum pro ea parte pertinent, pro qua parte quisque eorum dominus sit* (iii. 59); *aut calatis comitiis testamentum faciebant, quae comitia bis in anno,* &c. (ii. 101), &c. (More instances in Kalb, p. 84.)

Kalb also points out that Gaius regularly uses *quatenus* after *ea tenus,* e. g. Inst. iii. 161 *eatenus cum eo habeo mandati actionem, quatenus mea interest implesse eum mandatum;* D. iv. 2. 1 19; 3. 1 26; 4. 1 27. § 1; xiv. 3. 1 10; 5. 1 1. So also other Jurists, e.g. Proculus, D. xviii. 1. 1 69, &c. Ulpian very frequently has *quatenus* after *hactenus,* e.g. ii. 14. 1 49, *si quis hactenus desideret conueniri, quatenus facultates patiuntur;* viii. 5. 1 8. § 5; xviii. 4. 1 2. § 3; &c.

A repetition of the substantive with the demonstrative is found in Gai. i. 29; 32 *si nauem marinam aedificauerint…eaque nauis…portauerit.* In both places of Gaius the words are apparently copied from a law or senate's decree. D. vi. 2. 1 11. § 4 (Ulp. from Julian) *ex qua causa…ex ea causa;* ib. 1 13. pr. (Gai.); *id senatus consulto demonstratum est, quo senatus consulto comprehensum est* (xl. 5. 1 22. § 2. Pap.); *qua in re…in ea re* (Cic. *Tull.* 11. § 27): and see Lat. Gr. § 1002. The extent to which this kind of repetition was carried in laws may be readily seen in Bruns' *Fontes* (passim), e.g. *quem quomque* *ante suum aedificium uiam publicam h(ac) l(ege) tueri oportebit, quei eorum eam uiam arbitratu eius aedilis, quoius oportuerit, non tuebitur, eam uiam aedilis, quoius arbitratu eam tueri oportuerit, tuemdam locato ; isque aedilis diebus ne minus x, antequam locet, aput forum ante tribunale suom propositum habeto, quam uiam tuemdam et quo die locaturus sit et quorum ante aedificium ea uia sit ; &c. (Lex Iulia munic.* § 10 : Bruns p. 97 ed. 4).*

Quos pontifices quosque augures C. Caesar, quiue iussu eius coloniam deduxerit fecerit ex colonia Genetiua, ei pontifices eique augures coloniae Genetiuae Iuliae sunto, eique pontifices auguresque in pontificum augurum conlegio in ea colonia sunto, ita uti qui optima lege optumo iure in quaque colonia pontifices augures sunt erunt (*Lex Ursonens,* § 66 : Bruns p. 113).

36.　The repeated prefixing of relative clauses, shewn also in the last extracts, is very common in laws. A good instance is the following :

Quae colonia hac lege deducta quodue municipium praefectura forum concilliabulum constitutum erit, qui ager intra fines eorum erit, qui termini in eo agro statuti erunt, quo in loco terminus non stabit, in eo loco is, cuius is ager erit, terminum restituendum curato, uti quod recte factum esse uolet (*Lex Mamilia,* Grom. ed. Lachm. p. 263), i.e. 'it is the duty of the owner of any piece of ground within the territory of any colony established under this law to restore any boundary stone which shall have been set up in that territory and shall be missing in that piece of land'.

Uses of Particles and Pronouns.

37.　*Nec* is very frequently used for *non* or *ne...quidem,* e.g. *non quasi adempta, sed quasi nec data* (D. XXVIII. 4. 1 1. § 4. Ulp.) ; *libertinus nullo modo patri heres fieri possit, qui nec patrem habuisse uidetur* (Ulp. *Reg.* XII. § 3) ; *ut quemadmodum incipere alias non possunt, ita nec remaneant* (D. XLVI. 1. 1 71. pr. Paul.); *non quasi precario usum sed quasi nec usum* (D. XLIII. 1. 1 1. § 6. Ulp.) ; *si in metallum datus in integrum restitutus sit, perinde ac si nec damnatus fuisset, ad munera uel honores uocatur* (D. L. 4. 1 3. § 2. Ulp.); *senatores hanc uacationem habere non possunt, quod nec habere illis nauem ex lege Iulia repetundarum licet* (D. L. 5. 1 3. Scaev.); *qua ratione nec emancipando filium peculium ei aufert, quod nec in familia retento potest auferre* (D. XLIX. 17. 1 12. Pap.): &c.   Kalb says, Gaius uses *nec*, as a mere negative, only in the phrases *nec mancipi* and *furtum nec manifestum*.   The usage is found in Seneca, Martial, Quintilian, &c., see Lat. Gr. § 2232 ; Dräger, *Hist. Synt.* II. 73 ed. 2 ; and Halm's Index to Minucius Felix.

Kalb says that in coordinated clauses Gaius almost always uses *neque...neque*, not *nec...nec*.   (In IV. 150 *nec ui nec clam nec precario* is an old formula.)

38.   The use of *ne quidem* together and prefixed to the emphatic word is certainly frequent in the lawyers, though not perhaps peculiar to them.   (Koffmane *Gesch. d. Kirchenlat.* p. 136 quotes Faustin. *lib. prec.* 2.)   See my note on p. 126 and add to the references there given Gai. II. 218; D. XXIII. 2. 1 60. § 5. Paul.; XXV. 2. 1 1. Paul.; XXX. 1 114. § 11. Marcian.; XL. 1. 1 8. § 3. Marcian.; XLIV. 7. 1 58. (59) Licin. Ruf.; XLVIII. 18. 1 1. § 5. Ulp.; 19. 1 9. § 3. Ulp.; L. 2. 1 12. Callistr.; 6. 1 6. § 12. Callistr.

So also *non quidem :* e.g. *non quidem ad agendum sed ad administrandum* (D. III. 3. 1 43. Paul.).   So also Curt. III. 11. § 10 ; Sen. *Ir.* II. 10. § 3.   *Et quidem* (e.g. D. XXIX. 2. 1 42. pr. Ulp. *et quidem impune*) is common in lay writers : see Lat. Gr. § 1623.

39.   *Ceterum = alioquin : Quod circumspecte erit faciendum : ceterum nemo accedet ad emptionem rerum pupillarium* (D. IV. 4. 1 7. § 8. Ulp.); *quod sic accipiendum, si non dolus ipsorum interueniat : ceterum cessabit restitutio* (ib. 1 9. § 8. Ulp.).   So XXXVII. 10. 1 5. § 4. Ulp.   Other instances in Klotz *Lex.* s. v.   In the ordinary use of *ceterum* the other alternative is explicitly set out, e.g. *sed haec ita, si mandato domini procurator egit : ceterum, si mandatum non est,* &c. (D. III. 3. 1 27. pr. Ulp.); *sed hoc post litem contestatam : ceterum ante iudicium acceptum non decipit actorem qui se negat possidere* (VI. 1. 1 25. Ulp.); *ceterum aliter obseruantibus* 'if a different view were taken' *futurum,* &c. (XLIII. 8. 1 2. § 28.   Nerua ap. Ulp.).

40.   *Suus* is used not merely as a reflexive pronoun, i.e. as referring to the person who is the subject of the sentence, or at least the subject of the discourse (Lat. Gr. §§ 2262—2270).   It is used technically of a man's own heirs, i.e. of the children in his power (D. XXXVIII. 16. 1 1. § 2), *suus heres, sui heredes* (see note, p. 226).   In this use *suus* precedes *heres*.

Pro suo (D. XLI. 10) was used technically where *pro meo, &c.*
would be more natural, e.g. *Donata uel legata uel pro donato uel pro
legato etiam pro suo possideo* (D. XLI. 10. 1 1. pr. where indeed strict
construction would require the plural *pro meis; pro meo possideo*
follows just after).

(*Inter se* is becoming technical in Minuc. Fel. 18. § 1 *inter se...
singuli dissimiles inuenimur.* Cf. Sittl *Die loc. Versch. d. lat. Spr.*
1882, p. 115.)

For such uses as *suis nummis hominem emi* (D. II. 4. 1 10. pr.),
where *suis* refers to *hominem,* there are classical parallels. Cf. Lat.
Gr. § 1265. Cf. D. XXXIII. 10. 1 7. § 2 *non tamen a Seruio dissentio,
non uideri quemquam dixisse, cuius non suo nomine usus sit,* where
suo refers to *cuius* 'that of which he has not used the proper name'
cf. notes, p. 225.

41.   On *perinde* and *proinde* see notes, p. 149.

puta, ut puta, ib. p. 55.

quisque attracted into the case of *suus* (e.g. *sua quaque die* D.
XIII. 7. 1 8. § 3 ; *Tab. Baet.* ap. Bruns p. 200), see Lat. Gr. § 2288.

Formation of inflexions and words.

42.   Some unusual forms are found which are probably not due
to the copyists or to the compilers, but to a corruption or forgetfulness of the proper form, e.g. *praestauimus* (D. III. 5. 1 18. § 4. Paul.);
praestauit (v. 3. 1 36. § 1. Paul.); *praestarim* (XXII. 1. 1 37. Ulp.).
So also *praestatu* D. XVIII. 1. 1 66. Pomp.; XIX. 1. 1 11. § 18. Ulp.

Also *accederat* (D. XXIX. 2. 1 99. Pomp.), for which Mommsen
reads *accesserat; adpulserit* (XLIII. 20. 1 1. § 18. Ulp.); *expulsisse*
(L. 17. 1 18. Pomp.).

domu (abl.) is found frequently in the Digest, e.g. VII. 4. 1 22 ;
XIX. 2. 1 60. pr.; *Edict.* ap. XXV. 4. 1 1. § 10. It is also found in
Plaut. *Mil.* 126 and in some inscriptions (Neue *Formenlehre* I. p.
520 ed. 2).

43.   Stems in *-torio- (-sorio-)* are in very frequent use by the
lawyers, some being words of ordinary life, others formed for technical expressions. I have noted the following : *absolutorius, adiu-
torium, aestimatoria (actio), amatorius, ambulatorius, aratorius,
adsessorium, auditorium, balneatorius, captatorius, cenatorius, cen-*

*sorius, cocinatorius, cognitorius, collusorie, commissoria (lex), con-
fessoria (actio), constitutoria (actio), contestatorius, coopertorium,
defunctorie, delatorius, derisorius, derogatorius, deuersorium, dila-
toria (exceptio), dimissoriae (litterae), dormitorius, ereptorius, excep-
torius, exclusorius, exercitoria (actio), exhibitorium (interdictum),
fideiussorius, fraudatorium (int.), frustratorius, indutorius, institoria
(actio), interrogatoria (actio), interusorium, iuratorius, lusorius, man-
datorius, meritorium, messorius, moratorius, negatoria (actio), notoria,
nugatorius, obligatorius, olitorius, peremptorius, petitorius, pictorius,
piscatorius, pistorius, portorium, possessorius, potorius, praeparatorius,
praetorius, procuratorius, prohibitorius, putatorius, quaestorius, recu-
peratorius, redhibitoria (actio), repositorium, rescissoria (actio),
restitutorius, sectorium (interdictum), secutorium (iudicium), sena-
torius, signatorius, stratorius, successorius, tectorius, territorium, tri-
butorius, tutorius, uenatorius, uiatorius, uindemiatorius, uxorius.*

The list might be greatly increased, if the Codes were included.

Stems in *-ario-* are twice as numerous (over 150), but they are
not so largely legal. Some however have this aspect: e.g. *arbitraria
(actio), compromissarius, depositarius, fideicommissarius, fiduciarius,
fructuarius, hereditarius, honorarius, hypothecarius, iudiciarius,
legatarius, collegatarius, partiarius, peculiarius, priuilegiarius, pro-
prietarius, sequestrarius, superficiarius, testamentarius, triticiaria
(condictio), uenaliciarius, usuarius, usufructuarius, usurarius.*

44. Adverbs in *-ter* are also very freely formed. I have noted
these, many however being in common use elsewhere. Indeed, this
formation is rather a prevalent use of the time than specially of the
lawyers: *acriter, aequaliter, aliter, atrociter, audacter, audenter,
breuiter, ciuiliter, clementer, communiter, competenter, condicionaliter,
congruenter, consequenter, constanter, continenter, conuenienter, cor-
poraliter, criminaliter, difficiliter, diligenter, dissimiliter, dupliciter,
efficaciter, eleganter, euidenter, fataliter, fauorabiliter, feliciter, fide-
liter, fortiter, fraudulenter, frequenter, frugaliter, generaliter, graui-
ter, habiliter, immutabiliter, impersonaliter, impotenter, imprudenter,
inaequaliter, inciuiliter, inconsideranter, incunctanter, indifferenter,
indubitanter, inefficaciter, ineleganter, infauorabiliter, instanter, inu-
tiliter, largiter, leniter, leuiter, libenter, liberaliter, licenter, medioc-
riter, militariter, naturaliter, neglegenter, notabiliter, patienter, pecu-
liariter, pecuniariter, peruicaciter, petulanter, principaliter, prudenter, quadrifariter, qualiter, qualiterqualiter, regulariter, salubriter,*

sapienter, segniter, similiter, simpliciter, singulariter, solenniter, specialiter, subtiliter, sufficienter, turpiter, uehementer, uigilanter, uiolenter, uniuersaliter, utiliter.

45.   The formation of verbs from adjectives of the comparative degree is noticeable : e.g. *certiorare* (D. XII. 4. 1 5. § 1 and often); *meliorare* (VII. 1. 1 13. § 5); *minoratus* (XVIII. 7. 1 10); *peiorare* (Paul *Sent.* II. 18. § 1, but see Krüger *ad loc.*).

CHAPTER XVII.

AUTHORITIES FOR TEXT OF DIGEST.

FORTUNE has favoured the great work of Justinian. The multitude of MSS. which are found at the present day, containing the whole or part of the Digest, is no indication of the chances of its having been lost.   The great mass of them, indeed almost all, have been directly or indirectly copied from one MS. still existing at Florence, and have been written since the tenth or eleventh century ; so that with slight qualifications it may be said the line of authentic knowledge of the words of the Digest consists of a single thread.   An accident in the ninth or tenth century might have destroyed any authentic knowledge of the bulk of Roman law.

The examination and criticism of MSS. have been conducted of late years so much more thoroughly, and on such improved methods, due to a clearer comprehension of the problem, that it would be a matter of very great regret if the Digest had not been edited critically by some competent philologer of the present or recent times. Happily this task has been admirably performed by the scholar best fitted for it.   Th. Mommsen's edition (in 2 vols 4to., Berolini, 1870) is founded on a new collation of the Florentine MS. made by Ad. Kiessling and Aug. Reifferscheid, which has been verified in all doubtful passages by P. Krüger, R. Schöll, and others, so as to leave now no doubt as to the reading of the original scribe, or of the correctors of it.   And Mommsen has made such an examination and selection of other MSS. as to enable their value, or, as it may almost be said, their general worthlessness, to be ascertained.   The account I proceed to give of the authorities for the text of the Digest rests mainly on Mommsen's Preface to this edition.

The Florentine MS. was at Pisa in the middle of the twelfth century, and its preservation was carefully provided for in the statutes of that city, dated 1284. Whence or when it came there is not known. It has been said that it came there from Constantinople: it has also been said that the Pisans carried it home as booty after the capture of Amalfi: but there is no sufficient authority for either statement. The Florentines on their conquest of Pisa in 1406 carried it off with other booty to Florence, where it was kept in the public treasury in the Old Palace till 1786, when it was transferred to the Laurentian Library. The MS. is in two volumes, of which the first contains 441 leaves, the second 465. One (additional) leaf containing the Greek constitution Δέδωκεν has been lost from the first volume, but it was copied in the sixteenth century. Each leaf is written on both in front and back and (excepting the three Latin prefatory constitutions) in two columns. Each column contains 44 or 45 lines, the lines containing a various number of letters, according to Mommsen's estimate from 27 to 38, i.e. an average of about 32. The size of each leaf is about $14\frac{1}{2}$ in. high, and $12\frac{1}{2}$ in. wide: each column of writing is 10 in. long, and nearly $4\frac{1}{2}$ in. wide. Twelve scribes have been employed on the MS., of whom ten have written the Digest proper, the prefatory constitutions being written by two others. The letters are all uncial, about $\frac{1}{8}$ of an inch high, of a plain rounded character. There is as a rule no space or interpunctuation between the words. Each extract[1] commences a new line, one letter usually projecting, and there is usually a colon at the end of the extract; and sometimes a point or empty space after the name of the authors and before the commencement of a new clause. Marks similar to our own inverted commas are usually put where the words of laws or of the edict are quoted. No numbers or abbreviations are found, unless some ligatures of letters at the end of a line are considered such. The inscriptions and subscriptions of the several books, the titles (rubricae) and the names of the authors of the extracts (occasionally, by mistake as it seems, the following word also) are with few exceptions in red paint.

The MS. was executed in the sixth or seventh century by Greeks, and, probably at the same time and place, was corrected by two other Greeks, the first correcting Books i.—xviii., or thereabouts,

---

[1] i.e. what was taken by the scribe for a separate extract: but there are not a few instances of extracts being improperly divided and of others improperly united (Mommsen Praef. p. xxxiii.).

the second correcting the remaining books. For our purposes they may be treated as one. It is due to this correction that the work, as we read it, is pretty free from gross copyist errors. Whether the corrector had the identical copy before him, which the original scribes had, or another copy is not certain. There are appearances which speak for either theory. Mommsen inclines to the opinion that the corrector had a different copy before him.

There is no other MS. of any considerable portion of the Digest, which can be put on the same plane of evidence as an independent authority. But there are MSS. of small parts which are invaluable because they are independent. Four leaves of a Naples palimpsest, of about the same age as the Florentine MS. contain X. 2. 1 3. fin.— 1 16. pr.; 3. 1 23. fin.—1 29. pr. med.; 4. 1 12. fin.—1 19. Seven fragments of papyrus in Count Schönborn's library at Pommersfeld near Bamberg, of similar age, have preserved some broken bits of XLV. 1. 11 35—73. Both these are copied out in the Appendix to Mommsen's first vol., and a facsimile of the Pommersfeld fragments is given in the Appendix to the second vol. A third independent source are two MSS. of the *Gromatici Scriptores* which contain the title *finium regundorum* (X. 1). They are of the ninth or tenth century, and shew that the compiler of these writings of the land-surveyors had a different text before him from that exhibited by the Florentine MS.

These three independent MS. sources have a special value besides their bearing on the particular correction of the parts of the Digest contained in them. They shew that the Florentine MS., good as it is, and carefully corrected as it has been, yet is not a perfectly faithful copy of the original. In the short title *finium regundorum* Mommsen counts five passages where the reading of the Florentine MS. requires correction, and seven others where it requires supplementing from the text given in the *Gromatici*. Similarly in 133 lines of Mommsen's edition, seven passages receive correction or supplement from the Naples palimpsest, and this number would probably be increased if the palimpsest were not mutilated or illegible in parts. Even the MSS. of the Code, which contain two of the prefatory constitutions of the Digest, do not agree entirely with the Florentine MS.

The other MSS. are all in small characters. One written in the ninth century contains the end of the Institutes and about half of the first book of the Digest. This fragment is one sheet, inserted in a MS. containing Julian's Epitome of the Novels, and now in the public library at Berlin. It was either copied from a copy of the Florentine, or more probably from a MS. closely resembling the Florentine.

All the other known MSS. come from the Bologna school of law, and are therefore called *Bononienses*. Very few contain the whole Digest; the great mass contain, more or less completely, one or other of the three volumes, into which the Digest was divided during the middle ages. These are (1) *Digestum uetus* which contained Books I.—XXIV. 3. 1 2 as far as the words *Ulpianus libro trigesimo*[1]; (2) the *Infortiatum* containing Books XXIV. 3. 1 1 to end of XXXVIII.: but the latter part of this, beginning with the words *tres partes* in Book XXXV. 2. 1 82, is often spoken of as a separate portion, and called (from the initial words) *Tres Partes;* (3) *Digestum nouum*[2] containing Books XXXIX.—L. (There is no trace of such a division in the Florentine MS.) There are at least 200 MSS. of the *Digestum uetus*, and, if the three volumes be reckoned separately, probably 500 MSS. of the Digest in all: the oldest of these being of the time of Irnerius the founder of the Bolognese school, who lived at the end of the eleventh and beginning of the twelfth century. Only the older and better of these MSS. contain the inscriptions of the laws in full, and even these have not the Greek parts complete. Some MSS. leave a blank, others insert a Latin version. The Bolognese MSS. of the *Digestum uetus* are both older and better than those of the rest of the Digest.

---

[1] So Mommsen's oldest MSS. Others stop at the end of XXIV. 2.

[2] The origin of this division and of the names is unknown. According to Odofredus (who died A.D. 1265) they are connected with the gradual way in which Justinian's works became known at Bologna. First the *Codex* I.—IX. and *Digestum uetus* and *nouum* and the Institutes: then the *Infortiatum* without the *Tres Partes:* then the Three Books (i.e. Cod. X.—XII.) and last the *Authenticum* (i.e. Latin version of the Novels). Savigny (*Gesch. des röm. Rechts* III. p. 431 sq) suggests that the *Dig. uetus* was first found, then the *Dig. nouum* ; then the *Infortiatum* which was so called (" strengthened ") when the *Tres Partes* was added to it, whether that was found subsequently, or, as Savigny thinks, previously placed at the head of the *Dig. nouum*. Mommsen assigns no weight to Odofred's account (*Pref.* p. lxxii.). Scheurl (*Z. R. G.* XII. p. 146. sqq.) points out that the course of study as settled by Justinian may have led to such a division of the Digest MSS. as is found in the Bolognese copies. Books I.—XXXVI. were all that were intended *for study*. This coincides with the *Uetus* and *Infortiatum* (exclusive of the *Tres Partes*), if we suppose a few leaves lost at the end. Books I.—XXIII. were all to be *lectured* on ; of the remaining books only XXVI. XXVIII. and XXX. The *Uetus* omits only these last scattered books, and contains all the continuous portion, and only two titles more, these titles being closely connected with the preceding. Hence he thinks it may well be that the Bolognese found at first only a copy of the *Uetus*, and then of the *Infortiatum* less the *Tres Partes*, and, after obtaining the Florentine MS. or a copy of it, used the old MSS. only to correct it. Hence it comes that there is in the Bolognese MSS. no valuable correction of the Florentine text in the *Tres Partes* or *Nouum* (see below, p. ccxli).

Mommsen employed five MSS. of the *Dig. uetus* and rejected not a few others, all of the end of the eleventh or beginning of twelfth century.   Of the *Infortiatum* he had only one, of the *Dig. nouum* none, earlier than the thirteenth century.

The relation of these Bolognese MSS. to the Florentine is a matter of much difficulty.   The distribution into three or four volumes, certain transpositions common to all the older of them, innumerable identical omissions, insertions, corruptions, shew that they are of common origin, variously corrected by conjecture or reference to a better MS.   This common original, was it the Florentine or another? Mommsen holds it to have been not the Florentine itself, but one copied from it.   Not the Florentine itself, because one notable transposition in Book XXIII. 3 does not accord with the pages of the Florentine MS., and the nature of the mistakes in the older MSS. points to a MS. written in a different character.   But this original of the Bolognese MSS. must have been copied from the Florentine, because, amongst other reasons, (1) the Bolognese MSS. agree with the Florentine as against the Naples palimpsest and against the Gromatic MSS. of X. 1 (*Finium regundorum*); (2) they supply none of the larger gaps[1] in the Florentine and exhibit perpetually its errors; (3) they shew transpositions which are clearly explained by the Florentine MS.   Of these, two are caused by an omission in the first writing of the Florentine, which was then supplied by the corrector in the margin, and the words thus added have been introduced, not into the right place, but into one in which a careless copyist from the Florentine would very naturally insert them. These are D. XXIII. 3. 1 10. pr., shewn in facsimile appended to Mommsen's 2nd vol.; and XXXVIII. 7. 1 1 for which see Momms. *Pref.* p. lxvii.   A third transposition is in the last title of the fiftieth book.   All known MSS. have this order of the extracts : 1 117, then 1 158.—1 199; 1 118. —1 157 ; 1 200.   The Florentine MS. explains this precisely, a fact first noticed by Taurelli.   Two leaves, viz. 463, 464 have been transposed by the binder and have thus led to the inversion[2].

But this is not a complete account of the relation.   For there are a fair number of passages in which these Bolognese MSS. give us

---

[1] These larger gaps are (a) a space of 2½ lines between § 1 and § 2 of D. XXXVI. 2. 1 19; (b) a space of 17 lines and a single column at the end of XLVIII. 20; (c) a space of more than four columns at the end of XLVIII. 22. Some smaller gaps are filled by the corrector (Mommsen, p. lv.).

[2] Savigny (*Gesch.* III. p. 461 sq.) adopts a suggestion that the inconvenience of a different order in one copy from another led to all MSS. being made to follow the Florentine order.

the true reading where the Florentine does not, and yet this true reading is such as cannot be reasonably attributed to conjecture. In particular there are a number of passages in which words evidently, or at any rate probably, genuine are supplied by the Bolognese MSS. and are absent from the Florentine. Savigny gives a list of 26 such passages (*Gesch.* III., p. 455). Mommsen enumerates 30 (*Pref.* p. lxx.), but disallows some of Savigny's. The most probable explanation of the facts is therefore, according to Mommsen, that Irnerius, or some one yet older, noted on his copy, mediate or immediate, of the Florentine, some readings of another MS. different from the Florentine, and that this copy has been the parent of the Bolognese MSS. (*Pref.* p. lxviii.). Whatever be the precise truth on this matter, it is clear on the one hand that the mass of variations from the Florentine readings are due to error or conjecture, and on the other that, being right in a few places, the Bolognese readings cannot be wholly neglected. Mommsen considers that there is no instance after the thirty-fourth book (and therefore no instance in the *Tres Partes* or in the *Digestum nouum*) in which the Bolognese reading, even if right, can claim to be superior to a conjecture. Curiously enough in the seventeenth book where the ordinary corrector of the Florentine is wanting (viz. from tit. 1. 1 27 to tit. 2. 1 30 inclusive; see however Mommsen *Pref. ad ed. mai.* p. lxxxvii.) the Bolognese recension is of real value.

But there is another aid to ascertaining the real text of the Digest which is of greater value than the Bolognese MSS., and that is the old Greek commentators. For they were not only commentators, but translators as well. It was all very well for Justinian to consolidate the law of Rome, but the language of half the empire and of the court was Greek, and the law had to speak the language of the judges, the practitioners and the suitors[1]. The chief law-schools were Constantinople and Berytus, both in Greek-speaking countries. Justinian's Constitutions issued subsequently to the re-

---

[1] As a specimen of the mode in which law Latin was turned into Greek compare the following extract from Stephanus' commentary with our 1 25. § 7. ἐπειδὴ εἰρήκαμεν προσπορίζεσθαι τῷ οὐσουφρουκτουαρίῳ τὰ ἐξ ῥὲ αὐτοῦ βὲλ ἐξ ὀπέρις, οὐσουφρουκτουάριον τίνα νοήσομεν, πότερον ἐν ᾧ κατὰ διαθήκην ἢ λεγάτον ὁ οὐσούφρουκτος συνέστη, ἢ καὶ τὸν κατὰ τραδιτίονα ἢ ἐπερώτησιν ἢ κατὰ ἄλλον τρόπον τινὰ διὰ τῆς φαμιλίας νερκισκούνδαε ἢ τοῦ κομμοῦνι διβιδοῦνδο οὐσούφρουκτον λαβόντα; φησὶ τοίνυν ὁ Πήγασος, ἀποδέχεται δὲ αὐτὸν Ιουλιανος, προσπορίζεσθαι ταῦτα τῷ ὁπωσδήποτε γενομένῳ οὐσουφρουκταρίῳ. The law is thus briefly given in the text of Bas. Παντὶ τῷ τὴν χρῆσιν ἔχοντι τὰ ἐκ πράγματος αὐτοῦ ἢ ἐξ ὑπηρεσίας τοῦ δούλου προσπορίζεται.

vised Code were almost all in Greek, though some few of them were published in Latin also. Hence Justinian's Latin law books required interpretation into Greek. An early paraphrase of the Institutes still exists under the name of Theophilus. For the Code the most celebrated interpreter was Thalelaeus, and his version it is which was chiefly adopted in those passages of the Code which were taken into the Basilica. For the Digest we have substantial remains of four interpreters, Dorotheus[1], Stephanus, Cyrillus and one generally called Anonymus. Theophilus, a professor at Constantinople, and Dorotheus, a professor at Berytus, assisted Tribonian in compiling the Institutes, and were on the Commission for compiling the Digest. Theophilus was also on the Commission for preparing the first Code, and Dorotheus was on that for revising it. Both along with Thalelaeus are named among those to whom Justinian addressed his Constitution (*Omnem*) for reforming the course of legal education. Stephanus was a professor of law, according to Heimbach not the same as, but junior to, Stephanus the advocate, who was one of the compilers of the Digest. He appears to have lived and lectured about the middle of the sixth century. Cyrillus appears to have lived about the end of that century, but little is known of him. The nameless interpreter is in all probability identical with one called Enantiophanes, as the author of a book on the contradictory passages in the Digest (περὶ ἐναντιοφανειῶν). His real name was, according to modern scholars, Julian. Julian was author of a Latin Epitome of Justinian's Novels, and lived probably in the middle of the sixth century. Looking to the internal evidence and to the prohibition by Justinian (see above, p. xxv), we may conclude that the comments are reports of lectures: the versions may have been issued by the writers themselves.

Our knowledge of these versions and commentaries is chiefly due to the *Basilica* ('Imperials'). Basil (Βασίλειος) the Macedonian, emperor from A.D. 867 to 886, directed the consolidation of the Justinian law books into a single code of 40 (or 60) books, entitled Ἀνακάθαρσις τῶν παλαιῶν νόμων, 'Reformation of the old laws'. Whether this was completed or published is uncertain. He published a short institutional treatise called ὁ πρόχειρος νόμος, 'Handy Law', which was re-edited in 885 under the name ἐπαναγωγή ('New

---

[1] Zachariä dates Dorotheus' version 'after 542': that of Stephanus 'towards the end of Justinian's reign', those of Cyril and Anonymus 'in the reign of Justin' (565—578); the work of Enantiophanes 'in the reign of Heraclius' (610—641). See his *Gesch. des gr. röm. Rechts*, ed. 2. 1879, p. 5 sqq.

Edition') τοῦ νόμου. His son, Leo the Philosopher, either completed or revised and published, between 886 and 892 (Heimbach in Z. R. G. VIII. p. 417), the code in 60 books which was commonly called τὰ βασιλικά (from βασιλεύς, not from the emperor Βασίλειος). No one MS. has preserved to us the whole of this, but various MSS. have preserved parts, so that we have more than two-thirds of the whole, viz. Books I.—XVIII. (the last three, however, being mutilated), XX.—XXX. (the last being mutilated), XXXVIII.—XLII., XLV.—LII., and LX. Book XIX. has been partly restored from other works. The Basilica consist of large selections from the Digest, Code and Novels, arranged in this order under titles following in general the order of the Code, the matter, however, of Books VIII., IX., XI., XXXIX. 1—3, XLIII. and XLVII. of the Digest being put mainly in the last three books of the Basilica. In a few titles some passages from Theophilus' paraphrase of the Institutes occur. They usually are placed first.

About the middle of the tenth century a number of *scholia* or notes were added to the Basilica, and are found in the MSS. These contain many extracts from the *indices* ('short expositions') of the old commentators on Justinian's works, and also a number of more recent notes. The extracts from the old Greek commentators are of great value, both for the text of the Digest itself and for its explanation.

In those passages of the Basilica which were taken from the Digest, the Greek text is usually the version made by the anonymous commentator (Julian?), but Greek translations have been made of the Latin technical expressions which Anonymus and the others generally preserved[1]. Sometimes other versions, chiefly Cyril's, have supplied the text of the Basilica. The compiler appears to have had before him the works of Stephanus and Dorotheus. Stephanus is largely represented in the Scholia, but his version is mixed with his commentary. It is no doubt a report of his lectures, and it is in accordance with this that notes of his are found only on Dig. I.— XXIII., XXVI. and probably XXX. These, with the addition of Book XXVIII., are exactly the books on which, by Justinian's directions, lectures were to be given. Dorotheus' index has been used for the other books. Cyril's version and notes are also partially in the Scholia. All the older Scholia are adapted to Justinian's text, and the references are made to that. The versions differ from one another

---

[1] See, for instance, the passage quoted in the note on p. ccxli.

in point of fulness. Thalelaeus' version of the Code was literal (κατὰ πόδα). Dorotheus' version of the Digest approaches the same character, and is therefore the most useful for correcting the Latin text. Stephanus' version is a paraphrase, and hence obtained the name of τὸ πλάτος, 'breadth'[1]. The versions of Anonymus and Cyrillus, the latter especially, were concise (κατ' ἐπιτομὴν), and for the text of the Digest are of use chiefly when neither of the fuller versions is preserved. Mommsen has carefully used these sources for correcting the text of the Digest, and has made some useful remarks (*Pref.* p. lxxiv. sqq.) as to the caution necessary in using, for the ascertainment of the Latin text, Greek versions, and especially Greek versions mixed with comments, and in comparing the evidence of this inferential text with that of the Florentine MS.

The above account of the Greek writers rests on Heimbach's elaborate *Prolegomena* published in Vol. VI., a supplementary volume, of his edition of the Basilica. (See also an account in German by the same writer in *Z. R. G.* II. 318 sqq.) Appended to this is a *Manuale* in which he assigns, partly by internal evidence, an author to each of the older Scholia which are preserved, and refers them to the appropriate passage of the Institutes, Digest, Code and Novels. Four of the books of the Basilica (XV.—XVIII.) had previously been reedited from fresh MS. sources by Zachariä von Lingenthal, and these contain the Scholia conveniently arranged and named. (It is published as a kind of appendix to Heimbach.) Our present title, *de usufructu*, is contained in this, and forms by itself the whole of tit. 1 of the XVIth Book of the Basilica.

---

[1] Cf. D. XLVI. 3. 1 13 *Sed hoc ἐν πλάτει et cum quodam spatio temporis accipi debet*, i.e. 'must be taken broadly'.

CHAPTER XVIII.

OF THE MODE OF CITING THE DIGEST.

The Byzantine commentators cited a passage by the number of the book, title and extract, prefixing βι. for βιβλίον, τι. for title and διγ. (i.e. digest) for the extract. The Glossators, finding either no numbers or varying numbers in their MSS., cited by the rubric (abridged) of the title and the first words of the extract and of the paragraph. In the 16th century the numbers of the extract and of the paragraph were added, and, later on, the initial words were omitted. Until quite recently the practice continued of denoting the title by the rubric simply, but now the number of the book and title are usually given, and have sometimes superseded the rubric altogether. In Germany the rubric is usually given, except in books intended not so much for jurists as for philologers generally.

Editions of the Digest have an index of the rubrics, by which the book and title can readily be found. The older editions, e.g. Godefroi's, have an index of all the extracts by their initial words.

The order of arranging the parts of a reference also varies. The Byzantines generally put them in the order—book, title, extract. The Glossators did the like : rubric, extract, paragraph. But after them arose the practice of putting first the extract and paragraph and then the rubric. This is still the most usual way in Germany, though some have returned to what seems the more natural order.

The Digest is denoted by *Dig.* or *D* ; Π or π (for *Pandectae*): or in older books very often by *ff*, which has arisen by calligraphic development from a *d* with a line through it. (Transitional forms may be seen in *Z.R.G.* xii. 300 : see also xiii. 399.)

An extract in the Digest is usually denoted by *lex* or L or *l* : sometimes by *fr.* (for *fragmentum*). Sometimes *cap.* or *c.* for *caput* has been used. The paragraphs are usually denoted by §.

I have adopted the plan of denoting the book by roman numerals, the title by arabic numerals, and always prefixing *l* to the number of the law or extract, and § to that of the paragraph. I have omitted the rubric, as probably not of much service to English readers, and as adding much to the length of the reference.

It is not uncommon in modern jurists to prefix or affix the name of the author of the extract, e.g. *Ulp.* or *Gai.* Some even add the work and book of the author. There are occasions when such an addition is useful, but as a rule it complicates the reference greatly.

The following examples will show the principal modes. Further varieties are created by roman or arabic numerals, by addition or omission of brackets, and by different abridgements of the rubrics.

> βι. ς΄. τί α. διγ. κγ΄.   So Byzantine Commentators.
> *D* (or *ff*) *de rei uind. l in rem. § tignum.* So the Glossators.
> *l in rem § tignum ff rei uind.* (*D* or *ff* is often omitted, e.g.
> by Cujas.)
> *l in rem* 23 § *tignum* 6 *D de rei uind.*
> *L* 23. § 6. *D. de rei uind.* So Glück.
> L 23 § 6 *de rei uind.* (6. 1). So Savigny and Thibaut.
> fr. 23 § 6 *de R. V.* 6, 1 (Ulp.). So Bekker.
> *D. de rei uind.* VI. 1, 1 23 § 6. So Schrader.
> Paul. 21 ad Ed. (D. VI. 1, 23 § 6). So Voigt.
> Paulus *Dig.* 6, 1, 23, 6. So Mommsen in *Staatsrecht.*
> D. VI. 1. 1 23. § 6.

The three books on Legacies (XXX, XXXI, XXXII) are often quoted as *D. de legat.* I., *D. de legat.* II., *D. de legat.* III.

The rubrics are abridged, e.g. XXII. 1. is quoted as *de usuris* instead of *de usuris et fructibus et causis et omnibus accessionibus et mora;* XXIV. 3. as *sol. matr.* instead of *soluto matrimonio dos quemadmodum petatur;* VII. 1. as *de usufr.*, &c. Many are frequently quoted by initials, e.g.

> *de* I. et I. (for I. 1 *de iustitia et iure*);
> *de* O.I. (for I. 2 *de origine iuris,* &c.) ;
> *de* D.R. or de R.D. (for I. 8 *de diuisione rerum et qualitate*) ;
> *de* N.G. (for III. 5 *de negotiis gestis*) ;
> *de* H.P. (for V. 3 *de hereditatis petitione*) ;
> *de* R.V. (for VI. 1 *de rei uindicatione*) ;
> *de* S.P.U. (for VIII. 2 *de seruitutibus praediorum urbanorum*);
> *de* S.P.R. (for VIII. 3 *de seruitutibus praediorum rusticorum*) ;
> *de* R. C. (for XII. 1 *de rebus creditis,* &c.) ;
> *de* C.E. (for XVIII. 1 *de contrahenda emtione*) ;
> *de* A.E.V. (for XIX. 1 *de actionibus emti uenditi*) ;
> *de* R.N. (for XXIII. 2 *de ritu nuptiarum*) ;

de I.D. (for xxiii. 3 *de iure dotium*);

de H.I. (for xxviii. 5 *de hereditatibus instituendis*);

de A.v.O.H. (for xxix. 2 *de acquirenda uel omittenda hereditate*);

de B.P. (for xxxvii. 1 *de bonorum possessionibus*);

de A.R.D. (for xli. 1 *de acquirendo rerum dominio*);

de A.v.A.P. or *de* A.P. (for xli. 2 *de acquirenda uel amittenda possessione*);

de O. et A. (for xlvi. 7 *de obligationibus et actionibus*);

de V.O. (for xlv. 1 *de uerborum obligationibus*);

de I.F. (for xlix. 14 *de iure fisci*);

de V.S. (for l. 16 *de uerborum significatione*);

de R.I. (for l. 17 *de diuersis regulis iuris antiqui*).

The *de* is sometimes omitted.

In the older books, e.g. Godefroi's notes to Digest, earlier laws or titles are referred to with $\bar{s}$ prefixed (for *supra*); later laws or titles with $\bar{\imath}$ or $\bar{\jmath}$ (for *infra*). Thus (in a note on the earlier part) 1 6 $\bar{\mathrm{J}}$ *de iure dotium* refers to D. xxiii. 3. 1 6.

h. t. (*hoc titulo* or *huius tituli*) for the title on the subject on which one is writing. *Eod.* for *eodem titulo*, for the last title referred to. *Rubr.* where the rubric itself is the subject of the reference; *t. t.* (*toto titulo*) when the whole title is referred to. *Arg.* is added to a reference when the passage cited does not directly, but only by inference (*argumento*), support the proposition. *Uerbis* or *in uerbis*, (in the Glossators *uersi.* for *uersiculo*) is prefixed to any special words on which stress is laid.

When only one extract forms a whole title (e.g. xliii. 15) *l. un.* or the like (for *lex unica*) is given in place of the number of the extract. The last extract or paragraph is often denoted by *l. ult.* or *fi.* (*finalis*) or § *ult.*; the last but one by § *penult.*; &c.

When there is more than one paragraph in an extract the first paragraph is quoted as *pr.*, i.e. *in principio ;* and number 1 denotes the first-numbered, but really the second, paragraph. This probably arose from the notion, that it was unnecessary to begin numbering the parts of a law or extract, till you came to a new point or subject.

In the old times when they quoted by initial words, if it happened that several laws began with the same word, they were quoted thus, e.g. 1 5 of D. iv. 2 was distinguished as *l metum* i, 1 6 as *l metum* ii, &c.

The Constitutions printed at the commencement of the Digest directing its composition, &c. are still usually quoted by the final words, viz. Const. *Deo auctore,* Const. *Omnem,* Const. *Tanta* or Δέδωκεν (see above, p. xxiv). Similarly the constitutions prefixed to the code viz. *Haec quae necessario, Summa reipublicae,* and *Cordi.*

The other parts of the *Corpus Iuris* were quoted in analogous ways. The Codex was denoted by *cod.* or *c.* and the several constitutions either by *cap.* or more usually *l.* or *c.* or *const.* or *cost.* The Greeks have διατ. for διάταξις. The Institutes were denoted by *ist.* or *inst.* or I., e.g.,

C. *de pactis* l. *si pascenda*	Inst. *de rer. diu.* § *illud quaesitum.*
l. *si pascenda* C. *de pactis*	§ *illud quaesitum,* Inst. *de rer. diu.*
l 8. C. *de pactis*	§ 13 I. *de rer. diu.*
l 8. C. *de pactis* (2. 3) or (II. 3)	§ 13 I. *de rer. diu.* (2. 1) or (II. 1).
l 8 *de pactis* 2, 3.	
C. *de pactis* 2. 3. cst. 8	I. *de rer. diu.* 2. 1. § 13.
Cod. II. 3. l 8	*Inst.* (or Iust.) II. 1. § 13.

The Novels (or rather the Latin translation of them) are called in the older books *Authenticae,* and so referred to as *Auth.*; now as *Nov.* and the sections as *c.* 2, &c. (for *caput*) sometimes with subordinate paragraphs (§ 1, &c.).

For fuller accounts see Thibaut, *Civil. Abhandl.* p. 205; Schilling, *Inst.* I. §§ 39—42; Wächter, *Pand.* I. pp. 46—51.

CHAPTER XIX.

BOOKS RECOMMENDED.

IN conclusion it may be convenient if I name out of the large number of books on Roman Law some which seem to me especially useful to students of the Digest. Most, however, are in German.

1. For the text, Mommsen's critical edition in 2 vols. 4to is far the best: and, in a matter of text, everything depends on methodical examination and sifting of the authorities, followed by wise rejection of the bad and use of the good only. The stereotype edition in one

volume, including also Krüger's revision of the Institutes, is quite sufficient for most purposes, and is that which all students should have. It contains all the various readings which they need to care about; references to or citations of all passages extant from ante-Justinian jurists which have been incorporated in the Digest; references to the parallel parts of the Code and Basilica; and a brief statement, at the commencement of each title, of the distribution of the several extracts among the groups of works as ascertained by Bluhme.

2. Next to the text of the Digest in importance come the remains of the ante-Justinian lawyers and of laws and legal documents. The former are conveniently collected by Huschke (4th ed. 1879), whose abundant learning and ingenuity are shewn in the notes and conjectural restorations of the text. But another edition, less full and as yet incomplete, by Krüger, Studemund and Mommsen is more trustworthy, because the text is less conjectural. The Vatican Fragments have been twice edited by Mommsen, viz. an apograph and text with supplements (1860) and also a critical text in smaller form (1861). A third edition is to appear in the 3rd vol. of the last-named work. Gneist's *Syntagma* (i.e. parallel texts of Gaius and Justinian's Institutes) contains in the appendices and notes pertinent selections from Ulpian and Paul, and from other ante-Justinian sources. Of some other editions of Gaius I have spoken above, p. clxxx.

Bruns' *Fontes iuris Romani* (4th ed. 1879) contains all the extant laws outside of the Codes and Novels, specimens of conveyances, agreements, receipts, &c., some other inscriptions which have a legal bearing, and legal extracts from Festus, Varro and others. Since Bruns' death (1880), Mommsen has undertaken the charge of the book and has published a small supplement.

Hänel's *Corpus Legum* (1857) contains all the information we have respecting the imperial legislation not contained in the Codes (Theodosian, Justinian, &c.) or in the Novels. This information consists of extracts, from the Digest and historians and others, relating to the laws, digested in the chronological order of the Constitutions, with copious indices. Hänel has also edited critically the Theodosian code and the remains of the Gregorian and Hermogenian codes (1837) as well as the *lex Romana Uisigothorum* (see p. clxxiv).

Justinian's Code has been edited critically by P. Krüger (2 vols. 4to.). The stereotype edition, uniform with Mommsen's Digest, is convenient and sufficient for students. (A corresponding edition of the Novels by R. Schöll is only in part published.)

3. As to notes or commentary on the Digest I can refer to none except Godefroi's at the foot of his editions. I have sometimes found it useful in giving a reference to some other pertinent passage. Glück's *Ausführliche Erläuterung der Pandekten* (56 vols.) is not a commentary on the Digest, but a series of treatises on the subject-matter of the different titles of the Digest. On those particular passages which it happens to discuss the information is very good for the time, but the volume containing *De usufructu* is dated 1808. Some of the volumes recently published, e.g. Arndts on *Legacies* (1868—1878 unfinished), Leist on *Bonorum Possessio* (1870—1879), are valuable monographs, with close reference to the original authorities.

The Byzantine Commentators, published in Heimbach's *Basilica* and Zachariä's Supplement (see above, p. ccxliv) are sometimes of real assistance for the interpretation, as well as for the text, of the Digest.

4. There are three lexicons to the *Corpus Iuris*, all of which are excellent. Brisson's is the oldest, and as edited posthumously by Heineck (fol. 1743) is a very useful work. It contains references to other writers besides the Jurists. I regret that for some time I went without it under the false belief that it was superseded by the two others.

Dirksen's (4to. 1837) is more modern, and has some special features. It contains examples of expressions synonymous, and opposed to, the word in question. But it does not extend beyond the lawyers.

Heumann's is the most modern (6th ed. 1884, 8vo.), has the explanations in German, is well done and is a handy volume. But it is even more exclusive than Dirksen's, having comparatively few references outside the *Corpus Iuris*, and the passages are not quoted so fully as in the other two.

5. Of Histories and Institutional treatises there is none quite satisfactory. Zimmern's *Geschichte* (1826) is full, and good as far as it goes, but it is incomplete. It contains the external history and also the history of the law of persons and of the law of procedure. Schilling's *Institutionen und Geschichte* (1834—1846), also unfinished, in

some degree supplements Zimmern, as it deals with the Law of Things and of Obligations. Rudorff's is more modern (1857), and has a great deal of matter compressed into a small space, but is not free from rash conjectures, which are not sufficiently distinguished from what rests on fair evidence. It contains the external history and procedure, the latter very fully but concisely treated.

. Puchta's *Cursus* is a very able book, but the history of obligations, family law, and inheritance is published only from a brief lecture MS., his early death (1846) having prevented the completion of the work as intended. It has been frequently edited by Rudorff with additional notes, and lately (in 2 vols. 1881) by P. Krüger.

Walter's *Geschichte* (2 vols. 3rd ed. 1860, 61) is the work of an accomplished scholar, learned both in Roman, Ecclesiastical and German Law. It is complete and clear, with some peculiar views, but for the general reader is more suitable than any of the above. The author is however dead, and a good deal has been done by the publication of inscriptions, the verification of texts, and the discussions of lawyers and scholars since this work was last edited.

The most recent work of this kind is Kuntze's *Cursus* and *Excursus* (2nd ed. 1879, 1880). The 1st vol. (*Cursus*) is especially noticeable for containing among other matters a system of Roman private law at the time of the Classical Jurists. The *Excursus* is a collection of long notes on special points. Both volumes are full of the results of the most recent inquiries. There is a great deal of useful information and suggestion, but it is accompanied by a romanticism which largely obscures and perhaps sometimes distorts the ascertainable facts.

Danz's *Lehrbuch der Gesch. d. röm. Rechts* (1871) is very convenient for its analyses of various views on many controverted points (e.g. *iusiurandum, res mancipi, nexum, litterarum obligatio,* &c.).

Keller's *Institutionen* (1861) are admirable on the matters of which they treat. The book is in fact a series of *excursus*.

A good book, intended as a handbook for lectures, is Salkowski's *Institutionen und Geschichte* (3rd ed. 1880). It contains a continuous summary of the divisions and doctrines of Roman Law with a large number of illustrative passages selected from the original sources. Neither the history of the doctrines nor procedure is omitted. A convenient general book for those who have no other is Vering's *Geschichte und Pandekten* (4th ed. 1875) which also gives a brief account of German feudal law.

6. The passages in the Digest bearing on any particular subject or point are often scattered in different, and sometimes in not very obvious, titles. Hence a dogmatic treatise with ample references is necessary. Of such there is in Germany no lack. Monographs are too numerous to mention. Savigny is always admirable for learning and thought, and incomparable for grace of exposition. Puchta's (edited by Schirmer, 1877), Böcking's (1853—55, unfinished), Keller's (posthumous, 1866), Arndts', Windscheid's, Vangerow's and Wächter's *Pandekten* are all excellent. The last two can be specially recommended both for matter and style. Vangerow's is not a continuous exposition, but a series of critical and analytical discussions of controverted questions of Roman law, very carefully and clearly written. Nothing however has been done to it since Vangerow died in 1870. Wächter's *Pandekten* (based to some extent on Arndts) is not so well known, because it was only published in 1880, after its celebrated author's death. But it is clear and masterly. Arndts died in 1878, but his work has been reedited since. Windscheid is happily still alive. Both his and Arndts' works are in current use and high esteem. Other works might easily be named; but all of them deal with the law as now received in Germany, and not, except occasionally, with the special exegesis of the Digest, and thus (e.g.) matters relating to slaves receive but slight attention. An able and elaborate book in French by Maynz in 3 vols. called *Cours de Droit Romain* (4th ed. 1876) may be especially recommended to those who do not read German.

7. The application of the Digest &c. to modern life is illustrated by a collection of cases from German law-courts, edited by Girtanner (4th ed. by Langenbeck, 1869), and adapted to Puchta's *Pandekten*. The decisions are not given, but a *Pandekten-praktikum* by Pagenstecher (1860) furnishes a guide to the solution.

My references will, I think, be intelligible to those who wish to refer to the books. But it is well to mention that *Z.G.R.* means the *Zeitschrift für geschichtliche Rechtswissenschaft*, edited by Savigny and others (15 vols. 1815—1850): and *Z.R.G.* the *Zeitschrift für Rechtsgeschichte* by Rudorff and others (13 vols. 1861—1878). The avowed successor of this is *Zeitschrift der Savigny-Stiftung für Rechtsgeschichte* by Bruns, Pernice and others (1880, and still continued). I have quoted this usually as *Z.R.G.* with continuous numbers (Vol. i. being *Z.R.G.* xiv. &c.). I regret not to have had access to some other German periodicals.

APPENDIX A.

Book VII. 1—9.   Personal servitudes.

VIII. 1—6.   Real servitudes.

IX. 1—4.   Damage by fault and negligence (*Lex Aquilia*).

X. 1.   Ascertainment of property (*Finium regundorum*).

2, 3.   Partition of property (*Famil. ercisc.* and *Com. diu.*).

4.   Production of disputed property (*ad exhibendum*).

XI.   (Supplementary.)

1.   Interrogatories.

2.   Consolidation of suits.

3, 4.   Spoiling or concealing slaves.

5.   Dice playing.

6.   Fraudulent surveyors.

7, 8.   Tombs; funeral expenses : rights of burial.

B.   Suits on contracts.   (Commercial dealings.)

Book XII. 1.   Money lent (*mutuum*).

2, 3.   Oaths.

4—7.   Money unduly paid.

XIII. 1—5.   Other suits for recovery *in genere*.

6.   Recovery of loan *in specie* (*commodatum*).

7.   Recovery of thing pledged (*act. pigneraticia*).

XIV, XV.   Suits against principals on agents' contracts.

XIV. 1.   Shipmaster's contracts (*act. exercitoria*).

2.   Particular average (*Lex Rhodia*).

3.   Shopkeeper's contracts (*act. institoria*).

4. ⎫
XV. 1—4. ⎬ Children's and slaves' contracts.

XVI. 1.   Guaranties by women (*S. Uelleianum*).

2.   Set-off (*de compensationibus*).

3.   Deposit.

XVII. 1.   Unpaid agency (*mandati*).

2.   Partnership (*pro socio*).

XVIII. 1—7. ⎫
XIX. 1. ⎬ Purchase and sale.

2—5.   Hire, exchange, and the like.

XX. 1—6.   Pledge. Rights of pledgees.

XXI. 1—3.   Rescission of purchase, and eviction.

XXII.   (Supplementary.)

1.   Interest; mesne profits : delay.

2.   Loans on bottomry.

3—5.   Presumptions, documentary and personal evidence.

6.   Ignorance of law and of fact.

C. **Suits arising from family relations.**

　　a. HUSBAND AND WIFE.

　　Book XXIII. 1.　　Betrothal.
　　　　　　　　2.　　Marriage : who may intermarry.
　　　　　　　3—5.　　Dowry.
　　　　XXIV. 1.　　Gifts between husband and wife.
　　　　　　　　2.　　Divorce.
　　　　　　　　3. ⎫
　　　　XXV. 1, 2. ⎬　Claims on dissolution of marriage.
　　　　　　　3—6.　　Rights of unborn children, and claims for aliment.
　　　　　　　　7.　　Concubines.

　　b. GUARDIAN AND WARD.

　　Book XXVI. 1—6.　　Appointment of guardians.
　　　　　　　7—9.　　Guardians' management and responsibility.
　　　　　　　10.　　Removal of guardians.
　　　　XXVII. 1.　　Excuse from appointment.
　　　　　　　　2.　　Maintenance and education of ward.
　　　　　　　3—6.　　Suits for and against real and assumed guardians.
　　　　　　　7, 8.　　Suits against guardians' sureties and local magistrates.
　　　　　　　　9.　　Prohibition of sale of ward's land.
　　　　　　　10.　　Appointment of *curator* to lunatics, &c.

D. **Succession to deceased pater(mater)familias.**

　　a. SUCCESSION BY WILL : TESTATOR, HEIR, LEGATEE.

　　Book XXVIII. 1—7.　　Wills : power and duties of testator.
　　　　　　　　8.　　Time to heir to deliberate.
　　　　XXIX. 1.　　Soldiers' wills.
　　　　　　　　2.　　Acceptance by heir named.
　　　　　　　　3.　　Opening of will.
　　　　　　　　4.　　Will protected against heir's disregard.
　　　　　　　　5.　　Punishment of testator's murderer to precede opening of will (*de Sc. Silaniano*).
　　　　　　　　6.　　Interference with testator.
　　　　　　　　7.　　Codicils.
　　　　XXX. ⎫
　　　　XXXI. ⎬　Legacies in general.
　　　　XXXII. ⎭

Book XXXIII.   1—10.⎫ Special Legacies.
       XXXIV.   1—3. ⎭
                 4.   Ademption and transference of legacies.
                 5.   Matters of doubtful interpretation.
                 6—9.   Invalid legacies.
       XXXV.   1.   Conditional legacies.
                 2, 3.   Heir's right to a fourth (*Lex Falcidia*).
       XXXVI.   1.   Universal legacy (*Sc. Trebellianum*).
                 2.   Vesting of legacies.
                 3—5.   Legatees' right to security.

b. SUCCESSION IN SPITE OF AND BESIDE WILL.

Book XXXVII.   1—10.   Succession of relatives in spite of the will
                        (*Bonorum possessio contra tabulas*).
                 11.   Praetorian succession in accordance with
                        will (*Bon. poss. secundum tabulas*).
                 12.   Succession to emancipated child.
                 13.   Wills of sailors and others like soldiers.
                 14. ⎫ Patrons' right to services and to suc-
       XXXVIII. 1—5. ⎭   cession to property of freedmen.

c. INTESTATE SUCCESSION.

Book XXXVIII.   6—15.   Succession by praetor's grant (*Bon. poss.
                        ab intestato*).
                 16.   Succession by statute (*de suis et legitimis
                        heredibus*).
                 17.   Succession of mothers and children (*Sc.
                        Tertullianum et Orfitianum*).

E. **Suits between neighbours, and some other matters.**

Book XXXIX.   1—3.   Suits between neighbours (*Op. nou. runt.;
                        damn. inf.; aq. pluu. arc.*).
                 4.   Suits against taxfarmers.
                 5, 6. Gifts *inter uiuos* and *mortis causa*.

F. **Claims to freedom arising from manumission or otherwise.**

Book xl.   1—6.   Manumission in various modes.
                 7.   Slaves manumitted on condition (*de statu
                        liberis*).
                 8.   Freedom without manumission.
                 9.   Ineffectual manumissions.
                10, 11. Grants to freedmen of freeborn privileges.
                12—16. Assertions of freedom.

G. **Acquisition, especially by possession.**

Book XLI.	1.	Acquisition of ownership.
	2.	Acquisition and loss of possession.
	3—10.	Acquisition by possession (*de usucapione*, &c.).

III. **JUDGMENT AND EXECUTION.**

Book XLII.	1.	Judgment.
	2.	Confession.
	3.	Voluntary liquidation (*cessio bonorum*).
	4—8.	Execution: Possession by creditors: bankruptcy.

IV. **INJUNCTIONS, SPECIAL PLEAS, BONDS AND SURETIES.**

Book XLIII.	1.	Injunctions in general (*interdicta*).
	2—5.	Injunctions in connexion with inheritances.
	6—15.	Injunctions in protection of public rights.
	16—28.	Injunctions in protection of private rights.
	29—30.	Injunctions for production of freemen or children.
	31—33.	Injunctions on behalf of moveables, lodgers' goods and pledges.
XLIV.	1.	Pleas in general.
	2—6.	Special pleas, viz. matter decided, length of time, fraud, intimidation, oath, unfair conditions on liberty, &c.
	7.	Obligations and actions in general (introductory to stipulations).
XLV.	1—3.	Stipulations.
XLVI.	1.	Sureties.
	2.	Novation.
	3—4.	Release of stipulations.
	5—8.	Bonds required by praetor (*de stipulationibus praetoriis*).

V. **PUNISHMENT OF WRONGS.**

Book XLVII.	1.	Private wrongs in general.
	2—9.	Theft and robbery.
	10.	Insult.
	11—21.	Extraordinary offences.
	22.	Clubs.
	23.	Popular suits.

Book XLVIII.	1.	Crimes.
	2, 3.	Indictments and imprisonment of accused.
	4—15.	Treason, adultery, violence, murder, forgery, extortion, kidnapping, &c.
	16.	False accusations.
	17—18.	Criminal procedure.
	19—24.	Punishments.
XLIX.	1—13.	Appeals.

VI. SPECIAL AND PUBLIC LAW AND INTERPRETATION.

Book XLIX.	14.	Crown suits (*de iure fisci*).
	15.	Effect of capture by enemy and of release (*de postliminio*).
	16.	Military law.
	17.	Privileges of soldiers and veterans.
L.	1—12.	Municipal government and duties.
	13.	Claims of professional persons: suits against judges.
	14.	Brokerage (*de proxeneticis*).
	15.	Census of property.
	16.	Interpretation of special words and expressions.
	17.	Maxims.

APPENDIX B.

DIVISION AND ORDER OF WORKS FROM WHICH EXTRACTS WERE TAKEN
FOR THE DIGEST.

The following is a list of the works from which extracts were taken for
the Digest, arranged in the order in which the several Committees dealt
with them.   A bracket denotes the simultaneous handling of the works or
parts of works there named.   The list is compounded of the tables framed by
Bluhme, pp. 266 and 445, and is given here as slightly emended by Krüger,
whose list forms the 5th Appendix to Vol. II. of Mommsen's larger edition
of the Digest, and is also in the later issues of the stereotype edition.
(I have however written *Gai, Pomponi*[1], &c., not (as Krüger does) *Gaii,
Pomponii,* &c.)   In the case of works, from which only one or very few
extracts occur, the evidence on which the place in the list is assigned is
necessarily very slight.

The works are numbered consecutively on their first appearance in the
list.   Those printed in italics are not named, at least separately, in the
Florentine Index.

PARS SABINIANA.

							libb.
1	ULPIANI ad Sabinum		.	.	.	.	I—XIV.
2	POMPONI	„	'	.	.	.	I—IV.
3	PAULI	„	.	.	.	.	I, II.
	ULPIANI	„	.	.	.	.	XV—XXV.
	POMPONI	„	.	.	.	.	V—VII.
	PAULI	„	.	.	.	.	III, IV.
	ULPIANI	„	.	.	.	.	XXVI—XXIX.
	POMPONI	„	.	.	.	.	VIII—XI.
	PAULI	„	.	.	.	.	V.
	ULPIANI	„	.	.	.	.	XXX.
	POMPONI	„	.	.	.	.	XII, XIII.
	PAULI	„	.	.	.	.	VI.

[1] If any justification is needed for my writing this form of the genitive, I
would refer to the numerous *Priuilegia Ueteranorum* in *Corp. I. Lat.* III. p. 843
sqq.   They were written in Rome from the time of Claudius to Diocletian, and
the reading is certain.   They are thus among the best evidences of orthography.
They invariably give the genitive in *i*, not in *ii* (Mommsen ib. p. 918).

libb.

	ULPIANI ad Sabinum	. . . .	XXXI—XL init.
	POMPONI „	. . . .	XIV—XVII.
	PAULI „	. . . .	VII, VIII.
	ULPIANI „	. . . .	XL fin.—XLIII.
	POMPONI „	. . . .	XVIII—XXII.
	PAULI „	. . . .	IX, X.
	ULPIANI „	. . . .	XLIV—L.
	POMPONI „	. . . .	XXIII—XXVII.
	PAULI „	. . . .	XI, XII.
	ULPIANI „	. . . .	LI.
	POMPONI „	. . . .	XXIX.
	PAULI „	. . . .	XIII.
	POMPONI „	. . . .	XXX—XXXVI.
	PAULI „	. . . .	XIV—XVI.
4	ULPIANI ad edictum	. . .	XXVI—XXX.
5	PAULI „	. . . .	XXVIII—XXXI.
6	GAI „ prouinciale	.	IX, X init.
7	PAULI breuium	. . . .	VI.
	ULPIANI ad edictum	. . .	XXXI, XXXII.
	PAULI „	. . . .	XXXII—XXXIV.
	GAI „ prouinciale	.	X fin.
	ULPIANI „	. . . .	XXXIII, XXXIV.
	PAULI „	. . . .	XXXV—XXXVII.
	GAI „ prouinciale	.	XI.
	PAULI breuium	. . . .	VII.
	ULPIANI ad edictum .	. . .	XXXV, XXXVI.
	PAULI „	. . .	XXXVIII.
	„ breuium	. . . .	VIII.
	GAI ad edictum prouinciale	. .	XII.
	ULPIANI „	. . . .	XXXVII, XXXVIII.
	PAULI „	. . . .	XXXIX, XL.
	GAI „ prouinciale	.	XIII, XIV init.
	ULPIANI ad edictum	. . .	XXXIX—XLV.
	PAULI „	. . .	XLI—XLIII init.
	GAI „ prouinciale	.	XIV fin., XV.
	ULPIANI ad edictum	. . .	XLVI—L.
	PAULI „	. . .	XLIII fin.—XLVI.
	GAI „ prouinciale	.	XVI, XVII.
8	„ de testamentis ad edict. praet. urbani	.	I, II.
	ULPIANI ad edictum	. . .	LI.
	PAULI „	. . .	XLVII, XLVIII init.
	GAI „ prouinciale	.	XVIII.
9	„ de legatis ad edictum praetoris .	.	I—III.
10	ULPIANI disputationum	. . .	I—X.

		libb.
11	ULPIANI de omnibus tribunalibus . .	I—X.
12	„ opinionum	I—VI.
13	„ de censibus	I—VI.
14	IULIANI digestorum	I—XC.
15	ALFENI UARI digestorum	I—XXX.
16	PAULI *epitomarum Alfeni digestorum* .	I—VIII.
17	IULIANI de ambiguitatibus . . .	lib. sing.
18	„ ad Urseium Ferocem . . .	I—IV.
19	„ ex Minicio	I—VI.
20	AFRICANI quaestiones	I—IX.
21	FLORENTINI institutionum . . .	I—V.
22	MARCIANI „ . . .	I, II.
23	ULPIANI „ . . .	I.
24	GAI „ . . .	I.
25	„ aureorum . . .	I.
26	PAULI institutionum	I.
	FLORENTINI institutionum . . .	VI.
	MARCIANI „ . . .	III.
	GAI „ . . .	II.
	„ aureorum	II.
27	CALLISTRATI institutionum . . .	II.
	MARCIANI institutionum . . .	IV—IX.
	FLORENTINI „ . . .	X, XI.
	ULPIANI „ . . .	II.
	FLORENTINI institutionum . .	VII—IX.
	GAI institutionum	III.
	„ aureorum	III.
	PAULI institutionum	II.
	CALLISTRATI institutionum . . .	III.
	MARCIANI „ . . .	X—XVI.
28	ULPIANI de adulteriis	I—III.
29	PAPINIANI „	I, II.
30	„ „	lib. sing.
31	PAULI „	I, II.
	ULPIANI „	IV, V.
	PAULI „	III.
32	ULPIANI de sponsalibus	lib. sing.
33	PAULI *de dotis repetitione*	„
34	„ *de adsignatione libertorum* . .	„
35	„ *de iure patronatus*	„
36	NERATI regularum	I—XV.
37	ULPIANI „	I—VII.
38	SCAEUOLAE „	I—IV.
39	PAULI „	lib. sing.

libb.

40	MARCIANI regularum	.	.	I, II.
41	ULPIANI responsorum	.	.	I, II.
	MARCIANI regularum .	.	.	III, IV.
42	PAULI ,,	.	.	I—VII.
	MARCIANI ,,	.	.	V.
43	POMPONI ,,	.	.	lib. sing.
44	ULPIANI ,,	.	.	lib. sing.
45	ULPIANI de officio proconsulis	.	.	I—X.
46	PAULI ad. Sc. Silanianum .	.	.	lib. sing.
47	,, de portionibus quae liberis damna-			
	torum conceduntur	.	.	lib. sing.
48	,, ad legem Iuliam	.	.	I, II.
49	,, *de conceptione formularum*	.	.	lib. sing.
50	MACRI publicorum iudiciorum .	.	.	I, II
51	UENULEI SATURNINI de iudiciis publicis	.	.	I—III.
52	PAULI ,,	,,		lib. sing.
53	MARCIANI de publicis iudiciis .	.	.	I, II.
54	MAECIANI ,, ,,	.	.	I—XIV.
55	⎰MARCIANI ad formulam hypothecariam	.	.	lib. sing.
56	⎱GAI de formula hypothecaria	.	.	,,
57	MARCELLI responsorum	.	.	,,
58	NERATI membranarum	.	.	I—VII.
59	MACRI de officio praesidis .	.	.	I, II.
60	ARCADI CHARISI de testibus	.	.	lib. sing.
61	MARCIANI de delatoribus .	.	.	,,
62	⎧ULPIANI de appellationibus	.	.	I, II.
63	⎨MACRI ,,	.	.	I.
64	⎩MARCIANI ,,	.	.	I.
	⎧ULPIANI ,,	.	.	III, IV.
	⎨MACRI ,,	.	.	II.
	⎩MARCIANI ,,	.	.	II.
65	PAULI ,,	.	.	lib. sing.
66	RUTILI MAXIMI ad legem Falcidiam .	.	.	,,
67	PAULI *ad legem Fufiam Caniniam*	.	.	,,
68	,, ad legem Aeliam Sentiam	.	.	I—III.
69	ULPIANI *ad legem Aeliam Sentiam*	.	.	I—IV.
70	PAULI de libertatibus dandis	.	.	lib. sing.
71	,, *de liberali causa*	.	.	,,
72	,, de secundis tabulis .	.	.	,,
73	,, de iure codicillorum	.	.	,,
74	,, de centumuiralibus iudiciis	.	.	,,
75	,, de adulteriis .	.	.	,,
76	,, de senatus consultis	.	.	,,
77	,, ad Sc. Uelleianum .	.	.	,,

		libb.
78	PAULI de intercessionibus feminarum	lib. sing.
79	„ ad orationem diui Antonini et Commodi	„
80	„ de excusationibus tutelarum	„
81	„ ad orationem diui Seueri	„
82	„ *de uariis lectionibus*	„
83	ULPIANI *pandectarum*	„
84	MACRI de re militari	I, II.
85	PAULI de poenis militum	lib. sing.
86	ULPIANI de officio curatoris rei publicae	„
87	„ *de officio consularium*	„
88	PAULI de officio proconsulis	I, II.
89	UENULEI „ „	I, IV.
90	CLAUDI SATURNINI de poenis paganorum	lib. sing.
91	UOLUSI MAECIANI *ex lege Rhodia*	„
92	IAUOLENUS *ex posterioribus Labeonis*	I—X.

PARS EDICTALIS.

ULPIANI ad edictum		I—VI.
PAULI „		I—V.
GAI „	prouinciale	I.
ULPIANI „		VII.
PAULI „		VI, VII.
GAI „	prouinciale	II.
ULPIANI „		VIII—X init.
PAULI „		VIII—X.
GAI „	prouinciale	III.
ULPIANI „		X fin.—XII.
PAULI „		XI, XII init.
GAI „	prouinciale	IV.
PAULI breuium		III.
ULPIANI ad edictum		XIII, XIV.
PAULI „		XII fin.—XVI.
GAI „	prouinciale	V init.
ULPIANI „		XV, XVI init.
PAULI „		XX.
GAI „	prouinciale	V fin., VI.
ULPIANI „		XVI fin., XVII.
PAULI „		XIX—XXI.
GAI „	prouinciale	VII.
ULPIANI „		XVIII.
PAULI „		XXII.
GAI „	prouinciale	VII.

libb.

ULPIANI ad edictum			XIX.
PAULI ,, ...			XXIII.
GAI ,, prouinciale . .			VII.
ULPIANI ,, ...			XX, XXI.
PAULI ,, ...			XXIV.
GAI ,, prouinciale . .			VII.
GAI ,, ,, .			VIII.
ULPIANI ,, ...			XXI, XXII.
PAULI ,, ...			XXV, XVII, XVIII.
GAI ,, prouinciale . .			v fin.
ULPIANI ,, ...			XXIII.
PAULI ,, ...			XVIII, XIX.
GAI ,, prouinciale . .			VI.
ULPIANI ,, ...			XXIV.
PAULI ,, ...			XXV, XXVI.
GAI ,, prouinciale . .			VIII.
ULPIANI ,, ...			XXV.
PAULI ,, ...			XXVII.
93 GAI ,, prouinciale .			VIII, XIX.
,, ,, praetoris urbani .			
ULPIANI ,, ...			LVI.
PAULI ,, ...			LIV.
GAI ,, prouinciale . .			XXI.
ULPIANI ,, ...			LVII.
PAULI ,, ...			LV.
GAI ,, prouinciale . .			XXII.
ULPIANI ,, ...			LVIII, LIX.
PAULI ,, ...			LVI, LVII init.
94 GAI ,, prouinciale .			XXII.
,, ,, praetoris urbani *titulo qui neque sequantur neque ducantur.*			
ULPIANI ad edictum			LX.
PAULI ,, ...			LVII fin.
GAI ,, prouinciale . .			XXIII.
ULPIANI ,, ...			LXI.
PAULI ,, ...			LVIII.
GAI ,, prouinciale . .			XXIII.
ULPIANI ,, ...			LXII.
PAULI ,, ...			LIX.
,, breuium			XVI.
GAI ad edictum prouinciale . .			XXIII.
ULPIANI ad edictum			LXIII.
PAULI ,, ...			LX.
,, breuium			XVI.
GAI ad edictum prouinciale . .			XXIV.

					libb.
	ULPIANI ad edictum	.	.	.	.	.	LXIV, LXV.
	PAULI	,,	.	.	.	.	LXI.
	ULPIANI	,,	.	.	.	.	LXVI.
	PAULI	,,	.	.	.	.	LXII.
	,, breuium	.	.	.	.	.	XVI.
	GAI ad edictum prouinciale	.	.	.	XXIV.
95	,, ,, praetoris urbani *titulo de re iudicata.*
	ULPIANI ad edictum	.	.	.	.	.	LXVII.
	PAULI	,,	.	.	.	.	LXIII.
	GAI	,,	prouinciale	.	.	XXV.
	ULPIANI	,,	.	.	.	.	LXVIII.
	PAULI	,,	.	.	.	.	LXIV.
	GAI	,,	prouinciale	.	.	XXV.
	ULPIANI	,,	.	.	.	.	LXIX.
	PAULI	,,	.	.	.	.	LXV init.
	GAI	,,	prouinciale	.	.	XXV.
	ULPIANI	,,	.	.	.	.	LXX, LXXI init.
	PAULI	,,	.	.	.	.	LXV fin., LXVI.
	GAI	,,	prouinciale	.	.	XXV.
	ULPIANI	,,	.	.	.	.	LXXI fin.
	PAULI	,,	.	.	.	.	LXVII.
	GAI	,,	prouinciale	.	.	XXVI.
	ULPIANI	,,	.	.	.	.	LXXII, LXXIII.
	PAULI	,,	.	.	.	.	LXVIII.
	GAI	,,	prouinciale	.	.	XXVI.
	ULPIANI	,,	.	.	.	.	LXXIV.
	PAULI	,,	.	.	.	.	LXIX.
	GAI	,,	prouinciale	.	.	XXIX.
	ULPIANI	,,	.	.	.	.	LXXV.
	PAULI	,,	.	.	.	.	LXX.
	ULPIANI	,,	.	.	.	.	LXXVI.
	PAULI	,,	.	.	.	.	LXXI.
	GAI	,,	prouinciale	.	.	XXX.
	ULPIANI	,,	.	.	.	.	LXXVII, LXXVIII.
	PAULI	,,	.	.	.	.	LXXII—LXXIV.
	GAI	,,	prouinciale	.	.	XXVII.
	ULPIANI	,,	.	.	.	.	LXXIX.
	PAULI	,,	.	.	.	.	LXXV, LXXVI.
	GAI	,,	prouinciale	.	.	XXVII.
	ULPIANI	,,	.	.	.	.	LXXX, LXXXI.
	PAULI	,,	.	.	.	.	LXXVII, LXXVIII.
	GAI	,,	prouinciale	.	.	XXVIII.
96	ULPIANI	,,	*aedilium curulium*	.	I, II.
97	PAULI	,,	,,	.	,,
98	GAI	,,	,,.	.	,,

libb.

99   Παπινιανοῦ ἀστυνομικὸς μονοβίβλος.

    ⌠Ulpiani ad edictum . . . . .   LIV, LV init.

    ⎰Pauli   ,, ...   L, LI.

    ⎱Gai   ,,   prouinciale . .   XX.

100 Gai   ,,   praetoris urbani *titulo*
           de liberali causa.

    ⌠Ulpiani ad edictum . . . . .   LV fin.

    ⎟Pauli   ,, ...   LII.

    ⎰Gai   ,,   prouinciale . .   XXI.

101 ⎱,,   ,,   praetoris urbani *titulo*
           de publicanis.

    ⌠Ulpiani ad edictum . . . . .   LII, LIII.

    ⎟Pauli   ,, ...   XLVIII fin., XLIX.

    ⎟Gai   ,,   prouinciale . .   XIX.

102 ⎨,,   ,,   praet. urb. titulo *de*
           op. nou. nunt.

103 ⎟,, *de damn. infect.*

104 ⎳,, *de aquae pluu. arc.*

105 Gai ad edict. pr. urb. *de praediatoribus.*

106 Pauli ad Plautium . . . .   I—XIV.

107 Iauoleni   ,, ...   I.

108 Pomponi   ,, ...   I.

    Iauoleni   ,, ...   II.

    Pomponi   ,, ...   II, III.

    Pauli   ,, ...   XV—XVIII.

    Iauoleni   ,, ...   III—V.

    Pomponi   ,, ...   IV—VII.

109 Pauli ad Uitellium . . . .   I—IV.

110   ,, de iure fisci . . . .   I, II.

111 Celsi digestorum . . . .   I—IV.

112 Marcelli ,, ...   I—III.

    Celsi   ,, ...   V.

    Marcelli ,, ...   IV.

    Celsi   ,, ...   VI—VIII.

    Marcelli ,, ...   V, VI.

    ⌠Celsi   ,, ...   IX—XII.

    ⎱Marcelli ,, ...   VII, VIII.

    Celsi   ,, ...   XIII—XVI.

    Marcelli ,, ...   IX—XII.

    Celsi   ,, ...   XVII—XXI.

    Marcelli ,, ...   XIII—XV.

    Celsi   ,, ...   XXII.

    Marcelli ,, ...   XVI.

    Celsi   ,, ...   XXIII.

    Marcelli ,, ...   XVII.

libb.

	CELSI digestorum	XXIV—XXVII.
	MARCELLI ,, ...	XVIII—XXI.
	CELSI ,, ...	XXVIII—XXXV.
	MARCELLI ,, ...	XXII—XXIX.
	CELSI ,, ...	XXXVI—XXXIX.
	MARCELLI ,, ...	XXX, XXXI.
113	ULPIANI de officio consulis . .	I—III.
114	MODESTINI differentiarum . . .	I—IX.
115	,, de manumissionibus .	lib. sing.
116	,, regularum . . .	I—X.
117	,, de ritu nuptiarum . .	lib. sing.
118	,, de differentia dotis . .	,,
119	,, excusationum . . .	I—VI.
120	ULPIANI de officio praetoris tutelaris .	lib. sing.
121	,, *excusationum* . . .	,,
122	MODESTINI *de praescriptionibus* . .	I—IV.
123	,, responsorum . . .	I—XIX.
124	,, de enucleatis casibus .	lib. sing.
125	,, de praescriptionibus .	,,
126	,, pandectarum . . .	I—XII.
127	,, de heurematicis . .	lib. sing.
128	,, de inofficioso testamento .	,,
129	IAUOLENI ex Cassio	I—XV.
130	,, epistularum . . .	I—XIV.
131	POMPONI ad Quintum Mucium . .	I—XXXIX.
132	PROCULI epistularum	I—VI.
133	POMPONI uariarum lectionum . .	I—XV.
	PROCULI epistularum . . .	VII—XI.
134	CALLISTRATI de iure fisci . . .	I—IV.
135	PAULI de censibus	I, II.
136	CALLISTRATI de cognitionibus . .	I—VI.
137	TERTULLIANI quaestionum . .	I—VIII.
138	ULPIANI ad legem Iuliam et Papiam .	I.
139	PAULI ,, ,, .	I.
	ULPIANI ,, ,, .	II—V.
	PAULI ,, ,, .	II—V.
140	GAI ,, ,, .	I, II.
	ULPIANI ,, ,, .	VI—XV.
	PAULI ,, ,, .	VI—X.
141	TERENTI CLEMENTIS ,, .	I—XX.
	GAI ,, .	III—XV.
142	MAURICIANI ,, .	II, III.
143	MARCELLI ,, .	I—III.
	ULPIANI ,, .	XVI—XX.

libb.

144 MACRI ad legem uicesimam hereditatium . I, II.
145 GAI *ad legem Glitiam* . . . lib. sing.
146 PAULI ad legem Cinciam . . . „
147 ARRII MENANDRI de re militari . . I—IV.
148 TARRUNTENI PATERNI „ . . I—IV.
149 TERTULLIANI de castrensi peculio . lib. sing.
150 MODESTINI de poenis . . . . I—IV.
151 LICINI RUFINI regularum . . . I—IV.
152 CALLISTRATI edicti monitorii . . I—IV.
      LICINI RUFINI regularum . . . VIII—XII.
153 PAPIRI IUSTI de constitutionibus . I—XX.
154 *AELI GALLI de uerborum quae ad ius*
          pertinent significatione . . . I.
155 IULI AQUILAE responsorum . . . lib. sing.

PARS PAPINIANA.

156 PAPINIANI quaestionum . . . . I—XXXVII.
157   „   responsorum . . . . I—XIX.
158   „   definitionum . . . I, II.
159 ⎰PAULI quaestionum . . . . I—III.
160 ⎱SCAEUOLAE „ . . . . I, II.
     ⎰PAULI   „ . . . . IV—VIII.
     ⎱SCAEUOLAE „ . . . . III—VI.
     ⎰PAULI   „ . . . . IX—XI.
     ⎱SCAEUOLAE „ . . . . VII—IX.
     ⎰PAULI   „ . . . . XII—XIV.
     ⎱SCAEUOLAE „ . . . . X—XII.
     ⎰PAULI   „ . . . . XV.
     ⎱SCAEUOLAE „ . . . . XIII.
     ⎰PAULI   „ . . . . XVI—XX.
     ⎱SCAEUOLAE „ . . . . XIV—XVIII.
     ⎰PAULI   „ . . . . XXI—XXVI.
     ⎱SCAEUOLAE „ . . . . XIX, XX.
161 CALLISTRATI quaestionum . . . I, II.
162 PAULI responsorum . . . . I—VII.
163 SCAEUOLAE „ . . . . I.
      PAULI   „ . . . . VIII—XV.
      SCAEUOLAE „ . . . . II—IV.
      PAULI   „ . . . . XVI—XIX.
      SCAEUOLAE „ . . . . V.
      PAULI   „ . . . . XX—XXIII.
      SCAEUOLAE „ . . . . VI.

libb.

164	UALENTIS fideicommissorum	. . .	I—IV.
165	ULPIANI	„ . . .	I—IV.
166	MAECIANI	„ . . .	I—VIII.
167	GAI	„ . . .	I, II.
168	PAULI	„ . . .	I, II.
169	POMPONI	„ . . .	I, II.
	⎧MAECIANI	„ . . .	IX—XVI.
	⎪UALENTIS	„ . . .	V—VII.
	⎨POMPONI	„ . . .	III—V.
	⎪ULPIANI	„ . . .	V, VI.
	⎩PAULI	„ . . .	III.
170	„ sententiarum	. . . .	I init.
171	HERMOGENIANI iuris epitomarum	. .	I.
	PAULI sententiarum	. . . .	I fin., II.
	HERMOGENIANI iuris epitomarum	. .	II.
	PAULI sententiarum	. . . .	III.
	HERMOGENIANI iuris epitomarum	. .	III.
	PAULI sententiarum	. . . .	IV.
	HERMOGENIANI iuris epitomarum	. .	IV.
	PAULI sententiarum	. . . .	V.
	HERMOGENIANI iuris epitomarum	. .	V, VI.
172	GAI de casibus	. . . . .	lib. sing.
173	UENULEI stipulationum	. . .	I—XIX.
174	NERATI responsorum	. . . .	I—III.
175	PAULI ad Neratium	. . . .	I—IV.
176	TRYPHONINI disputationum	. . .	I—XII.
177	PAULI manualium	. . . .	I, II.
	TRYPHONINI disputationum	. . .	XIII—XXI.
178	PAULI decretorum	. . . .	I—III.
179	GAI *regularum*	. . . . .	I—III.
180	„ regularum	. . . . .	lib. sing.
181	PAULI *de cognitionibus*	. . .	„
182	„ de concurrentibus actionibus	. .	„
183	„ de usuris	. . . .	„
184	„ *ad Sc. Turpilianum*	. . .	„
185	MARCIANI ad Sc. Turpilianum	. . .	„
186	PAULI ad Sc. Libonianum	. . .	„
187	„ *ad Sc. Claudianum*	. . . .	„
188	„ de poenis omnium legum	. . .	„
189	„ de poenis paganorum	. . .	„
190	„ ad regulam Catonianam	. . .	„
191	„ de forma testamenti	. . .	„
192	„ de inofficioso testamento	. . .	„
193	„ de tacitis fideicommissis	. . .	„

		libb.
194	PAULI de instrumenti significatione . .	lib. sing.
195	„ ad Sc. Tertullianum . . .	„
196	„ ad Sc. Orfitianum	„
197	„ ad legem Falcidiam . . .	„
198	GAI *de tacitis fideicommissis* . . .	„
199	„ *ad Sc. Tertullianum*	„
200	„ *ad Sc. Orfitianum* . . .	„
201	„ de manumissionibus . . .	I—III.
202	„ de uerborum obligationibus . .	I—III.
203	„ ad legem duodecim tabularum . .	I—VI.
204	POMPONI enchiridi	I, II.
205	„ *enchiridi*	lib. sing.
206	PAULI de iure libellorum	„
207	„ *de articulis liberalis causae* . .	„
208	„ de iuris et facti ignorantia . .	„
209	„ de iure singulari . . .	„
210	„ de gradibus et adfinibus et nomini-	
	bus eorum . . .	„
211	„ *de officio adsessorum* . .	„
212	„ de officio praefecti uigilum . .	„
213	ULPIANI „ „ . .	„
214	„ de officio praefecti urbi . .	„
215	PAULI „ „ . .	„
216	ARCADI CHARISI de muneribus ciuilibus .	„
217	AUR. ARCADI CHARISI de officio praefecti	
	praetorio .	„
218	ULPIANI de officio quaestoris . .	„

N.B.   The place in the lists of the last seven books is not ascertained.

APPENDIX PARTIS PAPINIANAE.

219	PAULI imperialium sententiarum in cog-	
	nitionibus prolatarum . .	I—VI.
220	QUINTI MUCI SCAEUOLAE ὅρων .	lib. sing.
221	LABEONIS posteriorum a Iauoleno epitoma-	
	torum . . .	I—X.
222	PROCULI *ex posterioribus Labeonis* . .	I—III.
223	SCAEUOLAE digestorum[1] . .	I—XL.
224	LABEONIS pithanon a Paulo epitomatorum	I—VIII.
225	POMPONI epistularum . . .	I—XX.
226	„ S. consultorum . . .	I—V.

[1] Sometimes before, sometimes after, LABEONIS Pithana.

227 Scaeuolae quaestionum publice tracta-
　　　　　　　　　　　tarum　.　　.　　.　lib. sing.
228 Ualentis *actionum* .　　.　　.　　.　I—VII.
229 Uenulei Saturnini actionum　　.　.　I—X.
230　　　,,　　　　　,,　　interdictorum .　.　I—X.
231 Furi Anthiani ad edictum　.　　.　　.　I.

The above-named 231 works are thus accounted for.

In the Florentine Index there are named　　.　　.　　. 206 works.

Of these, the following are not represented in the Digest:

Sabini　　　de iure ciuili libri tres
Scaeuolae de quaestione familiae lib. sing.
Gai　　　　dotalicion βιβλίον ἕν
Ulpiani　　Πανδέκτου βιβλία δέκα
Pauli de officio praetoris tutelaris lib. sing.
　,,　de extraordinariis criminibus lib. sing.
　,,　ὑποθηκάρια μονοβίβλος
　,,　ad municipalem lib. sing.
　,,　ad legem Uellaeam lib. sing.
　,,　de iure patronatus quod ex lege Iulia et Papia
　　　　uenit lib. sing.
　,,　de actionibus lib. sing.
　,,　de donationibus inter uirum et uxorem lib.
　　　　sing.
　,,　de legibus lib. sing.
　,,　de legitimis hereditatibus lib. sing.
Modestini de legatis et fideicommissis lib. sing.
　　,,　de testamentis lib. sing.
Deduct these .　.　.　.　.　.　.　.　.　16

Separate treatises named in Index and represented in Digest　190
Add, not named in Index at all　.　.　.　.　.　27
　　named under other heads, viz.:
　　　　Gai ad edictum aedil. curul. (with 'ad edictum')⎫
　　　　Ulpiani　　　,,　　　　　　　,,　　　⎪
　　　　Pauli　　　　,,　　　　　　　,,　　　⎬　.　4
　　　　　,,　*ad Sc. Claudianum* (with 'Libonianum')⎭
　　titles (out of 'Gai ad Edict. pr. urb.') separately named
　　　here .　.　.　.　.　.　.　.　.　10

　　　Number of Works from which extracts appear in
　　　　the Digest .　.　.　.　.　.　.　.　231

APPENDIX C.

The proportion, in which the several jurists were used in order to form the Digest, is here given according to my own calculation. The figures differ slightly from those given in other books.

In counting the pages of Hommel's *Palingenesia*, I have omitted all extracts not taken from the Digest, and all citations as distinguished from extracts. These citations are properly included in the extracts of the author citing them, and cannot therefore also be included among the extracts of the author cited. Hence my estimate differs from that given in the *Dict. Antiqq.* The amount of print in each page of Hommel is not the same when the extracts are short, as when they are long and continuous, so that the estimate must be regarded as only approximate. (Five of Hommel's pages contain about as much matter as three of Mommsen's stereotype edition.)

In counting the extracts I have not resorted to Hommel, but to the Digest itself in Mommsen's stereotype edition. I have followed the inscriptions as there given, without conjectural alteration. But such extracts as XXXIII. 4. 1 13 I count as Paul's, not Labeo's; XXXIX. 6. 1 15 : XLIX. 17. 1 10 &c., I have referred to Marcellus, not to Julian or Pomponius; XLVIII. 5. 1 8 (Mommsen) I count as Marcian's; 1 9 as Papinian's. The extracts from Saturninus (XL. 16. 1 2) and Claudius Saturninus (XLVIII. 19. 1 16) I have counted with those of Venuleius. The numbers here given differ but slightly from those given by others, e.g. Rudorff, and may well be accounted for by the changes in Mommsen's edition: but as he gives Pomponius 7 more and Marcianus 8 less, I have in their case verified my figures by counting again.

	Number of Hommel's pages.	Extracts.
Ulpianus	590	2464
Paulus	268½	2081
Papinianus	92	601
Scaeuola	74½	306
Pomponius	70½	578
Iulianus	68	456
Gaius	63	535

	Number of Hommel's pages.	Extracts.
Modestinus	$40\frac{1}{2}$	344
Marcianus	$36\frac{1}{2}$	283
Iauolenus	23	206
Africanus	23	131
Marcellus	21	161
Tryphoninus	$18\frac{1}{2}$	80
Callistratus	15	101
Celsus	14	141
Uenuleius (including Cl. Saturninus)	11	72
Macer	10	65
Hermogenianus	$9\frac{1}{2}$	107
Labeo	9	61
Alfenus	9	54
Neratius	$7\frac{1}{2}$	63
Maecianus	$7\frac{1}{2}$	44
Proculus	6	37
Florentinus	4	42
Terentius Clemens . . .	$3\frac{1}{2}$	35
Ualens	3	20
Arcadius	$2\frac{1}{2}$	6
Papirius Iustus	2	18
Menander	2	6
Licinius Rufinus . . .	1	17
Tertullianus	1	5
Iun. Mauricianus . . .	1	4
Furius Anthianus . . .	$\frac{1}{3}$	3
Q. Mucius	$\frac{1}{4}$	3
Tarruntenus	$\frac{1}{4}$	2
Iul. Aquila	$\frac{1}{6}$	2
Rutilius Maximus . . .	$\frac{1}{12}$	1
Aelius Gallus	$\frac{1}{40}$	1
Anonymous (*in our* MSS.) . .	$\frac{1}{2}$	5
Total . . nearly	1510	9142

APPENDIX D.

CHRONOLOGICAL TABLE OF EMPERORS AND SOME PRINCIPAL EVENTS
(from Rudorff, Fischer, &c.).

A. U. C.	B. C.	
1	753	Rome founded.
245	509	The first Consuls.
260	494	1st Secession of *Plebs*.
303—4	451—0	The Decemuiri. XII Tables.
305	449	2nd Secession of *Plebs*.
311	443	Censorship established (A. U. C. **319** Mommsen).
387	367	*Leges Liciniae Sextiae*.
388	366	First *Praetor Urbanus*.
390	364	Rome taken by Gauls.
442	312	App. Claudius *censor*.
450	304	Cn. Flavius publishes *formulae actionum*.
467	287	3rd Secession of *Plebs*.
490	264	1st Punic war begins.
cir. 512	242	*Praetor inter peregrinos*.
513	241	*Sicilia* the first Roman province.
		End of 1st Punic war.
523	231	*Sardinia* made province.
527	227	First Provincial Praetors.
536	218	2nd Punic war begins.
538	216	Battle of Cannae.
550	204	*Lex Cincia*.
553	201	End of 2nd Punic war.
557	197	*Hispania citerior* and *ulterior* made provinces.
570	184	M. Porcius Cato *Censor*.
585	169	*Lex Uoconia*.
after 587	167	*Illyricum* made province.
605	149	3rd Punic war begins.
		M' Manilius *cos*.

A. U. C.	B. C.	
608	146	Carthage destroyed.
		Africa ⎫
		Macedonia ⎬ made provinces.
		Achaia ⎭
621	133	Tib. Gracchus killed.
		P. Mucius Scaeuola *cos.*
		Asia made province.
631	123	C. Gracchus killed.
634	120	*Gallia Narbonensis* made province.
637	117	Q. Mucius Scaeuola (augur) *cos.*
639	115	M. Aemilius Scaurus *cos.*
649	105	P. Rutilius Rufus *cos.*
652—3	102—1	Marius defeats Teutones and Cimbri.
652	102	*Cilicia* treated as province (organised A. U. C. 687).
659	95	L. Licinius Crassus ⎫
		Q. Mucius Scaeuola (pontifex) ⎬ *coss.*
663	91	Social war begins.
666	88	Social war ends.
672	82	Sulla *dictator. Leges Corneliae* (before 675).
673	81	*Gallia Cisalpina* made province.
675	79	Sulla retires.
680	74	*Bithynia, Cyrene*, made provinces.
687	67	*Creta* made province.
688	66	C. Aquilius *praetor.*
690	64	*Syria* made province.
691	63	M. Tullius Cicero *cos.*
694	60	Triumvirate of Caesar, Pompey and Crassus.
695	59	C. Iulius Caesar *cos.*
702	52	Milo kills Clodius.
703	51	Ser. Sulpicius *cos.*
705	49	CAESAR crosses Rubicon.
		Lex Rubria (before 712).
706	48	Battle of Pharsalus.
709	45	*Lex Iulia municipalis.*
710	44	Caesar is killed.
711	43	Triumvirate of Octavius, Antony and Lepidus.
		Cicero is killed.
712	42	Battle of Philippi.
714	40	*Lex Falcidia.*
723	31	Battle of Actium.
724	30	*Aegyptus* made province.
725	29	Octavian receives *ius trib.* and *imperium* for life. *Trib. pot.* part of his title, first in 731.

A.U.C.	B.C.	
727	27	Octavian called AUGUSTUS.
736	18	*Leges Iuliae de adulteriis* and *de maritandis ordinibus* passed by Senate.
751	3	
	A.D.	Birth of Christ.
754	1	
757	4	*Lex Aelia Sentia.*
758	5	C. Ateius Capito *cos.*
761	8	*Lex Fufia Caninia.*
762	9	*Lex Papia Poppaea.*
763	10	*Sc. Silanianum.*
767	14	TIBERIUS *imp.*
772	19	*Lex Iunia Norbana.*
780	27	*Lex Iunia Uellaea.*
783	30	C. Cassius Longinus *cos. suff.*
786	33	M. Cocceius Nerva dies.
790	37	CALIGULA *imp.*
794	41	CLAUDIUS *imp.*
799	46	*Sc. Uelleianum.*
807	54	NERO *imp.*
809	56	*Sc. Trebellianum.*
817	64	Burning of Rome.
818	65	Conspiracy of Piso.
821	68	GALBA *imp.*
822	69	OTHO *imp.*
		UITELLIUS *imp.*
		UESPASIANUS *imp.*
823	70	Destruction of Jerusalem.
832	79	TITUS *imp.*
834	81	DOMITIANUS *imp.*
849	96	NERUA *imp.*
851	98	TRAIANUS *imp.*
859	106	L. Minicius Natalis *cos.*
870	117	HADRIANUS *imp.*
882	129	P. Iuuentius Celsus *cos.*
		Sc. Iuuentianum.
891	138	ANTONINUS PIUS *imp.*
		M. Uindius Uerus } *coss. suff.*
		Pactumeius Clemens }
914	161	M. AURELIUS } *impp.*
		L. UERUS }
922	169	Verus dies.
930	177	M. Aurelius } *impp.*
		COMMODUS }

A.U.C.	A.D.	
931	178	*Sc. Orfitianum.*
933	180	Commodus alone *imp.*
945	192	PERTINAX *imp.*
946	193	DIDIUS IULIANUS *imp.*
		SEPTIMIUS SEUERUS *imp.*
951	198	with CARACALLA.
965	212	Severus dies.
		Caracalla at first with GETA *impp.*
		Papinian killed.
970	217	MACRINUS *imp.*
971	218	ELAGABALUS *imp.*
975	222	ALEXANDER SEUERUS *imp.*
981	228	Ulpian killed.
988	235	MAXIMINUS *imp.*
991	238	GORDIANUS I. *imp.*
		GORDIANUS II. *imp.*
		GORDIANUS III. *imp.*
977	244	PHILIPPUS *imp.*
	249	DECIUS *imp.*
	252	GALLUS $\Big\}$ *impp.*
		UOLUSIANUS
	252	UALERIANUS $\Big\}$ *impp.*
		GALLIENUS
	260	Valerian dies.
	268	CLAUDIUS *imp.*
	270	AURELIANUS *imp.*
	275	TACITUS *imp.*
	276	PROBUS *imp.*
	282	CARUS
		CARINUS $\Big\}$ *impp.*
		NUMERIANUS
	283	Carus dies.
	284	DIOCLETIANUS *imp.*
	286	with MAXIMIANUS *imp.*
	305	CONSTANTIUS $\Big\}$ *impp.*
		GALERIUS
	306	Galerius $\Big\}$ *impp.*
		SEUERUS
	307—8	Galerius
		LICINIUS
		MAXIMINUS
		Maximianus $\Big\}$ *impp.*
		CONSTANTINUS
		MAXENTIUS

A. D.

310   Maximianus dies.
311   Galerius dies.
312   Maxentius dies.
313   Maximinus dies.
324   Licinius dies.
330   Constantinople the seat of Government.
337   CONSTANTINUS II. ⎫
        CONSTANTIUS   ⎬ *impp.*
        CONSTANS   ⎭
340   Constantinus killed.
350   Constans killed.
355   Constantius ⎫ *impp.*
        IULIANUS ⎭
361   Constantius dies.
363   IOUIANUS *imp.*

	WEST.	EAST.
364	UALENTINIANUS I. *imp.*	UALENS *imp.*
367	with GRATIANUS *imp.*	
375	Gratianus ⎫ *impp.*	
	UALENTINIANUS II. ⎭	
379		THEODOSIUS I. *imp.*
384		with ARCADIUS ⎫ *impp.*
		and HONORIUS ⎭
392	Theodosius over whole empire.	
395	HONORIUS *imp.*	ARCADIUS *imp.*
402		with THEODOSIUS II. *imp.*
408		Arcadius dies.
410	Alarich king of West Goths in Rome.	
425	Ualentinianus III. *imp.*	
426	Law of citations. (Cf. p. lxxxiv.)	
439	*Codex Theodosianus* comes into force.	
450		MARCIANUS *imp.*
455	MAXIMUS *imp.*	
	AUITUS *imp.*	
456	MAIORIANUS *imp.*	
457		LEO I. *imp.*
461	SEUERUS *imp.*	
467	ANTHEMIUS *imp.*	
472	OLYBIUS *imp.*	
473	GLYCERIUS *imp.*	
474	NEPOS *imp.*	LEO II. *imp.*
		ZENO *imp.*
475	ROMULUS AUGUSTULUS *imp.*	

A.D.	WEST.	EAST.
476	ODOUACER.	
491		ANASTASIUS *imp.*
493	Theodoric king of East Goths in Italy.	
518		IUSTINUS I. *imp.*
527		IUSTINIANUS *imp.*
528		Code ordered.
529		Code published.
530		Digest ordered.
533		Digest ⎱ published. Institutes ⎰
		New Course of study.
534		Revision of Code.
565		Justinian dies.